*The Pageant of
Stuart England*

IN SERIES WITH THIS VOLUME
BY ELIZABETH BURTON AND FELIX KELLY

The Pageant of
Elizabethan England

THE PAGEANT OF
STUART
ENGLAND

By Elizabeth Burton

ILLUSTRATED BY
Felix Kelly

New York

CHARLES SCRIBNER'S SONS

Library of Congress Catalog Card Number 62-17724

Time which antiquates Antiquities, and hath
an art to make dust of all things, hath
yet spared these *minor* Monuments.

(*Sir Thomas Browne:* HYDRIOTAPHIA: Chapter V)

ACKNOWLEDGEMENTS

I HAVE to thank His Grace the Duke of Devonshire and the Trustees of the Chatsworth Settlement for permission to read and to quote from the Family Papers and Accounts of the Cavendish Family, preserved at Chatsworth. I am also greatly indebted to Mr. T. S. Wragge, M.B.E., T.D., Keeper of the Devonshire Collections, for his tireless assistance.

I am most grateful to The Right Hon. the Lord Saye and Sele and to The Lady Saye and Sele for permitting me to see and examine the MSS. Journals of Celia Fiennes at Broughton Castle.

I am greatly indebted to Professor Donald F. Bond, of the University of Chicago, who has been more than kind in answering all the questions concerning *The Spectator* and its times which I have put to him over a period of four years.

To a former Lord Mayor of York, Councillor A. L. Philipson, for allowing me to see certain bequests made to the city by Marmeduke Rawdon; to the office of the Lord Mayor of Norwich for otherwise unobtainable information; to the Keeper of the Public Record Office and in particular to Dr. R. L. Storey of that office; to the Essex Record Office and the County Archivist Mr. F. G. Emmison for invaluable assistance; to the National Trust and to Mr. John Kenworthy-Browne I am deeply in debt. As indeed I am to the Librarian and staff of the London Library; the Librarian and staff of the Bodleian Library, particularly Mr. R. G. Chapman; as well as to the Librarians of the Oxfordshire County Library, especially of the Witney branch.

I am more than grateful to Mr. Felix Kelly, not only for his enchanting illustrations but for his enthusiasm and for the help he gave me with Chapter II. I am very grateful to Dr. Margaret

Acknowledgements

B. Noble for reading Chapter VI and to Miss Désirée Grotrian whose advice I constantly sought and often took.

Lastly, I am fortunate in my agents and publishers on both sides of the Atlantic: Miss Margot Johnson of New York, and Mr. Donald Hutter of Charles Scribner's Sons; Mr. George Greenfield of John Farquharson Ltd., and Mr. David Farrer of Martin Secker and Warburg Ltd., have all shown me the utmost kindness and understanding.

CONTENTS

*The Pageant of
Stuart England*

CHAPTER ONE

The Queen is Dead—Long Live the King

WHETHER the sun danced for joy on Easter Day in the year of James I's accession—the year that brought about the marriage of England and Scotland—is a matter for conjecture.* But on Easter Monday, April 25th, 1603, two things happened which are simple matters of fact. In Rutlandshire, the king fell off his horse; in Huntingdonshire, the nephew and namesake of the squire of Hinchinbrook celebrated his fourth birthday.

The first occurrence caused great, if momentary, alarm among the king's courtiers and attendants. They had not yet realized that their new monarch had an unfortunate proclivity for falling off horses—a proclivity he was to indulge with almost monotonous and even ridiculous regularity for the next twenty-two years. The second event occasioned neither alarm nor interest. Indeed, no one from the Duke of Lennox down to the most beggarly Scot or place-seeking Englishman in the king's obsequent train, had even so much as heard the name of this obscure boy

*"Her feet beneath her petticoat
　　Like little mice peep out,
　　　As if they feared the light;
　　But oh! she dances such a way,
　　No sun upon an Easter Day
　　　Is half so fine a sight"

(Sir John Suckling, 1609-1642.
Ballad upon a Wedding)

celebrating a birthday—as he was to do for the next fifty-five years. Yet everyone in the huge, unwieldy cortège now pulping the April roads into bog and morass had heard of the child's uncle, the Squire of Hinchinbrook.*

That he was, at forty-one, four years older than the king; had three children; was M.P. for Huntingdonshire and had recently married (for the second time) the widow of the Elizabethan financier, Sir Horatio Palavicino, were details which, if known to the king, were of no interest at all. But of great interest and importance—and known to everyone—was that the squire, son of the lately dead and fabulously rich "Golden Knight", was thought to be worth "neere 5,oooli per annum".[1] This meant he had one of the largest incomes in the whole of England. As he was also famous for his hospitality and prodigality he had made lavish preparations to receive and entertain the king on his journey south—an entertainment which so easily might have been postponed by the king's fall. But God, in His Wisdom, suffered his divinely ordained vice-regent to escape with nothing more serious than a badly bruised arm and so the royal party rode on, hunting all the way, stopping for a night at Exton Hall† and at Burghley House‡ before arriving at Hinchinbrook.

This vast, rich, Elizabethan mansion, islanded in a great park and lapped round by its own farm lands and forests, was one of many still visible and solid symbols of wealth accumulated by—and since—the dissolution and spoilation of the monasteries

---

*or Hinchingbrooke.

†Belonging to Sir John Harington, later first Baron Harington of Exton, and cousin to Queen Elizabeth's "saucy poet" and godson also Sir John Harington. It may be the king stayed the night of the 25th at Harington's other house, Burley-on-the-Hill as the two houses were close together, for he was certainly at the latter house to hear a very long welcoming poem by Samuel Daniel. Burley later became the property of George Villiers, 1st Duke of Buckingham.

‡Belonging to Thomas, second Lord Burghley, elder son of Queen Elizabeth's chief minister, William Cecil, and elder half-brother of Robert Cecil. Thomas was later created first Earl of Exeter. Robert became first Earl of Salisbury.

The Queen is Dead—Long Live the King

long ago in the time of Henry VIII. Here the king—a great-
nephew of the original dissolver—found among other pleasures
fine hunting and hawking, sports he enjoyed above all others,
while a great concourse of people from nearby shires flocked to
see him or merely to be within the magical *ambience* of a king.
Outdoors where great ancient trees had unfurled new, green
flags and where the earth was freshly embroidered with primroses, cowslips and violets, booths were set up to feed the poor,
the diffident—or the merely greedy—with all the free bread,
beef and beer they could eat. Inside the house, where a huge
bow window had been espccially added to the room used for
feasting, and where new windows of painted glass displayed the
Palavicino and Cromwell arms, ample provision had been made
for the king's immediate entourage as well as for those of any
importance in Huntingdonshire or adjacent shires who cared to
pay their respects to his "princely grace" on this, his first, progress
in his new realm. Scores of servants in fresh liveries saw to the
needs of all guests. The sun and moon had been captured and
beaten into gold or silver plate enchased with leaves, flowers and
foliage, or fretted with pearls on which splendidly and richly
decorated food was served in prodigal abundance. Rivers of
various wines—none "riffe-ruffe"[2]—all fine, were drawn from
casks in the cellars into pottery or glass bottles and from these
were poured into delicate Venetian glass goblets standing on gilt
feet, silver cups and tankards of all sorts and sizes, and even into
old-fashioned, silver-mounted drinking horns. Music "the
mosaique of the air"[3] fell upon ears and brains dulled with food,
wine, and fresh air; richly jewelled clothing suffered the inevitable fate of careless crowded eating and drinking while at
night thousands of sweet smelling wax candles gave such light
that morning scarce paled them.

But better far than any of these things were the "many rich and
respectable gifts"[4] which the king received from the squire.
Among them "a very great, and very faire wrought standing cup
of gold, goodly horses, fleete and deep mouthed hounds, divers
hawkes of excellent wing"[5] and fifty pounds distributed among

15

"His Majesties Officers". Small wonder then, as he prepared to leave this hospitable house on the morning of the 29th, that his majesty gave his host "many Regall thanks for his entertainment".[6] A shade less regally, perhaps, but with that genuine emotion which never failed to move him at the sight of great riches or handsome young men—for he loved both—the royal visitor exclaimed in his broad Scots accent "Morry, mon, thou has treated me better than any since I left Edinburgh".[7] This spontaneous if tactless remark which burst from the king cannot have endeared him greatly to those who had already plunged deep in debt in order to entertain the new sovereign—either out of ostentation or hope of preferment. Nevertheless, it was true and was generally remarked that "this was the greatest feast . . . given to a king by a subject".[8]

And so, after farewells and Regall thanks, the subject, "Maister" Oliver Cromwell, returned to his recently inherited estates of Hinchinbrook while James VI, King of Scots and—by the Grace of God and the able assistance of Sir Robert Cecil— now King James I of England* rode on his royal and leisurely way toward the southern capital of his recently inherited kingdom. Both men, in time, squandered their rich inheritance.

The country through which the first of the seven Stuart sovereigns† rode differed little, at least in outward aspect, from the England which his great predecessor, Elizabeth Tudor, had inherited forty-five years before. It was still almost completely rural, untamed, wild, beautiful and sparsely populated. Mountains and hills to the north and on the Welsh borders formed natural, difficult barriers; the great central spine of the

---

*By Proclamation 19.V.1603 James assumed the title of King of Great Britain (the first in our history). North Britain (Scotland) and South Britain (England) became one country within the circle of the crown. Parliamentary Union was long delayed and did not take place until 1707.

†Counting William and Mary as two: they were first cousins, both were great grandchildren of James I, as was George I.

Men's hats, c. 1620-90.

Pennines was as yet unbroken by usable roads; narrow, rushing valleys in Yorkshire and Lancashire were hidden and secret, their boiling streams untroubled by mills. Enormous stretches of moorland and marsh tenanted only by wild fowl and beasts, lay barren, undrained and, as yet, un-needed. But there were champion fields too, in autumn brown-gold with barley in the north, pure gold with wheat in the south, or lake-blue with flax where the menacing and eponymous linnet sang so beautifully. And if new green hedgerows and plantations of trees now superimposed tentative and irregular outlines upon the countryside, mapping the slow spread of the new economy of enclosure "it is probable" that "more than half the acreage under corn was still open land, cultivated by the common efforts of the villagers".[9] True, the great primaeval trees had all but vanished, yet there were vast forests in many areas—albeit they too were diminishing to our great hurt. Mixed farming had increased and now flourished on land enriched by centuries of treading and dunging sheep, for wool had declined (it was to decline still further) and Elizabeth had, wisely, encouraged mixed farming on old grazing land. Even so, there were still wild, lonely stretches in Lincolnshire and the Cotswolds, in Wiltshire and Somerset, clouded with sheep and able to supply the raw material for the finest kersies, bays and broadcloth.

But these slow changes had not been, and were not, enough to disturb the face of the most beautiful and best country in the world—for we were then quite sure that this was so. The age old balance between countryside and town still held good and continued to hold for another 150 years. We considered ourselves fortunate above all people because we lived in England. And, naturally, because we were English.

In fact, at the opening of the Stuart century, the younger son of a country gentleman who had to work for his living (as younger sons did) because he inherited nothing "but that which the catte left on the malte heape" writes: "England, for the commoddities itt yields, is known to be inferior to no Country, saving that itt wanteth wine and spicery".[10] These were hardly grave disadvantages in a land abounding with "more sorts of other things then (than) any other country".[11] Among the more sorts of other things used at home and shipped abroad were iron, steel, lead, copper, tin and "all other kind of mineralls" except gold, and silver; flax, hemp, wool, corn, flesh, "fish of all sorts"; leather, cloth, salt, butter, cheese, beer; "fruites and herbes of all kindes", to say nothing of "wholsom and medicinable zaffran". Curiously, there is no mention of coal.*

Coal, once used only by those too poor to buy wood but fortunate enough to live but a mile or so from the nearest outcrop,

*Curiously, because Wilson seems at one time to have worked as a foreign correspondent in Italy for Robert Cecil and also for Thomas Sackville, Lord Buckhurst, and 1st Earl of Dorset (1604). The latter, when Lord Treasurer, was most anxious to have records of coal production and set about getting them—but see *The Rise of the British Coal Industry* and also *The Cultural Foundations of Industrial Civilization* both books by Prof. John U. Nef for information on Coal, and *Knole and the Sackvilles* by V. Sackville-West for information about Thomas Sackville.

The Queen is Dead—Long Live the King

had, during Elizabeth's day, come into much more general use. By the beginning of the seventeenth century it had certainly become a well-known "minerall" and an asset of national importance. Although the smelting of iron and steel still required wood—and continued to do so to the further detriment of our forests—many industries such as brewing, dyeing and hat making (men's hats were in particular very varied and unusual—one of Sir Francis Bacon's looked like a "close-stool pan"—while hat bands became almost a status symbol) had turned from wood to coal. During the whole of the Stuart era coal played an increasing part in the development of national wealth. One of the great raw materials necessary for the so-called industrial revolution of the late eighteenth century was being brought to light and use during this period when men were learning about coal mining, how to invent pumps to keep mines from flooding, and trying to understand the dangers of fire-damp and explosions.

Coal had to be carried by boat (which is why it was called seacoal) as did all heavy commodities.* It came, chiefly from Newcastle, around the coast and up the Thames or Severn, the Humber or the Exe (Exeter also boasted the first canal, built in 1566 by John Tew) enriching the cities and towns on these rivers. Wheeled transport was still virtually unknown for large-scale, long distance carrying although crude stage or long wagons drawn by six or eight horses were used. They were broad wheeled, had no springs, were covered with leather or sailcloth supported by iron hoops, and could carry twenty passengers and some goods. There were also smaller, privately owned wagons and carts, which were often commandeered by the monarch on his progresses or whenever he moved from one palace to another. Then much furniture including pots, pans and even the coals from the kitchen (kitchen menials were known as "black guards" solely because of their sooty faces) was moved too.

*Railways belong to this century. In some places horse-drawn wooden carts ran on wooden rails laid from pithead to loading point. In Mediaeval times according to Agricola man power not horse power was used.

The Pageant of Stuart England

Two-wheeled carts and wagons were also borrowed for the king's purpose, so were horses, to the great detriment of the owner who if he happened to be a farmer—as he nearly always was—suffered great loss by this.

Pack horse trains were in operation in many places, and records in Lancashire and Yorkshire during the early Stuart period show that in this district they were owned and operated by Mr. Pickford whose name as a goods carrier is better known now than it was then. Such trains, of some thirty or forty horses, each carrying up to 350 lb., straggled in single file across the Pennines. The jingling bells of the leading horses which announced the train's approach; the chink of horse brasses—worn to ward off the evil eye to which horses are very subject; the commands of the guards, armed to ward off more human evils, was a welcome and exciting event in the life of tiny village or lonely farm in the Holme or Colne valleys. Long-distance travellers often joined up with a pack horse train for safety and guidance when travelling in wild and remote parts of the country.

As always, roads were deplorable. The Roman roads or what was left of them were still the best but the rest were boggy, full of potholes winter and summer, unless summer happened to be dry, when they remained deeply rutted but thick with dust. Secondary roads were no more than cart tracks. Lanes straggled narrowly here and there and were much the same as in Anglo-Saxon times. There were few signposts to point the appalling way, and the length of a mile varied in different parts of the country. Horse ferries operated in the estuaries—that between Lambeth Palace and Millbank in London (hence Horseferry Road) belonged to the Archbishops of Canterbury who let it out at around £20 per year. Fording rivers or streams was often dangerous. Bridges were few, far between and frequently such ancient or carelessly built wooden structures that crossing by a bridge could be hazardous too. Poor Lydia Priestly, aged twenty, was killed when her horse caught its foot in rickety Godly Bridge and threw her into the river and this as late as December 17th, 1681! Even by Queen Anne's day when traffic was heavier, little had been done to improve roads. The Great North Road out of London which bore much traffic was fairly good in summer, but beyond Grantham it was no more than a stone causeway. In the Sussex Weald, roads between North and South Downs were a sea of mud until midsummer and lanes almost impossible in summer were quite impassable in winter.

Late in the Stuart century, the Rev. James Brome (d. 1719) of Cheriton, Kent, set out to explore and record England as a geographer and observer, but each winter, although he could afford a guide, he had to abandon his project because the roads were so bad. One winter found him in Devonshire and although he planned to go on to Cornwall it was quite impossible to get there. Small wonder that the Gubbings clan—"pure heathens" living near Brent-Tor on the edge of Dartmoor—had managed to survive undisturbed for two centuries or so. The Gubbings were a "race" founded in the fifteenth century by "two strumpets (who) being with child fled hither to hide", or so Thomas Fuller tells us. They can hardly have hidden themselves very thoroughly because certain "lewd fellows" resorted to them, pretty constantly one imagines, as this is the way the Gubbings increased. They seemed to be regarded as most peculiar by every one else because "they multiplied without marriage" and by Fuller's day (1608-1661) numbered many hundreds. They were exempt from ecclesiastical and civil authority; they lived in "cots" like swine, and by stealing, chiefly sheep; could run faster than horses (no wonder they were "exempt" from authority which was often too fat to run and too pompous to appear other than on horseback); they held together "like burrs"; spoke the "dross and dregs" of vulgar Devonian, and their "vivaciousness"[12] allowed them to outlive most other men. Furthermore, they seem to have been a sort of Mafia in themselves for if any member of the clan were offended all would avenge his quarrel. Happily or unhappily, by the time Fuller writes, the Gubbings were becoming civilized and even offering their offspring—still illegitimate, no doubt—for baptism. So it may be that by the time the Rev. Mr. Brome visited and recorded Devon they had finally ceased to be "exempt" from authority—and bitterly regretted it.

But if the traveller escaped death by drowning or suffocation in mud; or injury from pot holes, and ruts; or being forced to stay where caught by winter, there was still danger from highway men and footpads who flourished greatly. Some were professional thieves, some were men of better families who fell upon bad times and took to worse ways. So the educated and well born had a certain sympathy for highwaymen and not a few had relatives who had undertaken the profession. The well-born highwayman was often courteous, well-mannered and even quixotic. So the glamorous highwayman legend arose. Of course, if caught he was hanged—Sir George Sandes, or Sandys, was hanged in 1617 for "purse taking" and horse stealing—and people were sorry, just as we are sorry today for those who are caught evading income tax, although this is not yet a hanging matter.

Private coaches had appeared in Elizabeth's time (and perhaps even before, Stow says the first one was built in 1555 for the second Earl of Rutland). Hackney coaches* (that is coaches for hire) were in use in London from 1625 at least, and this, in time, led Sir Sanders Duncombe to introduce the sedan chair in 1634†

*It is said there were twenty coaches for hire in London in 1625. They did not wait in the streets but at the principal Inns. By 1635 coaches for hire were so common Charles I limited their number (fares were regulated too). In 1637 there were fifty in London and Westminster; by 1652, 200; in 1654, 300 (plus 600 hackney horses); in 1694, 700 and in the year of Queen Anne's death about 800. These were in addition to innumerable private coaches and as streets were very narrow "traffic jams" were chronic during the whole century.

†It is often claimed that the Duke of Buckingham introduced the sedan chair a dozen years earlier but in April 1619 James I was carried from Royston to Ware "in a kind of Neapolitan portative chaire (given him by the Lady Elizabeth Hatton) and the rest of the way in a litter" Jno. Chamberlain writes to Sir Dudley Carleton on April 24th, 1619. This does not, of course, mean the sedan chair was common but it does mean it was seen in England before either Buckingham or Duncombe introduced it.

The Queen is Dead—Long Live the King

(a French idea) in the forlorn hope of relieving the problem of traffic congestion in London. It didn't. It merely helped the decline of the Thames as London's great highway. Public coaches for distance travel did not appear until around 1637 when a weekly service linked Aldersgate and St. Albans. But by the end of the era most towns of any size were linked to London by coach.* There were no night journeys by public coach though, so it was indeed fortunate that inns were excellent, clean, comfortable and, in those days, willing and glad to supply quantities of food at any hour. Stage coaches were uncomfortable and slow by our standards but to most of our ancestors they were the marvel of the age. Despite the fact that over-nice and spineless travellers found it most unpleasant to ride in a public coach "all day with strangers, oftimes sick, antient, diseased persons or young children crying; to whose humours they are obliged to be subject, forced to bear with, and many times poisoned with, their nasty scents and crippled by the crowd of boxes and bundles",[13] one really only had to endure sickness, smells and crippling for four-and-a-half days now to get from London to Chester and for only six days to get to Newcastle. By 1669 the "Flying Coach" took Anthony à Wood from Oxford to London in a mere thirteen hours! By Anne's reign it took only six days to get from London to Edinburgh, and fifteen hours from London to Cambridge.

But during the early years of the era even if public coaches had been available for long-distance travel, which they weren't, a horse was infinitely preferable on a long journey. A large, heavy, square box swaying sickeningly on leather straps was not conducive to comfort. These box-like coaches were also springless and jolted horribly as they swayed; in addition, only leather flaps protected one against the rain, wind, sleet and snow of winter and the rain, wind or thick dust of summer. Hence, in 1635, when a certain Lieutenant Hammond set out on a journey from Norfolk into Western Counties he went on horseback and, arriving in Wiltshire, he took his "Nag . . . over the pleasant

*The word is perhaps, a corruption of the Hungarian "kocsi"; Kocs is a small village between Vienna and Budapest.

23

Plains to goe to see one of our Island wonders, whose admir'd, strange, confus'd, huge, fixt, astonishing Stones"[14] as he vividly describes Stonehenge which he thought had been erected by King Aurelius* as a memorial to his people slaughtered by the invading Saxons a thousand years before.

Thirty-three years later, Sam Pepys, his wife Elizabeth, Will Hewer and Captain Murford also went travelling, by coach, into the west country. Coaches had improved greatly and were general now even in remote districts; they were stronger and lighter and window glass had supplanted leather flaps, springs were also known though they did not come into general use until nearly a century later. But even with more coaches none, seemingly, was available in Salisbury for the Pepys party couldn't find coach horses to take them to Stonehenge so "got saddle-horses, very dear" instead. Then they, like Hammond, went "over the Plain and some great hills, even to fright us" and finally came to those stones which Pepys says are "as prodigous as any tales I ever heard of them and worth going this journey to see" although, unlike Hammond, he is unsure of their origin or purpose. "God knows what their use was!"[15] he exclaims, and adds, "they are hard to tell, but may yet be told".† And, after giving a shepherd-woman 4d. for leading their horses, the party returned via

*Traditionally—and improbably—the son of Constantine the Great. Geoffrey of Monmouth says Ambrosius Aurelianus was the son of Constantine (III) the Usurper, known as Constantine of Brittany, (c. A.D. 407), who had three sons Constans, Aurelius Ambrosius and Uther (the father of Arthur) which may account for the confusion as to parentage. Aurelius seems much more than a semi-mythical figure and there are good grounds for believing he did lead the resistance against the Saxon invaders under Hengist. He may also be the proto-type of Arthur. Both Gildas and Nennius speak of this hero but Gildas refers to him as *dux* not as king.

†Pepys had bought a guide book in Oxford which may have been Inigo Jones' "Stone-Heng Restored", if so he seems not to have agreed with Inigo's theory that Stonehenge was a Roman work, a temple dedicated to Coelus or Coelum (son of Aethera and Dies) and senior to all gods of the heathens. The architecture, Jones proved to his own satisfaction, was Roman and followed Vitruvius.

The Queen is Dead—Long Live the King

Wilton but, less fortunate than Lieutenant Hammond, were unable to see inside Lord Pembroke's house as his Lordship had just arrived. But Pepys did not care for the outside of the house— altered by Inigo Jones and John Webb since Hammond's visit— nor did he think much of its situation. We can however see from these two by no means isolated instances that the passion for seeing the houses and palaces of the noble and the rich is not exclusive to our own post-war era. What is new today, is that viewing country houses has become big business for the owners, many of whom couldn't keep the places up if it weren't.

It might reasonably be thought that as travel increased during the century*—and more particularly after the postal system was first reorganized in 1635†—that roads would have been improved, but not a bit of it. Bad roads and inept or out-of-date highway legislation were as typical of England and the English then as now.‡ Nevertheless, after the Restoration, fast post horses could be hired at 3d. per mile from government postmasters— slower ones cost less—and as lanes were often too narrow to permit coaches, coach travellers often had to finish a journey on a post office horse or nag hired from the postmaster situated nearest their destination. But if roads improved little, maps

*It should be remembered that never before in our history had more Englishmen travelled throughout the length and breadth of their own country than during the Civil Wars.

†In 1635 it became possible to send a letter to Edinburgh and have a reply within six days. By 1680 penny post was introduced and hourly collections were made at receiving offices in London. There were four to six deliveries in "greater" London per day and ten or twelve per day in the business sections.

‡Highway legislation then seems to indicate that roads were an institution in their own right and did not exist as prepared ways for vehicles. They were, supposedly, maintained by the parishes through which they ran and although each parish was bound to maintain its roads by six days free labour a year busy farmers whose duty it was to give this labour can hardly have been expected to comply with such a law, particularly as they had small interest in roads and were not paid for their labour.

improved a great deal. The famous maps by John Speed, brought out in 1611, remained in use until the end of the century and were full of information about the various counties. They were, and are, highly ornamental, with detailed decoration on border edges and in blank spaces—town plans, coats-of-arms, strap work, puffing winds, sea monsters and ships. Yet due to their scale and nature they cannot have been very convenient as road maps. But by 1675 the traveller had the advantage of John Ogilby's maps, which charted all the post roads in the country. These were specifically road maps and were engraved on strips drawn to resemble ribbon—so they are indeed "ribbon" roads. Ogilby's maps are fascinating and can still be used in places, although many roads have disappeared and certainly the "arrable", the forests, the bogs, the ponds are largely gone too. We can indeed no longer recognize the wild, sparsely populated northern half of the kingdom from them, although many a famous house serving as a landmark then still stands today.

All this sounds as if our seventeenth century ancestors took to the vicious roads in hordes and rushed about the country in coaches at a reckless thirty miles per day. But this is not so. Although it certainly seemed so, after the Restoration, to many an older man like Thomas Tyndale, who complained bitterly of the decadence of the time and put it all down to effeminate coaches. Certainly after mid-century more people of the middling sort did take to travelling—and for sheer pleasure too—but the majority stayed at home in their own towns and villages and went abroad only to attend the nearest market or fair. One is also inclined to think that improved coach transport must have led to an increased traffic in goods carried by road, but this can have been only a marginal increase as coaches were still small. The rich or the middling man might send a parcel by coach or carrier but the poor man probably hadn't a parcel, let alone the wherewithall to send it. The most disastrous parcel in our history was a bundle of flea-ridden, old clothes sent from plague-stricken London to Eyam, in Derbyshire, in 1665. It was a kind, well-meant gesture which wiped out the whole village.

Villages and towns themselves were not too greatly affected by transport improvement and so remained much the same, retaining an individuality and a separate identity throughout the whole of the century. London with perhaps 250,000 people to cheer James when he first entered it in May 1603, had probably 500,000 to regret the passing of Queen Anne in August 1714. Norwich with a population of around 10,000 at the beginning of the century was ousted as the second largest town by Bristol. Both had populations which grew to perhaps 15,000 during the first third of the century but by 1640 Bristol had become "the greatest town for shipping after London".[16] This was due to the fact that James made peace with Spain in 1604 and the town became a great sea-port. Among other things its soap industry flourished because Bristol could once again import olive oil from Spain and make "Castile" soap instead of trying to make do with train oil (whale) which stank abominably, and was much more difficult

Early seventeenth-century coach.

to procure. It manufactured sugar and brass pins (Gloucester manufactured pins too). Its Xeres or "sherry" sack was famous and known as Bristol milk because it was the first "moisture" given to infants and, after London's monopoly of the sole right to import tobacco was broken in 1639, Bristol, and other ports, started importing tobacco and also began to manufacture tobacco pipes. It was Thomas James, a Bristol man of Welsh extraction backed by the Bristol Merchant Venturers, who beat Luke Foxe a Yorkshireman (backed by London merchants) to the bay which bears his name. This was in 1631 and both men were endeavouring to discover the elusive North West passage. The two met in Hudson's Bay in August and although so far from home did not take to each other at all. Foxe returned to England in November but James bravely wintered in his bay on an island which he named Brandon Hill. There he set up a cross and the royal coat of arms, together with the arms of Bristol, and then, in October 1632, returned to England. His ship the *Henrietta Maria* displaced 70-80 tons! It was crewed by twenty-two men, a boy and two dogs. The dogs and four men never returned.

By 1660 Bristol's population was enormous at, perhaps, 30,000—which means that it had trebled in sixty years—even so, it is very unlikely that, after London, Bristol, Norwich and York, any town exceeded 10,000. Liverpool was a small port, one of the ports for Ireland. Birmingham, "a town so generally wicked" Lord Clarendon says, "that it had risen upon small parties of the king's and killed or taken them prisoner and sent them to Coventry", was small but already noted for its forges and for making excellent nails. Coventry, a stronghold of Puritanism, was also tiny—the Great Rebellion ruined its cloth and cap trade—but it was making a new reputation for itself with its Coventry blue dye. Huddersfield had scarce been heard of, save by the Ramsden family to whom Queen Elizabeth had sold it in 1599, and although it had long produced raw wool, (in the seventeenth century it began making woollen kersies) yet it was not until 1670 that King Charles II granted John Ramsden the right to hold a market there every Wednesday where,

The Queen is Dead—Long Live the King

doubtless, the dudderies* attracted more than purely local buyers.

But cloth manufacture did not mean a factory. There were no industrial centres as we know them, there were innumerable small industries scattered throughout the country and more often than not those who ran them lived on the premises. For those engaged in any trade there was no such thing as a private residence. The place of business was in the house or adjoining it. No such thing, either, as being despised for being in trade or for living "over the shop" as it were. That particular silliness belongs to a later era. Apprentices, bound to a master, lived with the family and often had a bad time of it but often did not. Although they were frequently beaten for trivial offences (so were children) and had no proper sleeping quarters, yet they belonged. They were part of a still patriarchal family way of life. Rich and middling people alike apprenticed their children to a trade. Fatherless Marmeduke Rawdon of York was early apprenticed to his uncle, Sir Marmeduke Rawdon, the London wine merchant, by whom he was treated just like a son and one of his jobs was to wait on table. Later he became very rich and a benefactor to his native city. But apprentices when they banded together could be difficult and often rioted in the streets of London, doing much damage and frightening sober citizens out of their wits . . . perhaps they were unhappy about pay and conditions or perhaps they were just young and liked to roister. But industry generally, with or without apprentices—and leaving aside such things as soap boiling and glass manufacture—was really a part of village life. Industry was predominantly cottage industry in which members of a family engaged. It was the church spire or tower, not the factory chimney which stood out as a land mark to travellers. Villages were still almost self-contained units, small islands in a sea of countryside, and the countryside was still the

*The sections or booths where cloth and clothes were sold at a market. Hence the word "duds" meaning clothing and probably also the word "dude" meaning a very dressed up person (male) as in "dude-ranch".

great universal provider which came almost to one's door. Its fields supplied food; its forests and trees, firewood and the raw material for furniture; its clay or stone provided houses. Village men were not farmers or carpenters or builders, they were more often than not all three rolled into one. A man could turn a hand to almost anything, just as his wife could cook, bake, doctor; brew home beer, wine, medicine; sew, spin and embroider; look after hens and the dairy; launder; raise vegetables and flowers, and make her own beauty aids. These were useful and necessary accomplishments at home, and they were to prove vital to that small band whom history now refers to as "The Pilgrim Fathers" (they were never so pompous as to call themselves that) who left these shores on September 6th, 1620, in a rickety ship called the *Mayflower* bound for the New World.

But all these were just everyday usual skills picked up by, or taught to, every child, and many were the basis of home industry which was encouraged everywhere. As there was no such thing as universal education, children at the age of six or seven were considered old enough to begin learning some "arte". The children of Norwich, for example, could earn as much as 4/- a week from the age of seven by knitting fine jersey stockings which Norwich merchants sold in London or exported to France. That these merchants made high profits by the exploitation of child labour horrifies us, but it was then regarded as an excellent thing (there were too few mines to send women and children into in those days). It taught the child a trade; the 4/- helped the family and improved the standard of living* and total production was increased. thereby enriching the community as a whole.

Children did everything at an earlier age in those days—even dying. The education of children began early. John Evelyn's boy, Richard, who died at five years and three days, knew Latin and Greek, "several propositions of Euclid" and was well versed in scripture. Rich men's sons went up to Oxford or Cambridge

---

*As a farm labourer earned 6d. a day, or 3/- for a seven day week, 4/- was a good wage for a child—or almost anyone.

The Queen is Dead—Long Live the King

at fourteen, and the sons of yeomen who wanted to move up into the category of gentlemen went to the Inns of Court very young too. Marriage at sixteen was not uncommon but during the century it became less usual to marry one's child off at ten, twelve or fourteen as had been customary in Elizabethan times. And, as the century grew older so, it seems, did the age for marriage. Among the rich and the powerful, family alliances were often cemented by marrying off children at a very early age but love marriages were certainly not unknown. Early marriages in Royal circles, that is dynastic marriages, were no longer arranged when children were still in their cradles. Where Henry VIII had angled for the four-year-old Mary Queen of Scots for his eleven-year-old son Edward, Mary's son, James VI and I, did not marry Anna of Denmark until he was twenty-three—and thereby acquired incidentally the Orkneys as well as a wife. Charles I was twenty-five when he married Henrietta Maria, and was given Quebec as a present—but gave it back again later. Oliver Cromwell, nephew and namesake of the Squire of Hinchinbrook who gave that stupendous feast in 1603, was twenty-one when he married Elizabeth Bourchier. Charles II, already vastly experienced and some said (wrongly) already married, was thirty-two before he took Portugal's daughter as his bride and with her Tangier and Bombay. James II, who succeeded his childless brother, was twenty-six when he married a commoner, Anne Hyde (Lord Clarendon's daughter); and forty when he married Princess Mary Beatrice of Modena (she was fifteen) whose beautiful little crown is one of the three Queen Consort crowns of England. William of Orange, or William III, was an old, cold twenty-seven when he married James II's and Anne Hyde's daughter, Mary, who was nineteen.* Mary's younger sister, who became Queen Anne, was fifteen when she didn't marry the unpleasing Prince George Lewis of Hanover, and eighteen when she married the monolithic and stupid Prince George of Den-

*She was, of course, the direct Protestant heir to the throne and so, correctly, or courteously, we should speak of Mary and William not William and Mary.

mark.* Anne, who died in 1714, like Queen Elizabeth but for quite other reasons, left no heirs and the nasty George Lewis, by then Elector of Hanover, a foreigner, and a foreigner to English ways which he never understood nor attempted to understand, succeeded to the throne. Just as James VI, King of Scots, also a foreigner who never attempted to understand his subjects, their ways or their country, had succeeded to the throne of Elizabeth in 1603.

If in 1603 England had changed but little on the surface since the accession of Elizabeth in 1558, it had changed greatly underneath and in spirit. James either could not or would not realize this (nor was he alone in his blindness). All he saw on his first progress from Edinburgh to London was a rich country—rich by Scots standards—full of great people with grand houses and estates who entertained him with far greater civility, richness and flattery than his Scots nobles had ever done. For, in truth, although James in his own person united the kingdoms of Scotland and England and so put an end to border savagery as well as to the age-old alliance between Scotland and France (always so perilous to England), Scotland was, in many respects, still a feudal country where chieftains and their clans, with or without the support of the kirk, struggled for supreme power. It was quite usual for Scottish kings to be killed at home in feudal wars. James himself, during his infancy had been little more than a political football in the long struggle for power, just as the crown of England had been a football during the endless Wars of the Roses which, in themselves, were an expression of the social and political anarchy which affected most countries during the transition from late mediaeval to early modern times.

The genius of the Tudors—or at least of the three great Tudors, Henry VII, Henry VIII and Elizabeth I (and what subsequent

*Luckily for Anne, the plan to marry her to her cousin Hanover fell apart; he was perfectly beastly to another cousin he married, the wretched Sophia Dorothea, whereas Anne and Denmark were quite devoted to each other.

Late seventeenth-century royal coach.

dynasty has ever produced three greater monarchs?)—lay in a remarkable political insight plus, in the case of Elizabeth and her father, a magic touch with people. They saw or sensed the terrible dangers of transitional anarchy and knew that only a strong monarchy could create a nation out of the exhausted and warring factions left over from the wars between the Houses of Lancaster and York. They were, in our terms, despots. Henry VIII has been called "a despot under the forms of law" and it is probably very true that, technically speaking, he committed no illegal action. But the two Henries and Elizabeth—although it was touch and go when Elizabeth came to the throne—made the monarchy a symbol of national unity. Out of regional loyalties—loyalties to feudal lords—they created a larger and greater single loyalty—loyalty to the crown. Elizabeth, more than either her father or grandfather, accomplished this and further, she turned a nation which under her half-brother Edward VI and her half-sister Mary Tudor had been nearly broken and in fact lay in economic ruins, into a prosperous and united country. She laid the foundations of England's future greatness. England was not loved—far from it—and I doubt if it has ever been dearly loved by any foreign country—but that didn't matter. England was strong. England was feared. England was respected. This may be regrettable but it was absolutely vital to her survival.* Her ships sailed around the world, traded everywhere, amassed fortunes—legally and illegally—and laid the foundations of the colonies in America. It was probably impossible that anyone could be a worthy successor to Queen Elizabeth, unless Alfred the Great had been re-incarnated, but James was unfortunately largely influenced by the fact that his own country, Scotland, was roughly in the same divided feudal state in which England had been at the end of the Wars of the Roses. And, further, he had the disadvantage of never having been a subject himself (he became king at eleven months) as Elizabeth had been. What Scotland needed was a Tudor dynasty; a strong, despotic monarchy to unify the country after its centuries of violence and bloodshed, and indeed, it must be said for James that he had done much to achieve this end in Scotland. But this was not now what was needed in England. Yet, in a sense, this is what England got in James. James' best years were behind him but he didn't know it. Nor did the people. For England by now was moving toward a more democratic form of government. Elizabeth and her Council had ruled the country and ruled it well, but during the last years of her reign she was at logger-heads with her parliaments. That the split did not become open is due in great measure to the fact that she could wheedle and cajole them and tell them she loved them and her people—which is absolutely undeniable—until they gave way. And if they didn't give way and she saw it was hopeless she sometimes gave way herself and snatched a personal victory out of defeat with a magnificent speech which dissolved Parliament—often in tears.

Nevertheless, the old Parliamentary machinery was creaking to a stop when Elizabeth died—and James was no Tudor. The only point James and Elizabeth had in common is the purely fortuitous fact that the mother of each had had her head chopped off. And although James had been canny enough to survive as

*England was not any of these things again—except hated—until Cromwell's day.

The Queen is Dead—Long Live the King

King of Scots for thirty-seven years—in itself no small achievement—he displayed neither political insight nor acumen as King of England. He saw the monarchy as "absolute", and absolute, strictly, means not dependent on anyone or anything. Parliament in Scotland, which he knew, was little more than a court of record and he never grasped that Parliament in England was far more advanced and had, or thought it had, age-old privileges—some of which had been done away with by the Tudors and which members wanted re-affirmed. James also believed in the divine right of kings. Kings were God's vice-regents to whom a subject owed total and humble obedience, as St. Paul seemed to state quite clearly in Romans: Chapter 13, verses i-vii.* The Tudors had certainly been regarded as semi-divinities, but they had never been so silly as to believe in divine right or even that they were semi-divine. James believed it profoundly, which was unfortunate. It was equally unfortunate that he possessed the fatal flaw common to all the Stuart sovereigns of England—he was an extremely bad judge of character (as, indeed, was his mother). His favourites had no qualification for the high offices thrust upon them other than looks and dress. A king who valued handsome, greedy, young men like Robert Ker and George Villiers above men like Robert Cecil, Bacon, Ralegh and Elliot was not likely to understand either the spirit of England or the English people.

James is an exasperating monarch. A man of many parts—too many of them unprepossessing—he was intelligent, shrewd and quite often he meant well. He had a robust sense of humour but tended to be maudlin and he really much preferred hunting to business. As early as June 1603 Thomas Wilson is busy writing to Sir Thomas Parry "Sometymes he comes to Counsell, but most tyme he spendes in the Feilds and Parkes and Chases, chasing away idleness by violent exercise and early rysing . . . The people according to the honest English nation approve all their Princes actions, words, savinge that they desyre some more of

*God, James told his first Parliament, had bestowed his blessings upon them all "in my own person".

35

that gracious affabilitye which ther good old Queen did afford them''.[17] Unhappily when it did come to business of state, to ordinary everyday king's business, or even friendly conversation, James was quite positive he knew everything about everything and he loved to argue, not for the sake of sifting opinion and arriving at a truth or a reasonable facsimile thereof, but merely to show how logical were his processes of thought and how divine his reason. This was very delaying—eristic argument always is. James argued with everyone on everything. He argued with Parliament, with Puritans, with Bishops, with his Council, the Church, his fancy boys. He never stopped, and he loved above all things to argue in Latin. Ambassadors and scholars replied in Latin and the cleverer ones were clever enough to make deliberate mistakes so that the king could have the pleasure of correcting them. This may have been intellectually dishonest, but it often paid off. James was flattered and it made him feel even cleverer and more condescending than he already felt. In short, James was an enthroned and extremely conceited Scots school-master and the English soon found him a ridiculous bore. But not at first.

At first the new monarch was welcomed with open hearts and arms and with such joy that James' not very attractive nor stable head must have been quite turned. The joy was quite genuine but was based chiefly on an enormous feeling of relief. It is difficult for us to imagine or understand why this was so great, but the truth is that relief and joy were due almost wholly to the fact that the succession had passed off quietly. The great question of who would succeed had worried and alarmed everyone·since the days when it had become quite clear that Elizabeth would leave no heirs of her body, and had also stubbornly refused to be badgered into naming an heir—although often implored to do so by the prayers and sometimes even the tears of her parliaments and her advisors. She was far too wise to do this and so set up a focal or rallying point for any opposition (a situation which was chronic in Georgian times). Nor was she going to risk assassination so that the named heir might succeed if any splinter group got tired of her. Hence, for the past thirty years, the question of who would succeed had worried the country—a worry which increased proportionately with the Queen's age—any hint of an illness threw the country into a panic, and when she died the people were nearly frantic.

There were a number of people abroad—including, improbably, the King of Spain; and at home—including Arabella Stuart —who might lay some sort of claim to the throne and receive interested foreign backing for that claim. Then, there was the Pope. He had no claim, but he was thought to have a nominee or two, in petto, and anyway, everyone expected he would support almost any Roman Catholic claimant no matter how wild or feeble the claim. It was even believed that the Pope had a fleet lurking and ready to attack our shores the moment he knew of Elizabeth's death. It all sounds absurd and melodramatic now. But it wasn't then. There was a fear of "popery" not wholly because it was Roman Catholic but lest it lead to any return of clerical rule—and that's what popery meant then. This is where poor Charles I made his really fatal mistake. He attempted to impose—or it was feared he was attempting to impose— clerical rule via Archbishop Laud and the Anglican Church. It didn't make a ha'porth of difference then whether it was a Roman Catholic Pope or an Anglican Archbishop who ruled—it was still clerical. And it was anti-clericalism as much as anti-Roman Catholicism which moved and molded public sentiment. So in 1603 all that the people were concerned about was that the successor shouldn't be a papist or a foreigner, and James was neither. Or rather, they knew he wasn't the first. They were to learn, bitterly, that he was the second.

In truth, James VI's claim to the English throne was undoubtedly the soundest of all the possible claimants. He was nearest in blood, descending as he did from Henry VIII's sister Margaret. Even so when Elizabeth died, without definitely naming James as her successor, it was not to be wondered at that great anxiety, apprehension and fear prevailed everywhere in England. That trouble did not come was chiefly due to Robert

The Pageant of Stuart England

Cecil who managed to get things settled privately to his and to James' satisfaction some years before the old Queen's death:—

> "A wonder 'tis our sunne is set, and yet there is no night;
> Darke stormes were feared around about, and yet all over
> bright
> Blest God; when we for feare scarce lookt to have seen
> Peace's moonshine.
> Thou sents from North, past all our hopes, King James
> his glorious sunshine . . ."

was the way one, R. Parker, put it in his thirty-eight lines of *England's Farewell to Elizabeth*. One might have expected a little better scansion from a member of "Caigon", but if the scansion is faulty and the couplets lame almost to the point of total immobility, R. Parker was certainly expressing what everyone thought and felt. "Nothing was looked for but war on all syds"[18] a Scots historian says flatly and the same thought is repeated and expressed in every ode written to lament Elizabeth and welcome James. Truly, many expected that "Upon the setting of that bright Occidental Star, Queen Elizabeth . . . some thick palpable clouds of darkness would so have overshadowed this land, that men should have been in doubt which way they were to walk, and that it should hardly be known who was to direct the unsettled state".[19]

To be honest, the state was unsettled by more than genuine and horrid fears about the succession. The long war with Spain had dragged on and was costing a great deal of money. Money itself was depressed in value. Prices were high. Wages were low. Parliament was restive. And if older men still saw, undimmed, the might and majesty, the glory and the greatness of Elizabeth, many a young man saw her only as a tiresome, autocratic old woman who had reigned too long and had blocked the way to much-needed parliamentary, social, political, economic and religious reforms. So the old welcomed James because the accession had been bloodless, but the young welcomed him because the death of the Queen was expected to solve all these pressing problems. Death, however, rarely solves problems, save for those who do the dying.

Thus the seventeenth century began with a wave of hysterical relief, superabundant hope and a popular successor. Relief, hope and the successor's popularity soon declined. James, although this

Small Merchantman, *c.* 1660.

had not been foreseen, was a foreigner and remained one. Neither he nor his unfortunate second son, Charles I, ever seem to have had the remotest idea of what the English were like (or if they had James at any rate didn't care, and Charles was too withdrawn to show that he did). Neither father nor son ever understood that religion and money are key words in English history; two things over which men who held power or who desired to hold power quarrelled and were to quarrel for years. Even today, mention of those two things will touch some hidden nerve in even the mildest of the English because this is a part of our Englishness. Religion, money, and power turned out to be the triune goddess of Civil War in the Stuart century.

It is always very easy to gain a reputation for profundity by taking the simple and translating it into obscure or grandiose language. But it is quite fatal to take what Carlyle called "that unspeakable puddle of a time"[20] and try to turn it into a small manageable pool of clear water. All one can say is, that there are probably as many views about history as there are historians or people who write about history, or, even, who think about history. We are all influenced by what we read acting upon our given temperaments. All I can do, here, is to say that politically the whole of the Stuart era, as we now see it and from this distance, is a struggle for sovereignty between crown and Parliament; between the King's prerogative and the rights of Parliament; between the doctrine of the divine right of an absolute monarch and what were believed to be the ancient rights of a non-representative but elected body of "Commons". Money comes into it because the Stuarts were wildly extravagant. James I particularly so, although in fairness it must be said that he inherited a national debt* of some £400,000, left over from the last Irish campaign, along with the throne. Parliament comes in here because Parliament was needed to vote the king extra "supplies" but Parliament refused to grant extra supplies unless the monarch granted or allowed Parliament certain rights and privileges which Parliament claimed had been theirs since the time of Edward IV—or even as

---

*Nevertheless, Elizabeth had managed to make do with less than James who managed to spend between £500,000 and £600,000 a year and incurred a deficit thereby of some £50,000 to £150,000 per annum. There was, however, great need for a more productive and better system of taxation provided the money didn't go to the king. Still, James did spend £10,000 on his journey south and gave away a further £14,000. In the first four years of his reign he spent £92,000 on jewels (and in the first ten years, the Queen, Anna of Denmark, spent £40,000 with George Heriot the goldsmith alone). By 1610 James had given away £220,000 to Scotsmen and some of the aristocracy, so Parliament had some justification for its attitude.

The Queen is Dead—Long Live the King

far back as Magna Carta and bad King John—but which had been abrogated by time and the Tudors. One of the things Parliament wanted was the sole right to levy taxes and men went to the Tower and died there for this right. That this has turned out ironic today does not lessen their heroism nor their achievement.

Religion comes into it because the country was divided on how far the Reformation went or should go. At the beginning of the century there was no such thing as a Puritan "party". England was a Protestant country and the church was that established by the Elizabethan Settlement. It was Anglican. And it was "unthinkable that there should be more than one Church; the discussion centred on the question in whose hands the Church should be" while "every religious party held that the ideal of the Church was inseparably bound up with the ideal of a rightly ordered state, and coercion in religion was applied as a matter of course".[21] Unfortunately, Crown and Parliament became more and more estranged and opposed on this question. Parliament was for puritanism, the Crown for Arminianism. To put it over-simply—it was predestination against free-will. But at first there was no real split, there were only certain climates of opinion within the established Church and within the country which ranged from rigid Calvinism on the left to what we would call High Church on the right. In the middle were varying degrees of moderates, including the Anglican Calvinists. Thus there were those who were satisfied with the Elizabethan *status quo*, as it were, and those who believed that the Reformation hadn't gone far enough and that the church still needed purifying. Elizabeth had said "There is only one Christ Jesus and one faith; the rest is a dispute about trifles", an attitude which led John Knox to brand her as "neither good protestant nor yet resolute papist"; but the disagreement within the Anglican church was, in the beginning, largely a matter of disagreement about forms. For example, the moderates disagreed with such forms as the sign of the cross in baptism, the ring in marriage, the wearing of copes and surplices by the clergy and "the longsomeness of the service". They had no desire to separate from the church, they

41

merely wished to do away with certain ritual and liturgical things which, to them, smacked of popery if not paganism. They were not separatist, they were non-conformist—as were the Pilgrim Fathers. But the extreme purifiers, the rigid Calvinists, who believed in the terrible doctrine of pre-destination, which meant that the individual was chosen or elected by God before birth for salvation or damnation, held that only the elect should have authority—presbyters and deacons in church and state— and that the non-elect (damned before birth) known to them as the Reprobate should be under their jurisdiction, primarily so that they should not annoy the elect by their sinful ways while on earth. When dead they could, literally, go to the devil.

These were the separatists or Dissenters. They saw no hope of purifying the church from within. They wanted to start anew and go back to what they believed the government of the early church had been, as re-interpreted by Calvin. The established church with its hierarchy of Archbishops, Bishops and priesthood was rotten with the non-elect and with papistical forms and doctrines. Dissenters, for example, considered it a weakness to use the Lord's Prayer when the spirit could, and did, move any man to extemporaneous praying and preaching and they laid great stress on preaching, discipline, and Sabbatarianism.*

*The emphasis was on preaching as against emphasis on sacramental and liturgical forms. So when writing or preaching on controversial matters was forbidden the Puritans took to lecturers. They established lectureships (paid for out of their own pockets). Laud put down lecturers. Discipline and hard work they believed would overcome poverty and Puritanism was always strong in areas such as London and the home counties—which were economically prosperous. In a way it became a handy tool for employers and, curiously, capitalism and puritanism were allied which was no bad thing. It was a duty to work hard and perhaps this accounts partly for the strict Sabbatarian attitude. There were too many saint's days, holy days or holidays in the mediaeval church (and in the Roman Catholic Church), above 100 in the year, on which no work was done. Only the Sabbath, according to the Ten Commandments, should be kept as a holy-day (not a holiday) hence the gloomy Sabbath. This is, on the face of it, a perfectly tenable point of view . . . whether one agrees or not.

The Queen is Dead—Long Live the King

On both sides there were many men of complete and absolute sincerity and integrity. On both sides there were a few self-seekers and canting or gilded hypocrites. But, since the King would not listen or even give an inch to the moderates at the Hampton Court Conference of 1604, it became inevitable that the purifiers—moderates and extremists—would, and could, achieve their ends only by uniting, hence the Puritans as a "party" (and there were many sects within this party including the lunatic fringe Fifth Monarchy men, ready to bring in Christ's Kingdom by fire and sword) came into being. And, since the King was head of the church and of the government, and church and politics were not separate, they could achieve their aims through politics only. If war is an extension of politics then, in this century, the two religious "parties", Anglican and Puritan, gave rise to political parties.

Here one must remember that in those days of poor communications, the parish was the real social unit and the church represented the core and centre of village life. It was also the centrè of local taxation and administration. Titles of property were held in the church. In times of war or threat of war arms were stored there and men were trained in the church yard. Church bells called the parish to service, they also pealed out for joy or to call out the able-bodied in times of trouble or disaster. As for the parson and the pulpit? The pulpit was the logical place for government announcements, just as it is used today to announce the date of the annual Sunday School picnic, or the next meeting of the Mothers' Union. The monarch, as head of the church and sole appointer of bishops (still today a function of the crown) could use the pulpit to make a firm announcement of policy or for more oblique propaganda purposes. For example, in 1620, James the head of the church (and also of an extremely debauched and profligate court) ordered the Bishop of London to instruct London's clergy to preach against "the insolence of our women, and their wearing of broad-brimmed hats, pointed doublets, and their hair cut short". This was, doubtless, annoying to women but it was trivial. It was far less trivial when six years later, under Charles I, the clergy was told to preach sermons indicating that to refuse the king financial support was sinful. One can see at once that those parsons who believed that it was no such thing would have a tender conscience, and when so instructed might refuse to do as they were bid and so might be turned out. "If the patron be precise so must his chaplain be" says Robert Burton, "and if he be papist his clerk must be so, else he be turned out". No matter how good, how learned, how virtuous, how sincere a man in holy orders, he had small chance of preferment unless willing to compound with his conscience and also to enter by the "simonaical gate"* for many patrons "by right of inheritance" were a "debauched, corrupt, covetous, illiterate crew . . . a sordid, profane, pernicious company, irreligious, impudent and stupid . . . enemies to learning, confounders of the Church and the ruin of the Commonwealth".[22] Many members of the clergy were shockingly underpaid, since they "bought" their livings, some had no more than £8-£10 per year and, of course, many parsons were almost illiterate.

This was the unfortunate situation in many livings, but there were less corrupt patrons who did not sell livings and who were honest, earnest men. Yet they, too, used the pulpit for what they considered to be the best interests of the commonwealth— economically and politically. Puritan patrons, naturally, appointed parsons of puritanical and parliamentary leanings but in the beginning, as far as doctrine went, most incumbents were Anglican. Religious radicalism, as such, did not appear until around the 1640's and then chiefly among those who rejected entirely the patronage system, probably because under Laud ecclesiastics were more and more being put into the offices of civil government. In 1637 the Bishop of London, William Juxon, was made Lord High Treasurer of England—an office which had not been held by a churchman since the pre-Reformation days

---

*There was what the Earl of Clare called "temporal simony" as well. The established price of a barony under James I was £1,000; an Earldom cost £30,000.

of Henry VII. This was seen as a long step backward into the feared and hated clerical rule—it was as unpopular then as it is unthinkable now. And, with the influence patrons had on parsons, and parsons on the parishes; and the influence of Puritan preachers, now proscribed but functioning underground, as it were, as "lecturers", it becomes relatively simple to see how a

Warship of 100 guns, *c.* 1670.

country could become so split, so fragmented, so divided, and finally so harrassed and desperate as to plunge into the most dreadful of all wars, civil war. For the great majority had no desire to live in the "state ecclesiastical", as John Robinson, pastor to the Pilgrim Fathers, put it. And a state ecclesiastical meant to them, rule by the Bishops and by ecclesiastical courts, and money controlled by the Bishops and the king.

So the Puritan Revolution, which is yet another name for the Great Rebellion or the Civil Wars, was inevitable . . . religion, money, power became inextricably muddled. So muddled that even during the wars themselves, the issues were not very clear to most people, or they became overlaid, as issues do. Men changed sides and then changed back again because of some point or another. Perhaps some did so out of expediency, but others did it bravely and of conviction, for as a very great modern statesman has said it takes a brave man to rat and re-rat.

Through it all one feels desperately sorry for the second Stuart King. Not because Van Dyke's paintings of Charles I are the best pieces of propaganda any monarch ever had, but because the king appears so often to have been untrustworthy and treacherous. But was he? Or was it merely a matter of conscience or rather consciences? For as the Bishops explained to him over the terrible business of Strafford, his private conscience and his public conscience were two different things and his public conscience might require him to do what his private conscience forbade. To allow Strafford's execution was the duty of his public conscience, although privately he had given Strafford his word that he would not allow Parliament to impeach him. This has often been held against Charles (and indeed he held it against himself). But wherein did this differ from the conduct of, say, the good citizens of Gloucester? who, when asked to surrender to the king and promised a free pardon replied, "We do keep this city according to our oaths and allegiance, to and for the use of his Majesty; and his royal posterity: and we do accordingly conceive ourselves wholly bound to obey the commands of his Majesty signified by both Houses of Parliament; and are resolved by God's help to keep this city accordingly".[23] As Samuel Butler makes his Roundhead say, "We make war for his Majesty against himself". Again, this sounds a fearful muddle and very two-faced to say the least. But if the king had two consciences the Parliamentary party with great subtlety—the subtlety of theologians—drew a fine distinction between the "natural" person of the king and his "official" person. To the "natural" person belonged the King's private conscience and the death of Strafford, to the "official" person belonged Gloucester's oaths and its resistance to the "natural" person. The end of it all was the tragedy of Charles' death upon the scaffold—and when faced with death the natural and official combined and no man was ever more king-like. The

The Queen is Dead—Long Live the King

end was also in the assembled crowd which had clamoured for his death and which, when his severed head was exposed, sent up the most terrible great groan of pity and horror. To whom now did they owe allegiance?

There are so many ifs in history that it is idle—if interesting—to use the word speculatively. But in this seventeenth century there are two great ifs which may be usefully inspected. If James I had been less interested in showing off his theological knowledge; less frightened of falling into the hands of the Presbyterians (dissenters), from whom he'd escaped in Scotland; less consumed with his own idea of divine right at the Hampton Court conference; and more willing to listen or accede even in a very small way to the moderate demands made by the reforming party within the Anglican church then, probably, extreme radical Puritanism would not have come into being and the Puritans who beset his son Charles would not have "harried him out of the land"* via the headsman's axe. Again, if James II had not become a convert to Roman Catholicism—and a stupid and bigoted one at that, who attempted to put Roman Catholics into high office—there would have been no Glorious Revolution of 1688 when finally the swaying scales in the long battle for sovereign power came down on the side of Parliament. William of Orange became William III by the invitation and CONSENT of Parliament. So here, in this century, is the beginning of modern constitutional monarchy. Here we have the beginning of what everyone likes best . . . the eating of the cake and the having of it too. For certainly the English learned one very important thing about themselves in the Stuart era. They had kings ruling without parliament in the first half of the century and they didn't like it at all. That was absolute monarchy, a thing which was developed to its

*At the Conference James said to Dr. Reynolds, the Puritan Leader, "If this be all your party hath to say, I will make them conform themselves or else will harry them out of the land." With these words James, as Professor Gardiner says, sealed his fate and that of the country. He also signed the death-warrant of his son. For muddled and tardy as usual we beheaded the wrong king.

highest point by Louis XIV of France. They didn't approve of it there or at home. They then had six years of Army/Parliament rule and, finally, five years with a Lord Protector to save them from the rule of the saints militant which had turned out so badly. But in 1689, after a Restoration of one King (Charles II), and the removal of another (James II), they got what they wanted—the king back in Parliament again, but with the rôles reversed. It was Parliament and not the King which held the power. It has done so ever since and Queen Anne, the last of the Stuart sovereigns, was also the last monarch to act as Prime Minister. The last to touch for the King's Evil. Divine right was as dead as James I— so was the age-old magic of kings. And, as a curious concomitant of this, from Anne's day on, the court never again led the way in anything at all. It set no standard either of splendour or corruption. It neither displayed nor enshrined the cultural ideals or aspirations of the country. It wasn't even particularly fashionable and, save for a brief and very limited revival of artistic interest a century later under the Regency, court patronage of, and interest in the arts and sciences ceased forever.

But the court was not representative of England, even in the Stuart era, in any larger sense of the word. Nor were kings, courtiers, political leaders, army Generals, great merchants and bankers the only outstanding figures of this brilliant, fragmented, restless, insurgent century—perhaps the most important in our modern history and in many instances the most like our own. For men were thinking in new ways about things other than the internal balance of power. Their minds were stretching in all directions. They were no longer satisfied with the formalized and fossilized knowledge of scholastic philosophy beloved by Aristotelean schoolmen. There was a great movement within the spirit of man everywhere and this movement, in England, did not express itself wholly in the struggles between Kings and Parliaments, between Anglicans and Puritans, between Tories and Whigs. But if the century blew up at half time, so to speak, it soared in other ways and right from the beginning, too, like

The Queen is Dead—Long Live the King

the great magnificent rockets which always ended the fireworks displays which were so adored and with which, and the ringing of bells, were celebrated everything from Royal Weddings to the Lord Mayor Shows throughout the whole of the era.*

But now the rockets, with their miniature and imitative comet's tails, burst against the dark perimeter of a sky which, for the first time in English history, was being carefully explored and charted, as the great Elizabethan seamen and navigators had once sailed and mapped hitherto unknown seas. Man, with an extra-corporeal and enlarging eye, had multiplied Sappho's Pleiades, had looked upon the beautiful and ravaged face of the moon while the earth, so recently round,† slept like a top and moved, elliptically, about a sun which would never again dance on Easter Day. And high "Above the smoke and stir of this dim spot which men call earth"[24] are men like Milton and Boyle and Newton and Harvey; Donne, Dryden, Hooke, Marvel, Bacon, Wren and so many other "immortal shapes of bright aerial spirits"[25] who, in their different ways and in every field, burn with such a glorious light, that the sad "unspeakable puddle" is transmuted, by and upon reflection, into a sheet of burnished gold. For Milton touches Shakespeare and Jonson with one hand and Congreve and Addison with the other, while Dryden's life overlaps the lives of Donne and Pope. Inigo Jones was fifteen, William Harvey ten, when the King of Spain made his "piratical brain-sick attempt" with the Armada; both men lived into the Commonwealth, and Harvey into the Protectorate. Newton's life touched Charles I at its beginning and comes within a few months of George II at its end. Wren's year of birth saw Thomas

*One example only; to celebrate the Peace of Ryswick in 1697 a great fireworks display costing £12,000 was given. There were 1,000 sky rockets of from four to six lbs. in weight; 200 sheets; 2,400 pumps with stars; 1,000 cones; 7,000 Reports; 15,000 swarms; 400 Light Balls; twenty-three Rocket chests containing sixty rockets each, and a large number of casualties, some fatal.

†Confirmation by American space flights, of the Van Allen radiation belt now (1961) reveal, rather shatteringly, that the world is not round, it is pear-shaped.

The Pageant of Stuart England

Wentworth, Earl of Strafford, as Deputy in Ireland and the year of his death saw the birth of Adam Smith. Robert Hooke was a young man when Galileo died, an old one when "Longitude" Harrison was born. Francis Bacon died in 1626 and Robert Boyle, the greatest disciple of the Baconian method of the new "natural philosophy", was born the next year. Centuries are never isolated and remote—although they seem so—we have all linked hands in a great chain since Adam.

Again such names as these, taken at random, are great names and far better known to us today than to the century which produced them—every modern school child must have heard of Shakespeare and Milton, of Newton's apple and Boyle's law. But in the Stuart century the great were known—to what percentage of the population? It is impossible to say with any accuracy. The plain fact is, that probably seventy-five per cent of our Stuart ancestors lived just on or below subsistence level. And of the more fortunate twenty-five per cent, only a very small proportion were rich or well educated enough—and had sufficient opportunity or leisure—to interest themselves and participate in an era which is the first era of really creative science in our history (our own is the second), or to produce or acquaint themselves with, say, the enormous literary output of the time. For the few, then, it was a magnificent century "the best of all places for an Englishman to be", as Sir Arthur Bryant puts it. But for the many it must have been sheer, grinding misery.

We know a great deal more about the few than we do about the many because the few by now had become for the first time self-conscious and highly articulate, and a great many of them took to keeping journals and diaries and account books. And, probably because of the new, improved and improving postal system they took to writing countless letters too. How their quills flew across the paper which is so much better and more plentiful in this century than in the last. What oceans of gummy, inferior ink they used. Their spelling is quite unorthodox—the same word is spelled half a dozen different ways in the same letter. Their punctuation is equally light-hearted. Sentences end with a

Seventeenth-century spinning wheel.

comma, a semi-colon, colon, or full stop with a mediaeval virgule added. Their use of words differs from modern usage; their pronunciation differs too. But we owe so much to the letter writers, the diarists and to those who wrote histories and pamphlets—and, thank goodness, their handwriting is far easier to read than Tudor handwriting for there is so much more of it to read. So we can eavesdrop on their private lives as they write letters of a gossipy nature; exchange recipes for home-made wine or against the plague; give news of inheritances, debts, curtain materials, feasts, new flowers from outlandish parts, the births and deaths of children (both appallingly frequent). We hear about the weather. It is wet. It is the coldest winter ever. The Thames is frozen and a great fair takes place there with coaches going on the ice from Westminster to the Tower, and oxen roasted over blazing fires, and all manner of booths set up to sell all manner of things. Or it is hotter and drier than any man can remember, the crop yield is poor and cattle waste in the drought. We read of the terrible divisions in families during the Civil Wars when husband was on one side and son on another. "O my deere son", Lady Denbigh writes, "that you would turn to the king . . . I cannot forget what a son I had once, I do more travall with soro for the grefe I suffer . . . than ever I did to breeng you into the world". And we know that, before this, Ann Stagg, a Brewer's wife, tried to prevent the great grefe falling upon England by leading a procession of women as "sharers in the public calamity" to present a Petition against the war to Parliament. They were entreated to return to their homes and turn their petition into prayers.

Through so many and so varied writers of letters, histories, diaries and "characters", we are given a glimpse of the small, the personal, the absurd and the touching. There is King James I, shareholder in the New River Water Company, falling headlong into the New River* which he and Sir Hugh Myddelton had had dug to bring a better water supply to London. There is Sir Francis Bacon, who "much fancied . . . arm chairs covered and arched over the head"[26] because he maintained that all air was "predaetory". And old, debt-ridden Sir Oliver Cromwell, who loathed his nephew and namesake, the Protector, who falls into the fire and dies in an attempt to dry his clothes after going for a brisk walk—aged ninety-three—on a summer's day in August 1655. There is Nell Gwynn surrounded by the hostile mob at Oxford, which mistook her carriage for that of Charles II's French mistress, Louise de Kéroualle, crying out, "Pray, good people be civil; I am the Protestant whore". And the Earl of Lauderdale—a fierce-tempered red-headed man—who used to pinch Charles's snuff, trying to cheer the king up after the Dutch had burned our fleet in the Medway by dancing before him dressed in women's petticoats. The Earl of Melfort writes to Mary of Modena that King William is "a new Herod"[27] and Prince George Augustus of Hanover (later George II) writes in French to his cousin, now Queen Anne, to express his gratitude for being given "l'Ordre de la Jarretière"[28]—which, one suspects, she probably didn't want to give him at all! While Dean Swift eats a Chelsea bun "Rrrrrrrrrrare Chelsea Buns"? he tells Stella, on May 2nd, 1711, "it cost one a penny; it was stale, and I did

*On January 9th, 1621/22 near Theobalds.

not like it." And there is William Blundell, of Crosby, Lancs., who, in a way, sums up the difference between the old, secure world and the new, with a sad little entry made in his journal, perhaps in 1659, "I do not know in what part of the world dragons are to be found" he says, "nor do I know their shape or size."

And it is William Blundell who, while we are thinking about Chelsea buns and dragons, plunges us suddenly into that below-subsistence-level world. The world where from three-and-three-quarters to four-and-a-half million out of a total population of five or six million of our Stuart ancestors lived. For one day, in 1684, meeting a poor woman he asked her how many children she had and was told six. "Here" he said "is sixpence for them" . . . "No sir" she replied simply, "I will not sell my children for sixpence." And, indeed, in most diaries and account books, we become conscious of the poor, the submerged three-quarters. They emerge as constantly recurring items in gifts to "a poore woman", "man" or "ragged boy" and this is about all we do know about them. Search as we may we cannot find them else-where. They are shadowy, unsubstantial figures who appear, briefly, anonymously, to be given 2d. or 4d. or 6d. and some-times even a shilling. Or they appear, again in other people's words and records, as in Parish Overseers accounts, if they are paupers like the Widow Siggars, deceased, of Hornchurch whose small effects are sold and the money spent to clothe her children. "Laid out for the widow Siggars youngest child" in Restoration year is $8/4\frac{1}{2}$ to provide a coat, petticoat "whale-bone" and other "instruments", as well as "1 pair of hose, 1 pair of shoes and a cap"[29]—hose, shoes and cap cost $1/8\frac{1}{2}$. Or we see them as they appear before the King's justices for various misdemeanours; such as that committed by Margaret Edwards, wife of a fisherman who, in Fishers Street, Barking in 1645, did call Edmund Palmer (a Draper) "in a violent and outraigious manner . . . roundheaded rogue" and "used many other reviling words whereby a great tumult was raised".[30] Or there is Mr. William Poole presented for "not doing his worke in the highway with his carte this year''; and the wretched Pannells—a family of brothers, wives, and children—tradesmen—nineteen of them burned out with ''theire working loomes, bedding and household stuffe to the valewe of One hundred pounds and upwards, to the utter undoing of the said parties and their wives and children, they being lefte without any places to reside, but upon the charities of some neighbours neere dwellings''.[31] This kind of disaster spelled complete ruin for many a small tradesman in the days before fire insurance which wasn't thought of until after the great fire of London.

Then there is Jane Earle, a widow, who stayed away from church one Sunday in 1641/2 because she was ''very weary and Sicke'' having come on foot fifteen miles the day before. For this they carried her by force to the Parish Cage and imprisoned her, happily for only ''a quarter or halfe an hower''—one hopes it was only for that time. There is also Edward Mayer—possibly poor, possibly just eccentric—who, ''obstinate and refractorie'' fellow that he was, refused to live soberly in a house near Wivenhoe but persisted in inhabiting a boat drawn up on dry land. He'd made his boat very comfortable, too, with a fireplace. But the neighbours thought this a danger. His chimney might set fire to a nearby thatched roof and so they petitioned to have Edward removed. One appreciates Edward's desire to live in a boat. One also sees the neighbours' point of view. Fire was a terrible hazard everywhere.

Yet even these people whom we find misbehaving were still so much better off than many. The Pannells were probably not below the subsistence level until after the calamity of the fire, and all of them, including Jane Earle, obviously had settled homes. Even she was apprehended at home ''lying upon her bed.''

But what of the cottages occupied by ''the poore'' who ''lived in houses such as a man may build in three or four hours''? Squalid ramshackle huts, built on waste land on some moonlit night, so that by morning smoke could be seen issuing from a hole in the roof and the legendary squatter's right established.

The Queen is Dead—Long Live the King

How did they live? What were their lives? Where do we find
them? Some must have been even worse off than the weaver of
Hastings with whom John Taylor, the water poet, found lodging
one bitter winter's night:

> "No meat, no drink, no lodging (but the floor)
> No stool to sit, no lock upon the door,
> No straw to make us litter in the night,
> Nor any candlestick to hold the light."[32]

This is no exaggeration. It is the plain truth and there were
thousands like the weaver who, it should be noted, was carrying
on a cottage industry in circumstances of such terrible poverty
and misery that not even John Taylor's subsequent adventures on
his water journey from London to Salisbury can deflect our
minds from this picture.

And so we have a century of enormous contrasts. Of a few
great people—and of many anonymous, faceless ones. Of a new
scientific spirit of inquiry—and of hanging harmless old women
as witches. Of splendid houses like Hatfield and Chatsworth—
and the dreadful cottages of the squatters on waste land. About
the twenty-five per cent we know more than we have ever known
in our previous history, but about the seventy-five per cent we
still know virtually nothing. They are still submerged. Still
hidden. They speak to us because they do not speak. Like ancient,
worn, carved angels in cathedrals who play, with calm indiffer-
ence, a silent music upon broken instruments of stone, they too
are of a different order—remote and lost in the semi-darkness of
history. For them, as for most of us, "Oblivion is not to be
hired: The greater part must be content to be as though they had
not been, to be found in the Register of God, not in the record
of man".[33]

CHAPTER TWO

Of Houses—Great, Middling, and Small

THE high point and the end of court festivities celebrating the investiture of Henry Frederick as Prince of Wales came on the evening of June 5th, 1610 when, in the ramshackle old palace of Whitehall, a long-rehearsed grand masque was given. The masque, *Tethys' Festival*, was written by Samuel Daniel—poet laureate "at jealousies" with Ben Jonson—but the moving spirit behind it, as well as in it, was undoubtedly the prince's mother, Anna of Denmark* who adored masques above all things. As this was a most romantic, traditional occasion (there hadn't been a Prince of Wales for more than a century†) the court's favourite designer for the royal theatre, Mr. Inigo Jones, had devised a romantic setting rather than a classical one—although there were a few classical touches here and there.

The principal piece, a magnificent rocky grotto cascading with water, had a great central niche supported on each side by two subsidiary ones. These lesser niches were ornamented with "pillasters of gold mingled with rustick stones".[1] Inside, and

---

*Although we call her Queen Anne, the Queen consort of James I always signed herself "Anna" and I use this throughout to distinguish her from her great-granddaughter, Anne, who was of course, Queen regnant.

†The previous holder of the title was Henry VIII, created Prince of Wales in 1503.

presumably in the dry, tritons and water nymphs were decoratively displayed. The nymphs were really ladies of Anna's court but as children of Tethys, Empress of Streams, personified the rivers of their fathers' estates. Among them, Princess Elizabeth, not yet the unfortunate Winter Queen, represented the Thames; Arabella Stuart, soon to make a marriage which led to the Tower, madness and death, was the river Trent; the beautiful fourteen-year-old Countess of Essex, later infamous as an adulteress and poisoner, was the Lea; and Anne Clifford, Countess of Dorset who fought so long for her rightful inheritance, personated the Aire. In the central niche where a finny entablature of dolphins with wreathed tails supported huge golden vases, stood the rocky throne of Tethys—six steps up, with golden cherubim as arm rests and flanked by great silver whales, sea horses and tridents. Above, a giant silver scallop shell with rich folds of drapery made a "state" or canopy while in the arching roof jewels of coloured glass—fabulous diamonds, emeralds, rubies and sapphires—let in the fugitive light of rainbows meshed in sea spray or caught glittering in the jetted plume of a whale. The throne's occupant "Love inspiring Tethys" was, ironically enough, Anna herself.

Very probably no one noticed how absurd she looked except perhaps poor Mr. Jones who had so carefully designed a bodice of sky-coloured silk to be worn with a flowing train and a half tunic of silver gauze embroidered with sea-weed. This costume symbolized the nature of the mythological Empress—even more importantly it cleverly disguised the very un-nymph-like figure of the real Queen. But silly, frivolous, extravagant Anna didn't care a jot about symbolism or suitability. As Queen she was automatically the leader of fashion (a rôle she greatly enjoyed) and Mr. Jones was much mistaken if he thought a leader of fashion would appear on such a great occasion—or at any other time for that matter—half swathed in an unostentatious gauze garment which concealed rather than emphasized and exaggerated the most prominent parts of the figure. So the Queen ordered an enormous wheel farthingale and a high starched ruff to be added

Typical Jacobean house, *c.* 1620.

to her costume. The effect must have been acsthetically disastrous—but it was a typical Jacobean gesture.

Fortunately Mr. Jones outlived the Queen, farthingales and ruffs; and one shudders to think what might have happened to English architecture in the succeeding centuries if he hadn't. For early Jacobean architecture was an elaboration and a crystallization of the late Elizabethan style, and the late Elizabethan style was largely and unhappily hideous. Even so, boastful and vulgar as it often was—and is—there is no mistaking its virility, animation and enthusiasm. If rich Elizabethans built for show, which they did, so did the Jacobeans; but they built for "state" too, and there were more rich Jacobeans than rich Elizabethans. So houses as status symbols were even more numerous. "No kingdom in the world" says Bishop Goodwin "spent so much in building as we did in this time".

By now, houses had often achieved a more symmetrical look, but "in this time" came a much more definite feeling for the massing

First Italianate style classical house, Inigo Jones, 1616/1629-35.

of shapes which was due to the clearer and better understood
influence of the Renaissance. A great house might, and often did,
cover more ground than earlier houses but it certainly rambled
less. The E or H plan with its recessions, elaborate corner turrets
or bays rising like small towers, was still a firm favourite, but the
cross-bar of the "H" was often pushed down to make elongated
wings or pavilions on one front and a shallow depression on the
other. The rectangular or square plan was also favoured, em-
bellished with projecting bays, towers or turrets; yet interior
and exterior bore little relation to each other. Rooms varying in
shape and size within the plan were, as they had been for centuries, intercommunicating. Privacy was unknown. To get from
one end of a house to the other one might have to pass through
bedrooms, parlours, dining-rooms or great Hall, the chapel, if
any, and even sometimes the kitchen. This must have been always
tiresome and frequently embarrassing, but no one had thought of
interior passages as yet, although an open loggia known as a

"purgola", with gallery above, served this purpose for ground and first floors in large houses. The only interior innovation of any significance in the time of James I was in the positioning of the Great Hall. Formerly on left or right of the main entrance, it had been reached only through a bogus passage made by placing an elaborately carved screen across the hall at right angles to the entrance. But in new Jacobean houses the Hall was placed on the central axis of the house and was entered from either end or from the side. Paradoxically, as it became the centre of the house it ceased to be the centre or heart of the home. But the Great Hall had been in a gentle decline for years while the Long Gallery (in this century always on the first floor) gained in importance. The Hall continued its decline, rather more rapidly, until it became an elaborate though smaller entrance hall in which no one now ate meals, played shovel board, danced or exercised with the broad sword during bad weather, a fact lamented by John Selden the famous "parliamentary" lawyer and orientalist who believed that the old custom of dining with servants and tenants made for better understanding between master and men.

As a smaller hall left more internal space this was used for extra rooms. Thus many great houses now had two parlours, one for winter, the other for summer, adjoining the diminished hall. A bit later these parlours became a dining-room and a small withdrawing-room. Above the Hall was the Principal Chamber where owner and wife received and entertained guests—even if it did contain a large florid bed. This became the principal drawing-room in houses of a later date. Ordinary bedrooms themselves were unimportant, inconvenient and uncomfortable, but in great state houses lodgings—that is apartments of two or more rooms—were provided for members of the family and guests. In houses such as Hatfield there were an enormous number of lodgings.

But most prodigy houses, although varying slightly in shape, size and plan, had one thing in common—ornamentation of the most stupendous impurity. So-called classical elements were outrageously contorted and distorted. Columns resembling fat

Of Houses—Great, Middling, and Small

giant snakes or gargantuan corkscrews squirmed and writhed upwards. Bases were hideously swollen, notched, carved or otherwise mutilated. Capitals had involutes buried by great coarse leaves. Entablatures were denticulated, notched or snipped out of all recognition and, in addition, too often swarmed with garlands (of the clump kind), masks, lozenges, bold curly strap work, heraldic devices and grotesques. Like the Elizabethans, the early Jacobeans, broadly speaking, felt that no surface inside or out should be left unornamented. And, as their houses were larger there was far more surface to be filled up as fancy or Flemish designers dictated. The farthingale and starched ruff mentality was not exclusive to Queen Anna, nor did it apply to clothing alone. It was evident everywhere. Decoration was piled upon decoration, Pelion upon Ossa, horror upon horror. It wasn't until the end of the reign of James I (and he didn't die until 1625) that, architecturally speaking, things began to sober down. Inigo Jones had a hand in this.

Jones, the son of a cloth worker was, we are told in the preface to *Stone-Heng Restored*, "naturally inclined to study the arts of design" and "passed into foreign parts to converse with the great masters thereof in Italy".* It was less a conversation than a complete conversion. Yet the work of Jones and his pupil Webb

*Jones visited Italy twice. The first time he studied the wonderful buildings of Andrea Palladio, which in addition to the Villas of the Veneto, had transformed Vicenza into a town of exquisite beauty. After this he, possibly, went to Denmark and may have come from there to England where, under Anna of Denmark's patronage, he became a member of Prince Henry's Establishment. During this period his principal work seems to have been in designing settings (many with revolving scenes and other modern devices) and costumes for the masques so popular with the court. These drawings (many are at Chatsworth) are architectural and also characterized by a wonderfully free draughtsmanship. Some are based on the famous stage scene created for the Teatro Olimpico, Vicenza. After Prince Henry's death in 1612 Jones returned to Italy and studied Palladio's great books on architecture which were based on the precepts of Vitruvius. In 1615 he came back to England and was made surveyor-general of the Royal Buildings. At the age of forty-two, his real career as an architect began.

does not really represent the architecture of the first half of the century. Jones was so far in advance of his time in England as to be an almost isolated phenomenon. Time—and taste—did not catch up with him for nearly a hundred years. It must be remembered too that Jones was, chronologically, an Elizabethan; born in 1573 he was only nine years younger than Shakespeare. And here we must look back in order to understand why Jones was so extraordinary.

The soaring vertical lines of Gothic ecclesiastical buildings carry the eye ever upwards to the highest point. Tudor buildings are secular but they are also essentially gothic in form and feeling—one is always conscious of vertical lines and high points. The Elizabethans were also Tudor-Gothic builders but the late ones were greatly influenced by what they fondly imagined to be Italian Renaissance architecture, the symmetrical façade, to which they added all sorts of classical Renaissance detail with a wonderful and almost slapdash disregard for proportion and suitability. Never did they understand the five orders of architecture as such; they used them, tortured and debased, as applied ornament. The result was a fantastic vigorous romantic muddle. The more so because these classical details both of form and design had been a long time reaching England and had finally turned up via the Lowlands looking rather coarse and with considerable Flemish accretions. This kind of building persisted well on into the seventeenth century. Where Inigo Jones is wholly remarkable is that he completely ignored the fashionable architecture of his day and built in the pure Italian manner according to Palladio's rules of classical proportion with as few modifications as possible. This difference, between the usual style and that of Inigo Jones, is perhaps best seen in Hatfield House and the Queen's House at Greenwich. They seem to belong not only to totally different centuries but to quite different civilizations. Yet a mere five years lie between the finishing of one and the beginning of the other.

Hatfield was built by Robert Cecil who, like his father, was a canny politician, cunning in statecraft and a great builder of

Of Houses—Great, Middling, and Small

houses. Having been forced by James I to exchange the wonderful palace of Theobalds—built by his father—for the old Episcopal Palace of Hatfield (where Elizabeth had lived as a girl) he commenced, in 1607, to build the new Hatfield which we today visit in our thousands. The new prodigy house, set on higher ground than the old palace, took but four years to build. This in itself is refreshing. Elizabethan houses of a similar kind were often ten, twenty or thirty years abuilding and, not surprisingly, ended as a weird and wonderful mélange of styles. Nevertheless Robert's last house is mixed and transitional. It is a Janus house, two-faced (and so, I fear, was Robert). It is a three-storied house, the north front square with extruded corners from which projecting bays rise, tower-like, above roof level. Another two bays stand on either side of the entrance to break the front but rise only on two storeys. The entrance, another bay, stops at roof level. Behind all this and at some distance rises the clock tower, so the eye does not slip very easily across the front, it leaps from bay to bay finding no resting place.

The south front is quite different. Here two great wings or pavilions extend from the central building and end in ogival towers. Across the face of the central block an arched loggia runs, its upper storey containing the Long Gallery. In the middle is a most elaborate storied structure as a "centrepiece"—half tower, half gateway with double columns carrying each storey. The whole thing rises above a roof ornamented with ogee gables. Behind this rises the equally complicated clock tower. Certainly one cannot complain that nothing rivets or carries the eye upward. Eye and mind are stunned and overwhelmed.*

Not so the "Queen's House". Here lines are horizontal, unbroken and uninterrupted by turrets, towers, bays or recessions. Although it took far longer than Hatfield to build, it is all unity, simple, symmetrical, subtle and of great elegance. It is an

*Blickling Hall, Aylsham, Norfolk is a Hatfield in little. Built 1616-28 to designs by Robert Lymings, Hatfield's architect, it lacks the brio and magnificence of Cecil's house, but has a wonderful still quality all its own which is enchanting.

organized whole; inside and outside are related. The foundations were laid in 1616 and we catch a first glimpse of the house in a letter written by John Chamberlain to Sir Dudley Carleton on June 21st, 1617. "The Quene", the letter runs . . . "is building somewhat at Greenwich, W<u>ch</u> must be finished this sommer. Yt is saide to be some curious devise of Inigo Jones, and will cost about 4,000<u>li</u>." This was only twice the average cost of one of Anna's masques and cannot be considered excessive, but for some reason, possibly financial, work was stopped soon afterwards and then, in 1619, Anna died. Building was not recommenced until 1629 when Anna's daughter-in-law, Henrietta Maria was Queen consort. She is the Queen of the "Queen's House". Nevertheless, as its foundations were laid in 1616 and the first floor possibly completed before work stopped, the Queen's House can be regarded as Jones' first really important building and, more significantly, the first classical house in England.*

What a plain, unprepossessing little box it must have looked then, with its rusticated ground floor, its stuccoed walls, swept clear of all ornamentation save for balusters under the windows; its plain cornice and simple balustraded roof. Like Hatfield, the south has a loggia, but it is pillared not arched and is set on the first floor facing the slope of the park where later in the century Wren's Royal Observatory was built.

Yet the problem Jones had to solve was certainly not simple. At the old palace of Greenwich, gardens and park were separated by a much used road running from Deptford to Woolwich. The Queen's House had to straddle this public highway so that royal occupants had free access to garden and park without crossing

---

*But not the first classical building. In 1619 Inigo Jones began work on the Banqueting House in Whitehall (the Gothic one was destroyed by fire in 1617) and the building was finished three years later. Providentially it has escaped ruin by time, builders and bombs. The need for a new Banqueting House may have stopped work on the Queen's house. Charles I was executed on a scaffold built just outside one of the new banqueting house windows.

the road. Jones' solution was to divide the ground floor into two quite separate halves, one half in the garden the other in the park, connected by a covered bridge. All principal rooms were sited—Italian palazzo fashion—on the first floor, excepting the two-storied entrance hall on the north front, so the road, in a sense simply ran through the house.* Today with the road diverted

The "Dutch" House, later Kew Palace, 1631.

we can scarcely imagine how essential or original this "curious devise"—nor, indeed, how revolutionary the house—was.

Jones here made the complete break with traditional "Jaco-bethan" architecture. For him there seems to have been no transitional period, and although his buildings seem very English

*As the house is nearly square it was possible in 1661 to add two further bridges to the perimeter of the square. The division was then no longer apparent nor was the original design spoiled in any way. The original bridge is now the central room, first floor.

to us today he was European in his approach and leaped forward where other and lesser men were content to compromise with the past. The lesser men probably found his buildings flat, spare, and almost indecently naked or even pretentious: Ben Jonson called Jones "Vitruvius Hoop" and "Lanthorne Leatherhead"—they "quarrelled greatly"—but it must be remembered that Jones was a Court Architect. His style was not "popular", nor did it spread very much beyond court circles. Although Jones lived during three reigns and part of the Commonwealth he worked almost exclusively for the court and the nobility, but ninety-five per cent of our ancestors lived a very long way outside the *ambience* of the court, so English building jogged along much as it had done for years.

Houses for the most part, and particularly in the country where the majority still lived, were built to the centuries' old pattern. And here it is necessary to point out that many of the "Olde Worlde" sixteenth- and seventeenth-century cottages advertised for sale today are not cottages at all. They are farmhouses— and rather grand ones at that. It is highly probable that no cottages of the period survive, but we know pretty well what they were like, and it is quite wrong to picture them as enchanting and nostalgic bits of pastoral England—all thatch, firelight, lowing cattle, with a hey nonny nonny and woodbine round the door. Some, no doubt were. Many were not. Throughout the whole of a century which "spent so much in building" there were "Poore cottages . . . on which the sun had never shone"[2] and villages, particularly in the north, of "sad little hutts";[3] genuinely mistaken by one traveller for cattle stalls. It was impossible to believe they could be dwelling houses; dry walled "slatt" roofed with "little or noe tunnells for their chimneys".[4] They were small, cold, poor, wretched hovels for the small, the cold, the poor, and the wretched.

Basically, a cottage consisted of one room only. This was known as the house-room or house-part and here the family lived, slept, ate and looked up at bare rafters provided they could be seen through the smoke. Unaware of the advantages, if any, of this early equivalent of the open floor plan, cottagers if and when they prospered added other rooms at the ends or side of the house-room; these were called "outshuts". One, near the fireplace, might be the buttery where food, pots and cooking utensils were kept. Another might lead to "chambers", a single room with partitions half-way up to make sleeping cubicles or bed-rooms. Rarely was there an upper floor, although occasionally if the house-room were large and its roof high enough, a cock loft (attic) was built with it or "ceiled off "later, and reached by a ladder. Many cottages had the barn attached, often separated from the house by nothing more than a wooden partition, and in some cottages the entrance was through the barn. Naturally there were variations in shape, size and building material but as a statute of 1589 forbade more than one family to live in a cottage it is possible cottages increased in number from then on. More farmhouses were built too, and more small houses of the minute manor type. These were not built by architects or surveyors but by master masons and carpenters responsible for both design and building. Many must have been men of the greatest talent; anonymous artists whose work still gives us such joy and delight when we stumble across it in the countryside. Rural building was still conditioned, as it always had been, by local materials, but timber was no longer handy and plentiful. Charcoal burners, iron workers, and farmers had all made terrible inroads into once great forests.* Transport was poor, roads vile. So it would be an extravagant folly for a farmer or husbandman in, say, Gloucestershire to send to East Anglia for building brick. It would be equally ruinous for an East Anglian to build his house of Cotswold stone (although the rich imported Caen and Portland stone). It was not until canals were dug in the eighteenth

---

*Thomas Fuller (1608-1661) is very sad about the vanishing forests and expresses himself in the following melancholy verse.

"Jove's oak, the war like ash, veined elm, the softer beech
    Short hazel, maple plain, light asp, the bending wych;
    Tough holly and smooth birch, must altogether burn
    What should the builder serve, supplies the forger's turn;"

century and railways laid in the nineteenth that it became possible for rural houses to be built in anything other than local materials. Thus, quite literally, small houses and cottages sprang from the chalk or clay upon which they stood or from the substratum of rock beneath the soil. This is why such houses look and feel as if they belonged.

Some local materials are, by nature, better for building than others. The hard granites of Cornwall and Wales are difficult to work, so houses there were—and still are—strong, simple and unornamented. Midland and Yorkshire sandstones are either too hard or too friable. The first leads to the same rugged simplicity found in Wales and Cornwall but the second does not well survive the weathering of centuries. Dorset houses, according to Thomas Fuller, were to be lived in rather than "looked on" being "very low" in situation. And he thought the old rhyme "The north for greatness, the east for health, The south for neatness, the west for wealth" was still very true in those days.

Chalk districts produced plaster houses—like the black and white ones in Cheshire—but now beaming became less frenzied and plastered areas were more often rectangular or square whereas earlier they had been diamond-shaped. Clay districts produced brick houses as they had once produced oak—the oak like the rose prefers clay—so once the oaks had vanished the clay which fed them was turned into bricks and, curiously enough, it is in this century that bricks really come into their own as an independent building material.* Hitherto they had been chiefly regarded as very useful in making walls, chimneys, and ovens, but otherwise rather limited and undistinguished.

*The history of brick in England is a strange one. Like central heating brick came in and went out with the Romans. We didn't rediscover brick until sometime in the thirteenth century, which sounds rather unenterprising of us—but we are only just re-discovering central heating. What is surprising, in view of the corkscrew chimneys of the Tudor period which certainly displayed the versatility of brick no less than the skill of the bricklayer, is that it took so long before the real potentialities of brick as a comprehensive building material was realized.

Of Houses—Great, Middling, and Small

Brick couldn't be worked or carved like stone or wood. It wasn't in itself decorative, apart from the colour and the way it could be set in patterns or diapered, nor were brick walls strong enough to uphold the great weight of roof timbers unless supported and reinforced by piers or stone quoining—or so it was thought. Hence, stone masons were more important than bricklayers and the Stone Mason's Company was very rich and very powerful. The Bricklayers' Company wasn't and, not unreasonably, wanted to rival the Masons in power and wealth, so a series of "discoveries" was made about brick and it soon became known as a most versatile building material. It was strong. It could be moulded, cut and used for all sorts of ornamental detail. The first all-brick house in Leeds was built, rather nervously one imagines, in 1628, by Alderman Metcalfe. Three years later the Dutch House (we call it Kew Palace) was built by Samuel Fortrey, a Flemish merchant with Dutch interests. The house is small, charming and entirely brick down to the last detail. Pilasters, mouldings, architraves, key stones and string courses illustrate the new use of brick. Even the voussoirs of the curly Dutch gables are banded with brick instead of stone and curly pedimented gables were very fashionable now (there are many beautiful ones surviving, particularly in Norfolk). Broome Park, near Denton, Kent (begun perhaps in 1635), displays a roof line of fantastically elaborate Dutch gables, and dormers all in cut and moulded brick. Brick had arrived! At Broome Park too, if one ignores the gables, one begins to see how classicism in architecture was developing in England. Classical symmetry and horizontal lines are there, although overtopped by a wildly romantic roof.

Classicism of the Italianate variety might well have begun to flourish from then on instead of being delayed for half a century or so, but in 1642 the Great Rebellion, as Lord Clarendon called the Civil Wars, began and this put a stop to building. Unhappily, it also caused the destruction of many existing houses. Some were burned or battered to death, others irretrievably ruined by soldiers of both sides. Contrary to popular belief,

Parliamentary soldiers were not the only destroyers of houses (they could claim that unenviable distinction when it came to churches)* the King's men were just as bad and many a house which had survived the ill treatment given it when occupied by soldiers of one side perished when occupied by those of the other. The same is true today. The interior of Ashdown House (built in 1665) was almost entirely ruined by British and allied soldiers during the 1939-45 war.

The Commonwealth and Protectorate (1649-1660) was not a notable period for building; in fact many great houses were destroyed at the time. The marvellous palace of Theobald's was torn down and the building materials sold off to pay the army. Holdenby suffered the same fate, and it seems hardly necessary to multiply examples of what, to us, seems foolish and wanton destruction. We, ourselves, are too often guilty of the same offence.

Of the few houses built during the time, and they were built chiefly by men who held high office, or who were (probably temporarily) in favour, Thorpe Hall is an excellent example of what might be called non-Inigo classical. It was built by Chief Justice Oliver St. John, the ship money lawyer, a relative by marriage and close friend of Cromwell, who refused to act as a Commissioner for the Trial of Charles I. John Evelyn en route to Peterborough passed Thorpe when it was very new, or still unfinished, and notes in his diary that it was "a stately palace of St. John's (one deep in the blood of our good king) built out of the ruins of the bishop's palace and cloister".[5] This comment

*Although Parliamentary soldiers wrought terrible destruction upon churches, and rifled tombs for jewels, gold and silver, in fairness it should be noted that not all the defaced or mutilated statues in churches are necessarily the handiwork of these soldiers. Many a saint's statue was believed to work cures and quite often bits were secretly chipped off by parishioners or travellers, taken home and used either in medicines or as amulets against disease. This sort of thing had been going on for centuries. In fairness too, the New Model Army was expressly forbidden to loot houses. But much damage was done before the New Model came into being.

The first London square: the "piazza" Covent Garden.

about St. John falls curiously from the pen of Mr. Evelyn. St. John, at least, had the courage of his convictions (and a patently illegal trial wasn't one of them) whereas Master Evelyn, a royalist, scuttled off to Europe at the beginning of the Wars. But first he went to the King's capital at Oxford to kiss the King's hand. He was, he told Charles I, loyal but his estates lay near London and, as London was the Parliamentary capital, if he took up arms for the king they'd be confiscated.

Thorpe is not a stately palace. Evelyn was just probably suggesting it was to make St. John look like a man who had profiteered out of blood and ruined Anglican bishops. Marmeduke Rawdon of York visited Thorpe and, as his biographer tells us, saw "a very fine house of Mister Sent Iohn's built of free stone, in which thir is a stair casse made with much arte and hath fine gardens, grotts and fish ponds"—one particularly likes the grotts and fishponds. This, though brief, is a much sounder description. As the house is classical (but not wholly so) it has often been ascribed to Inigo Jones or John Webb, but it was in fact designed by a London bricklayer, Peter Mills (1600-1670).

London even by the middle of the century was still essentially Tudor, Elizabethan (and even mediaeval) in appearance, with innumerable narrow-fronted houses where jettied upper floors overhung the dark, narrow, twisted and filthy streets. But London was expanding—old houses were torn down (or added to, where possible at the back), new ones put up and certain "undeveloped" areas were being developed. Notable among developers was William Newton, a rich Bedfordshire man who in 1637 decided to make even more money by developing unoccupied land in the region of Great Queen Street and Lincoln's Inn Fields. So he put up fourteen large houses on the south side of Great Queen Street (none survive) and Peter Mills designed them.

Perhaps Mills was influenced by the brand new buildings in Covent Garden designed by Inigo Jones and Isaac de Caux (or de Caus). The "piazza", the first formal planned London Square, had tall houses unornamented save for flat stone pilasters, and the first floor faced the street with open vaulted and arched loggias, reminiscent of that "ample piazza" at Leghorn. The Leghorn piazza "very fair and commodious . . . gave the first hint to the building both of the church and the piazza in Covent Garden with us, though very imperfectly pursued".[6] Imperfect perhaps, but at least they didn't sell slaves there.* Whatever the influence, the Newton-Mills houses were remarkable—and classical; devoid of gables and with unornamented Corinthian pillars rising from first floor to a mercifully discreet cornice. Principal rooms on the first floor had higher ceilings and longer windows than on the other floors, but the plan probably was little different from the

*The preferred place to sell them, particularly when they were British, was in the Barbados. In 1648 Cromwell did this; after Monmouth's rebellion (1685) James II permitted it, and so did George I after the rising of 1715. This, one of the nastier bits of our history, at least proves we were not bent on exploiting the Negro only. Slavery was common and remained common. Barbary pirates raided the Devonshire coast for slaves, while many an Englishman died in foreign galleys due to the hazards at sea or the misfortunes of war.

Of Houses—Great, Middling, and Small

old; two interconnected rooms, front and back, and a narrow side staircase. More unusually, each house had a 40-ft. frontage.

The houses have long since vanished but of the much grander houses in Lincoln's Inn Fields (not designed by Mills) Lindsay House still stands—it may be by Jones, certainly it is still very beautiful. Such houses had a strong influence on later architecture. But to the average Londoner these houses probably looked quite hideous, flat-fronted, cold and formal. He probably much preferred the old familiar squalor, darkness, clutter, mess, smell and overcrowding to which he was accustomed and indeed in many ways still is.

Similarly, the rural inhabitants of wildest Berkshire must have thought the house built by fashionable Roger Pratt for his cousin Sir George Pratt just as odd and ungrateful to the eye . . . and nothing like so good as the old Coleshill which had recently burned down (fire was a hazard in country districts as well as in towns). The new Coleshill, built sometime in mid-century, perhaps around 1650, was also classical and, like Thorpe Hall, was once attributed to Inigo Jones. Pratt discussed the plan with Jones but the house is his. He had travelled abroad during the Civil Wars (had lived with Evelyn in Rome) where he made notes on the architecture of the countries visited. And Coleshill probably owes as much to Pratt's foreign travels as it does to his discussion with Jones. It is—or was for it is lately deceased— what Pratt called a "double-pile" house. By this odd term he meant two rooms deep (most smaller houses and a good many great ones were only one room deep) with a central corridor running the length of the house—the corridor idea wasn't all that new, Chevening, Kent, had been built to this revolutionary plan some thirty years before. From this corridor the rooms opened. Thus Sir George did without windows on one side of his rooms but he had the blessed advantage of a corridor which, although it may have been draughty, guaranteed privacy. The exterior of Coleshill was absolutely symmetrical with delicate emphasis on horizontal lines. There were no recessions, wings, bulging bays, romantic turrets or gables, no columns, caryatids or telemones, to break its serene front vertically. No curly strap work, heraldic devices or misbegotten if mythological beasts were set about to add "interest". The house was rectangular, plain, without affectation. There was a fine Italian touch about its big exquisitely spaced and proportioned windows (and in the cornices too); and more than a hint of French in the chimneys and the roof which was hipped, balustraded, and had a very French-looking lantern. Yet it was, as those of us who are fortunate enough to have seen it know, superbly and unmistakably English. Alas, this Coleshill was burned too, in 1952. It is said that it could have been restored but it was torn down and the stone sold off. Only the gate piers remain to remind us that minor masterpiece of English architecture* once stood there.

Roger Pratt built only a few houses† just to occupy himself until he came into his inheritance, was knighted and retired to his native Norfolk. But before retiring he had built Clarendon House, Piccadilly, one of the first of the great classical houses.

The Grand Duke of Tuscany, who certainly must have known a classical house when he saw one, remarked that it was "commodious and sumptuous" square, light, cheerful, "regularly

*Ashdown House, Berks, although not like Coleshill has tall chimneys and a lantern reminiscent of Roger Pratt's house. It is an enchanting house, high and narrow. Visitors may go up to the roof via the original staircase which occupies one quarter of the whole smallish house. The staircase is so solid that presumably it could not be ruined by troops billeted there. Or perhaps they realized that a staircase—even a beautiful one—is a necessity.

†Among these was Horseheath (Cambs.) built for Lord Allington. On July 20th, 1670, John Evelyn dined with Allington "who had newly built a house of great cost, I believe a little less than £20,000. His architect was Mr. Pratt. It is seated in a Park, with a sweet prospect and stately avenue; but water still defective; the house has also its infirmities". One suspects that Evelyn and Pratt did not always see eye to eye over things and certainly they didn't over repairing St. Paul's. Horseheath contrary to Evelyn's note is said to have cost £70,000. Eighteen years later it, together with the estate, was sold for £42,000 and had another £30,000 spent on it. In 1777 it was sold to be pulled down, the price being the value of the materials!

disposed according to the rules of architecture''. Less know-
ledgeable about men than houses he also thought the, by then,
fugitive Lord Chancellor was a ''secret Presbyterian''—tantamount to saying he had horns and a tail. Clarendon House was
pulled down in 1683 and we know little about it, but it had an
enormous influence on future architecture. It was replaced by
Albemarle Street and Old Bond Street—laid out by Robert
Frith, John Hind and Sir Thomas Bond. Lord Berkeley, too,
built a grand house in Piccadilly, the new favourite locality for
''new Palaces'' (Evelyn), and later began to lay out a square and
various streets on his land. Hence Bruton, Farm, Hill, and
Charles streets.

By the time the Lords Clarendon and Berkeley began their
houses, both in 1664, a number of things had happened. Inigo
Jones and Cromwell were dead. Charles the second had been
restored in 1660 and in that year Sir John Denham, royalist,
gambler and poet* became ''Surveyor of the Works'' (royal
architect). A verse in his tragedy ''The Sophy'', makes one
wonder a trifle uneasily what kind of architect he was:

> ''Somnus the humble God that dwells
> In cottages and smoky cells,
> Hates gilded roofs and beds of down;
> And though he fears no prince's frown,
> Flies from the circle of the crown.''

More than Somnus had fled the circle of the crown when this
was written (1642) and although these lines may not have
expressed Denham's more mature view of architecture—he
built old Burlington House for Richard Boyle, first Earl of Burlington between 1663-68—it is at least interesting to note he thought
a sad little hut and a smoky cell a sure cure for insomnia.

William Harrison, a century before believed a good smoky

*''Cooper's Hill'' is his best known poem. It describes the country-
side about Egham and is reputedly the first descriptive poem of that
genre in English.

room not only preserved the timbers of a house but prevented its inhabitants from contracting "rheums, catarrhs and poses". Unfortunately Denham although "not suspect to be a Witt"[7] at the age of fifty took the greatest gamble of his life and married pretty young Margaret Brookes who shortly after became the Duke of York's mistress. Denham, distracted and provoked by this occurrence, couldn't very well challenge the Duke so, it is said, he poisoned his wife's chocolate. Mr. Evelyn, according to Mr. Pepys, called Lady Denham's conduct "bitchering". Although a *post-mortem* revealed no trace of poison (how good were they at finding such traces one wonders?) rumour was not silenced and Sir John then became sadly demented. He believed himself to be the Holy Ghost, which was a great trial to his friends, and died in March 1669.

Fortunately, the really influential man in early Restoration architecture was not Denham but Hugh May, Paymaster in the Office of Works, who very probably sponsored a new Dutch style, now free of curly gables. It wasn't a difficult style to sponsor. Many English exiles had lived in the Netherlands during the Commonwealth, had seen the Mauritshuis at the Hague or the nearby Huis ten Bosch (as we can see them today) and had acquired a taste for what Sir John Summerson so aptly calls "Dutch Palladianism". Furthermore, with brick now such a versatile building material, the new Dutch style which made great use of brick—with stone—had much to recommend it. Brick was cheaper too, and many people had lost much during the wars. So brick houses now had flat stone pilasters running from ground floor (not first floor) to cornice which gave beauty and formality to a façade just as in their giant size they give such dignity to the solid, comfortable brick-built, beautiful Mauritshuis. Little of May's work survives (he built Lord Berkeley's house, now destroyed), the best example is Eltham Lodge, Kent. Mr. Evelyn saw it while it was being built in 1644 and thought it "not well contrived; especially the roof and rooms too low pitched, and the kitchen where the cellars should be". What was to become the Victorian black hole of Calcutta—basement or semi-basement kitchen—came in during this century (Coleshill had a basement kitchen). In great houses before now, kitchens were usually in a wing on the ground floor and food was trundled through miles of interconnected rooms to hall or dining-room to arrive stone cold or, worse, tepid. But no one minded in those days.

In the field of non-domestic architecture come the Royal Palaces. Hugh May made some alterations at Windsor where he took to Mediaevalism and not Domestic Dutch. John Webb, Jones' pupil who really should have been Surveyor instead of Denham (he and Jones built part of Wilton), added a beautiful new block to Greenwich (we call it King Charles' Building) and Henrietta Maria, by now a rather bossy and tiresome Queen mother, had a new gallery built (1661–2) at her old residence Somerset House, Strand. By this time Somerset House must have needed refurbishing as it was already 200 years old. The new gallery was built to a plan made long before by Inigo Jones (who

Middling manor house, 1640.

died at Somerset House in 1652) and must have been very beautiful, judging from surviving drawings. A century later Somerset House was demolished to make room for Government offices.

Generally speaking, we may say that early Restoration houses carried on from the immediate pre-Commonwealth period. The influence of Inigo Jones was apparent in the work of Webb and others while Classicism, as we have seen, had become more widespread. But, like religion, this classicism was of a distinctly northern brand, neither Mediterranean nor French in character. It is just possible that this type of classicism might have flourished and persisted in the reign of Charles II (for it appealed to the English more than did the Italian manner) but it was not in the stars.

The stars at this time—constantly consulted by astrologers for the benefit of clients and themselves—were also being looked at for very different reasons by the Gresham Professor of Astronomy, Dr. Christopher Wren. Dr. Wren had early come under the influence of John Wilkins, the famous Warden of Wadham and leader of a small group of men who during the Great Rebellion and after turned their minds neither to politics nor religion (both were very unsafe and by then practically indistinguishable), but to the new study of science. Wren was interested in mathematics, medicine, physics and astronomy, and there is little, if anything, in his early career to indicate he would become England's most famous architect. It is not clear just how or when Wren did become an architect, but in accordance with a new idea of the time, an architect needed to be a mathematician. Wren was a brilliant one.* His first important job was the Sheldonian Theatre, Oxford and here he based his design on a Roman theatre. Then,

---

*A good architect, says Vitruvius, should have natural ability but should also be "educated, skilful with the pencil, instructed in geometry, know much history, have followed the philosophers with attention, understand music, have some knowledge of medicine, know the opinions of jurists, and be acquainted with astronomy". Wren had most if not all of these qualifications.

in 1665, he went to France and was much impressed by French architecture even if he found Versailles too feminine and preferred the more masculine Palais Mazarine. In France he met the Italian sculptor and architect Bernini (who fostered the high Baroque style in Italy) in Paris to make designs for the new Louvre for Louis XIV. Louis didn't like the design but Wren, who saw it briefly and noted it in his memory, said that he would have given his skin for it! When he returned to England bringing, among other ideas, that of the Mansard roof* he became involved in the discussions on how to repair St. Paul's, now in an appalling state. Long needed repairs had been started by Inigo Jones, had been interrupted by the war, and the cathedral had suffered further damage and mutilation at the hands of Parliamentary troops quartered there.

Wren did not want "to follow the Gothick Rudeness of the old Design", he wanted to remodel "after a good Roman manner"[8] and on August 27th, 1666 he, John Evelyn, Roger Pratt, Hugh May, Thomas Chicheley and others met to discuss plans and "plumb the uprights". Pratt and Chicheley were all for repairing the old steeple as it stood. Evelyn and others were against this; they thought the steeple "very mean" and wanted "a noble cupola, a form of church-building not as yet known in England".[9] The argument might have continued indefinitely but ten days later nothing remained of St. Paul's. It, together with eighty-seven parish churches and 13,200 houses, was a heap of smoking ashes and blackened rubble. So great, so complete was the destruction by the Great Fire which raged "as if it had a commission to devour everything that was in its way"[10] that even those who knew the city well and had lived there got lost

*More correctly Mansart, said to have been invented by François Mansart (1598-1666) a Fr. architect who designed many Paris churches and private houses of great size. The modern Fr. word "mansarde" a garret or attic chamber, is derived from his name as a mansard or curb roof allows more floor space on the top floor. François is not to be confused with his distant relative Jules-Hardouin Mansard (his name does end with a "d") Louis XIV's brilliant architect who designed the palace of Versailles which Wren found too feminine.

among the ruins and could not distinguish where houses or warehouses, churches or taverns or any other familiar building had stood, unless the skeletal pinnacle of some church or another had survived to serve as a landmark.* And "the people who now walked among the ruins, appeared like men in some dismal desert, or rather, in some great city laid waste by a cruel enemy".[11]

Wren rebuilt St. Paul's and many of London's churches but he seems to have built few private houses although many claim him as their "onlie begetter", perhaps correctly. Fawley Court, near Henley, is for certain a Wren house and set the pattern for Wren style country houses.†

But Wren, who succeeded Denham, was a Royal Builder, a builder of Churches. He was what we call a civic architect, and civic building—although it influenced private building—is outside the scope of a domestic history. What concerns us here is the rebuilding of those 13,200 houses. Not surprisingly, very few remain to tell us what they were like, but the first "Act for the Rebuilding of the City of London‡ shows that there were many innovations. The act provided that new houses must be of brick, wall thicknesses and floor heights were specified. Brick and wall thicknesses reduced the risk of fire; floor heights made for a standardization which had hitherto been lacking. New floor heights must have changed the face of the whole city as they made gabled fronts uneconomic. Perhaps most important of all, the new standard specifying brick for domestic building became country wide. London's fire outshone all others because London was so large, but other cities and towns of the realm habitually

---

*This was not London's first great fire by any means. A previous and equally catastrophic one occurred in 1135. It destroyed nearly the whole of the city which then consisted almost entirely of wooden buildings.

†Marlborough House may be by Wren or by his son. Winslow House, Bucks, may also be by Wren. Across the Atlantic, William and Mary College, Williamsburg, is generally attributed to Wren's design.

‡After the fire that is; acts specifying materials and kinds of building had been passed from time to time long before and had been largely ignored.

Middling manor house, *c.* 1680.

suffered extensive fire damage from time to time. Northampton was destroyed in 1675 and Warwick in 1694, and when a devastated city or town was rebuilt the London Building Act was often quoted in local agreements. As for London herself? A typical post-fire house had windows of the same size on each floor (unlike the Peter Mills house) with, occasionally, smaller windows on the top floor of a three-storey house. There were keystone blocks over the windows, a modillion eaves cornice to a pedimented rather than gabled roof, and a classical portal. Such houses were very attractive, as anyone who saw Carlisle House* (built *c.* 1670), Soho before it was bombed (1941) will remember. There were of course many variations within the

---

*During the next century, Theresa Cornelys, a quondam love of Casanova, made a pretty fortune by opening an Assembly room in Carlisle House. Admission was two guineas which allowed one to attend the ball and partake of the lavish supper provided.

specifications laid down by the act, as the taste or pocket of the private or small speculative builder dictated.

The small speculative builder, who might be bricklayer, carpenter or mason, could build two or three houses and probably built them much to the same pattern, but patterns would differ with each builder. The large scale speculative builder—and it is at this point that large scale speculative building first enters our history—had other ideas. Nicholas Barbon (Barebone or Barebones), the son, it is said, of old Praise-God Barebones,* was a financial wizard, economist, doctor of medicine, and rather a scoundrel. He founded a land bank, instituted fire insurance in England, wrote treatises on economics, one of which propounded the novel idea that exports could only be paid for by imports, and died in 1698 leaving firm instructions that none of his debts should be paid. He was also, very probably, the first really big speculative builder in our annals and obviously saw at once the great advantages of uniform building; the saving in time and money and the consequent larger profit.

Although the houses in Great Queen Street and Lincoln's Inn Fields enunciated the principal which Jones had impressed upon the "piazza", Barbon went much farther. He laid out streets of contiguous houses with every house built to the same plan and identical down to the last detail inside and out. Such streets were the progenitors of those terraces which were to become so characteristic of London, Bath, Buxton and other cities in Georgian times—and of course, squares were laid out too. London was rebuilt in four years "to the amazement of all Europe" and "with so much beauty and magnificence that we who saw both states, before and after the fire cannot reflect on it without wondering where the wealth could be found to bear so vast a loss as was made by the fire" says Bishop Burnet.

What is so curious about post-Restoration-architecture is, that

*Praise-God, a man of substance, was an anabaptist politician, one time M.P. for city of London and later a Fifth Monarchy Man from whom the the "Barebones Parliament" derives its derisive nickname.

Of Houses—Great, Middling, and Small

although there were more architects, as we define the word, many gentlemen still designed their own houses—or said they did—as they had been doing in a sporadic sort of way for centuries. Designing a house seems to have been considered an accomplishment like playing a musical instrument or dashing off a play or a poem, or arguing about the new philosophy. And if a gentleman were not accomplished enough to design his own house he must at least profess to know something about architecture. Still, even a gentleman had to depend upon masons, carpenters and bricklayers, and these craftsmen were, as before, often the real architects of a great house. They lived and worked in London, in other major cities, in towns, and in the country. Some were very conventional and did not take kindly to new ideas and so adopted a safe and time-tested style, which is one of the reasons why the classical style was a slow starter. But one noble gentleman builder of the time decided to employ an architect not to build him a new house but to furbish up an old one. He was William, fourth Earl (later first Duke) of Devonshire. The architect was Talman who succeeded Hugh May as Comptroller of the Works in 1689, the house was Chatsworth.

Elizabethan Chatsworth had been built by the Duke's great grandmother, Bess of Hardwick, and the Duke seems to have been as autocratic and arrogant as this magnificent and thoroughly disagreeable old woman. Although he didn't inherit her shrewdness about money he had her passion for building and the same fatal tendency to quarrel with his builders. Bess's last quarrel with hers, on a bitter winter's day in 1608, ended in pneumonia and death. The Duke's ended less dramatically but more wearingly in endless lawsuits.

It was not the Duke's original intention to rebuild the old house completely, but an attempt to modernize it (1676-80) by altering rooms and enlarging windows, so weakened the structure that it was necessary to rebuild the south front. For this job he chose William Talman—a difficult and arrogant man with a feeling for French and baroque styles. By the time the south front was finished and Talman dismissed, the Duke was infected with the building fever.*

The Duke, educated abroad, spent some time in France, as well as in the Tower, and Chatsworth owes much to the second of these three happenings. But it is well to remember that from shortly after the Restoration there were two quite strong influences at work in English architecture—French and Dutch. Speaking almost too broadly, grandest houses were more French in style; middling and smaller houses more Dutch. Perhaps the curious love-hate relationships with these two very different countries account for their influence in so many different spheres. In any event, English architecture absorbed many things from both of them and produced something typically English. Hence the east front of Dyrham Park, Glos. which Talman built for William Blathwayt looks English to us,† so does his wing at Chatsworth. This wing (1686-89) took three years to build and is three stories, plain, uncomplicated and very lovely. Corners are extruded, but with great reticence and serve to break what otherwise might be a too box-like look. Windows are set between flat pilasters and above is a balustraded roof— typical of Talman's work—the balusters topped by urns. Unfortunately the side facing the courtyard had no windows at all, no galleries, no openings save two doors at ground level. What had been forgotten, either by Talman or the Duke, was that the old Jacobean interior plan was démodé. The outside was beautifully classical, the inside was just old inconvenient Jacobean. To get from the chapel on the west corner to the dressing-room on the East one passed through a living-room, the entrance passage,

*Chatsworth was built in five stages and took twenty years to complete. Although it preserved its outward unity, inside it proved so disconcerting and difficult to live with that in the eighteenth century the 4th Duke converted the kitchens into the entrance hall. At the beginning of the nineteenth century the 6th Duke doubled the size of the house and corrected many of its deficiencies—and has been called a vandal for his pains.

†But not to the average foreign tourists. Tudobethan or Jacogothic are typically English to them.

a bedroom, and a "Stag parlour". This was true of the upper floors too, and in 1703 a gallery had to be added over the court-yard to help overcome this defect.

It was, perhaps, unusual for the Duke to have employed Talman for this job. Even more unusually, all but two of the master craftsmen employed came from London—and it was a

New style civic architecture, *c.* 1670-1714.

long way from London to Derbyshire in those days. So Chatsworth has the additional distinction of being one of the first of the great English houses to be built by contract. Building contractors, like speculative builders, begin here. Hitherto most great houses had been, and still were, built by master craftsmen and artisans belonging to the estates of rich men. Even if a house were designed by an "outsider", the outsider was directly employed and paid by the owner-builder. But in the building of the south front of Chatsworth the artisans were neither responsible to nor paid by the Duke; all this was handled by the contractors. Once the Duke got into this arrangement, he simply hated it. He liked being boss. He was just as feudal in his ideas as old Bess. The idea of a contract with one side supplying capital, the other labour and materials, and wherein both had equal rights he simply did not understand. Nor was this unusual. On his estates, as on many others, his own officials received an annual wage plus a "gift". This gift, as the Chatsworth accounts show, was as regular as the wage—but it was nevertheless a gift which could be withheld at any time if the Duke were so minded. Furthermore he could deduct any amount he pleased at any time for any offence or dereliction—real or fancied. But when bound by a contract which he either could not or would not understand the Duke was miserable—and so, no doubt, were the unhappy contractors. This led to endless sackings, law suits and bad temper.

But the minute the Talman front was completed the Duke—who seems to have been able to see a thing only three dimensionally and not in the flat—was so stimulated that he had a better idea how the next front should look and, quite forgetting that his original idea was to have only the south front done, he set about doing the next one. This is why Chatsworth was built in five separate stages—four fronts and a staircase—each new stage stimulating the Duke's imagination to go on with the next. This is also partly why it took so long to build. The other reasons were that often the Duke happily docked wages because the men were lazy; often the men went unpaid because the Duke lacked money. Even more often the Duke lacked money because the horses he backed at Newmarket lacked speed. This was in the long run useful because by the time the Duke worked his way around to the much grander west front, he had fortunately been inspired to incorporate an internal passage on the courtyard side of each front. Narrow passages they were but they made for a certain amount of convenience and privacy.

The West front was finished in 1704 and the Duke, despite increasing infirmity and increasingly heavy losses at Newmarket, was inspired to finish the job and do the north or last front. There wasn't much to do; West and East fronts had crept around their corners and encroached upon the brick of the old house, so the Duke just spanned the space between encroachments with a bow "of Singular Ornament and Service". This Singular Ornament, designed by William Archer, was the kitchen and it cannot have been of great Service as in the next century it was turned into the entrance hall.

Still, in spite of illness, lawsuits and dreadful debts the first Duke lived to see the Singular Ornament finished and old Elizabethan Chatsworth become a great new Classical one. It was completed in 1707, the year of his death. But, like Robert Cecil, the Duke did not die at his beautiful new home. He died at Devonshire House, Piccadilly at 9 a.m. on April 18th, and this particular Devonshire House was that fine "new palace" built back in 1664 by Lord Berkeley. The sad news of the Duke's death reached Chatsworth in a letter written by Mr. Moore, Keeper of the Stables. "I am sorry," he wrote, "this letter Brings you the Mellankoly news of my Lord Duckes Beeing Ded."

"Beeing Ded", the Duke fortunately did not have to face his creditors. His successors did and no more could be done to Chatsworth for some time. Yet the rebuilding of Chatsworth, great house though it is, illustrates in a very personal and individual way the growth of classical architecture in England. A growth spanning three reigns—James II, William and Mary, and Queen Anne. When the Duke began rebuilding, in 1687, Wren, at the height of his power, was busy rebuilding among other things fifty-three of London's churches,* assisted by his talented young clerk, Nicholas Hawksmore. By the time Chatsworth was finished, in 1707, Wren was an old man of seventy-two; Talman,

---

*In the 271 years between 1668 and 1939, twenty of these churches were destroyed; roughly one church every thirteen-and-a-half years. Between 1939 and 1945 German bombers destroyed or gutted another seventeen; roughly one every four months. At the earlier rate of destruction it would have taken 229½ years to accomplish what the Germans did in six.

its first architect had been succeeded as Comptroller by Sir John Vanbrugh who, with Wren's one-time talented young clerk, was producing some of the most astounding, massive, dramatic English Baroque houses in the country. Vanbrugh, like Inigo Jones, had once been connected with the theatre.

And in 1707 London theatre-goers were being highly diverted by "Lady Bountiful", that "old, civil Country Gentlewoman that cures all her neighbours distempers"—as played by Mrs. Powell; no less than by "Mrs. Sullen" who muddled the treatment of a sore leg with a "receipt" for baked meat—as played by Mrs. Oldfield. Queen Anne, however, was NOT amused. She did not care for the theatre. It was indeed a far cry from Anna of Denmark and *Tethys' Festival* to Queen Anne and *The Beaux-Stratagem*. It was just as far a cry from the Queen's House to the Queen Anne House.

And it is with the so-called Queen Anne house that Domestic architecture, as we know it, first comes into its own. Somewhere along the difficult road of this brilliant, fragmented century— possibly after the Great Fire or later—builders and architects at last discovered the solution of a problem which had long vexed them. They discovered how to translate the grand classical manner of palace, great house and civic building into plain, everyday, beautiful English prose. They learned, in fact, how to reduce proportions without destroying them. It was no longer a question of putting a semi-classical front on to a still mediaeval interior plan. And so small, dignified all-of-a-piece houses, suitable to the moderate state and fortune of town or country gentlemen of the middling sort, began. Rich powerful Whigs or rich impotent Tories could build great palaces and great houses in the French or even English Baroque style; farmers could go on building traditionally and in local materials, adding perhaps a new fashioned touch in string course or architrave of window, but the gentleman of moderate means was unable to do either of these things, it just wasn't suitable. And all over the country now there were gentlemen of moderate means. Men who had nothing whatever to do with politics or court circles, and who

The Queen Anne style small house.

had no desire to have anything to do with them. Men who were neither farmers nor great land owners. Small squires, merchants, lawyers and agents; good country stock for the most part with a bit of money made, perhaps in some commercial venture, or inherited as the portion of a younger son, or even won in a state lottery.

So the Queen Anne House came into being mainly for the *gentes minores* and nearly all these houses share certain well-defined architectural characteristics, no matter where built or what the building material. They are simple and rectangular and topped by a hipped roof; that is a roof which slopes up on all four sides from eaves to ridge. There are no cupolas or lanterns, no balus-traded bits. The eaves line on all sides is horizontal and treated like a cornice with modillions or brackets which imitate the ends of roof beams found in ancient Roman building. If a house were three or four stories high and might therefore look disproportionally tall and narrow for its width, the third or fourth floor is set above the eaves and light admitted by dormers wearing tiny steeply pitched roofs with small triangular or curved pediments. The façade was generally plain, but the entrance door usually had a canopy. Sometimes canopies were in the form of a pediment which was often elaborated and supported by pillars or brackets. But most enchanting and delicious of all are canopies, deep, round and fluted so that they look like great ribbed shells—the canopy or "state" for the Englishman's home.

Windows were regularly spaced with heavy wooden or stone frames and thick glazing bars. If the angles of the house were "quoined" then this pattern in brick houses was usually followed around the windows. And probably the greatest improvement of all was that the sash window had come into general use. Sash windows changed the face of English domestic architecture more than any other single detail. At first they were wedged open, but once sash cord and weight were invented sash windows became popular and remained popular until the nineteenth century. Ashstead Park, Sir Robert Howard's* new brick house, built in 1684 out of the gains made as Auditor of the Exchequer (he couldn't really have made sufficient money from his plays, poems or historical works) had the new kind of window; "all the windows are sarshes and large squares of glass" Celia Fiennes says, and notes further they were double sashes "to make the house warmer for it stands pretty bleak". She probably meant the double hung, vertically sliding sash rather than the transom or casement sash.

*Shadwell satirizes him as Sir Positive At-All in "The Sullen Lovers". This Sir Robert mustn't be confused with his uncle who, long before, ran off with poor Frances Coke, the Lord Chief Justice's daughter, who by her father's wish had been forced into a distasteful marriage with Viscount Purbeck, the half-mad brother of the first Duke of Buckingham.

Of Houses—Great, Middling, and Small

What we call Queen Anne architecture did not begin with the accession of Anne in 1702, nor did it die with her in 1714. Mompesson House, Salisbury, was built probably in the last years of William III's life but one would be hard put to call it anything other than Queen Anne (it is often ascribed to Wren but there is no documentary evidence to support this). While a small house in High Street, Burford (now a chapel retaining only its front) was built possibly in 1710 (no evidence here, either) and it could no more be called Queen Anne than could Hatfield House. It is small, classical, semi-basement with corinthian pilasters from ground floor to balustraded roof. It looks backward to Inigo Jones, forward to the great Palladian era. In its very tiny, enchanting way it contains both the beginning and end of Stuart era architecture. For it was Inigo Jones who discovered Palladio and Vitruvius for us at the beginning of the seventeenth century; and at the beginning of the eighteenth century Jones and Palladio were on the point of being re-discovered. Hard on Queen Anne's death came the Palladian-Inigo Jones revival—if revival it can be called since few had, until then, followed either Palladio or Jones—and Palladianism became all the rage. It owed little to Wren, May, Hawksmore or Vanbrugh or to any other English architect other than Inigo Jones. It was new, modern, beautiful . . . and it harked back a century.

Seventeenth-century village houses.

The Pageant of Stuart England

In 1614, young Inigo wrote in his sketch book, "In all designing of ornament one must first design the ground plain as it is for use . . . then adorn and compose it with decorum according to its use". It was a rule he applied to more than ornament. By 1714, when Queen Anne died, this rule had been accepted. It was then England entered that period of domestic architecture for great, middling, and small house still unsurpassed by any other country in the world.

CHAPTER THREE

Of Furniture and Furnishings

THE year 1662 began traditionally enough at court level, with the usual Lincoln's Inn Revels, attended by the King and his brother James, Duke of York. On a less exalted level, Mr. and Mrs. Pepys, together with "young Mr. Pen and his sister" after eating "a barrel of oysters" went to the Duke of York's theatre to see "The Spanish Curate",* a good play, well acted but "Diego the Sexton did overdo his part too much".[1]

The year ended, untraditionally, when the king startled his subjects—on December 26th to be exact—by announcing that until a Bill for the Indulgence of Tender Consciences could be laid before Parliament, he, out of his mercy, would dispense with the penal laws against religious dissentients. Mrs. Pepys, on this date, spent the whole day making Christmas pies. Mr. Pepys bought Samuel Butler's "Hudibras" for 2/6 but, oddly, thought it "so silly an abuse of the Presbyter Knight" that he promptly re-sold it to Mr. Townsend for eighteen pence. Between the beginning and end of the year† a number of things of national, international, and purely personal interest happened. Parliament voted a 2/- chimney tax as a constant revenue to the Crown forever. It was unpopularly called "hearth money", and forever lasted until 1689. Charles Sackville (Lord Buckhurst), his brother Edward and other aristocratic, brawling wits were

*by John Fletcher (1579-1625) of Beaumont and Fletcher, as it were.
†I have taken the year as beginning on January 1st, officially it began on March 25th. The events listed are neither in order of importance nor in chronological sequence.

93

clapped into Newgate for killing and robbing a tanner named Hoppy, near Waltham Cross. A Grand Jury decided it was manslaughter not murder. Some two thousand parsons, or about one fifth of the total clergy, were driven from their pulpits as nonconformists; in 1646 a victorious Parliament had done roughly the same thing to 2,000 Anglican clergy. The widow of Frederick, Elector Palatine, died aged sixty-six—long, long ago she had impersonated the nymph of the Thames in *Tethys' Festival*. John Tradescant, the younger, died too and his famous Ark went to Mr. Elias Ashmole, not without some trouble.

Dunkirk and Mardyke were sold to Louis XIV for 500,000 pistoles. The Duchess of Richmond called the Countess of Castlemaine Jane Shore (surely a slander upon Jane's name) and piously hoped the Countess would come to the same squalid end. She did, rather, but not until 1709. Lord Clarendon's daughter, Anne Hyde, Duchess of York, was brought to bed of a girl, Mary. No one was pleased. Even less pleased was Admiral Sir William Penn, when his son "young Mr. Pen" got sent down from Oxford for Nonconformity. The second edition of *New Experiments, Physico-Mechanical* newly revised by its author Robert Boyle, youngest son of the great Earl of Cork, appeared—it contained what is now known as "Boyle's Law". Thirteen plays by "Mad Madge" Duchess of Newcastle also appeared in a folio volume which ran to 679 pages.

Samuel Pepys first heard, saw and commented upon the dulcimer* "played on with sticks knocking of the strings, and is very pretty". The Royal Society received its first charter of incorporation, the Lord Viscount Brouncker was nominated president and "The Longest Tyranny" was at an end—or so Mr. John Dryden a newly elected member wrote.

The Queen Mother, Henrietta Maria, with Lord St. Albans (gossip ran that he was her husband, or if he weren't he certainly should be) honoured Mr. John Evelyn's "poor villa" with her presence. She graciously accepted a "collation . . . and staid till

*The dulcimer is the direct parent of the pianoforte, as the psaltery is of the harpsichord.

Farthingale chair, c. 1610. Carved oak chair, c. 1615.
Cromwell chair, c. 1655.

very late in the evening".[2] Marmeduke Rawdon of York went
abroad to see the sights—among the sights he saw at Leyden was
"the skin of a Scotsman dried". At Chatsworth, Mr. Thomas
Hobbes the unpopular philosopher gave James Wheldon an old
silk robe valued at £1.[3] At Earles Colne, the Rev. Ralph Josselin
saw some townsmen digging on the Sabbath and noted that this
would lead straight to "flat athiesm".[4] Old Subtlety, otherwise
known as Viscount Saye and Sele, who according to Lord
Clarendon had "the deepest hand in the rebellion" died, aged
eighty, but his granddaughter Celia Fiennes was born. The
effects of the widow "Pery" lately dead at Roxwell, Essex,
were valued at £21.15.6. It was rumoured that thirteen-year-
old James Crofts* was legitimate . He wasn't. But James Crofts'
father gave the boy a kind stepmother when he married the
Infanta of Portugal, Catherine of Braganza, and on his thirty-

*In November 1662 James was created Duke of Monmouth and the
following year married Lady Anne Scott daughter of the Earl of
Buccleuch. He subsequently discarded the surname of his guardian
Lord Crofts, to take that of his wife. He subsequently discarded his
wife too.

second birthday, the second anniversary of his Restoration, he and his bride arrived at Hampton Court Palace.

It was fortunate that the late and still largely unlamented Lord Protector had liked Hampton Court and reserved it "for uses of state" otherwise like most of "the late Charles Stuart's"[5] effects it might have been sold for a psalm. But the late Charles Stuart's eldest son was now in safe possession of the Palace. He had recovered some of his father's paintings and tapestries, had been busy about the gardens and a new tennis court and so the old Palace of some 1,500 rooms was equipped to receive the new Queen Consort. She arrived, it was noted with gleeful malice by some and genuine disquiet by others, with too many ill-favoured ladies, a handful of Portugese priests, a wardrobe of perfectly splendid but absurdly old-fashioned farthingales and a most curious hair style. Her complexion was an unfashionable and "unagreeable . . . olivander". And, if her eyes were fine and dark, her mouth was marred by a front tooth or two which (like her mother-in-law's) stuck "a little too far out".[6] Furthermore, the wretched woman was foreign. Her English was woefully inadequate—and who were we to learn Portuguese of all languages! She was also Roman Catholic, not very intelligent and had been bred "hugely retired".[7]

That she brought to England as part of her official dowry, Tangier and Bombay, and free trade with the West Indies and Brazil did little to offset her personal defects in the eyes of cynical courtiers or in near court circles. She also brought with her, as part of a personal dowry, a cradle, unhappily destined to remain empty—the disagreeable Spanish said it would remain so—and the finest Indian Cabinets ever seen in a country just beginning to know about Indian Cabinets. Such exquisite furniture might have looked a trifle out of place in that wonder of rooms, known as the gallery of horns—a gallery which would have delighted Queen Victoria with its "one hundred Twenty seaven hornes of several sorts of Beasts. One picture of a large pair of hornes from Amboiz. Twelve branches for candles"[8] (antlers turned into candle holders?). But there were other,

Of Furniture and Furnishings

splendid rooms where the cabinets could be displayed more fittingly, and these must have delighted Queen Catherine.

They were richly furnished and hung with tapestries and pictures. "The Story of Abraham", ten pieces of Arras which had escaped the sale,* were there; so were the Raphael Cartoons; so was a new bridal bed—all crimson velvet embroidered with silver—a gift from the States of Holland to her husband and valued at £8,000. There was also the handsome toilet set, a gift from the Queen Mother to her new daughter-in-law. It was of massy, beaten gold and had a large mirror among its pieces.

Catherine was probably deliriously happy for the first six weeks at Hampton Court. Charles was tall (about six ft.), weighed thirteen stone (at least he went to scale at that when riding races at Newmarket), dark, with a curly cynical mouth and possessed of an ugly handsomeness which most women find far more attractive than conventional good looks. He had also inherited all the Stuart charm and seems to have done all he could to amuse her. There were balls and theatricals in the evenings, expeditions to the surrounding countryside by day, and lots of visitors. Charles appeared quite devoted and probably was; Lady Castlemaine was still confined to her chamber after producing a son whom she declared, rightly, to be the king's—a fact which he cheerfully admitted. Or perhaps he was just relieved to be married and have done with being badgered by his advisors who had never ceased urging him to marry (as Queen Elizabeth's badgered her, fortunately for the Stuarts without effect) and had sought suitable matches for him all over the Continent. Of two German Protestant Princesses raked up Charles merely said "Odds fish! they are dull and foggy". The Princesses of Parma had also been on offer but one was too fat, the other too ugly.

*Parliament sold some of the finest pictures and art treasures in the world for a grand total of £180,000. They were bought by Continental Sovereigns and can now be seen in European art galleries and museums . . . instead of in England. Nevertheless Mantegna's *Triumph of Caesar* which escaped the sale is so badly and disgracefully displayed at Hampton Court (in the Orangery) that perhaps it is just as well.

The Pageant of Stuart England

Henrietta, daughter of Prince Henry Frederick of Orange, was quite out of the question. Charles when an exile had wanted to marry her but had been turned down by the girl's silly mother because he had no prospects. It was an insult Charles never forgave. So Catherine of Braganza, despite her religion, seemed the best of a rather poor lot. There was the further attraction that Louis XIV favoured Catherine to the extent of offering his cousin, Charles, 300,000 pistoles if he married her . . . nearly as good as the price for Mardyke and Dunkirk. Thus England and Portugal once more became allies as they had been in the time of Henry the Navigator.

Catherine, who may or may not have understood these things, was happy anyway, but she made one unfortunate error. She fell in love with her husband. Charles couldn't bear this. His temperament could neither sustain the responsibilities nor the boredom of the conjugal state.* Being incapable of love himself— save for his sister Minette—he believed no one could love him except out of self-interest. There is little to suggest he was mistaken in this.

Whether the widow "Pery" loved her husband we do not know. But in the year Catherine arrived she departed, and the usual inventory of her effects was made by George Bayly and Abell Baker.[9] These two, whose spelling does them credit, valued the effects at £21.15.6. This included "monney in her purse" plus "wearing cloathes" total valuation £5. There were no desperate debts.

Yet widow Perry was not classed as a pauper, otherwise she would have been drawing parochial relief, and her inventory would be found in the records of the Parish Overseer. She wasn't even poor. She had a six-room house with a "Butry and Dayre".

---

*Although an indifferent husband, often careless selfish and deliberately wounding, he was very grieved when Catherine was ill. He also refused with contempt any suggestion that he should divorce her when she failed to produce a child. There is something rather touching about these two who must have been as unsuited to each other as were Mr. and Mrs. Pepys—and for similar reasons.

Of Furniture and Furnishings

It had an upper floor and was well furnished throughout by ordinary standards. In the hall there was "One Joyned tabell with 2 formes and a sid bench, 2 litl tabells and one Joynd stoll, 4 chayers, one Joynd cubert, a litl glascase, 2 tramells (adjustable chains with pot hooks), 2 cobyrons, a fier shovell and tonges, a curbine, a musket, a rest and banddoleres, one warming pane, 2 smoothing yrons, 3 cushins, one cubert cloth" at a total value of £3.14.10. In the chamber over the parlour was a joined "bedstedl", a feather bed, two blankets, one coverlet, two bolsters "curtaines and valianc" valued at £5.6.8. Elsewhere were "6 payer of shets", two pillow beres, "half a dossen of napkins", two tablecloths, six pewter spoons, six pewter dishes, one salt, two porringers, one candlestick, various pots and kettles, a chest, another "tabl and tressells" and two more beds. One of these with a bolster, flock mattress, and two blankets was valued at 10/-.

What is revealing about this inventory, apart from the contrast it gives us between the world of the £8,000 bed and the world

Wing chair, c. 1680. Carved walnut chair, c. 1685. Oak chair table, c. 1660.

where the household effects of a fairly well-off widow are valued at £21 odd, is that widow Perry's furniture, with the possible exception of the two little tables, the glass case and the firearms, might have belonged equally well to the previous century and this was 1662. The joined table with its forms and side bench, the joined stool, the "tabl and tressells" (value 6/8) sound, and perhaps were, Elizabethan. Indeed the trestle table is even earlier. The joined bed had four posts and a tester, as curtains and valance are listed as part of its "furniture", but the bed with the flock mattress was probably the old-fashioned boarded bed with head and foot made either of rough boards or of solid panels perhaps carved with initials. Or possibly it was a solid frame with truncated posts at each corner—a bijou four-poster in fact—all of which had been in common use for many years. More importantly, widow Perry had four chairs. These are not described but one may very well have been an "old" chair such as the one possessed by Mary May, widow, who lived at Writtle. *Her* total effects were valued at £8.0.2 and she was not a pauper either. The "old" chair would almost certainly refer to a wainscote or box chair dating back to Elizabeth's day. But the four chairs in the Perry house was a large number even in 1662. When Cosimo III, Duke of Tuscany, came over in 1669 (he was then only a Tuscan Prince) and entertained the King and the Duke of York at supper in the Earl of St. Albans' house where he was staying, he ordered a chair to be placed at the oval table for the king, but Charles ordered it removed and insisted upon sitting on a backless stool just like the rest of the very distinguished company.

This was certainly harking back to the time of the old Queen when chairs were scarce and given only to important people—her courtiers sat on stools, unpadded ones at that! Even in the reign of James I chairs were still not plentiful and they were never very plentiful in poorer homes throughout the whole Stuart era. So the widow's four chairs give us an indication of her status. This is also borne out by the little tables, the glass case and the candlestick. Ignoring the firearms, doubtless used by her husband during the Civil Wars, widow Perry's furniture

Of Furniture and Furnishings

sounds a mixture of Elizabethan and early Stuart.* Perhaps one of the chairs was upholstered, for the upholstered chair, although known in Elizabeth's day only gained popularity in the reign of the first two Stuarts. The farthingale chair, for example, was upholstered and was the direct outcome of the hooped petticoat which in the reign of James I increased to such fantastic, cartwheel proportions that this special, oddly-shaped chair was invented to meet the requirements of the fashionable dress of the day. Small wonder that the English thought Catherine of Braganza's trousseau of farthingales absurd, ugly and wildly old-fashioned; the farthingale was forty years out of date.

Anna of Denmark was indirectly responsible for the farthingale chair for, as we know, she was enamoured of farthingales (and yellow starched ruffs). Where the Queen led, court ladies followed, and the fashions of the court were soon imitated or envied by women all over the country—as they often are today. Poor Margaret Hardman, a simple Lancashire girl who thought herself bewitched, was perhaps one who envied and could not afford such a costume. In describing the dress which she asked her "familiar" to provide, she said "I will have a French Farthingale. I will have it low before and high behind and broad on either side that I may lay my arms on it".[10]

James, as disgusted by farthingales as he was fearful of witches, once issued a proclamation which forbade anyone, man or woman, to appear at Whitehall clad in this "impertinent garment" as it took up too much room. Gentlemen didn't, of course, wear farthingales but not to be outdone by the ladies they used padding or bombast and sometimes as an economy even sawdust to puff out their clothing. James himself was addicted to quilted clothing chiefly because he feared being stabbed. His proclamation had not the smallest effect. Ladies continued to

*Going through rural inventories of the middling and near middling sort one is struck by their similarity—allowing of course for regional variations. There are always quite a few pieces qualified by the adjective "old". As furniture was scarce, these had probably been handed down. Wills of the rich too are full of legacies of furniture and clothing.

Walnut "scriptor", carved, turned walnut chair, both *c.* 1675.

be fire hazards and to cause complete chaos as they got stuck in the narrow passages or tried to pass on a staircase at Whitehall and the farthingale continued popular until James's death. As for the ruff? "The cobweb lawn yellow starched ruff (which so much disfigured our nation and rendered them so ridiculous and fantastical) died at the gallows with her who was the supposed inventrix of them".[11] "Her" is the disreputable Mrs. Turner who assisted Frances Howard—the nymph of the Lea in *Tethys' Festival*—to rid herself of an unwanted husband by spells, to marry James's fancy boy Robert Ker (Earl of Somerset) by the aid of love potions, and to remove Sir Thomas Overbury, who stood in her way, by the means of poison. But a ruff did not particularly limit movement whereas a farthingale did. Obviously farthingaled women couldn't squeeze into the close box chair, the solid-backed armchair, the X-shaped Glastonbury, or the spool-back triangular-seated chair, all of which were well known during the early years of the century. To gauge with any accuracy just where the relevant portion of one's anatomy would come in relation to the object to be sat upon, must have been rather like a snail attempting to sit, shell side down, on a pin

Of Furniture and Furnishings

head. Hence the farthingale chair, peculiar to James's reign. It was armless, had a high, wide padded seat, low padded back, plain or columnar legs, and was upholstered in expensive imported velvet or rich Turkey* work—curious but not out of place with the rich hangings which covered the newer larger-paned windows, or the tapestries† which hung from tenterhooks against the walls of the more noble rooms.

The close or joined chair, impossible for the farthingale, went on developing by itself. It became lighter but still can't have provided much comfort with its solid-panel back often richly and bumpily carved. The panel was framed and topped by a crested rail. But on this chair, around the turn of the century or earlier, a most important development took place. The top rail instead of being confined within or between the uprights escaped and was sometimes placed, cresting and all, upon the uprights.

This, initially, made for an undeniably hideous and top-heavy look, particularly in chairs where ears or ear pieces were added just below the crested rail. But it was a development of the first magnitude because it ultimately freed the chair from the limits imposed upon it by its Tudor grandparents. With a free top rail, chair back and chair could and later did become, graceful, light and elegant. Carved chairs with crested top rails went on being

*Turkey work, not to be confused with Turkey carpets, was often made at home and is classified as embroidery although carpet knotting was used. It was the early century favourite for chair backs, curtains, hangings and cushions. In the latter half of the century Crewel work was the rage. This was done on linen or twill with thin wools and the designs came from Indian cottons imported in such quantity. The "tree of Life" was a favourite, so was the asparagus pattern, and twisting seaweedy looking stems. Often the work was in various shades of green although bright coloured wools were also used.

†Eleanor of Castile, wife of Edward 1st is said to have introduced the fashion for hanging tapestries and carpets on walls. It was a Moorish custom which had been adopted by Spain. Eleanor is also the "chere reine" from which it is also said Charing Cross derives. This may not be true, it may come from "Char rynge", which was a ring or parking place for horses and "cars" when their owners attended levees or their equivalent or had business at Westminster Palace.

popular for half a century and more but by 1640 we find that leather held in place by brass studs is being used for seats and backs of lighter chairs, and upholstery too became much less uncommon. By 1645 the Verney family had dining-room furniture upholstered in green velvet;* they also had "stooles with nailes guilt". The stool was still (and continued to be) in constant use. Grand ones were upholstered "as nailes guilt" tells us, but ordinary oak stools were in every house and they were changing also. Stretchers which on chairs had begun to move from instep or ankle up towards the calf were, on stools, moving down, possibly to strengthen legs which were becoming much slimmer and were sometimes even fluted. Tables, presses, court cupboards went on much as before, which means they remained unswervingly ugly—John Hayne of Exeter, in 1639, bought himself a "Wainscot Press" for storing linen and clothes "with lock and iemies" (hinges). It cost him £3, "iemies" and all. At that price it was probably carved in the demented fashion of the day—the further west the more demented the carving. Smaller tables, however, improved greatly in design and also increased greatly in number. Side tables came into more general use, square, round, octagonal, rectangular. Those with hinged tops—they were called falling tables or flap tables and were once quite a novelty—had the flap supported by a moveable bracket or leg and so it was not long before the gate-leg table, once only for the rich, came into more general use. But even these small tables did not escape the carver's relentless chisel. Excessive as usual, friezes were over-ornamented with the favourite lunette design of the period—that is, semi-circles repeated in a band and filled in with almost anything—or with strapwork and jewel carving, or with whorls and roundels and, of course, guilloche, which is supposed to look like entwined ribbons but at this period more often than not didn't. Small tables had also lost weight since

*The finest collection of seventeenth-century upholstered chairs are in the brown gallery at Knole. The brocade, velvet, silk and damask coverings are original which is most unusual. Each chair has its own footstool—even more unusual.

Elizabeth's day, so had other furniture. This meant that furniture could be moved about more easily and grouped more attractively. As it often took two men to move a good solid box chair —and half a dozen to shift a refractory refectory table—this newer lighter furniture was a double boon. It could be shuffled about and rearranged as and when one liked, and it must also have meant fewer ruptures and slipped discs among the servants.

This slow but happy change from dropsical to delicate leg, from heavy, lowering stretchers to higher, lighter ones seems to have been made possible because rush matting now began to supercede strewn rushes as a floor covering. At all events, low ponderous stretchers helped to hold rushes down. Slim legs, higher placed stretchers—to say nothing of gate-legs—would have become hopelessly entangled in loose rushes but rush matting stayed down by itself and matting must have begun to replace rushes quite early in the century. In the household accounts of Naworth Castle for the year 1624 the sum of 18/- is paid out for six bundles of rush mats each of six yards; in the same year "6 pair of matts to mat chambers with at 30 yards apiece" were sent to Knole. Carpets were still not in general use on floors. They covered tables, beds, formes, settles and almost every other bit of all too solid furniture.

Lord William Howard, of Naworth, in 1619, bought six Turkey carpets to cover furniture and paid £1.0.6 apiece for them. Farmer Robert Loder of Harwell, some five years earlier, paid 10/- "for a rugges weaving", he also bought a court "couberd" for 25/- and "a Chaire of small Roddes for my chamber" for 2/-; his woven rug was probably intended as a bed covering.

In 1640, Lady Sussex, whose elderly husband the sixth Earl had hired Lord Bacon's house at Gorhambury, is engaged in the tricky business of buying carpets by letter and writes: "the woulde bee very fine for a bede", but if the ground were dull and the colours of the flowers not pleasant she very much doubted that they would: "suet with my haninges and chers".[12] She does, however, speak of a small carpet which, if it wouldn't do for a "windo", would "sarve for a fote carpet". By this time, 1640, when Lady Sussex is so engaged, the Great Rebellion was close at hand, and when war broke out Lady Sussex and others feared they would be "ransakede". Her fear was never realized, others were less fortunate. Thus the first half of the Stuart century and of an old established world came to an end.

A quick summing up of the first half of the century may be useful here so, speaking very broadly, we may say that during this time furniture became more plentiful and in the early years of the century there was often more elaboration, more tormented, swollen and degraded detail than there had been during the most immoderate excesses of the Elizabethan era, but toward the end of the first quarter of the century—the quarter ended with James's death—and as the times became more troubled, paradoxically, ornamentation calmed down. Carving became flatter, more restrained. Sometimes, but not frequently, pieces were even left uncarved. In the plainer, more classically designed houses enormous over inflated furniture must have begun to look rather vulgar if not childishly boastful. The richer one gets, or rather the more accustomed one becomes to riches, the less need there is to emphasise the fact by sheer size and blatant show.

The rich were by now very rich indeed and the poor, very poor. Further, the rich had been getting about more on the continent, they were collecting or importing pictures, sculpture, furniture and objets d'art. Mr. Jones helped many people to select treasures, including Charles I, and Charles was the first monarch to collect with a connoisseur's eye. As Mr. Jones and others seem to have preferred Venice and the Veneto above all places a certain amount of Venetian furniture was imported by the court, by rich merchants, and nobles. Such pieces were beautifully carved and had wonderful velvet upholstery trimmed with fringe and closely woven gold, silver or silk braid.

Then came the Commonwealth and Protectorate which did not go on for long enough to set a furniture style of its own. This may be a pity, and one feels it is, when one sees what remains of the really early American furniture. The Pilgrim Fathers of 1620 took with them the Puritan idea in furniture as well as in other things and when cabinet makers and joiners had leisure enough to make furniture in the new country it was plain and beautiful.

What furniture was made during the Commonwealth was also plain and unornamented but a great deal of it cannot be called either beautiful or simple. For some reason, possibly

Gate leg table, *c.* 1670. Ebony table with silver mounts, *c.* 1670.
Queen Anne stool.

economic, "turning" was permitted and bobbin turning was brought to a very high pitch of perfection before it spun over the edge into absurdity. Legs, rails, stretchers, uprights positively twirled with balusters, bobbins and balls. Arms would have twirled too, only armless chairs were the rule rather than the exception. There was to be no slovenly lolling about in the new era. The new era lasted eleven years.

The Pageant of Stuart England

Then in 1660 came the Restoration, and in 1666, the Great Fire of London. Both had a far reaching effect on furniture. The fire in destroying thousands of houses also destroyed a good deal of Elizabethan and Jacobean furniture. Those who rebuilt and refurnished, built and furnished very differently. The age of oak lay in ashes. The golden age of English furniture, an age which was to last for nearly a century and a half, began.

London it is true, was not England, but London was the pace setter for the rest of the country, even if it did take remoter areas fifty years to catch up. The restored King and his brother, James, Duke of York, had during their exile acquired a taste for the luxury, elegance and manners of the court of Louis XIV, a court which was the admiration of all Europe. So the royal brothers, who were half French (Louis was their cousin) and less English by birth and education than either their father or grandfather, were the arbiters of taste and fashion. Where the new court led, others as usual followed, and the court—many of whose members had also been in exile—had as little use for solid oak as for solid virtue. Walnut soon became the favourite wood. The French did not influence by conquest in 1660 as they had in 1066, they influenced by example. They were loathed but at the same time were emulated in matters of taste, fashion, distinction and all the appurtenances of civilization, just as in the Elizabethan era the Spanish were emulated although loathed too. This apeing of foreign manners and customs was deplored by many, but there were many more who found it all very new and exciting after the undeniable dreariness of the Commonwealth. And so French influence spread more rapidly outside court circles than it might otherwise have done due to the Great Fire.

Thus from the time of Charles II there is an almost complete break with the past and from the Restoration on, furniture design moved steadily and rapidly forward. Indeed one feels, rightly or wrongly, that during the fifty-four years between the Restoration and the death of Queen Anne, furniture changed more than it had during the whole 118 years of the Tudor Dynasty plus the forty-six years of the first two Stuarts. Chairs of walnut

Of Furniture and Furnishings

or beech with caned back or seat made their appearance—possibly in plague year, although a very rough sort of caning had been known in Charles I's day. These soon began to oust the heavier upholstered and leather seated chairs. In addition, chairs now began to be made in "sets"—two armchairs and a half dozen or more single (armless) chairs to the set—and a certain uniformity, hitherto lacking, was achieved. Backs became higher and were, in early Restoration times, fashionably crown-crested. Arms began to take on a graceful feminine curve and where walnut proved too expensive birch wood painted black made a pleasant substitute. By the end of Charles's reign chairs were still elaborate but in a very different way. Pierced work, in backs, was fashionable, so was caning held in a panel between ornamented or barley twist uprights. Stretchers were carved and, like front legs, were often curved and scrolled. The wing chair made what must have been a most welcome appearance, richly upholstered in velvet or needlework; carved chairs were gilded after the French fashion like the pair of upholstered chairs at Ham House with dolphin legs and arms.

These were, of course, chairs for the rich (and it should be remembered that right up until 1660 the average house had boasted one or perhaps two chairs so widow Perry was certainly above average). Dr. Claver Morris, who lived in Devonshire, was neither rich nor poor. He was a successful and well-to-do physician who notes in his diary for 1686 that he bought one and a half dozen "Turkey work chairs" for £7.2.6 and "10 leather chaires"—old fashioned as both leather and Turkey work had by then become—for the unbelievable sum of one pound, or 2/- per chair. So chairs had become plentiful and, to us, cheap but we must multiply by perhaps twenty or twenty-five to get the present day equivalent in money. Dr. Morris's chairs, although they may not have been brand new, were new style chairs; the quantity indicates this and the Turkey work chairs were evidently a "set". Dr. Morris may have wanted a rather large number of chairs for the musical evenings which he so enjoyed.

By the time the Duchess of York's girl, Mary, came to the

throne as co-ruler with her dour husband, William, chairs and indeed all furniture had become very tall and stately. Again, fashion probably influenced this. Women were wearing very high head-dresses and men adopted larger and larger wigs. If one wanted to be fashionably psychological about this one might suggest that the high head-dresses and the large wigs were symbolical of emphasis on the brain, whereas in James I's day the emphasis was on the buttocks. One might, however, be just a little too clever here, because by now women had taken to hooped petticoats again (though much much smaller ones) and were as usual being lectured for it with dreary monotony. But possibly the hooped petticoat made the spoon-back chair a necessity, it came in during Mary's time; or perhaps a severe lordosis was more common in women then than now.

The cabriole leg, typically Queen Anne, was also first introduced in the time of William and Mary, but it is barely recognizable as such because the legs are tied by stretchers—bandy legs must at first have looked as if they needed holding together. But by Anne's time stretchers had disappeared and chairs looked as if able to trot lightly away on colts' fetlocks, lions' paws and even on the claw and ball foot. Incidentally, the latter is of Persian origin. It is a dragon's claw holding a great pearl, which is why we sometimes find scaling above the claw.* In Anne's reign chair backs became lower again (so did head-dresses) and the vase splat-back was popular, but the spoon-back remained fashionable and continued to do so until Chippendale.

Stools changed throughout the period. Although they continued to remain *de rigueur* for dining until as late as 1680 they were lighter, more graceful, well upholstered, handsomely fringed and

---

*I have often heard this called feathering above an eagle's claw. But Dragons are scaley and nearly always have feet like those of a buzzard or falcon, with sometimes four toes and a spur toe. Certainly the great dragon, very properly killed by Rustem for attacking his horse Raksh, has bird feet claws. So have most of St. George's dragons. I do know, however, one or two dragons with lion-like, or perhaps Chimaera-like paws.

Japanned cabinet on silvered stand, *c.* 1670.

had delicate legs. The settle, for so long a good solid exceedingly hard and uncomfortable piece, was modified and became a less rigid, uncompromising affair. First its seat was upholstered and loose seat cushions were added, next the hard back (still high) was curved and arms were lowered. By Anne's time it had become the settee, its back was again straight but lower and the frame is supported by three cabriole legs in front and two straight ones behind. The love-seat, so called by us, made its appearance around the end of the seventeenth or beginning of the eighteenth century. It was an upholstered settle for two, perhaps the English equivalent of the French Marquise chair which suggests, no doubt quite wrongly, that the French nobility was either very fat or very amorous—probably both. But hardly fatter or more amorous than the English.

Day beds too became fashionable, although surviving ones look neither comfortable nor "lewd", as Shakespeare once described a royal one. They had caned seats and a carved or caned back, the caning on the back held between two boldly carved uprights. They cannot have been very restful even with the back let down. But they were probably made bearable and even mildly sinful by loose cushions. Sensibly, such cushions were often leather-backed to keep them from slipping (chairs, when not upholstered, often had dished seats to hold a flat squab cushion).

As for great or State beds, they still had four posts and a tester but here the resemblance to the Elizabethan and early century bed ends. All the wooden parts of the bed were now concealed by costly fabrics. The headboard, no longer recessed and arcaded was, in effect, a half headboard; sometimes curved like a great shell, sometimes built up with scrolls or amorini and topped by feathers, or a crown (crowns supported by amorini were, understandably, very popular). This half headboard was set against a backboard carefully draped with silk, or figured velvet caught back by rosettes or other ornaments. The whole inside of the tester was silk lined and although frieze and cornice were carved they too were silk covered, the covering concealing the wood but often revealing the carving. Four slender posts also covered with material supported the tester. Finials of various shapes surmounted the four corners. Vase-shaped finials were popular and often contained great plumes of feathers which needed special feather dressers to keep them looking fresh, or alternatively, feathers were just clumped at the corners and tied with ribbon bows. The "pennaches" or tufts of plumes ornamenting one of the beds of the "Dutchesse of Chaulmes" cost 14,000 livres[13]— almost £1,000. That was in France in the 1650's. In the 1650's we obviously couldn't go in for such panache but we more than made up for it after the Restoration.

Valances became deeper and, together with the curtains, which could be drawn to enclose the bed, were wonderfully rich. In fact the value of the bed now depended almost entirely on the materials used to cover and enclose it. When they rotted away with the centuries the bed looked a poor bare thing. This is why carved wooden beds of the sixteenth and very early seventeenth century are far more frequently seen in museums and great houses than beds of subsequent eras. Coverlids or counterpanes

Of Furniture and Furnishings

were either fitted or loose and often gold or silver fringed. And all this passion for covering every bit of the bed with fabric led to a boom in the home manufacture of brocades, damasks, broadsilks, silks and all "soft" furnishings—although fashionable women flatly refused to wear such home-produced fabrics and imported them from France. The richer you were the more elaborate and expensive the bed. Royal beds were and always had been fabulous (as are the wonderful beds at Knole) and the £8,000 bed at Hampton Court was really not all that unusual.*

In fact even in the 1659 inventory of Hampton Court—the one made after Cromwell's death but before Charles' return—there was in the "Rich Bedchamber" a bedstead "furnished" in "rich incarnadine velvett, imbroidered very rich with gold and silver". There were also two "elbow Chaires" and six back stools upholstered in the same velvet and embroidered. The head cloth and linings of the curtains were cloth of gold and window curtains were of scarlet cloth lined with "Taffety and laced about with gold and silver needlework lace, like acorns". In the "Room Appointed for Strangers", strangers were suitably impressed by a bedstead with "furniture" (furnishings) of "needlework of poetical fancyes"; forty-four pieces of crimson velvet and cloth of gold, to say nothing of "curtains of grene satin" branched with gold and silver flowers. The room also contained an elbow chair, two back stools, a foot stool, a long seat with a cushion. There were also seven gilt cups dotted about and seven feathers which suggests that the cups were there to hold the feathers, one cannot think why.

As bedrooms were still reception rooms, those with any pretentions to fashion or who hoped to get on—one way or another—simply would not have been caught dead in an old-fashioned Elizabethan or Jacobean tomb-like bed. So crude, so

*The great State bed at Chatsworth, possibly made by Lapierre in 1697, was more modestly priced at £470. Even so, the first Duke seems to have paid for it on the Hire Purchase system at the rate of £6 per week. The canopy of this bed is now at Hardwick Hall.

heavy, so barbaric, made for and handed down by one's nouveau riche great grandparents; dark and depressingly connubial. One was after all *riche* oneself, but not all that *nouveau*, although certainly the nouveau nouveaux riches abounded after the Restoration because Charles sold titles like a pedlar selling trumpery wares at a fair. Hideous old beds were good enough for country squires (or poor relations) rotting away in the provinces, or for gloomy old nobles in their gloomy old castles and fortresses in the far north or west who had been ruined by supporting Charles's father (many received small recompense from his son) but they wouldn't do for the newly ennobled; the rich merchant, the fashionable, modern, and worldly Londoner. They were not for men and women, who, if we are to believe Restoration comedies regarded having to live in the country as a fate infinitely worse than death. "This is more dismal than the country . . . pity me who am going to that sad place"[14] says Harriet Woodvil. Poor Harriet couldn't even endure to hear the word "Hampshire" spoken.

These lavish and beautiful beds, so elegant, so costly, so covered with silks and velvets had, however, one grave disadvantage. They became as easily infested with bugs as their no less elegantly dressed owners became infested with lice. We tend to forget that the past, no matter how elegant and glamorous it appears to be, or with what acute nostalgia we view it, was rat-ridden, flea-ridden, bug-ridden and, due to the sanitary or rather insanitary arrangements of the day, it stank abominably.

Rat-ridden or no, however, new, plainer, better proportioned and smaller houses demanded an altogether different type of furniture and just as the introduction of rush matting had affected the position of stretchers and the shape of legs in the first half of the century so the introduction of the smaller private dining-room in all new-built houses affected the shape and size of dining-room furniture, while the introduction of new beverages begot newly designed small tables and various other special and necessary appurtenances.

The long solid dining-board was completely ousted and the

Of Furniture and Furnishings

smaller oval, round or square table came in. By the end of the century a better-made and more delicate gate-leg table was a firm favourite—and firm is the key word—in dining-rooms of the moderately well to do. Carpets, metaphorically speaking, were no longer on tenterhooks, they crawled off walls and furniture onto polished oak floors . . . and were almost invariably placed under the dining-room table or under the bed or any other large piece of furniture.

Parqueting of floors was known but was not general until after the Restoration. Sir John Danvers (d. 1655) who laid out the Italian gardens at Chelsea (he also signed the death warrant of Charles I) had a floor in his house at Chelsea "chequered like a chesse board of Box and Ewgh panels of about six inches square".[15] Perhaps the floor was already laid in 1644 when the unfortunate eight-year-old Princess Elizabeth, namesake of the Winter Queen, and four-year-old Prince Henry, Duke of Gloucester, children of the king, were lodged in the house with Sir John as their keeper. Seven years later, in confinement at Carisbrooke Castle, the little Princess quietly laid her head down on the Bible her father had given her and died.

From about 1680 parquetry floors were fairly usual and by

Carved walnut day bed with caned seat, c. 1680.

The Pageant of Stuart England

Anne's time handsome inlaid floors of floral or geometric pattern became fashionable, although hall and a downstairs room or two might still have a sanded tile or stone floor. Carpets were still imported from the East and from Europe but by 1701 the weaving of the tougher floor carpets became established here and the famous Wilton carpets began to be made. Smaller rugs or "fote" carpets were in more general use, yet carpets and rugs on floors did not really become plentiful even in the homes of the wealthy until the first quarter of the eighteenth century. In humbler homes rushes remained the usual floor covering.

But to return to the smaller dining-rooms in which people were eating larger meals. The monstrous side tables, court cupboards and presses vanished, to be replaced by bureau cabinets, china cabinets and other smaller and more graceful cupboards. By the end of the century a wide range of cabinets, bureaux and cupboards were being made and being used, not solely in the dining-room, but all over the house. The old chest, known since the beginning of time, which had developed in Elizabeth's day into a chest with a drawer, and later into a chest-of-drawers, now, by some inspired need to save space became the chest-on-chest or tallboy. By amalgamating with the early Stuart portable desk it became the bureau. By sitting a cabinet (itself a development of the hutch) on its head it became the bureau-cabinet. The dresser, perhaps invented in Cromwell's time, was probably the parent of the bureau bookcase. And the bureau bookcase was similar to the bureau cabinet, but whereas the cabinet part of the latter piece contained small compartments, the former was fitted with shelves. By now there were also free standing bookcases, straight-fronted and with glazed doors, although bookshelves along the walls were often a planned feature in big houses. Collecting books was not only the pastime of antiquarians or politicians like Harley, and if great houses had special rooms for books, smaller ones needed bookcases. Even if one weren't clever enough to understand all the political and philosophical works there were plenty of other books to be had (and scurrilous pamphlets too) all beautifully bound. Regrettably, some people

Of Furniture and Furnishings

followed the sad example of the Italians, commented on with scorn by Mr. Evelyn, and bought their books "by the yard", as some still do. In 1666 one Symson the Joyner made Sam Pepys various presses to house his rapidly growing collection of books so that Pepys might have "as noble a closett as any man". Symson's work still houses some of Sam Pepys' books in the Pepys Library at Magdalene College, Cambridge.

Big pieces by this time were nearly all made of imported yellow deal suitably prepared to take veneers—deal in those days held glue far better than oak. Veneering had originated on the continent and it showed off the beauties of walnut to perfection. The curl or crotch pattern came from a slice taken from a Y or L shaped junction of side branch and main trunk. The "oyster" was thinly sliced, like a cucumber, from an individual branch and showed the small ring pattern of the branch. The "burr", most intricately figured of all, came from the abnormal and swollen growths found at the base of the tree trunk. As successive slices taken from the same piece of wood often showed duplicate patterns, this enabled the veneer to be glued in matched sections, often four of such were quartered on a door, a panel, or a drawer. But it was not only walnut which was so used, elm, yew and mulberry made excellent veneers too. And olive and laburnum, like Colchester and Whitstable, produced the best "oysters".

Marquetry, a very advanced form of veneering, seems to have become very fashionable around the mid 1670's. It too originated on the continent—in Holland to be exact—and required the highest skill and greatest patience in the delicate cutting and fitting together of coloured woods to form the wonderful patterns of flowers, birds and foliage characteristic of early marquetry work. By 1700 arabesques were popular and also the incredibly complicated and beautiful "sea-weed" or "endive" marquetry, which looked so handsome on long clock cases (parquetry, on furniture, is a form of marquetry in which geometrical patterns are used). To get the right colour for a pattern the native colour of walnut could be altered by bleaching, staining, dyeing or by scorching with hot sand, but other woods of a suitable colour were used too. There was a great demand for apple, dogwood, boxwood, maple, plane and sycamore for the lighter colours such as yellow and white. These handily grew at home, but other woods had to be imported, from the East, from South America and the West Indies. Princewood (later elevated to Kingwood), snakewood, partridge wood, rosewood and lignum vitae gave the rich reds and browns; ebony was black; fustic, yellow, but it turned, like a potato, dead brown when exposed to air. The craze for elaborate marquetry began to die down in Anne's reign when there was a return to plainer veneering.

Indian lacquered or "japanned" furniture—like the cabinets Catherine of Braganza brought with her—was seldom "Indian", it came mainly from Japan or China and was enormously popular. Japanese lacquer-work was considered to be the finest and was brought to us first by the Dutch. But because the East India Company also handled Chinese and Indian lacquer-work (some was made in India) which was sold in their "Indian" stores it became known as Indian work. In Japanese lacquer-work the decoration is usually in higher relief than in Chinese and the design is usually of trees and water, mountains and rocks, birds and animals. Human figures are rarely seen in Japanese work but are frequent in Chinese lacquer. Another type of lacquer-work which was much admired was called Coromandel. Here the design is incised and this really did come from India. So popular did lacquer work become that English merchants feverishly exported English-made furniture to be lacquered and returned home or as a pattern to be copied and lacquered. So English-style furniture, made and lacquered in the East, was imported into England. It was also not at all unusual to import folding lacquer screens, intended to keep off the draughts which still knifed the inhabitants of even the most elegantly furnished new houses, but many cabinet-makers bought such screens and cut and converted them into cabinets. Cabinets were always placed on stands, but the stands were English made. Some are most ornate, carved and gilded or silvered, baroque fashion, as were William and Mary tables. There are many beautiful cabinets and stands still

Of Furniture and Furnishings

to be seen in private homes today. But one of the finest is in the Victoria and Albert Museum and dates from *circa* 1675. The carved silvered stand has a very fine frieze, and although the front legs are a mad combination of claw and ball foot, acanthus leaf from ankle to calf, from which pot-bellied and rather sulky telemones arise it is typical of the period . . . and oddly beauti-

Bedstead in the grand manner, *c.* 1680.

ful. While all this importing of lacquer work was going on a domestic lacquering industry had begun and in 1693, a company was formed calling itself "The Patentees for Lacquering after the Manner of Japan". As usual, the patentees (and other furniture makers) looked upon the importation of foreign furniture as a threat and by 1701 had persuaded Parliament to impose a heavy duty on imported lacquer. From then until around 1740 all japanned work was made at home and much of this we exported to other countries. It is now not always easy to tell the true Oriental from the Anglo-Oriental cabinet, but the Eastern ones generally have a black ground while domestic work often has a coloured ground—red being a firm favourite, although green, yellow and mock-tortoise backgrounds were favoured too. English japanned work also tends to lose its lustre more quickly than Eastern work.

All this new lighter furniture in new houses (and in altered old ones) would have looked rather odd and out of place against dark heavily-panelled walls. Enormous tapestry hangings were fine if you had the space, or the tapestries (many had both) but you could hardly hang pictures upon tapestry and people were having their portraits painted and buying pictures like mad. Dr. Claver Morris went to London again (in 1694) and returned home this time with four pictures, "Herodias's Daughter Dancing", "Our Saviour on the Cross", "Cardinal Wolsey" and a "Little Landskip", a very mixed bag for which he paid 14/6, 2/6, 2/6 and 3/- respectively. We cannot be sure these pictures were paintings, they may have been engravings but whatever they were they went straight on walls and walls too had moved with the times.

Wainscotting, plain or carved, was popular and where panelling was plain the framework was often painted red, while painted or stencilled designs in colour ornamented the panels, more particularly during the first half of the seventeenth century. In all great houses throughout the period there was much oak panelling and there were many tapestries too which hung now from cornice to dado only (Mortlake was continuing to turn out fine tapestries until the century's end). But in the new houses and the small houses panelling was as often of cedar or fir, and panels, as the century drew to its close, became larger and often had a raised bolection moulding around them. Mr. Rooth's new "neate" house at Epsom had a little parlour "wainscoted white in veins and gold moulding" and of a "neate booffett furnish'd with glasses and china".[16] A buffet in those days was an alcove cupboard let into the wall. Clothes cupboards were also let in

Of Furniture and Furnishings

and fitted with a door. But the chief change in walls came with the use of wallpaper and it wasn't until this century that wallpaper was used in any quantity. Due to its very nature it is not easy to judge just how general or how early its use. But certainly it was known before the "Stuart Century". The discovery that printing type could be cut in wood had early led to the idea of producing decorative printed papers and these early papers reproduced the designs of the brocades, the velvets, the damasks and the stamped and painted Spanish or Dutch leather, used in the palaces and great houses both in Europe and England.

Probably the earliest example of wallpaper here, was that produced by a printer, Henry Goes of York, who used as his "mark" a capital H and a goose—which tells us how to pronounce Henry's last name or perhaps indicates how much the pronunciation of the word goose, has changed. Anyway, Henry Goes's paper* is in small squares, because this economical Yorkshireman printed his design (brocade or velvet) on the backs of bills proclaiming the accession of Henry VIII! But wallpapers do not seem to have been much in use until a good century and a half later. It may be that they were used more commonly than we suppose, but failed to survive in the climate. We do know that in the sixteenth century decorative Italian papers, marbled or figured and used to line books and chests, had already inspired the French around Rouen to produce such papers for home decoration and these were eagerly bought by French peasants who couldn't afford any other decoration for a chimney breast. Later on, French papers were printed and hand coloured, as the name "papier-pient" suggests (papier-tincture, today), but it is not until 1631 that we have any real indication that our own ancestors were interested in wallpaper. In that year, Charles I granted to Jerome Lanyer the exclusive right to manufacture flock paper (invented it is said in France in 1620 by Le François of Rouen). Lanyer called his paper "Londriana" but strictly speaking it wasn't a paper at all. He used linen, cloth, leather,

*Found early in our own century during restoration of the entrance of Christ's College, Cambridge.

and many other substances as background for his wool flocks—perhaps because the paper we made wasn't then very good. Early wallpapers must have had a very haphazard appearance *in situ* as they were printed on small sheets, perhaps twelve by sixteen inches, and no attempt was made to key the sheets. They were probably chiefly used to ornament the centre of wood panelling instead of painting or stencilling the design.

What happened to wallpaper during the Commonwealth we don't know, although we can perhaps guess, but fifty years after Lanyer's flock-paper, a man called Dunbar had an enormous quantity of wallpaper in stock at Aldermanbury. There in the '80's Londoners could see and marvel at these papers, some "after the manner of real tapestry", others designed as damasks, yet others ornamented with sprigs and branches, suggesting embroidery and, most fascinating of all, the yard wide papers which simulated marble. By now flock-papers had gone out in France, but were all the rage in England. And if they were more economical than rich hangings (but economy was not the point, fashion was), they were infinitely more difficult to deal with. Early papers had been nailed onto walls with flat-headed nails, later papers had been pasted on, but when flock-papers became fashionable they were treated more carefully than the tapestries they supplanted. You couldn't just "hang" a flock-paper (even if, at least in the United States, they use paper-hanging as a verb) nor could you apply it as real damask was applied. Flock-paper wasn't hung at all, it was mounted. Stretchers were first made and nailed to walls, strong linen was stretched tightly over them, then a brown paper lining was pasted on to the linen and when this was dry the wallpaper was finally applied. It was during this century too that Chinese wallpapers first came to Europe (and led to the Anglo-Chinese designs of the next century). They were very probably first used as a panel to set off the new Chinese porcelains which Queen Mary II collected so avidly, or as a foil for Indian cabinets or other lacquered furniture.

Walls in the new, smaller houses, whether panelled or papered, would have been overshadowed by the pendative bossed ceilings

Commonwealth table, *c.* 1650. Queen Anne chair.

of the early years of the century, and certainly smaller rooms couldn't have stood menacing, giant, plaster stalactites. But ceilings had been changing too as the century grew older. Right from the beginning ribs were flatter and often delicately ornamented with leaves and flowers—the thistle was, naturally, a favourite motif—frequently interstices were left unornamented or in large rooms there would be a centrepiece showing an allegorical figure or a series of figures personifying the five senses. A woman playing a musical instrument, rather improbably, to a listening stag, was not meant to suggest "music hath charms", it symbolized hearing. A seated woman holding a vicious bird which pecks away at her hand indicated touch—and so on. The library ceiling at Blickling, an early one, is most interesting. All kinds of mythological and other figures are here, one panel shows Zeus with a very neat wedge-shaped slice removed from his head to allow Athene unhindered birth . . . or perhaps one should say Jove and Minerva as the century seemed to turn to the Roman not the Greek for its literary ideas. The Elements; Peace and

War; the three theological virtues—Faith, Hope and Charity; medallion heads of one or more of the Nine Worthies—Alexander the Great was a particular favourite; Time and Truth—all these were fit subject matter for ceiling figures modelled in relief against a tinted background. Unmistakably male amorini and equally unmistakably female angels were popular; strap-work, much restrained, was still in evidence. During the Common-wealth ceilings became almost plain, with emphasis, if any, on the centrepiece which, when not non-committal, generally and safely depicted the Virtues—all rather plain girls—or the pious Pelican. Edifying no doubt but one prefers Blickling.

After the Restoration, ribs divided the ceiling less frequently into square and triangular compartments and more often into ovals and rectangular shapes. Swags of fruit and flowers matching the carved fruit and flowers of mouldings or the patterns of marquetry work, ornamented and disguised the ribs and very beautifully too. Great houses with huge rooms could and did take ceilings with high relief on rib and panel but smaller houses couldn't, so in these houses ceilings achieved their effect by a nice feeling for delicacy and proportion. The ceiling of the oak room (1668) at Wroxton Abbey is a fine example of what lies between the extremes of heavy and plain. It is charming and each panel is ornamented with musical instruments.

Side by side with the development and refinement of plaster and stucco ceilings was the fashion for great houses and palaces to have ceilings and staircase walls painted with enormous, overpowering mythological or allegorical scenes. Both Inigo Jones's Banqueting house at Whitehall and Wren's Sheldonian had painted ceilings but of a very different kind from that which became fashionable sometime in the 1670's when the coarse and pretentious work of Antonio Verrio ruined many a fine ceiling and noble staircase. Fortunately Verrio's assistant, Louis Laguerre, was not corrupted by his master and so produced among other things some of the splendid ceilings of the State rooms at Chats-worth (and later the famous saloon at Blenheim). Verrio and Laguerre are probably the best known of the early foreign

Of Furniture and Furnishings

painters who worked here. (Pelligrini and the Ricci came slightly later under Queen Anne.) It was an English painter, Sir James Thornhill, who was most in demand but he is better known for the work done after Anne's death.

Staircases changed too. In the early years with the shifting of emphasis from Great Hall to Long Gallery and with the siting of State rooms on an upper floor, the staircase naturally became of much greater importance. Hitherto, it had been, for the most part, relatively modest with newels and other carved bits ornamented and picked out in colour, and speaking very generally it had been largely ignored as an architectural feature. It had been but a means of access and—apart from the winding stair of wood or stone which is defensive—the ladder was its near ancestor. In many a farm-house of two floors or in a cottage where an upper room had been added this ancestor was still very much alive and moveable. The ladder-stair in such houses had the great advantage that if for some reason you didn't like it where it was —perhaps it went up into the wrong bedroom, or perhaps you'd added a room above one of the outshuts—it could be moved, rough hand-rail and all, to wherever you wanted it. You merely cut a hole in the ceiling, boarded over the old one and there you were. The movement of this ladder-stair can often be traced by boarded up holes found in the upper floor of many a surviving farm-house.

With the increase in the building of prodigy and state houses in the late sixteenth and early seventeenth centuries and with the Great Hall, save in more conservative families, now little more than an outsize entrance hall, a mean little staircase leading from it would give the arriving guest—who must be suitably impressed—no idea of the hidden splendour awaiting him on the first floor. A grand staircase was needed for a grand house. Unfortunately, with the staircase our ancestors just hadn't the grand manner. They couldn't conceive of anything like the magnificent stone staircases developed in France and Italy in the fifteenth century (think of Chambord and Blois). They stuck to wood and fell back on their native talent for holding to the

Enclosed, pierced panel staircase, early century.

traditional and conventional with minor if flamboyantly modish alterations. Sometimes newels like bedposts supported a hand-rail fit for Goliath, sometimes balustrading was carved and arcaded. Newel posts—some were carried up to support the overhead landing—sprouted tall elaborate finials in the shape of heraldic beasts or mythological figures. At Francis Bacon's house at Gorhambury there was "a delicate Staircase of wood, which was curiously carved, and on the posts of every interstice was some prettie figure as of a grave Divine with his booke and spectacles, a Mendicant Friar, etc., not one thing twice".[17]

Later in the century the great Earl of Cork when improving Stalbridge, which he bought from the Earl of Bristol and which was subsequently occupied for a time by his son, Robert Boyle, notes in his diary that he employed Christopher Watt to make "twelve figures each three foot high to set upon my staircase, for which he demands 20s. apiece and I offer him 13s. 4d. And he is presently (immediately) to cut one of them with the figure of

Baluster, open string staircase, late century.

Pallas with a shield. One with a coat with a coronet is to be cut for a trial". Even at 13/4 the Earl was going to be sure of what kind of work he was getting. It is not surprising that when he took over Ralegh's estates which due to James I's shameful treatment of Ralegh had been utterly neglected, he made them pay. He was one of the greatest and best of Irish landowners; even Cromwell said that if all landowners had been like the Earl there wouldn't have been a rebellion in Ireland. But even an Irish rebellion did not deserve Drogheda, although the Irish often forget we too suffered the "final mercy" of Worcester.

Despite the passion for ornamentation, stairs were narrow and steep with square landings. Unaccepted were the bold curved sweep and spacious landings of the continent . . . landings which could contain furniture and mirrors and torchères. Everything was ornamented and overornamented. Sampson asleep with his head on Delilah's lap—Delilah with her shears at the ready; sub-human figures blowing trumpets; large fantastic flowers, amorini and stiff-legged beasts appear on the carved, enclosing panels of the balustrades, but the shape and form of the staircase remained much the same. It took many years for people to realize that arcaded balusters or even pierced slab panels although effective, when forming the rail to a gallery were most unhappy when attempting to climb a stair with many half paces. The effect is restless and disquieting. On the other hand the Great Painted Staircase at Knole (c. 1605) shows the soothing effect of the circular baluster where both base and rail follow the slope. The staircase at Knole is, probably, the finest of its kind in England. But Knole was ahead of its time.

From somewhere between 1620 and 1630 until the mid '70's the most usual type of balustrade was the pierced panel, carved with fruit, flowers, leaves and scrolls and although piercing made for some lightness the stair was still massive and solid. The staircase at Aston Hall, Birmingham, is a good example; hit by a cannon-ball in the Civil War it is still as solid as ever. During the Commonwealth the barley twist baluster came in. It too, was very heavy, with clumsy balusters set between a heavy, carved string and an equally heavy rail. Newel posts became lower though still elaborately carved. Toward the end of the century there was a return to the barley twist, the vase shape and the turned baluster, but they were much lighter, more graceful and slender, and designed for an "open string"—which sounds like something one does on a double bass but means that the bases of balusters (now grouped in two's or three's) were fixed on to stair treads instead of into the sloping plank or string which supported the treads (formerly the string had come above the treads). The staircase of Virginia walnut with parquetry half-paces at Dyrham Park in Gloucestershire* is a fine example of the open string with grouped balusters. Hand-rails and newel posts

---

*In the earlier, non Talman, west front of Dyrham Park; it was built for William Blathwayt by Alex Hunter of Piccadilly! The house is a recently acquired property of the National Trust. Unfortunately, the staircase was painted oyster white and gold by a previous tenant but the Trust hopes to be able to afford to have it stripped one day. Blathwayt was brought up by his uncle, Thomas Povey, Pepys' friend.

were also much lighter and finials all but disappeared. Indeed they did disappear in small houses.

But such modest staircases were not for great houses and palaces where marble and stone were at last being used freely. Here wrought iron balustrades were the answer—and wrought iron was becoming extremely beautiful. At Chatsworth around 1697 the hall was lofty and painted with "armoury" and, according to Celia Fiennes "there is 18 steps on each side goes up as an arch with iron barristers* tipt with gold which meets on top, large steps of stone, thence you enter a dineing roome two drawing rooms a bed chamber and closet which opens through the house a visto." Some four years later when the eighteenth century was perhaps twelve months old, Old Subtlety's grand-daughter, just turned forty, revisited Hampton Court—considerably altered by Wren since the day when the now Dowager Queen Catherine of Braganza first came there as a bride. Celia's rather downright powers of description are strained to breaking by the "lofty and spacious" royal staircase where Verrio had let his fancy run wild on wall and ceiling. The wall is "black and gold painted with armory like a wanscoate", she writes, "over that is a curious painting of the twelve Caesars, over that the banquet of the Gods all at length, with Ceres over the side board with plenty". There is a semicolon's pause for breath before she attempts the ceiling; "the rooffe is angells and cheru-bins", then a plunge down to the half pace where "is Julian and the spectre than appear'd to him, in a tent of green, the curtain drawn soe bold as if real with gold fringe."

And, looking back from this point in time to that fixed moment when Celia stands forever upon the stair, observing long-vanished gods and dead Caesars, we too can conjure up the past and see it as if in a mural. But it is our own past. And if some of the figures are still brilliant while others are faded, nevertheless none is mythological. Here is James Crofts' father, dead these fifteen years; and James Crofts' uncle, once Duke of York, then James

*Barristers, unlike chancellors, are rarely of iron. Miss Fiennes means banisters.

II, now an exile and stirring plots in France. And James Crofts himself . . . headless. For the self-proclaimed King of England lost his treasonable, handsome and foolish head on Tower Hill in 1689, and all Catherine of Braganza's pleas for mercy were in vain. Here, too, is the Duchess of York's girl, Mary—the infant who became Mary II and co-ruler of England. She too is dead (so is Mrs. Pepys) and with John Dryden they belong together in one group—for to be dead is to be neither near nor far and no man outranks another in the tomb.

Still living are: Charles Sackville, now sixth Earl of Dorset and Earl of Middlesex, master of Knole and, at the moment, Lord Chancellor to William III; the eighty-four year old St. Evremond who writes a letter to his ex-love and contemporary, Ninon de Lenclos, linking us back in time to the year of his birth—the year of Shakespeare's death. In a corner, the erstwhile Countess of Castlemaine and Duchess of Cleveland is indeed heading for a rocky shore, she is married to the disreputable "Beau" Fielding who has a wife living. Admiral Sir William Penn's son has turned out rather well after all, and Lord Somers is the not very distinguished head of the Royal Society. Mr. Pepys has retired to Clapham; Mr. Evelyn to Dorking.

As for Catherine of Braganza? She too has retired but to her native country.

And ironically enough she was most put out when her brother the King of Portugal requested her to adopt the dress of her native country once more. So poor Catherine discarded the long full-skirted dress with its train caught back in graceful folds and held by ribbon bows or loops to display a pretty, rich petticoat, for whatever grand ladies in Portugal were wearing in 1700. Just as she had once discarded the magnificent, old-fashioned Portuguese farthingale for the full skirt, worn over several petti-coats, the neat-waisted bodice, the low, wide décolletage worn by fashionable Englishwomen in 1662.

CHAPTER FOUR

Of Things—Curious and Commonplace

"THEY put into the Chimney certain Iron Stoves about half a Foot high with a Plate of Iron behind and beneath; before and on each side are Bars placed and fasten'd like the Wiers of a Cage, all of Iron". Thus a French Huguenot refugee, Henri Misson, describes that English commonplace thing a "seacole" grate. Everyone in England—save perhaps those unfortunate, unsophisticated sub-humans compelled to live in remote rural areas—knew what a grate was and had known for years. There was no need for them to describe it to each other; it grew out of a need to save wood* and so what was a natural development for the English was to M. Misson a great curiosity when he saw it in English homes in the late seventeenth century.

Having carefully pointed out that "none but people of the first quality burn wood at London" and "only in their bedchambers", whereas in other parts of this strange island, wood, turf and ling were still used (cow dung, dried leaves and grass were used by the very poor had he but known it) he goes on to tell his wide-

*Forests near coasts and waterways were by now denuded. It was difficult to transport timber over the still appalling roads. Coal lying near the Tyne and Severn could be shipped by barge by sea to the Thames. Since Elizabeth's time coal production had increased enormously and the amount unloaded at the Port of London rose from around 11,000 tons in the late sixteenth century to around 500,000 tons in the late seventeenth century. A levy on Londoners' coal largely paid for the new St. Paul's.

eyed countrymen about Coal; also, it seems, a curiosity to the elegant but obviously impractical French. Why, as early as 1606 we were saying of ordinary things which bored us, that they were "as common as coals from Newcastle", and by 1650 Thomas Fuller had invented the phrase "to carry coals to Newcastle" . . . meaning "owls to Athens".

But M. Misson is a stranger and so is at great pains to explain about coal and its qualities. "Their Common Fewel is Coal" he writes "which comes from Scotland and Newcastle".[1] Common coal, though not so "combustible", burned well, once lit, and was very convenient because it lasted "a great while with little repair". This was just as well. Common coal had little else to recommend it. Trying to set it alight in one of the seacoale grates was a most involved process as described by M. Misson. Even when successfully accomplished a most alarming result followed. Yet M. Misson writes about it with cheerful equanimity. "In proportion as the Coal grows hotter it dissolves" he says "becomes glutinous and sticks together . . . to keep it up and Revive it you now and then give it a stir with a long piece of Iron, made on Purpose". Presumably, that is, if you could get near enough to the glutinous, tar-bubbling mess without being choked by smoke, blanketed by smuts or overcome by sulphurous fumes to the point of needing reviving yourself. But once these hazards were braved and overcome one could, perhaps, even sit by the revived fire, or warm one's anatomy by slowly twirling in front of the baleful flames as if on an invisible spit. Hence, the honest and melancholy proverb "If you will enjoy the fire you must put up with the smoke".

Yet M. Misson is rather too jovial and irritatingly cheerful about it all, for he assures his countrymen that although the "Smoak" is terribly thick, if chimneys were well built (too often they weren't) the smoke is "carried cleanly (sic) away and consequently incommodes the Streets more than the Houses". Furthermore, the sulphurous smell is certainly offensive to newcomers but "one is soon used to it."

This, one can hardly credit. Perhaps M. Misson was just being

Of Things—Curious and Commonplace

polite and kind. Most foreigners spoke bitterly of the smoke and filth of London. That rather tiresome scholar and bibliophile von Uffenbach, a late Stuart visitor, complained that his cuffs became filthy whenever he handled a book in any Library, even in a private house. Although foreigners, as usual, detested the English quite as much as the English detested them and would rush any fault or vice into cold, bold print, it was not only they who complained of the dirt and smoke of London. That *English* gentleman and virtuoso, John Evelyn, was so exercised by the smoke menace that in 1661 he wrote a book about it. In his dedication "to The Kings Most Sacred Majesty" he says flatly that one day whilst walking in the Kings Palace at Whitehall "a presumptuous Smoake issuing from one or two Tunnels* neer Northumberland house and not far from Scotland yard, did so invade the Court; that all the Rooms, Galleries and Places about it were filled and infected with it"[2] to such a degree that "Men could hardly discern one another for the Clowd". This was not only a "hazzard" to the King's health, it was also bad for His Majesty's subjects. And canny Mr. Evelyn mentions that the King's sister the "Dutchesse of Orleans"—Charles's beloved Minette—complained while at the palace of the "Smoake" in her "Breast and Lungs". This was calculated to arouse Charles who worried about Minette's health to the point of writing to implore her to be careful of "strong broths and gravy in the morning". Following the dedicatory epistle, Mr. Evelyn then outlines his recommendations on how to rid London of smoke. Ever precipitate, the English did something about it exactly 295 years later.

*The word chimney was still used to describe what we now call the fireplace. In earlier eras, smoke, with luck—and unaided by pipes, flues or stacks—went out through a hole in the roof. Later when the hearth moved from the centre of the room to a wall it was hooded and had a tunnel (or chimney flue) to draw the smoke up through the hole. Ultimately these tunnels were built into the walls of the house and finally became known as chimneys. Evelyn speaks of tunnels in his *Fumifugium*. But earlier in describing "the old ragged city of Leicester" he speaks of "chimney flues" which were "like so many Smith's forges" (Diary. Aug. 9th, 1654).

Early century chimney piece.

Despite these disadvantages the early coal age had a two-fold effect upon domestic interiors. It made a desirable and necessary alteration in the sheer size of fireplaces with a consequent reduction in overwhelming ornamentation, it also produced new types of "hearth-furniture". Fireplaces in that vast rabbit warren, Whitehall, were probably as much to blame for the "obscuring Clowd" as were the smoking tunnels near-by. It is never easy to turn a great, old-fashioned, log-burning fireplace into a smaller one meant for a coal basket (and vice versa) without running into severe trouble. So in London and other places where coal replaced wood the choice probably lay between making an old fire-place smaller and risk being heavily smoked, or of leaving it enormous and risk being half whisked up the chimney by draughts whistling in under the ill-fitting doors and windows of an old house.

In new houses, new fireplaces—we hope—behaved rather better, although from contemporary accounts there seems to be singularly little evidence that they did. Nevertheless, if their behaviour was deplorable their looks had certainly improved.

Of Things—Curious and Commonplace

Vast, over-burdened chimney pieces—those enormous, tiered superstructures of wood, stone or plaster where biblical and mythological figures, birds, beasts, strap-work, medallion heads, armorial bearings and the like had burgeoned for so many years—disappeared. Their supports—fat writhing columns with cabbage capitals, heavy bosomed caryatids, and portly telemones with such unprepossessingly flat heads—also dwindled and faded away. New fireplaces were smaller, more sober and far better proportioned. From perhaps around 1620 mantling around the opening was divorced from the chimney-piece and some fireplaces even in great houses were surrounded by no more than a simple moulding with mitred angles. Above this, a picture, a piece of tapestry or a looking-glass replaced the old ornate chimney-piece. Even as early as 1647 we see this happening. Sir Clepesby Crew of Thistleworth, in addition to "fine Indian hangings" also had "a very good chimney-piece of water colours, by Breughel" says Evelyn. Fifty years later this was usual. At

Late century piece.

Hinchinbrook* where the dining-room was ceiled with Irish oak upon which "no spider will weave or endure", Miss Fiennes saw over one of the chimneys "a fine picture of Venus—were it not too much uncloth'd".

Not all those in advance of fashion used simple mouldings, some preferred columns but there was now nothing blatant or elephantine about them, they were plain or fluted with capitals and bases proper to their orders—which is where the true Italian Renaissance feeling comes in. Such columns supported a shelf above a mantletree often carved with swags of fruit, flowers, shells, rosettes or trophies. Or perhaps the shelf would be supported by curved brackets—carved, plain or ending in scroll, paw or similar mildly ornamental device. Flat wooden surrounds in middling houses were sometimes decorated with painted motifs, more often they were carved; sometimes left unpainted, sometimes picked out in gold or colours.

Marble moulding (like black and white marble floors) was for those who could afford it. And the Duchess of Lauderdale when she remodelled Ham House in 1675 had a new fireplace put in what is now the Blue Drawing-Room. Here a simple marble moulding frames the fireplace, while carved swags above frame a picture. It is a simple, beautiful, high, rather virtuous and prim-looking fireplace. The duchess too was beautiful but she was neither simple nor prim—nor virtuous. According to many, including Bishop Burnet, she had once numbered Oliver

*Hinchinbrook was by then no longer the late Elizabethan house where Sir Oliver Cromwell had so lavishly entertained England's first Stuart Sovereign. Spendthrift Sir Oliver, after vainly trying to sell the house to James I "at a reasonable price" in order to help pay his debts, finally sold it in 1627 for £3,060 to Henry Montagu, Earl of Manchester. Through Henry's youngest brother, Sidney, it passed to Edward Montagu, later first Earl of Sandwich (Sam Pepys was his secretary at the Admiralty) who rebuilt Hinchinbrook in the "modern" manner. But by the time the scantily-clad Venus was observed, Sandwich had been dead for years—blown up in his ship at Solebay in 1672. It is now (1961) on the verge of being bought by the Huntingdon County Council for a school.

Of Things—Curious and Commonplace

Cromwell among her lovers. The Bishop also says that Cromwell broke the affair off—and we can well believe it—when it became the subject for gossip. But the Bishop comments too on the Duchess's beauty, her quickness of apprehension, her vivacious conversation, her knowledge of divinity, history and mathematics but adds that she had a restless ambition, lived at vast expense, was "ravenously covetous", and stuck at nothing to get what she wanted. She was "violent in everything she set about—a violent friend but a much more violent enemy".

Hearth furniture, naturally, changed too. Those "Iron Stoves" described by M. Misson were dog-baskets, developed probably (and here I am guessing) by placing a grid iron or a brazier on fire dogs and, later on, adding a dwarf fire back. Andirons could be and often were very decorative. Far better proportioned than those of the early century, they were now often shaped as balusters, columns or obelisks topped by a bronze or silver finial knob or a flat pierced disk, while silver or bronze shields, leaves or lozenges might mask a plain upright and testify to the wealth and taste of the owner. Silver uprights were not unusual even early in the century. In Imogen's bedroom with its ceiling fretted with gold cherubims, the andirons were:

> ". . . two winking Cupids
> Of silver, each on one foot standing, nicely
> Depending on their brands".[3]

Such andirons were either cast from solid metal or built up, section by section, around an iron core. These may have been a curiosity in the first decade of the century but they became almost commonplace after the Restoration—commonplace that is among the very, very rich. In 1660 silver dogs and andirons are fairly simple; baluster shaped, chased with foliage and fruit and with flame or ball finials. By 1670 the balusters of andirons are truncated and stand between a most elaborate base and an upper part which holds a figure of man, woman or a beast. By 1680 balusters have disappeared and an annular knop holds together, by courtesy, a wonderfully embossed base, rioting with flowers, fruit, acanthus leaves, cherubs, lion masks, and a vase or cup-and-cover shaped top surmounted by a flame finial. Elaboration and ornamentation is with us again, but of a very different kind. It is less coarse but it is no less ostentatious than the over-elaboration of the first quarter of the century.

"The Long Piece of Iron made on Purpose" for stirring the fire might be a plain enough piece of the blacksmith's art but its handle, depending on purse or status, displayed the craft of silver or bronze-smith. Shovel and tongs became a prime necessity and they too were ornamented but the shovel was pierced like the lid of a warming pan so that the ashes could be sifted. Bellows—the old-fashioned still called them bellies—became smaller and more beautiful with their pear-shaped or rectangular boards often overlaid with silver or other metal and enriched with applied ornaments—cherubs, crowns, coronets, crests, fruit. Charles II, it is believed, gave Nell Gwynn a beautiful pair of bellows with his cypher below the crown. The handles are silver gilt with crossed sceptres, repoussé. These are in the possession of H.M. the Queen, but there is a pair in the Ashmolean Museum identical in design. There is elaborate silver hearth furniture at Burghley House and a rather less elaborate kind still at Ham House.

But what really is so exhausting to think about is how tiresome cleaning must have been. With all those sulphurous fumes silver must have tarnished in an hour. To clean silver in those days one mixed up ashes of wheat straw, whiting, and burned alum and applied it with a woollen cloth; or heated the silver up in a bath made of Sal Ammoniac, Alum, Sal Gem, Tartar and Roman Vitriol dissolved in water—which sounds easier but as unsafe for silver as for one's hands. Even so, it could hardly have been possible to warm up great heavy andirons in this, or to pop into the bath large silver tables and torchères like those in the King's bedroom at Knole. Paint work was simpler to clean, whether gold, silver or any other colour. Fresh urine and vine ashes did the trick. This might possibly work on silver too as it would contain mild lye and mild ammonia . . . and would be easier and less dangerous than the bath, which I do not like the sound of at all. And certainly, there was a great deal of silver to be cleaned, apart from hearth furniture and beautiful if rather vulgar andirons, tables, and even silver bedsteads. Silver was still a favourite metal and much of it had been melted down by both sides to pay for the Civil Wars. So there were many silver gaps to be filled and with the Restoration there was a great demand

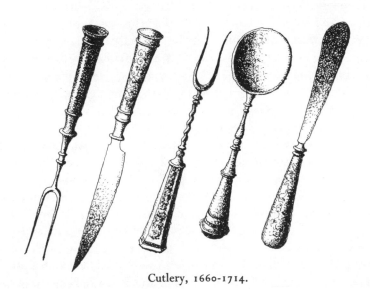

Cutlery, 1660-1714.

for silverware of all kinds. There was nothing like silver to show how well you were getting on in this new, getting on age. And a piece of plate was as good a way as any of indicating to a patron the hope one had of benefits or preferment to come, or of expressing thanks for benefits or preferment received. Plate was also still the usual gift to and from the sovereign on New Year's Day. Even if James I had made no bones about his preference for hard cash, his grandson Charles II did not follow suit—although he was always at loggerheads with a niggardly parliament. There is a Privy Seal dated May 21st, 1671 to Sir Robert Vyner for repayment of £9,063.15.7 and £22,865.8.8 for gold chains, medals, plate and jewels supplied to Charles "by the Grace of God, King of England, Scotland, ffraunce and Ireland, Defender of the ffaith etc". The £22,000 odd went for "white Plate for our Stores" most of it "curiously wrought and enchased" while the £9,000 covered "Angel and Crowne" gold given away in "Chains and Medalls" to Ambassadors and others, with "a George and Garter to the Prince of Orange". Not quite in the same class of orders and medals was the great silver bedstead which the King bought for Nell Gwynn in 1674. It weighed more than 3,000 ounces and was lavishly ornamented with two large figures, slaves, cupids, the King's own head, and four crowns— presumably those of "England, Scotland, ffraunce and Ireland". It was wildly expensive and does not survive.

If silver was too expensive there was a trick whereby tin could be made to resemble silver by mixing it with lead and Greek pitch; a lengthy process which at one stage required the use of mercury or quicksilver. Or iron could be made to look like gold by beating together burned Roch alum, Sal Ammoniac, and Nitre, boiling in strong vinegar in a brass pan until the liquid was reduced to a third; then, strain and apply to iron . . . and Lo! all that glistened was certainly not gold. Old-fashioned alchemists of the Hermetic variety, as opposed to new-fashioned "Sceptical Chymists", were still hoping to find the Philosopher's stone or elixir which transmuted base metals into higher ones (which is why base metals are so called). Even as late as 1701-2, the Rev. Abraham de la Pryme sent to Dr. Sloane "a bottle of Nostock or that hitherto unknown substance that is called Star Slough or Star Gelly".[4] This was supposed to be a sort of stellar scurf, very useful in chemistry as it "radically dissolved gold". Francis Bacon, Lord Verulam (says the Reverend gentleman) used this stuff and other things to make a "strang stone" which he presented to Prince Henry. This "Compound of Meteors" or "star shot jelly" was of use in diagnosing affections of the heart— amatory not medical. Can Bacon, the propounder of a new method of experimental science, really have believed this? As for his own heart, John Aubrey says it was given to young men like Thomas Bushell. True perhaps. And perhaps that's why when Bacon married, he turned up at his wedding clad from head to toe in purple, the old colour of mourning, and everyone thought it most curious. But it was no more curious than James I after the funeral of Anna of Denmark. He turned up gaily and newly dressed in Watchet (sky blue) satin with a feather in his cap.

But to return to more practical everyday matters. Just as the introduction of coal for domestic use changed the size and shape of fireplaces and necessitated new hearth furniture, so the introduction of three new beverages, chocolate, coffee and tea—of which more later—necessitated new equipment. As these drinks were very expensive only the rich or well-to-do could afford them and much of the new equipment was of silver.

Chocolate and coffee-pots, even as late as the eighth decade of the century, look very much alike and must often have been used without discrimination for both drinks. The only distinguishing mark of the chocolate-pot was in the lid finial which could be swivelled round or slipped forward or entirely removed to expose the opening for the "moliquet" with which chocolate was stirred. As chocolate came in hunks, it had to be grated, so a grater was often part of the equipment as were chocolate cups, some set in silver frames, Spanish fashion. Coffee "berries" had to be pounded in a pestle and mortar—a tedious business eased by the introduction of the coffee mill at the end of the seventeenth century. Londoners could buy mills from Nicholas Brook at the Sign of the Frying Pan in St. Tulie's Street (Tooley St., Southwark?). They cost from 40/- to 45/- apiece.

In December 1685 we know that Sir John Bankes who was, perhaps, that same Sir John whom Evelyn describes as "a merchant of small beginning but had amassed £100,000"[5] paid five shillings for a "chokalet pot".*[6] The equivalent today would

*Although I have referred to these particular account books throughout as belonging to Sir John Bankes (or Banks) this is an attribution by association rather than one based on direct evidence.

be perhaps £5 or £6. It is just possible that this was a second-hand silver pot, though it is more likely to have been pewter. But chocolate itself was then selling for 30/- a pound or more—six times the price Sir John paid for the chocolate-pot. The intervening centuries have at least made chocolate cheaper than silver. And indeed, as the seventeenth century pivoted into the eighteenth, chocolate began to fall in price, so that by 1712 it cost only 3/6 to 4/- a pound, unground. How one wishes that one had owned the silver chocolate-pot made by Peter Pemberton (hallmarked Chester) in 1703 which was sold in 1958 for £1,200.

Coffee-pots and tea-pots in the early days also looked very much alike before they parted company. They were plain, conical, with hinged dunce-cap lids, finials, straight spouts and loop handles like the chocolate-pot. Sometimes the spout was set low, sometimes high; sometimes the handle was set at right angles to the spout, sometimes directly opposite; sometimes the dunce-cap had straight sides, sometimes the sides curved slightly and gently inward, turning the dunce into a pierrot. The earliest example of a silver tea-pot known in England was made *c.* 1670-71 and is a $3\frac{1}{4}$ inch taller, more severe, and rather clumsy elder sister to a $10\frac{1}{4}$ inch slightly more rakish-looking brother coffee-pot made ten years later. Both these are in the Victoria and Albert Museum. Both once belonged to the East India company.

Some time later home-made tea-pots began to take on the more distinctive form by which we know them. Brown or red Yi-hsing stoneware tea- or wine-pots were shipped in with every chest of tea and we began imitating these in silver a good decade or more before a Dutch potter commenced making them of native clay in Staffordshire. Here it may be interesting to note that until the fourteenth century the Chinese made tea either by boiling tea dust in a kettle or by whipping tea leaves in boiling water in an open dish. The modern idea of instant tea is not so very different in principle from pre-fourteenth century Chinese tea dust.

Then in the early 1680's, the melon-shaped silver tea-pot made its appearance. A fine early one in the Ashmolean Museum has a curved spout and a spout cap chained to cover finial, but it is

Long case clocks, 1680-1714.

only $5\frac{1}{2}$ inches high, less than half the height of the earliest known tea-pot. By Queen Anne's day tea-pots had found the shape they were to keep for years—smooth or polygonal pear shape, or just plain globular. Spouts were sometimes plain but often resembled the neck and head of a strange bird or of a Loch Ness monster. Handles were of wood. The pear-shaped pots had high domed lids. Globular pots, slightly flattened on top, had flat lids sometimes flush with the pot, sometimes very slightly moulded. By our standards tea-pots were midgets $5\frac{1}{2}$ to 6 inches high and no bigger around at base, widest part of pear, or middle of globe. This meant constant refilling, hence a tea kettle on a stand with a lamp below became a necessity and in those days few hesitated to boil the pot itself. There are still some enchanting octagonal, pear-shaped pots to be had—at great price—which stand on a silver tripod with a small spirit lamp below. These measure no more than $8\frac{1}{2}$ inches, stand and all.

143

The Pageant of Stuart England

Coffee-pots and chocolate-pots, on the contrary, remained similar and did not so much alter as refine and improve upon their original shapes. The tapering or conical-shaped body took to angles too. Base and mouth were often moulded and handles were frequently set at right angles to a now curving spout with a hinged rather than a chained spout cover. These pots ranged in height from eight to twelve inches and could hold a pint or more.

Then there were silver tea caddies or "canisters" as they were called—and are still so called in many parts of Canada and the U.S.A. today. These were at first minute and often cube-shaped. By Anne's time they were taller and slimmer—sometimes five inches high—square, triangular, hexagonal or octagonal and came in sets of two or three designed to hold two kinds of tea and sugar. These twins or triplets were fitted into charming boxes of wood, leather, mother-of-pearl, shagreen or tortoise-shell with silver mounts and, with tea so costly, a very necessary lock. Although Henry Savile, a hearty type, thought tea drinking both effeminate and foreign "a base unworthy Indian practice"[7] he calls it, few can have agreed with him. In fashionable and near fashionable circles from the 1680's on, there is much talk of tea, tea-tables and tea things . . . and much business with them on the Restoration stage which reflected the narrow fashionable world. Women delight in taking tea and ruining reputations as they sip tea from "dishes". Men pretend, rather, to despise this, and are to be found in chocolate houses gambling, drinking chocolate, coffee, or brandy, and plotting to ruin women or to marry them to get control of their fortunes. But chocolate seems the non-alcoholic drink common to both sexes. "Two dishes of chocolate and a glass of cinnamon water"[8] are requested for the not so gentle women who seek out that professed "whoremaster", Petulant, at the coffee house. The Roxalana who ordered cinnamon water must have been suffering from indigestion as well as indignation.

Tea drinking also meant specially made smaller than usual spoons, and so teaspoons were first evolved in this century (although they are not found in sets before 1700) and were, at first, as great a curiosity as forks had so recently been. Forks had

Of Things—Curious and Commonplace

ceased to be the prerogative of the royal or the wildly rich towards the end of Elizabeth's reign, but no one really took to them much, and they did not begin to come into general use until the middle of the seventeenth century. In 1633 among Sir John Elliot's effects only one fork is mentioned—a "toesteinge fork of silver" and, curiously, no knives are mentioned other than "mincing" knives. Even as late as 1669, Cosimo III, Grand Duke of Tuscany (a Medici who, due to domestic difficulties, was seeing the world) says, or rather his secretary says it for him, "On English Tables are no forks". He also complains of our lack of refinement in having no vessels on the table in which to wash our hands. One miserable basin and ewer served for the whole company. Diners merely dipped their table napkins into a jug of water and then proceeded to clean their teeth and wipe their hands with them. Yet his statement about forks is clearly an overstatement. As early as 1633 Lord William Howard of Naworth bought ten silver forks for £3. 15. 6 and it cost him 2/6 to have his arms engraved on them. Though ten silver forks were not many for his large family.

If there were silver forks made in England in James I's day— and the key word is silver—none has survived. The earliest English silver fork is hallmarked 1632-33, which is when Lord William bought his. The fork, a long known Italian refinement (which is why poor, dull Cosimo was so shocked by their absence), was very slow to supercede knife or spoon as an eating tool; and the knife, itself, had only succeeded the dagger in the sixteenth century. In the late sixteenth and early seventeenth centuries, sets of a dozen knives and a single fork are often listed in the inventories of rich households indicating that the fork must have been used for serving and the narrow-bladed, sharp-pointed knife for spearing and carrying whatever was served to the mouth. Pairs of knives with steel blades set in hafts of crystal, bone, ivory, ebony, horn, jet, silver, jasper and agate and decorated with jewels or arabesqued with gold and silver at the shoulders, were the extra-corporeal eating tools of the early Stuart, rich Englishman. They were sold in leather or embroidered sheathes and one took them along when invited out to dine. And it had long been common custom for a bridegroom to present his intended bride with a pair of wedding knives as a gift which she wore for ever after in an embroidered tassled sheath at her girdle. In August 1634, John Hayne of Exeter, a dealer in serges, woollen goods, and cottons presented Susan Henley with a pair of wedding knives and Susan must have been vastly relieved that John had, at last, so openly declared himself.

John, a whirlwind lover if ever there was one, had opened a cautious courtship a good two years earlier when he presented Susan with Mr. Hildersham's Lectures . . . they cost 7/-. The Rev. Mr. Hildersham was a most pious and learned Protestant divine who published many works, including 108 lectures upon "The Fourth of John". The second edition of these lectures, published in 1632, is perhaps the edition John gave Susan. But the wedding knives cost more, they came to 8/6 and, in fairness, it must be said that John at this time made other presents too, among them, two etuis and the haft of a knife (total value 10/-). He may have bought the etuis in Paris; four of them are listed in his accounts as having been bought there for £1.16.0 or 9/- apiece. Later in the year, John gave Susan two "Sermon books" and fortunately for her—as sermons were often long and gloomy —a pair of "posie" bracelets made of "590 pearles and 590 curralls" (corals). They cost £4.18.0. In January 1634-5 he bought a marriage licence in London for 13/4 (surely an odd sum) and finally, in April of that year, John and Susan were married in Winsham Church by Mr. Wiatt who was given 10/- for his services. By February of the next year they were buying a cradle for 11/-, and in May their daughter, Susanna, was born "for whom the Lord make me thankful" John notes in his diary, perhaps a little equivocally. This may be due to the fact that the midwife cost him £1.10.0 and the monthly nurse, or Keeper, as she is called, £1.2.0. Nanny it seems, got 6/8 per month. Presumably she got her lodging and the run of her teeth as well.

What happened to Susan's wedding knives we do not know, but it is quite likely that one was converted into a fork, fairly usual thing by the time of Charles I. Many owners of beautiful pairs had one knife converted rather than buy a new knife and fork set. It was easily done. The blade was shortened, slotted down the middle and the knife became a two-pronged fork. Converted sets can usually be distinguished from separately made forks because the handles of both fork and knife are the same size. Separate forks have slightly smaller handles. Three-pronged

Bracket clock of Kingwood and brass, *c.* 1680.

forks came in about 1680, but wedding knives continued to be a suitable gift until the end of the century.

And by the end of the century the gentry, at any rate, were able to supply enough silver cutlery to make it unnecessary for a dinner guest to bring his own knife and fork to a feast. But knife, fork and spoon sets (some collapsible) were still a must for travellers. English Inns, good though they were, still did not rise to the heights of providing flat silver or cutlery for their guests.

Eating with a fork must have been a more efficient way of eating than spearing one's meat—and perhaps one's tongue—with a knife; and x-shaped scissors, which in this century finally ousted old-fashioned shears or spring scissors for everyday use, must have been an even greater boon. One can eat with one's fingers but one cannot cut with them. Like central heating and bricks, pivoting scissors were known to the Romans, but the English evidently forgot all about them too—or perhaps regarded them generally as a nasty foreign refinement and with true British devotion stuck to bronze age shears until the end of the Middle Ages. Even from then on—and the Middle Ages were still pretty near—pivoting scissors were a rarity, possibly because they were difficult to make.* As late as 1624, when the Cutler's Company of Hallamshire was formed, there were fewer than a dozen cutlers making scissors and shears in England. Even in the more sophisticated capitals of Europe central pivot scissors seem not to have come into common use until the beginning of the seventeenth century, although in China and Japan they had been known much earlier. It is possible that with the opening up of the East traders saw the advantage of pivot over the spring† and since everything which came from the East was an utter marvel and found a ready market, cutlers may have had to start making pivotal scissors in earnest or risk losing a large part of their domestic trade. That the Italians, who took to forks long before the English, did not also take to pivotal scissors earlier is illustrated by the charming "La Madonna Cucitrice" (by Caroto [1480-1555] Accademia, Venice) where the Infant Jesus, helping his Mother with the sewing, holds in his right hand a very beautiful and very small pair of shears—the embroidery scissors of the time. Nevertheless, by 1660 Samuel Pepys is privately rebuking his sister Pall "for stealing of such things such as my wife's scissors and my maid's book". As he had, only a fortnight before, bought himself "shears to cut silver" it seems

*I am aware that pivoted scissors were found near a skeleton at Avebury, but it is thought the skeleton was a barber-surgeon. Pivoted scissors were not common, they were specialist scissors.

†Shears were in ancient manuscripts the symbol for a woman. They were the mark of the professional embroiderer and in England on mediaeval grave stones shears denoted *hic jacet* a wool dealer or a stapler.

obvious that Elizabeth Pepys' stolen scissors were indeed scissors and not shears.

In 1694 (the year in which the Bank of England was founded) a pair of "sisors" cost Sir John Bankes 10d.; in 1696 he paid a shilling for another pair of "Cizars". Perhaps the first pair were lost or perhaps they were of poor quality, for just about this time M. Misson is busily noting that England made the best knives but the worst scissors in the world. Bad or good, Stuart century scissors ended up immortalized as that "two-edged weapon" which the Baron used with such devastating effect upon Belinda's hair.[9]

Other things were improving too and there seems no end to the elegant trifles and useful innovations for the household which made their appearances or became very popular. Most important was the great improvement in clocks and watches, and certainly it was an improvement which would be noticed by vastly more people than those who moved in select tea drinking circles. The real leap forward did not take place until after the Restoration and was due to the discovery of the pendulum, the balance spring (among other things), and to the Revocation of the Edict of Nantes (1685) which brought a fresh wave of Huguenot refugees to our shores. Many of them came from Blois which, in addition to being the very core of French Protestantism, was one of the four great watch-making centres of the time. The other three centres were Paris, Geneva, and London.

It would not be fair, though, to dismiss the first half of the century as of small importance because, in 1631, the first real advance was made in England when the Clock Makers Company was formed with David Ramsay as its first Master. It badly needed forming. Most clockmakers belonged to the Blacksmith's Company—which sounds a little odd—but most English clocks of the large church tower or even chamber variety were then weight driven and made of iron. On the continent spring clocks were in great demand but blacksmiths who work in hot iron, not unnaturally, found it difficult to make the finer wheels and, particularly, the spring which these new clocks required.

Locksmiths, who deal in cold metal, were the craftsmen for this kind of job—in England Love was laughing himself silly at our Locksmiths who were very far behind continental ones. So while blacksmiths went on forging and hammering away at large iron clocks the rich English were importing clocks from the continent, and continental craftsmen quick to see an opportunity came to England and set up in business here—to the intense fury of English clockmakers. It was all a great muddle but was sorted out after many an acrimonious dispute and great difficulties when clockmakers and blacksmiths separated into two companies, just as Grocers and Apothecaries had done some few years earlier. After that, clockmaking forged ahead. Next came a series of discoveries. Galileo Galilei discovered the isochronous properties of the pendulum. Christiaan Huygens, a Dutch mathematician, astronomer and physicist, applied the discovery to a clock (Robert Hooke seems to have done so here at the same time) but it was John Fromanteel, a member of a clockmaking family of English-Dutch descent, who first learned the "secret" of making the pendulum clock at the Hague and returned with it to England. So, in 1659, we find Ashaseureus Fromanteel advertising that he had for sale the pendulum clock "Clocks that go exact and keep equaller time than any now made without this Regulator".

This particular kind of advertisement has the quality of a sudden revelation. The seventeenth century—and indeed all centuries before it—is here at its most remote and possibly its happiest. Punctuality was impossible. Time, that arbitrary division made by man, varied from household to household, from public clock to public clock, from village church to village church. Time was a more or less affair. No one ever arrived or departed, nothing ever happened "on the dot". There wasn't any dot.

The pendulum helped correct this blissful state of affairs but not wholly. In 1675 those who owned the new regulator clocks and watches were advised to set them "continually by one Sun-dial because 'tis seldom that two Sun-dials go true together so

Gilt-brass and silver watch, *c.* 1700. Gold alarm watch, *c.* 1683.

that if set it sometimes by one, and sometimes by another you will never know when your Watch or Clock goeth right".[10] Happily for our ancestors, even those who had watches fitted with a tiny sun-dial as they sometimes were, our dull climate must have done much to offset this well-meant advice.

In 1670 the anchor escapement, invented by an Englishman William Clement, improved timekeeping so that it became sufficiently accurate to be used in astronomical observations by John Flamsteed, the first astronomer royal (sadly overworked and underpaid as usual). Due to this invention his observations were far superior to those of his European contemporaries. But Mr. Flamsteed, working at Greenwich in the new Observatory designed by Christopher Wren, was more concerned with Time as "the moving finger of Eternity" than with the regulating of the countless clocks and watches now being made in ever increasing number for household use. To this great period belong names such as Thomas Tompion "father of English clockmaking", a genius at complicated movements, whose finish is as meticulous as his clocks are beautiful. His repeating work was much more elaborate—and much more accurate—than that of other makers. Repeating clocks are those with a mechanism added to the string train, whereby if a cord is pulled the clock strikes first the last quarter then the last hour. In an age without matches or illuminated dials this was very handy for knowing the time at night. Equally handy for night travellers going about their lawful or unlawful occasions, were the newly invented lunar clocks which showed the moon's age and its face with phases.

As astrology was very important in everyday life not a few clocks were made with dials which showed the relative aspects of the planets. These too must have been useful to those who allowed astrology to govern their lives, as so many did. Potted horoscopes were not a feature of news sheets of the day.

The pendulum clock—running for eight days—had heavier weights and was altogether too heavy to be hung on a wall with weights dangling and pendulum exposed. So a wooden case was made to enclose the clock, weights, pendulum and all; and at this point with this English idea the parent of the grandfather and grandmother clock was born—although not so called at birth. It was known as the "long-case" clock and had a glazed hood covering a larger (and by now two-handed) dial; the hood slid upward to allow for winding and regulating. It looked very handsome standing in a corner or against the wall in room or hall of a middling house. Styles in cases reflected the changing architectural and furniture styles of the day; marquetry, parquetry and inlay were much used. Some trunks were, however, plain and had a Lenticle—a small bit of glass—let into the front through which the regulator could be seen moving—an always fascinating thing to watch. Hoods were topped with cresting, moulding or a pediment—broken or plain; spandrels became an area for ornamentation—heads of cherubim in silver or gold, fruit, flowers, leaves, and seaweed were much favoured from about 1675. The base, balancing the hood, stood on a moulding, on bun or cheese feet, on square feet or more grandly on ornamental feet scrolled like the hood cresting.

Of Things—Curious and Commonplace

Small clocks also became more beautiful. The lantern clock was often made in silver instead of brass (earlier days it had been made of iron or iron and brass). The bracket clock was still popular, but its bracket was now designed to match the clock case and frequently had a small drawer for the winding key. The upright, spring-driven, table clock was becoming even more fashionable and, like long case clocks, followed the prevailing fashion in architecture and furniture design. Delicate minute classical columns support chaste pediments; finely wrought caryatids in silver and gold raise tops like miniature testers with corner ornaments above exquisitely engraved dials. Clocks with basket, double basket, bell and inverted bell tops increased during the '80's and '90's. But horizontal table clocks—they had come in from abroad in the late sixteenth century—were still in use.

Watches improved enormously too. During the first part of the period, watches had movements or parts of movements made by different specialists and were assembled, perhaps, by someone else. Cases were also made separately (often they were imported) and were wonderful specimens of the goldsmiths', jewellers', enamellers' and engravers' art. Some watches were even contained in hollow rock crystal cases so that the time could be told without opening the case; this ultimately led to the watch glass, first introduced in the time of Charles I (c. 1630). Nearly all such watches had the verge escapement, were single-handed, very inefficient time keepers, and were really not much more than a splendid article of personal adornment; a portable status symbol, in fact, with erratically moving parts.

But with the invention and adoption of the balance spring—and Thomas Tompion was the first to apply this to watch movements in England—watches became far more efficient time keepers and had a second hand. They were still extremely beautiful. Dials were often enamelled with pastoral scenes, figures, fruit or foliage, and could be made to strike the hour and its quarters. Alarm watches were also made, but these were larger. Some watches had a sun and moon on each side of the dial. The sun stayed from 6 a.m. to 6 p.m., and the moon appeared at 6 p.m. and disappeared at 6 a.m. Thus the owner, no matter how or why confused, could at least be sure of knowing whether it was night or day.

Towards the end of the century cases were supplied in pairs. The inner case, which held the movement attached by a spring, was of gold or silver or brass gilt and another case, highly ornamented and decorated to impress one's grander friends, went over this. This second case was often so expensively and beautifully decorated that a third case had to be provided to protect it. Jewels which reduce wear and friction were introduced about 1704 and yet even with all these improvements inside, and out, in Anne's day it could still be said:

> "'Tis with our judgements as our watches, none
> Go just alike, yet each believes his own."[11]

Another thing which made a prodigous difference to daily life, or rather to night life, was that candlesticks improved in look and function—at least for the middling and the rich—the poor still made do with rush dips. There are many more candlesticks about in this century and, after the Restoration, candlesticks began to be made not individually but in pairs or in sets of four or more. They usually had baluster or columnar stems and greatly reduced wax pans—some had no wax pans at all because tallow continued to improve in quality while English wax candles (the finest it was said came from Doncaster) were better than any in the world—naturally as English bees produced the basic wax. Chamber candlesticks developed a circular flat base, the sconces had cartouche-shaped silver wall plates, often heavily embossed to reflect the light.

Chandeliers or "branches" added further brightness to rooms already much lightened by white painted walls. At Broughton Castle, the Elizabethan panelled oak drawing-room, or solar, was painted white by Lord Saye and Sele in honour of King Charles' return (the paint was removed early in this century and the oak walls so protected are the most beautiful original light colour). At Lord Orford's house, Chippenham Park, where the best drawing-room had a hanging of gold and silver tissue, and a looking-glass above the chimney-piece, there were reflecting glass panels set into the wainscot and other looking-glasses in nearly every room. In the dining-room, looking-glass panels between the windows were each so large that "it shews one from top to toe" Celia Fiennes says, perhaps disapprovingly, as she was, in every way, a most un-self-regarding person. They were "much talked off" and were a novelty which must have made proud and covetous Lord Orford's dining-room much lighter by reflecting both sun and candle light. There was also a great deal of beautiful carving about doors, sconces, mirrors and chimneys. Carving was no longer of the tight clump or bunchy swag sort. Grinling Gibbons, by some happy or contrived accident, had been discovered by John Evelyn in 1671 and his incomparable work freed carving from its tight, hard form and turned it into a thing of pure, delicate, imaginative poetry, with a life and quality of its own quite apart from its decorative function. This dual quality is perhaps best seen in all its beauty and purpose in the great carved room at Petworth.

Silver candlesticks, *c.* 1670 and *c.* 1690. Taperstick and extinguisher, *c.* 1680.

Another curiosity of the period were cream jugs. These did not appear before Queen Anne's day, but thereafter cream in tea did not cause our ancestors to shudder. They quite calmly continued to ruin tea with cream until the nineteenth century, a custom which still prevails in Canada and the United States. Coconut and ostrich egg cups were no novelty but were still undeservedly popular as ornaments, but their silver mounts were different, some were quiet and plain others were richly ornamented. From mid-century, children and invalids must have found comfort and possibly even sustenance in the newly invented feeding or spout cup. Infants were either breast fed to a late age or the old cow-horn feeding bottle was used. As bits of bread, lumps of flour, and currants couldn't get through the horn, this unattractive relic of the past must have preserved many a baby's life, if only for a short time. Grand feeding horns were probably silver-mounted, like old-fashioned drinking horns.

The "standish" became more elegant, and much more common . . . a flatter less ornate tray now held ink pot, sand or pounce box, and taper stick. Silver hand bells summoned servants from anterooms where they waited, although in the relative privacy of the bedroom, ladies summoned their maids by knocking, or stamping, with high-heeled shoes or slippers.

From the Restoration on, many a Whig merchant must have drunk damnation to a Tory squire in punch from a silver Monteith with its notched or indented rim. The rim became detachable around 1690 and Monteiths with rim attached could then also be used as a communal rinsing bowl for wine glasses, the notches proving handy for holding the glass with its foot outside and its bowl in the water; without the rim they served a variety of other purposes. The cruet frame crept in during Anne's reign too (cruet probably means pot). It was of silver with rings to hold sets of casters sometimes combined with oil and vinegar bottles. By this time too it was no longer *de rigueur* to wipe one's knife and fork on the tablecloth, they should be cleaned on the newly invented Doyley provided for that purpose (which took its name from Mr. Doyley the linen draper who also made a cheap cloth

Of Things—Curious and Commonplace

known as Doyley). Etiquette also now frowned upon the custom of picking one's teeth with the tines of a fork—a gold toothpick testified not only to the elegance of one's manners but to one's wealth.

In addition to silver, pewter, and wooden utensils there was also pottery—and porcelain. During the sixteenth century mediaeval shapes had been considerably refined and when, in 1567, two potters from Antwerp who knew how to make Italian Maiolica, established themselves in England, a greater variety of colour and design became possible. Such smooth, white paste made a fine, clean background for painting in metallic colours and so the stage was set for the advances of the seventeenth century, and for the home production of pieces hitherto imported such as vases, salt cellars, jugs and even candlesticks. Delftware, long known and imported, also began to be made here and the earliest piece of English manufacture appeared probably about the turn of the century. The "blue dash chargers", so called from the edging of blue dashes, were probably used purely for decorative purposes and stood beside pewter and silver on court cupboard or sideboard. They may even have been hung on walls. Nevertheless, there was an increasing abundance of pottery made for more or less everyday use.

Flowers and fruit were popular designs in the early years of the century and around 1614 figures began to appear. It was probably in the 1620's that designs first began to imitate those of contemporary Chinese porcelain and so birds, insects, and rocks—in blue and purple—began to be seen on native-made posset pots, mugs and cans. By 1634, as might be expected, Biblical subjects were much favoured, the most popular being the representation of the Fall. The Fall, of course, had everything in one go—trees, fruits, animals, humans, frilly leaves, and a sinuous serpent as a sort of decorative ribbon or banner. Furthermore, although admittedly decorative, the Fall could hardly be denounced by even the most rigorous of Puritans (although no doubt it was) since it was such a melancholy subject and a useful reminder of that first fatal mis-step which doomed all mankind—

save the Elect—for all eternity. Yet the Fall continued to be very popular among the Elect and the non-elect (or Reprobates as they were often called) until well into the eighteenth century.

In Charles I's day slip ware began to increase greatly. Slip is pipe clay, white or coloured, mixed with water and applied to pottery as icing is to a cake. So it was a very useful method for making simple designs and for writing quotations or Biblical texts on pottery.

> "Break me not in your hast
> For I to none would give distast."

a mud-coloured glazed pot implores in words handsomely lettered in white, while another highly glazed jug dated 1633 with a conventionalized fleur-de-lys design orders "Obay the King".* People might possibly have been willing to do so, but this was the year in which William Laud became Archbishop of Canterbury and William Prynne wrote his book of bigoted nonsense "Histriomastix" and had his ears lopped off for so doing . . . an unduly savage penalty even for that intolerant age. Ironically enough, Charles's head seems first to have appeared on a platter in 1653—four years after it had so shamefully rolled on the scaffold outside Inigo Jones' new banqueting house. In Commonwealth times, pottery was liberally adorned with the gloomier biblical texts.

Coronation pottery, which now floods the modern market, seems first to have appeared in this century. Mugs, plates, and pots bearing the date 1661 and made to celebrate the Coronation of the second Charles are still extant. The loyal rich could indulge themselves in big pieces where the king's head, crowned and sprouting a lavish array of black curls, was displayed. The less rich could have the same on a smaller, bulbous mug. From then on, all coronations produced suitably decorated pieces of the potter's art. Another brand new kind of ware was made from 1671, when John Dwight patented his discovery of stoneware

*Both in the London Museum.

Later seventeenth-century wine glasses and Biberon.

(hitherto called Cologne ware and imported from the Rhine). Dwight set up his pottery at Fulham, where it still flourishes, and in 1693 we find him defending his patent in a law suit against John and David Elers and Richard Wedgewood. English stoneware dates from this period and Dwight made some charming small stoneware fruit purely for ornamental purposes—melons, gourds, pomegranates—the fruit so loved by wood-carvers and plaster workers of the day.

Of course, all during the period the East India Company was bringing pottery—and some porcelain—back to England. Craftsmen could, and did, imitate the pottery, but porcelain was still beyond them.* This made porcelain very fashionable and very expensive. It was not of the best; nor was it antique Chinese porcelain—for nothing was known of these marvels until the Victorian era. Queen Mary II is often credited with making the collection of pottery and porcelain fashionable. But this cannot be strictly true for in 1652, long before Mary was even born,

*No porcelain is known to have been made in England until 1740 although it was produced in France from *circa* 1673.

159

Lady Gerrard gave a great supper and Evelyn says, "all the vessels which were innumerable, were of porcelain, she is having the most ample and rich collection of that curiosity in England". And, too, one remembers Lady Fidget who remarks that Harry Horner "knows China very well, and has himself very good but will not let me see it lest I should beg some".[12] The remainder of the famous speech appears to but does not, in fact, refer to China. Whether pottery or porcelain is meant by the word China we don't know but it seems reasonable to assume that porcelain *is* meant because the play appeared first in 1675 and was a cynical caricature on the social life of the time.

Nonetheless, Queen Mary was a notable collector and had "a vast stock of fine China ware, the like whereof was not then to be seen in England"[13] and at Hampton Court in the newly reconstructed Water Gallery (where Elizabeth had once been detained by her sister Mary Tudor) corner fireplaces were topped by stepped shelves to hold favourite pieces, and Cabinets were especially built by Gerrard Johnson for her "Delft Ware Closet".

Great advances were made in glassware and had been made ever since the law of 1615 which prohibited glassmakers from using wood for their works and forced them to take to much hotter coal fires. In the early part of the century the finest glass still came in from Venice despite a high tax and attempts to restrict imports for the benefit of English producers who were making bottles, decanters, jugs, beer and wine glasses. During the Commonwealth, glass was regarded as an unnecessary extravagance, but after the Restoration it flourished again and a novelty of the time, coin glasses, made their appearance. These, as the name suggests, had a coin enclosed within the stem. George Villiers, second Duke of Buckingham, set up glass factories at Vauxhall and Greenwich. He had the monopoly for making looking-glass and also the sense—although he was normally far from sensible—to employ Venetians to run his factories. By 1680, thanks to experiments by George Ravenscroft, a new method of making glass with oxide of lead was well under way, it was not so thin as Venetian glass but it had a wonderful hard,

Of Things—Curious and Commonplace

clear brilliance and sparkle. And if a lively gentleman, upon occasion, played the "Satyr" to a lady's "Nymph" by offering her a bottle of "Renish wine with sugar", or played "the Wag" by drinking his wine out of her shoe in a public tavern, as Mrs. Friske said her gallants did,[14] private cellars—now full of "Champaign, Chablee, Bergundy and Remedy Wines", instead of the old-fashioned "Ale, Cyder and March-beer"[15]—demanded a greater, more useful, more delicate variety of wine glass than ever before. And, quite suddenly, and for the first time in history, wine glasses became a particular speciality of English glass-makers, and different shapes and sizes of glasses became usual for different kinds of wine. On the death of King William III in 1702, the new Stuart sovereign, Queen Anne, "condoled . . . with her she Favourite over sparkling champaign".[16] that notorious scandal monger Mrs. Manley tells us and in this instance Mrs. Manley was probably right. Anne was, indeed, overjoyed at William's death—they had never got on—and one wonders if the new Queen and her "she Favourite", Sarah Churchill, soon to be Duchess of Marlborough, drank to William's final departure out of six ounce champagne glasses with a lipped, pan-topped bowl and a moulded pedestal stem, or from the larger cup-topped goblet with a hollow bobbin stem. But brandy was really the Queen's favourite (she was called, rather rudely, "Brandy Nan") and was politely known as "cold tea" because, rumour had it, she took it out of a tea cup to disguise the fact that it was brandy. This I think is doubtful, there weren't any brandy glasses in those days, as far as I know, and women always had tea cups handy anyway. But we made things other than wine glasses; the silver cup and cover turned into the covered glass goblet, stoppered decanters were made and serving bottles of "crizzled" glass (to bring casked wine from cellar to table) began to replace the pottery bottle: there were bowls and jugs, wavy-rimmed tazze, goblets, posset pots, biberons (a biberon is a terribly ornate vessel with a curved spout from which the sick were said to be able to drink) and candlesticks, to say nothing of jelly glasses, loving cups and a host of more modest and useful vessels. Glass by Anne's time was no longer the prerogative of the rich, it was in middling houses and in taverns, and English glass had become so good that glass was now exported instead of imported.

Yet in such basic things as sanitation the country was still in the dark ages. Indeed, the dark ages must have been considerably cleaner than the sixteenth and seventeenth centuries. It is true that water supplies had been improved in London and other cities. Water was laid on to many a house, although it was still brought to many another by paid water-carriers and was fetched by the poor for themselves from conduits and fountains. But there were no drains and unless you happened to live in a house or castle which overhung a stream, river, or moat the privy was in some dismal little windowless room and was little better than a large bucket which had to be emptied somewhere, sometime by someone. That someone was you—unless you could afford to hire a scavenger, or laistow man, to do the job. The overflowing privy was a commonplace. Small wonder that dysentery and the bloody flux were commonplace too. Many houses had a cesspit arrangement in the cellar and, where houses adjoined in a row, it was not uncommon for a cesspit in one house to overflow into the next.

If rich enough, sensible enough, or near enough to a good water supply you could have a w.c.—invented in the previous century by Queen Elizabeth's god-son who later became tutor to the young Phoenix (the Prince of Wales) and had a remarkable dog, Bungay, to whom he was quite devoted. But these w.c.'s were few and far between. At the newly built Chatsworth the accommodation was unusually spacious for the times—the Duke had grand ideas—there were at least ten close-stools and from the records it seems that several were water closets. Cisterns in those days were made of wood or alabaster, pipes and stopples of copper, and woodwork of cedar or "wanscot". The pots were alabaster too. At Chatsworth they were of marble. Alabaster was common stuff in Derbyshire and almost as cheap as gritstone.

The really elegant close-stool was a padded box made with a

Of Things—Curious and Commonplace

lid and handles so that it could be carried about the house as necessary. Pepys had a "very fine close-stool" in his drawing-room—and a cesspit in his cellar. Less nice than Sam were members of Charles's court who with the King removed to Oxford in 1665 to escape the plague. These courtiers, according to Anthony à Wood, were "gay in their apparell" but "nasty and beastly" in their habits. When they finally left Oxford they also left "excrements in every corner, in chimneys, studies, cole-houses cellars". Horrid as it sounds, this was nothing to the behaviour at the glorious and splendid court of Le Roi Soleil.

As to the humble chamber pot, it was often not humble at all. Magnificent ones came in gold. Less valuable were those made in silver. Pewter ones were fairly common and are frequently mentioned in inventories of the day, for some reason among kitchen utensils, earthenware pots were common too and cost about 2/- at mid-century.

Marmeduke Rawdon of York who died in February 1688-9, left £400 to the city to enlarge the market place; £100 to provide a standing cup for the use of the Lord Mayors of York; £60 for a gold chain for the "Lady Maioresse" and £10 to provide a silver chamber pot for the Lord Mayor. The standing cup is superb, it is now worth some £10,000. The gold chain, twenty-seven feet in length when open, is worth £3,000 and the chamber pot, which is not on view with the Civic plate except by request, is of hammered silver with an elegant handle and thumb piece. It is inscribed "The Gift of Marmeduke Rawdon Merchant of London, Sonne of Laurence Rawdon late Alderman of this City. anno 1672". It is a most handsome piece and there must have been hundreds of them belonging to rich houses of the time. Few seem to have survived in their original form. The Victorians added an extra handle and used them for flowers.

Bathing facilities were sadly lacking too, although there were certainly some very grand tubs. Queen Mary's Bathing Cabinet contained a fine white marble bath "suitable either to hot or cold bathing as the season should invite".[17] How often the season invited is not recorded, but it is a safe guess that it wasn't very often. At Chatsworth the bath was of white marble finely veined with blue "as deep as ones middle on the outside and you went down steps into the bath big enough for two people".[18] At the upper end were "two Cocks to let in one hott the other cold water to attemper it as persons please". The windows of this wonderful "batheing roome" were all of "private" (ground) glass. Things had improved a bit since the days of Queen Elizabeth who took a bath once a month whether she needed it or not, and since those of her successor, James I, who had as great an aversion to bathing as he had to naked steel. Yet in the nine years in which he kept his Diary, Pepys mentions only one occasion upon which his wife took a bath, "My wife busy in going with her woman to a hot-house to bathe herself, after her long being within doors in the dirt, so that she now pretends to a resolution of being hereafter very clean" and adds cynically "How long it will hold I can guess". We too can guess since he never mentions it again.

This was a public bath of which there were a number in London and other cities, some little better than stews. London had Turkish baths, "Hummums", hot as ovens but providing such extra attractions as private rooms, wine, women, and possibly, even, song at a price. The Hummum was, strictly, a hot air bath but there were bagnios providing hot and cold water baths too. A sort of do-it-yourself portable steam bath was invented very early in the century, or before, by Sir Hugh Platt. Something which looks like a large barrel or cask was placed outside and to one side of an old, open fireplace. Over the fire hung a pot full of water and herbs, from this a tube ran through the side of the fireplace and into the cask, which was fitted with a false, perforated floor. In this the bather or steamer sat, head protruding, while steam was forced from the pot through the tube into the cask (why didn't it condense en route?) But it should be remembered that being steamed was thought to be a cure for venereal disease, so it may be that this bath was really designed as a home treatment to replace having to go for more public

Of Things—Curious and Commonplace

treatment at the hands of those who provided curing tubs. Mrs. Overdone, the bawd, had to take the "tub cure"[19] and Timon of Athens in one of his usual splenetic fits urges the mistress of Alcibiades to . . . "bring down rose-cheeked young to the tub-fast and the diet".[20] Few cures for the Pox or Clap can have been as harmless to the sufferer as this one.

Early century close stool and chamber pot.

Then there was the problem of keeping the house clean. We do not really know, and have no means of knowing, what the standards of the day were, but if the court's behaviour at Oxford and the behaviour of Parliamentary and Royalist troops is anything to go by it is a sure indication that the standard in general cannot have been very high. In London, as we know, and in other cities the streets were little better than an open drain. The passer-by had to be careful not only where he stepped but of what might rain down upon him from above. Throwing slops out of windows was forbidden, but few took much notice of this and a

The Pageant of Stuart England

cry of "Gardy Loo" (*Gardez l'eau*) from an upper window followed by a shower of something unspeakable was not an infrequent cause of brawls in the meaner, tenemented streets of London and other cities (from this we get our euphemistic "Loo"). Every stream too, was an open sewer. Yet in household and contemporary written accounts we find many references to cleaning materials and things useful to laundering. Up at Naworth Castle they were paying 16/- to 19/- for a firkin of new soap during the first half of the century; 1/6 for a pail and dust basket, 3d. to 4d. per pound for starch, and 8d. for unspecified amounts of coarse sand. Brooms varied in price from 6d. to 1/-, and in 1612 someone was paid a shilling for cleaning out the privies—which is as much or as little as the cost of a broom. But prices varied greatly in different parts of the country.

By the second half of the century brooms had dropped in price, at any rate in London, where they cost 3d. apiece. They cannot have been very good as they are a constantly recurring item in the account books kept by our opulent friend Sir John Bankes. Coarse sand and whiting in unspecified amounts at 2d. each lot are also constantly recurring items, and indicate what hard work scouring must have been—expensive too as a scouring brush cost a shilling. Mops were less dear at 11d., but rotten stone, again no amount is specified, cost 8d. On June 6th, 1676 Sir John paid the Scavenger 8/6, probably for performing the same duties for which Lord William Howard had paid a shilling fifty-four years earlier —inflation was inescapable. The half year's rent for his house in Lincoln's Inn Fields also fell due in June. It came to £100, a very large sum in those days. But Sir John could afford it. He had a country house, The Friary at Aylesford, "an old Abbey . . . mighty finely placed by the river" (Pepys) and Sir John told Pepys how Oliver, the Protector, had once threatened some Dutchmen who owed him (Sir John) and Alderman Mico £64,000 so that the Dutchmen paid up. Small wonder Sir John could live in style and could pay Mr. Pointz £135 for "Don-quicksot hangings"—and no nonsense about pronouncing foreign names as foreigners did.

Of Things—Curious and Commonplace

In 1685 he paid 4/- to have five chimneys swept; Mary the kitchen maid received her (presumably) half yearly wages of 5/-, wash balls were around 6d.—a price which seems not to have varied much throughout the century—but half a year's rent for New River Water came to £1.

Up in Yorkshire where Sir Walter Calverley built his new house, Esholt Hall, a stream was dammed for £3 and the first work in bringing water to the place was completed by 1703; "2 tuns and 32 stone of lead" were used for pipes which, with the labour of laying and the supply of necessary cocks, cost above £40. He paid 3d. a yard for casting pipes "great and small" and 8d. a joynt for every joynt at 30 yards". Firth the plumber was employed to "uphold" the pipes "within the ground" for seven years for a fee of 12d. per annum paid at the end of each year. A Mr. Smith of Mitcham was more fortunate than most people, natural water ran right through his house and he was able to use this "most chrystal stream", not for bathing as we might have expected, but as water power to turn his spit. Dirty though we may have been we can hardly have been dirtier than Lewis XIV who took a bath once a year.

Dry cleaning—it wasn't called that then—was a chore. The old-fashioned housewife still swore by bull's gall, white of egg, burnt alum, salt, orris powder and soap made into a ball and dried in the shade. Rub this over a dampened spot or stain, rinse, and if the spot hasn't disappeared, repeat. More modern house-wives removed, or tried to remove, pitch, tar, resin or grease spots from clothing and hats with a feather dipped in the finest oil of turpentine—it cannot have been very effective. But per-haps bad dry cleaning is just part of the Englishness of the English. The washing of clothing and of household linen seems not to have been frequent. This is not surprising in view of the tedious and boring methods used to cleanse and bleach cloths. That washing and bleaching was needed we cannot doubt. Von Uffenbach who found England quite filthy, was horrified at the way in which meals were served both at Oxford and in the Middle Temple. Here wooden trenchers were still used—this was in

The Pageant of Stuart England

1710—crockery pots were placed on the table to receive the bones, a sensible if inelegant idea, there were no napkins, and the tablecloth looked "as if a sow had farrowed on it". This he found so revolting that he had no stomach for the meal and betook himself to a Library, to feed his mind and dirty his cuffs.

What could be done with discoloured tablecloths, napkins, sheets and the like? Mrs. Anne Blencowe (daughter of John Wallis the mathematician) gives minute instructions on the method she was using in 1694. First, soak the cloth from Saturday to Monday in a thick green mixture of soft water and sheep's dung; only summer dung will do. From Monday to Wednesday, dip repeatedly into a pond or river. On Wednesday beat out and leave to soak in pond or river until Thursday afternoon; then allow to dry. (Either the weather was better than it now is or drying took place indoors). Next day, put it into a tub, spread a buck sheet over it, make a thin paste of Dog's Mercury, Mallow, Kecks or Wormwood, spread this over the buck sheet, then pour strong boiling hot lye over the lot, cover and allow to stand overnight. By Friday it is ready to be spread out on the grass and watered all morning. Friday night, repeat the buck sheet process; do this again on Saturday. Saturday night, drop the cloth into lye and allow to soak until Monday morning. It is then ready to be laid out once more and watered every day with pond water until white enough!

One cannot help feeling from the number of processes, the labour and the time involved, that perhaps something was amiss with Mrs. Blencowe's recipe. Perhaps that initial soaking in the thick green mixture was a mistake. And the idea of dog's mercury makes one a trifle uneasy too. Dog's mercury makes a fine, bright yellow vegetable dye. Again, what happened to grass with all that lye washed on to it? And what happened to hands which lifted the cloth out of the lye solution without benefit of rubber gloves? Possibly rods or sticks were used but, even so, it must have been a messy, dangerous and distasteful business.

This method, fortunately, could not be used in London and other cities, even if sheep grazed in "High Park" and similar green areas. Lacking ponds and rivers—or rather with ponds and rivers as filthy as they were—town linen, coarse or fine, was washed (when washed) with black soap. The stink of "Soap Boylers" no less than that of the soap itself, and the linen washed with it added a not inconsiderable quota of smell to the polluted London air. For lye, as a bleaching agent, was no longer plentiful in that coal burning city where "Iron Stoves . . . with . . . Bars placed and fasten'd like the Wiers of a Cage" had long since turned from a curiosity into a commonplace.

CHAPTER FIVE

Of Eating and Drinking

IF the Bishop of Ely,* the king's pet theologian, had followed his royal master's example he certainly wouldn't have been "surprised by a sodain surfet of porke that had almost carried him away"[1] at Christmastide, 1617, for the "British Solomon", as James called himself, couldn't abide pork in any form whatsoever.† This was a food fad which those who had the expensive honour and dubious pleasure of entertaining the King had to remember. It was also imperative to remember that if the king didn't mind too much what kind of wine he drank, he certainly did mind if there weren't plenty of it. James had a very strong head and was never totally incapacitated (his falling about was due to weak, spindly legs), yet it seems unlikely that he could have been always cold, stone sober after dinner. This isn't surprising, for dinner was at midday and often went on for several hours. Even so, by Danish standards, this must have looked as if we bolted our food. Anna of Denmark's father thought nothing of sitting seven hours over a meal. Nevertheless, bolters or not, the rich English were certainly not going to "live like Natures bastards" and "in a pet of temperance feed on pulse"[2] either then or throughout the whole of the era.

So the Stuart Century when it came to food began with a bang, or possibly burst would be a more appropriate word. Admittedly,

*Lancelot Andrewes, later Bishop of Winchester. He was first on the list of divines appointed to make the authorized version of the Bible.

† James I's favourite dish was sheeps head boiled in the wool, flesh removed and served with butter.

Of Eating and Drinking

rich Elizabethans had set a standard for enormous meals (foreigners other than Danes thought us gross feeders) but the even richer early Stuarts simply gorged. The Master cook—the best were men—was a very important part of any grand household and when a feast was required he was both creative artist and general in devising and ordering dishes.

> ". . . he designs, he draws.
> He paints, he carves, he builds he fortifies.
> Makes citadels of curious fowl and fish,
> Some he dry-ditches, some moats round with broths;
> Mounts marrow-bones; cuts fifty angled custards;
> Rears bulwark pies; and for his outer works,
> He raiseth ramparts of immortal crust;"[3]

This sounds a flight of poetic fancy but it isn't. Food in great variety and abundance appeared in all sorts of fanciful disguises, elaborately decorated, often with gold or silver fringe while ramparts of immortal crust on a large pie—it was called a coffin in those days—often concealed something to amuse the guests. When a large venison pasty was set before Queen Henrietta Maria at a feast given by the first Duke of Buckingham no one was astonished at its size but all were startled when the pie was opened and a dwarf leapt out onto the table. This was the famous dandiprat, Jeffrey Hudson, nineteen years old and eighteen inches tall* for by now four and twenty blackbirds was not only a mingy dish to set before a Queen, it was definitely *di moda passata*. Italian recipe books, a century earlier, had given minute instructions on how to make a pie full of live blackbirds which,

---

*Hudson, when fully grown, was three feet nine inches and perfectly formed, which must mean he was a pituitary or acondroplastic dwarf. He became a captain of horse in the Great Rebellion; went into exile with the Queen and when a certain Mr. Croft unwisely forgot that a pistol is a great leveller and insulted Hudson, Hudson shot him. He was imprisoned for this misdemeanour, but lived to be sixty-three and died in 1682.

when the pie was opened, flew about and caused a merry *tafferuglio*. Bird droppings in the wine, birds ensnaggled in ladies' hair, candles put out—all produced a gay hurly-burly, guaranteed to enliven any party. It is surprising that the Italians, who regarded us as positively barbarous in our habits, should have thought this one up. But then one remembers that perfectly ghastly "coffin" in Shakespeare's Titus Andronicus . . . and passes hastily to more pleasant food.

Great feasts of the rich or royal were one thing, "a frugal dinner for the entertainment of a worthy friend" was quite another and could be managed by any relatively competent English housewife —or so Gervase Markham says. Markham, the Mrs. Beeton of the first half of the century, died in 1637, and among other things wrote a useful book called *The English Housewife* which went on being published after his death.* It gives an illuminating idea of what Markham considered a "humble feast" of the kind which "any good man may keep in his family".

The substantial part of this feast numbers sixteen items; a shield of brawn with mustard, a boiled capon, boiled beef, a chine of beef, roasted; a neat's tongue, a roast pig; "cheewits", baked; roast goose, swan and turkey; a haunch of venison, a venison pasty; a kid "with a pudding in its belly", an "olive pye", a couple more capons and a custard or "dowsets" . . . in that order. To this frugal repast were added side dishes— "Sallets", "Fricases", "Quelquechoses" and "devised past", together with "as many more dishes as to make the full service".† The full service (or full treatment as it was often called) consisted of thirty-two dishes which we learn without great surprise "is as much as can conveniently stand on one table".

From this one might reasonably be led to think that the word

---

*I have used that contained in *A Way to Get Wealth*, published 1647.

†Two or more services or courses constituted a dinner. Each service consisted of an equal number of dishes including sweet dishes. Guests were often seated in "messes"—groups of four—who were served with the same dishes, although a mess could also mean a portion, or could refer to dishes mixed about.

Of Eating and Drinking

"frugal" had a different meaning in the seventeenth century than it now has. Not so, as Markham next divulges the dishes which are suitable for a princely feast—within reach of the same good man who otherwise lived so frugally. Beginning with grand, green and compound sallets, princely feasters whetted appetites with simple and compound fricassees. Simple ones contained fried eggs, collops of bacon, ling, beef or young pork. Compound ones—and these were considered "things of great Request and Estimation in France, Spain, Italy and the most Curious Nations" were made of Tansies,* fritters, and "Quelquechoses". After this came all boiled meats; simple and "stewed" broths; roast meats; "jiggets" of mutton; seven other sorts of hot baked meats and three of cold; five kinds of domestic and wild fowl, to say nothing of simple and compound "Carbonadoes" (meat grilled or broiled over hot coals). Then followed the lesser wild fowl—mallard, teal, snipe; and the lesser land fowl--chickens, "pidgeons", partridge; merely to prepare the way for the greater, such as bittern, shoveler, peacock (Markham doesn't think much of the peacock as food, but in another book recommends it as "useful in keeping the yard clear of toads and newts") and other birds. The princely feast was rounded off with "Marrow-bone pye", quince pie, Florentines and tarts.†

Wines were no problem. There were those from "Burdeaux", such as Gascoigne, Anguelle, "Rochell" and, curiously, Galloway. There were Rhenish wines of two sorts—Elstertune

---

*However "Curious" the nations nothing could have been more curious than Tansies. They were a kind of scrambled egg made with cream and the juices of wheat blades, violet and strawberry leaves, spinach and walnut tree buds, plus grated bread, cinnamon, nutmeg and salt, they were sprinkled with sugar before serving. Tansy had once been an ingredient of this dish. Markham says to use it if you like but walnut buds are better.

†Marrow-bone pie was made by alternating layers of artichokes, currants, dates, sliced potato (probably the sweet potato), candied eringo roots and marrow, spiced with sugar. A Florentine consisted of kidneys, herbs, currants, sugar, cinnamon, eggs, cream and "crums" baked in special pastry and served in a deep pewter dish.

was by far the best, but nothing much could be said for the Brabant, except that addition of honey and cloves made it drinkable. There was sack (sec) from various countries but the best came from "Seres" (hence sherry); smaller sacks were imported from Galicia and Portugal. Muscadine and Malmsey were favourites too. Malmsey was pleasant, well "hewed" and fine. Bastard Malmsey was fat and sweeter; "tawney bastard" was the sweetest of all. There were all sorts of things you could do with a good bastard. You could revive or make an indifferent sack palatable by mixing it half and half and adding three gallons of Spanish "Cute". Or when you'd drunk the first forty gallons fill up the cask with the lags (lees) of any old white wine or a mixture of white of egg, bay salt and conduit water, then add aniseed, coriander, long peppers and licorice in a bag. The result tasted just like Osey (or Osy) which had been a favourite in Elizabethan times. One wonders why.

But whether a frugal or princely, drunken or sober feast, the housewife must dress the meat herself, a custom which persisted for a very long time. Even as late as 1706, Lady Mary Pierrepont, better known to us as Wortley Montagu, took carving lessons three times a week from a carving master so that she could act as hostess for her widowed father. Once dishes were dressed they were handed to a "Sewer"* whose job, failing a gentleman usher or other waiters, was to make an artistic or decorative arrangement of the dishes as received from the Dresser. He or

---

*A Sewer in this case is neither a seamstress nor a drain. The word comes from *servire*, to serve. One of its compounds is *desservir* meaning, to remove—with particular reference to removing from a table that which has been served. Hence our own word "dessert", or that which follows after the main course has been removed. Here, Canadians and Americans are more correct in their usage of the word than the English are, since dessert in North America *does* follow the main course and is a pudding or some form of sweet course. In England we use it for what comes after pudding or savoury. But this earlier usage must have persisted in this country for some time, otherwise we wouldn't have dessert spoons. One can hardly eat fruit or nuts with them.

Set piece for banquets.

she was instructed to set "the sallets extravagantly about the table, mix the Fricases about them, then the boyld meats amongst the Fricases, roast meats amongst the boyld, baked meats among the roast and Carbonadoes amongst the bak'd so that before every Trencher may stand a Sallet, a Fricase, a boyled meat, a Bak'd meat and a Carbonado". This, Markham states, not without reason, will give "a most comely beauty to the table and a very great contentment to the guests".

It is therefore perhaps a trifle surprising to learn that after such "sumptuous gluttonies and gorgeous feasts"[4] contented guests were frequently expected to stagger into another room to partake of a banquet. A banquet could round off a splendid feast or it could be a quite separate entertainment given in late afternoon or in the evening, after supper. It was generally held in a special room or, weather permitting, in the garden in a banqueting house, for a banquet in those days consisted chiefly of sweet dishes—cakes, fruits and wine. It sounds simple and unsophisticated. It wasn't.

Rules for "the ordering or setting forth of a banquet" were almost as strict as those for a feast. Marchpane took first, middle and last place and the banquet was ushered in by a dish "made for shew only, such as beast, bird, fish or fowl according to invention".[5] This set piece could be real (and eaten by the family next day) or a made up, inedible decoration painted and gilded and put away, like a stage prop, for further use. Then came marchpane, plain or moulded into all sorts of entertaining shapes, followed by preserved fruits and a "Past"; wet or dry suckets, marmalade (quince) comfits, apples, pears (boiled, raw, or roasted) sliced oranges and lemons; wafer cakes and another dish of preserved fruit "and so consequently all the rest as before, no two dishes of one kind going or standing together" says the indefatigable Markham. This, it seems, "will not only appear delicate to the eye but invite the appetite with the much variety thereof". As this was only the first course—other similar courses followed—a banquet must also have invited superfluous flesh, bad teeth, a liver which could be potted like *foie gras* and a prodigiously high level of blood sugar. But Markham, medically-minded though he is—and he provided a useful compendium on diseases and home remedies for his English Housewife—does not here warn his reader of the consequence of over-indulgence. Gervase Markham and Dr. Thomas Muffet certainly did not see eye to eye in the matter of diet and health.

Dr. Muffet* was all for "temperancy", good plain cooking and no nonsense such as making "quelquechoses of unsavoury, nay of bad and unwholesome meat". Nor does he approve either of "surfeiting or self-pining". The latter, among other things was apt to make the teeth wormy while the former led to soggy fat, no less than physical and mental weakness. Gross eaters he reminds us, quoting from Hippocrates and Galen, stand upon the "Raysors Edge". If they suddenly cut down they "Hazard their

---

*Dr. Thomas Muffet, Moffett or Moufet, practised at Ipswich and London and died in 1604. His book *Healths Improvement* was very popular for years after his death. I have used the edition "as corrected and enlarged" by Christopher Bennet, London 1655.

health" and if they continue so grossly they are "suddenly strangled with apoplexies". Our ancestors were certainly not going to hazard health by dieting. Far, far better to be struck down or strangled in the middle of a gargantuan meal like Sir Henry Fanshawe who, at dinner during Hertford assizes, was "sodainly stricken with a dead palsie that tooke him away in 40 howres".[6]

It did not matter that Dr. Muffet, at great length, deduced the fall of Rome from those vices brought about by or attendant upon sheer gluttony, England just went on eating and eating. No doubt Rome's fate would have overtaken the country right then had everyone in England been able to eat even a tenth as well as Markham's frugal feast suggests. Obviously this isn't so. Four to five million people couldn't and didn't eat that well even on feast days and in boom years.

The economic fluctuations of the era cannot be dealt with here[*] but there were often periods of terrible dearth and bad harvests. There were at least three major depressions—the worst between 1620 and 1624—and although we have no reliable statistics either about population or economic classes it is significant that during the first half of the century people thought that the country was overpopulated. In other words, many were unemployed, many were poor and many emigrated.[†] In 1615, a slump year, Sheffield had 725 "begging pore". Not a very large number we may think, but it represented a third of the population. Comparable figures today would mean, roughly, 166,000 begging poor in Sheffield alone.

---

*The interested reader should consult *A History of Agriculture and Prices in England* by Thorold Rogers; and Professor W. K. Jordan's *Philanthropy in England 1480–1660*.

†Although it is usual to think all emigrants left for religious reasons, this is not so. Between 1630 and 1643 some 20,000 went to New England, about 40,000 to Virginia. They were not all fleeing from "Laudian persecutions" by any means. Many yeoman and sons of yeoman went out to "better themselves". Besides, there was certainly no religious freedom to be found in Massachusetts in those days.

Prices went on rising, but.wages didn't until about mid-century. Up until then farm workers were paid from 6d. to 9d. a day (more at harvest time), although this rate varied from district to district as indeed did prices. By 1650 farm wages had risen to 1/- and artisan's wages to 2/-, not very adequate to feed a wife and family on, although wife and older children worked too. So farm workers' families lived chiefly on broth made of beans or salt meat, rye or barley bread, fish, a bit of cheese, occasionally a bit of bacon, augmented by what could be snared or poached.* If lucky, the family had a few hens or a pig and if really fortunate a cow to add milk, butter, and cheese—but certainly not in any quantity as a cow yielded perhaps a gallon of milk a day between Whitsun and Michaelmas.

Not surprisingly, with low wages and high prices, many a yeoman farmer prospered greatly and this particular part of the century is often called the golden age for the yeoman farmer. Many indeed were far more prosperous than gentlemen and sent their sons off to the Inns of Court to learn how not to be diddled out of land by gentlemen and how to "cast accompts". Who taught Robert Loder to cast accompts I do not know, but he kept very detailed ones ("item—culling my haires 4d.")[7] and was advanced enough to calculate the profit he would have made had he sown one crop in preference to another (Relative Value). Loder, whose fifty–one years stretch from 1588/9 to 1640 had a prosperous farm of perhaps 150 acres on, or near, the site now occupied by the Atomic Research station at Harwell. He was certainly not a subsistance farmer and he had no wish to be "gentry" . . . there were too many calls and too many taxes laid upon the gentry. He wanted to make a good profit and not

*But only until 1671. In that year new Game Laws were passed which made it an offence for any freeholder of under £100 per annum—which meant virtually the majority of freeholders—to kill game even on his own land. This wicked and iniquitous law meant that many poorer households were deprived of food which they had every right to enjoy. Equally selfish game laws were passed by William and Mary, too.

Of Eating and Drinking

just live on his own produce with enough money to buy a few necessities. He seems to have achieved his ambition as his net profits work out at between £200 and £300 per year. He paid his workers from 6d. to 8d. per day in winter and a penny or two more in summer. At mowing or reaping they got 1/2 to 1/4 a day.

His accounts show what crops he sowed, the yield per acre and what he paid for some things he did not grow or produce, such as "sope", "sinoment", "pieplates" and "watt-meale" (oatmeal). "I think it were a good course to buy salt and sope and fruite (dried)—yf we could, at London", he notes in 1618 when soap for the year cost him 12/3. That was a wonderful year for barley with a yield of 32.6 bushels per acre (it was to reach 42.6 in 1620), almost twice as much as in the dreadfully wet summer of 1613, which brought the lowest yield of wheat and barley it had ever been his misfortune to record. Worse, it brought his brother John's wife. She came, and her maid came too, for a six weeks' visit and their food alone cost him £3.10.0 or 5/5 per week each. As his accounts show, each member of of his household—family and help—cost him around £10 per year to feed (roughly 3/10½ per head per week); this must have seemed a fearful sum to Robert, particularly as clothing for himself, his wife and child cost but £7.12.11 for the whole year. It is possible that John's wife was thought such a gross feeder that she was never invited to stay again, for no mention of her is made in the later accounts. My own feeling is that Robert was rather ungrateful. Internal evidence suggests that John's wife came to be with Mrs. Loder (née Mary Andrewes of Sutton Courtenay) who was on the verge of producing a daughter, Mary. Mary's christening feast must have been elaborate. It cost 35/-.

Then too Robert is always willing to thank the Lord with fulsome praise and suitable Bible texts (inserted into the accounts) in a good year, but he is undeniably off-hand in bad years. When it came to casting "accompts" of this sort, things were strictly on a quid pro quo basis. For Loder was nothing if not a businessman farmer and in his small and local way, he reflected what was happening on a larger, national scale.

Taking it all round, agriculture had become "business". The great trading ventures of the late sixteenth century increased and became even more prosperous for investors in the seventeenth, and this led to the establishment of new country estates. Those made rich by trade and commerce invested a great deal of their new-made money in land. They spent lavishly on building houses, making gardens and creating farms. The purchase of land doubled between 1600 and 1688, as Charles Davenant, an early economist, pointed out (1698), and the rents of farm land trebled. As larger areas came into the hands of those who knew how to make money, it was natural that they should be as progressively minded about agriculture as about any other business. They were not afraid of new ideas nor of risking capital to implement such ideas. Doubtless many a farmer born and bred was horrified at the new-fangled notions of these merchant and business types who took to the land. But the fact is, these new men did much toward the steady improvement of agriculture and agricultural methods. There was, however, a bad side to this too. The small country squire (and he was usually Tory)* simply couldn't face the competition. Subsisting only upon the proceeds of his own land with no alternative source of income, lacking sufficient capital, brain power or education, he was—particularly towards the end of the century and in Anne's day when land taxes to pay for the wars of Dutch William and Marlborough ruined him—extremely unhappy economically and was often forced to sell out to those who were ever on the look out for additional land to add to their increasingly large estates. He received a good price for his land, but when he'd sold it all he had was money—and he was often not very clever at knowing what was best to do with that money. Thus, great estates gobbled up small, a process which continued until the time of George III

*The word was not in use, of course, until around 1678 when Titus Oates, the Senator McCarthy of the period, used it to describe statesmen of the Right.

and which in no small way accounted for the hatred impoverished Tories felt for rich and successful Whigs.

Although during this time the practical techniques of farming seem to have changed little, judging by the quantity of books published on the subject, the interest in good husbandry increased enormously and there was a slow but steady increase in the kind and quality of crops. During the latter half of the era experiments with "great clover" and turnips were well under

Kitchen trivet and bellows.

way. This was of first importance as it led directly to the solution of the age-old problem of how to keep cattle healthy over winter and, ultimately, changed the whole agricultural pattern—no less than the eating habits—of the country.

But this change did not come about until Hanoverian times and as there are other changes in food habits which took place during the Stuart Century we'd best return to them.

As we know, the price of food went up—it has been estimated that prices rose by 120 per cent in the 100 years between 1540 and 1640—and there was certainly no corresponding increase in wages. This caused much hardship but in one respect it has its comic side. Poultry, hitherto rather looked down upon by the rich, perhaps because it was the only meat a farm labourer could produce and eat, became fashionable in certain quarters because it was expensive. Poultry, in fact, became a status symbol.* To be able to afford it shewed you'd gone up in the world.†

> "When my Master got his wealth, his family fed
> On roots, and liver and necks of beef on Sundays.
> But now I fear it will be spent on Pultry
> Butcher's meat will not go down"[8]

—says Holdfast, with derisive scorn. But if butcher's meat did not accord with the social pretensions of my Lady Frugal and her kind it was nevertheless a predominant item in the diet of the grand and the middling sort of people.

Up in the Border Counties, or Middle Shires as James I preferred to call them, having united the kingdoms of Scotland and England in his own unpleasant person, Lord William Howard,‡ known as Bauld Willie to his contempories, was also keeping itemized accounts which show us the rise in meat prices —even risen they make melancholy reading today. Mutton rose from 2/8 to 9/—a whole mutton that is—a side went up from

---

*A curious echo of poultry as a status symbol is found in our own century. During the American presidential campaign of 1928, Mr. Herbert Hoover used as one of his slogans "a chicken in every pot". Thirty-odd years ago, the chicken was a status symbol in America as the motor car, swimming pool, yacht, etc. are today. It was a symbol here too. Now with the rapid rise in "broiler factories" here and the consequent lowering of price it is rapidly ceasing to be so.

†"At night my wife and I had a good supper by ourselves of a pullet hasjed which pleased me much to see my condition come to allow ourselves a dish like that", Pepys notes on Sunday, November 3rd, 1661. His "condition" in that year was around £600.

‡Lord William, Robert Loder, and Philip Massinger all died in the same year, 1640.

Of Eating and Drinking

5/- to 5/4; a quarter 1/2 to 2/-. Lamb, a whole one, rose by 4d. to 3/8; a whole veal from 6/4 to 9/-; a kid from 10d. to 2/-. It was cheaper, if less satisfying, to eat sparrows. They at least had gone down in price from the days when old Bess of Hardwick had paid 9d. for thirteen . . . they were but 2d. a dozen now. Beef, in London during the period seems to have averaged out at around 3¾d. per pound . . . and beef together with bread and beer had long been a staple in the diet of the "middling sort". But now they ate less of it, not much less it is true, and they ate more cheese than formerly.

Their meat was obviously not so good in quality as ours . . . and in winter it must have been pretty tough, since only the healthiest cattle could be overwintered; old and weak stock was slaughtered for winter use and the meat was powered (salted). It cannot have been very appetizing as it was "tough, hard, heavy and ill of nourishment, requiring rather the stomach of another Hercules (who is said to have fed chiefly on bull flesh) than of an ordinary or common ploughman", Dr. Muffet tells us, with just perhaps a touch of snobbery because it indicates that only the most vigorous and low class appetites could stomach the stuff. This is patently untrue, for what could even the rich do in an era when refrigeration was unknown? And it was unknown in the first half of the era even if Francis Bacon, Lord Verulam, had caught his death while stuffing a chicken with snow to see if it would keep.

Still, by mid-century or thereabouts we had learned—perhaps from the French or the Italians—how to preserve ice and snow during the summer months. It was then that a few of the rich learned how to build ice houses. These, either sunk in pits or enclosed in earth, had hollow, straw-stuffed walls (short barley straw was best) and a double floor with a straw closed drain. Once filled with snow or ice the doorway was also strawed, the door closed, tightly fastened and the contents left untouched until needed. Ice houses became more common among the rich as the century grew older and, according to Celia Fiennes, Mr. and Mrs. Rooth cleverly concealed theirs in the garden mount.* As the years between 1600 and 1850 are sometimes called "the little Ice-Age" ice and snow were readily available most winters even in southern counties.

Yet for the most part during the period, there was really small choice between salted meat in winter and bad meat in summer, particularly in towns. Civic authorities did their best to prevent the sale of bad meat, but they could do little about it once it was cooked and sold in cook shops. Cook shops were by no means new, they flourished in London and other towns and had done so for centuries. A French visitor makes them sound excellent. "Generally" he says, "four spits, one over another, carry round each five or six pieces of Butchers Meat, Beef, Mutton, Veal, Pork and Lamb; you have what quantity you please cut off, fat, lean, much or little done; with this, a little Salt and Mustard upon the Side of a Plate, a bottle of beer and a Roll; and there is your whole feast".[9].

Provided one wasn't poisoned it must have been very good value because the price was fixed, as was the "ordinary" or "set meal" provided by taverns. The ordinary usually consisted of a hot meat dish, bread, cheese and ale. Near Temple Gate was a tavern where Pepys used often to have an ordinary. It cost 1od. . . . and was obviously a better meal than the dinner he had at Sir William Penn's (Aug. 1st, 1667) where they ate "a venison pasty that stunk like a devil". He seems to have come to no harm though, for after dinner he went to see *The Custom of the Country* at Drury Lane; had a talk with the actress Knipp (whom he loved, dearly); took her and Mrs. Pepys by coach to Pimlico where they sat and sang and talked and drank . . . all but Mrs. Pepys who was "out of humour as she always is when this woman is by".

*In Restoration year an ice house was built in St. James's Park where summer drinks were kept and sold from a nearby stall. It is difficult for us to visualize an age which depended on ice houses to keep food fresh but in the centuries which succeeded the Stuart era, ice in summer developed into big business. Ice boxes replaced ice houses and ice blocks were imported from Norway right down to modern times. In northern Ontario where there is no electricity or gas ice houses are still usual.

Of Eating and Drinking

Pepys enjoyed a feast as much as he enjoyed work, wine, women, song, the theatre, fine clothes, books, painting, music and court gossip, and kept the anniversary of "being cut for the stone"—an operation which took place on March 26th in the year of Cromwell's death—as a festival.* In the year 1665, however, the feast was not held until April 4th. An entry in the diary on the true date undoubtedly explains why. "This morning did come a new cook-maid at £4 per annum, the first time I ever did give so much." Obviously Sam, who liked to do things well and to make a good impression, would not trust a new cook-maid with preparing a feast for this important occasion.

As it turned out the new cook-maid proved a treasure—if temporary.† The guests sat in the newly wainscoted dining-room around a new table (which cost 50/-), Pepys, no doubt in a fine suit and wearing silk stockings and a lace band which he had taken to in the previous October and Mrs. Pepys, one imagines, in that moiré over which there'd been such tantrums and trouble in January (moiré had recently superseded taffeta as the fashionable fabric). Possibly Pepys handed *the* stone around; it was the size of a tennis ball and they all must have seen it often before as Pepys frequently carried it about with him and even had a leather case made for it. In any event, they were all very merry "at, before and after dinner, and the more for that my dinner was great and most neatly dressed by our only maid". There was a fricassee of rabbits and chickens, a leg of mutton, boiled; three carps in a dish, a side of lamb, a dish of roasted pigeons, four lobsters, three tarts, a lamprey pie—"a most rare pie"—a dish of anchovies, several kinds of wine "and all things mighty noble and to my great content". After dinner they took coaches and went to Hyde Park where they saw King

---

*March 26th, 1660 he writes "it is two years . . . since I was cut for the stone . . . and did resolve while I live to keep it a festival as I did last year". By 1669 he was remembering the date but not the year of this anniversary. The stone carried him off in 1702 at the age of seventy.

†She left on August 17th of that year. Her name was Hannah and she does not appear to have been very honest.

Charles in one coach and Lady Castlemaine in another who greeted each other "at every tour".

Grand as this feast was . . . and they must have eaten a lot as there were only eight or nine of them to do justice to what appears a large quantity of food . . . it was a mere nothing compared to the usual table kept by the really rich. Or rather tables. Thomas Osborne, Earl of Danby and later Duke of Leeds, able and vastly corrupt, kept three tables at Wallingford House; one for himself and family, one for his Stewards and upper servants, and one for the women. The "Expence of the Household" for the Michaelmas Quarter 1677 amounts to a total of £1,304.13.9. Half of this was spent on Poultry (£254.2.8), Butcher's meat (£231.16.11) and wine (£201.9.1). On June 25th, when among other things ninety-four chickens were provided for "my Lord's table"—and five for the women's—the total cost for the day was £30.19.0. More than was spent on wax candles for the whole quarter (£21.17.6) or tallow ones at £24.8.0.

In this quarter bread and "flower" cost £52.19.6. The grocer received £40.8.5, the fishmonger £95.19.3, while wood and "cole" came to £36.3.6. Turkeys, duckling, quail, pigeon, sturgeon, salmon, lobster, eels, mutton, veal, lamb, geese, pullets and chickens and sweet breads figure largely in the accounts.[10] So does codfish.

It was in this year that Danby arranged the marriage of Mary, the fifteen-year-old daughter of James, Duke of York, to her twenty-seven-year-old cousin William of Orange. Mary cried immoderately at the very idea, but the match was extremely popular in the country (and subsequently with Mary herself). Mary's father had made a most unpopular match when, in 1673, he married as his second wife, young Mary Beatrice of Modena. James was a Roman Catholic, so was Mary. But James, being a convert, was so zealous that even the Pope wrote and asked him to moderate his zeal. From time to time it was less politically provocative to have James out of the country and so, in 1679, we find the loyal corporation of Edinburgh welcoming him as High Commissioner of Scotland with a fabulous feast which sounds

Of Eating and Drinking

much more as if it belonged back in the reign of James I than to the eighth decade of the seventeenth century.

This "treitt to his hayness the Duke of Albanie"* took place on December 29th—among the guests was the Master of the Duke's Robes, young Colonel John Churchill. In addition to the usual vast amounts of beef, mutton, ducks, hens, rabbits and neats' tongues, there was a perfect pageant of dishes which rivalled in their splendour the table decorations which were crowns, castles, and the royal arms. There was a large "turkey

Iron andirons.

pye all over giled rubby (ruby)", it cost £12,† a "potailzie" pie—whatever that may be—hung with gold fringe; a lamb's pie "a la mode", a Florentine, gilded, a shrimp pie with "vermiliane colour", a venison pasty and three gilded, trotter pies. Most of the pastry was painted and decorated and the large "salmond" pie was also fringed with gold. It is probable that George Porteous the herald did some of the decorating as he was paid twenty pounds for gold, gilding and painting. There were

*The Duke of York's title in Scotland.

†The Scots pound was worth 1/8d. The Scots shilling, of which there were twenty in the pound, thus worked out at 1d. English money. "What a masque I shall furnish out for forty shillings—twenty pound Scotch" cries Bartholomew Coke, "Esquire of Harrow" in 1614. (Jonson: *Bartholomew Fair*.)

diet pies, "teirts" and huge "minched" pies and countless other substantial dishes. Among the lighter things were oranges, almonds, raisins, 60 pounds of comfits and 567 pounds of confections. Truly a princely feast but a riotous one too, the breakage was shocking. Thirty-nine glass trenchers, a dozen jelly glasses, sixteen "stalked" glass plates, eight crystal glasses were either broken or disappeared. Dr. Irving loaned his two silver salts for the great occasion and cannily charged the corporation £12 for their use. In view of what happened to my Lord Provost's knives this does not seem an unreasonable charge for taking a risk with one's best silver. My Lord Provost was bereaved of two knives "mounted and twisted with silver" and the £5.6.8 (Scots) which the corporation paid him for this loss seems, in terms of English money, rather niggardly ($7/6\frac{3}{4}$).

Pepys' feast, Danby's accounts, and the "treat" given the Duke of York are all very different, yet they have one notable thing in common—an absence of potatoes. Although the Virginia potato was introduced in the late sixteenth century it completely failed to become popular (Spanish, or sweet potatoes were known but were a delicacy for the rich). Food prejudices die hard and there seems to have been a prejudice against the potato, perhaps it was thought to be "windy meat", but just why this should have been held against the potato in a country so given over to cabbage is not easy to understand. The Irish* potato, it is true, was grown in the North of England in the first half of the era but to a very limited extent. No one was enthusiastic, excepting a few wise men who thought it might provide cheap food for the needy and the poor. In 1664 John Forster wrote a book about the potato and its uses. Its title is long, accurate and prophetic, *England's Happiness Increased— or a Sure Way and Easie Remedy against all Succeeding Dear Years; by a Plantation of the Roots called Potatoes*. In it he advocated potatoes as a good cheap substitute for bread, in addition he

*It is the white-flowered Virginia potato which grew better in Ireland than the purple-flowered variety and thus became known as the Irish potato.

Of Eating and Drinking

gave a number of potato recipes designed to appeal to the taste and purse of the good housewife (these methods were brilliantly used by Lord Woolton during the last war). In this same year, the Royal Society did what it could to encourage potato growing, its members grew them and urged others to do so. But neither Forster's recipes nor the active blessing of the Royal Society could popularize the potato and increase "England's Happiness".

England obstinately refused (particularly in the southern half of the country) to be converted to the merits of the potato. Bad harvests might make bread scarce and dear, Dutch wars and debased coinage might push up the price of other foods, but "Those who had a will to win" definitely did not "eat potatoes in their skin"*—or in any way at all. No doubt if Charles II had been seen eating potatoes, when dining publicly, it would have become fashionable food and the fashion would have spread —Charles and his court popularized a new French drink called champagne. As it was, the poorer townsfolk during the last half of the seventeenth century subsisted largely on bread, salted or pickled herring, some cheese and occasionally a sheep's head or pig's trotters—the cheapest meat available. Nor did their lot improve greatly until Queen Anne's reign when a series of excellent harvests brought plenty.

But if our ancestors did not take to potatoes as a substitute for bread,† which during the century grew whiter and whiter,

*Younger readers may not remember that this was one of the verses used by the Min. of Food to urge us to cut down bread consumption and the importation of wheat during the 1939-45 war.

†Townspeople demanded bread of a finer quality than that eaten by their country cousins (or even the rich of the sixteenth century). As the century progressed even the working classes of southern England gave up the rye and bran bread to which they were accustomed and took to "wheaten flower"—save in times of dearth. Most of London's bread was white bread, we should call it wholemeal and it must have been far better than our present day bleached, pallid, steamed loaf. Dutch prisoners of war complained bitterly about London's fine bread. They preferred the coarser loaves of the poor which were more like the bread they ate at home.

they took to rice in fairly large quantities particularly after mid-century (although rice does appear earlier in Loder's accounts). An early rice pudding calls for cream, eggs, cloves, mace, currants, dates, sugar, salt, pepper, beef suet all boiled and served a day old; and a meal of rice, once a week, instead of "Water Gruell' was approved for the children of Christ's Hospital. Yet even in bad times, if C. Davenant can be believed, we were not so badly off as other European countries. "As to the common people" he says in a late century essay, "there is no country in the world where the inferior rank of men were better clothed, and fed or more at their ease than in this Kingdom—nor consequently where they propagate faster". This was probably true and parson Harrison had said much the same thing a century earlier.

Certainly the English thought that food and everything else was much better at home than abroad. And they seem to have believed that Spanish food in particular was very poor and scarce. Lady Anne Fanshawe, in her diary, tells us that this just isn't so. "I find it a received opinion" she writes, "that Spain affords not food either good or plentiful. Strangers who don't know how to choose or who are not well supplied with money may think so", but she herself says "there are no better wines in the Christian world than their midland wines". Water "tastes like milk", corn is "white to a miracle", bread is the best in the world, bacon, "good beyond belief". Segovia veal is larger, whiter, fatter than English; small birds incredibly fat as they feed on corn and grapes. Partridges and sausages are the best she ever tasted. Dolphins are excellent meat (but we ate porc-poisson, alias porpoise, at great feasts). Cream was thicker and sweeter; eggs, larger; salads, fruit and roots (vegetables) far superior, and she most admired Spanish melons (rightly), pears, grapes, oranges, lemons, figs and pomegranates. Above all Lady Fanshawe liked their "manger blanc"—obviously not the wobbly tasteless "shape" it now is. But the great catch about Spanish food was, and she admits it, only the rich could afford it. "The want is money, only" she says. So, contrary to the

Of Eating and Drinking

popular English belief, Spanish food was excellent—provided you were rich—and it looks as if both Davenant and Harrison were right in thinking the poorer people in England fed better than they did in Spain. If so, the Spanish poor must have suffered untold hardship and misery.

The English, on the other hand, now ate three regular meals a day for they had taken to breakfast again—or rather the idle and fashionable had. Farmers, artisans and hard working, early rising people like the old Queen herself, had always eaten breakfast. Nevertheless in late Elizabethan and early Jacobean times it had become a fashionable affectation to rise late and forgo breakfast. It is probable that during the hard-working Commonwealth and Protectorate the meal became more common among all classes and was taken early, between 6 and 7 o'clock. Farmers, of course, breakfasted before sun up, and Sam Pepys often rose at 4 a.m. And if the rich and idle, who after the Restoration took to staying up until the smallest hours of the morning, did not breakfast early, the newly emerging professional classes did. So did merchant princes, unprincely merchants, business-men, traders, shopkeepers and civil servants. Cold meats, cheese, salted, picked or dried herring (no kippers as yet) were popular breakfast foods. So were oysters.

Oysters, in fact, were cheap and plentiful and were an im-portant article of diet for the less well-to-do. In 1701—and one sheds a bitter tear to record it—oysters cost 2/- a hundred—less than 3d. a dozen. Colchester oysters were the best, par-ticularly those called Calliblephera or "The fair lidded oister" (Muffet). Alexander the Great may have been astonished to see oysters in the Indian seas a foot long but such a sight wouldn't have caused old Dr. Muffet to bat a fair eyelid. Hadn't he seen, at his own brother's wedding too, an oyster so large that "it divided into eight good morsels"? Oysters, but we may, I think, assume not quite such large ones, were sold in London's streets by hucksters together with gilt gingerbread, which sounds a slightly unusual combination. These barrow boys also sold Venus cockles, although the best were not to be found in England. They could be had at Compostella "where lecherous men and women resort to eat them for the kindling of lust" (Muffet)—regrettably under the guise of making a pilgrimage to the shrine of St. James. Hamlet, perhaps, made this pilgrimage. At any rate, verses one and two of Ophelia's song seem to suggest that he did.

Caviare was probably more appreciated by generals—certainly there were more generals and more caviare. The Jews, Thomas Fuller tells us, would not eat caviare "made of sturgeon" because a sturgeon lacked scales. But they would eat caviare made from carp "a stately fish but not long naturalized in England". The Italians, it seems, made great profit by selling red caviare to the Jews. Snails were not a recommended food, but frogs were all right. The "hinder parts" (Muffet) were best. This is true. Frog's legs or thighs are still a great delicacy in France and also in certain parts of Eastern Canada. Various other foods were also sold in the streets; oranges, lemons and other fruits. They were disposed from "moveable shops that run on wheels, attended by ill-looking Fellows".[11] These ill-looking fellows had sold costard apples for years and were called costard mongers—corrupted later to coster mongers.

Towards the end of the seventeenth century puddings became more widely used—sweet puddings that is—largely due to a fall in the price of sugar which was in turn due to our increasing trade with the East and West Indies. M. Misson is positively lyrical about our puddings "BLESSED BE HE THAT INVENTED PUDDING" he says in capital letters "for it is a manna that hits the palates of all sorts of People". But he was not unaware of our gluttony, for he also says "The English eat a great deal at Dinner; they rest a while and to it again till they have quite stuffed their Paunch. Their supper is moderate. Gluttons at noon and Abstinent at Night". Even so, we never seemed to be able to get through an afternoon at the theatre (and we still aren't) without a snack. The English habit of eating in the theatres was as strong and as much of a nuisance then as now. Oranges (at 6d. apiece) were the popular fruit, perhaps because

Silver gilt teapot, 1680. Standing salt, 1614. Sugar box, 1683. Tankard, 1620.

they were thirst quenching or, more probably, because the pungent smell helped cover the appalling effluvium of the audience.

There was quite a to-do in the King's Playhouse one November afternoon in 1667 when right in the middle of a performance of *Henry the Fourth* a certain "gentleman of good habit . . . dropped down as dead".[12] He had choked on a segment of orange. Fortunately, Orange Moll had the presence of mind to push her finger down the throat of the victim and restore him to life again.

It is not surprising in view of the amount we ate, to find in old recipe books—and most women kept recipe books—recipes for "Surfeit Watter". It must have been badly needed on many an occasion and Mrs. Anne Blencowe,* who compiled a book

*Born in 1662 daughter of John Wallis, famous mathematician, cryptographer and inventor of the symbol "∞" for infinity. Her book of *Household and Physical Receipts* was drawn up in 1694. She married John Blencowe, M.P. for Brackley, Northants in 1675.

at the latter end of the century includes· one which contains aniseed water, poppy flowers, "lickorices" saffron, figs, raisins and a handful of marigold flowers. We are also indebted to Mrs. Blencowe for a recipe for "Veal Glew". To make this a whole leg of veal was boiled over a low fire for seven hours, at the end of this time what remained was a very solid, concentrated "Piece of Glew". This, if wrapped in flannel and paper, kept for years and when a good broth was wanted you just hacked a bit the size of a nutmeg from the parent piece and poured hot water over it. Mrs. Blencowe's "Veal Glew" is certainly the ancestress of our bouillon cube. Though in view of the number of chickens that went into a "Foule Brauth" the veal bouillon must have seemed most insipid.

Other liquids were less insipid and the Stuart century saw an enormous change in what we drank because a number of things happened which changed our drinking habits considerably. The Navigation Act of 1651 (and the one of 1672) provided that no ships carrying goods from countries other than their own could enter English ports.* As the Dutch were great transporters of goods from other countries the act was designed to ruin the Dutch Trade—which it did. Unfortunately, it also ruined the wine trade, as a good deal of Rhine wines, Moselle and French wines were transported in Dutch bottoms.

This, among other things, led to war with the Dutch. It also gave the French wine trade a blow from which it never recovered. Recovery might have been possible had a further Act of 1688 not imposed a tax of £4 a tun on French wines, but the end result of this was to make wine so costly that ordinary people gave up drinking it and took once more to beer and ale. The rich continued to drink wines, but they were no longer from France or Germany. They were the sweet Levant wines, Portuguese wines, and those Canary wines out of which Marmeduke Rawdon of York made his fortune. These acts which put wines out of the reach of the "middling sort of people" had another

*The Act also provided that all colonial produce should be exported in English ships.

effect. They stimulated the making of home brew, just as the passing of the Eighteenth Amendment did in the United States back in the second decade of our present era. Recipes, wisely anonymous, appeared, telling one how to make wine from things like vinegar, blackberry water, clary juice and "pippin cyder".

In 1703 French wines were dealt another terrible blow, when a duty of £77 a tun was imposed on them,* but only £7 a tun was levied on Portuguese wines. The Portuguese, who had hitherto supplied us with the vin du pays, such as Colaris and Bucellas, were hard put to meet the enormously increased demand for these wines and so they began to ship us Port, in quantity. We took to Port at once. It was much stronger and sweeter than sack, the old favourite, and soon entirely supplanted it. But all wines in those days were drunk from the wood, drawn into a bottle as it was wanted—or into a narrow-necked pottery jug—stopped with a wooden peg, or a cork bark stopper.

In country districts people still brewed their own beer as they had always done but in the towns this custom fell into desuetude. Innkeepers made their own beer and each had his own special recipe. M. Misson records with some astonishment that there were hundreds of sorts of beer made in England.† It varied from strong beer which quickly knocked a man out cold, to a light lager type or "small beer" which even children drank. But many regretted the passing of the old English Ale and thought beer a "Dutch Boorish Liquor" and "Alien to our Nation". It was "a sawcy intruder in this Land" and unknown until the time that "Hops and Heresies came among us". Or so says John Taylor, the self-styled "water poet" in one of his innumerable works which, as everyone enjoyed a good pun, he entitled *Ale, Ale-vated into the Ale-titude* (1651). Hops and Heresies had been imported in the time of Elizabeth and forty-five years after her death hops, together with a handful of "heretics", emigrated to Virginia. Today the largest "hop-ranches" in the world are on

*By the Treaty of Methuen.
†Today there are about 3,000 different beers.

the Pacific Coast of the United States which also, curiously enough, seems to have the climate necessary to promote the growth of various new religious and occult sects.

Taverns assuaged the heavy thirsts of the day with the usual wines and beers and with specialities such as Mum, and Buttered Ale, which didn't contain butter but was made by warming the ale, sweetening it with sugar and spicing with cinnamon. Lamb's Wool, a drink made with the pulp of roasted apples, white wine, spices, and sugar was a country favourite and much liked by small squires. Cock Ale was much esteemed too, goodness knows why, as it was made by parboiling an excessively old cock, grinding it up and putting the mash in a canvas bag together with two quarts of sack, three pounds of raisins, mace and cloves. The sack was suspended for a week or so in a vessel holding ten gallons of ale. The ale was then bottled and left to ripen.

Spirits, although known in Tudor days, had not been drunk in any large quantity save in Ireland, where the brew was called Usquebaugh. But in the seventeenth century references to spirits or aqua vitae increase considerably. It is not easy to determine exactly what aqua vitae was, as the name is applied variously to any strong drink distilled from fermented grain, fruit, wine lees or old cider. Queen Elizabeth had granted a monopoly for the preparing of "Aqua Composita, Aqua Vitae, Vinegar and Alegar" to a certain Richard Drake, but by the first quarter of the seventeenth century there were some 200 distillers of these spirits and other "strong Hott-waters" manufacturing and selling the stuff. By 1638 the Distillers Company was founded and did much to improve the quality and methods used in making "strong Hott-waters". Gin or Genever also came in towards the end of the century. Expeditions to the Low Countries, friendly or otherwise, had for years made many familiar with the drink and its popularity spread until by the time Dutch William came to rule us we were importing half a million gallons annually—which doesn't sound much until one realizes that the total population was possibly six million and that gin was probably drunk only in sea ports and not in rural areas. Another end of the century drink was Punch (the name comes from the Indo-European "pan" meaning five, and the drink classically had five ingredients). For some reason punch drinking became the symbol of Whiggery, so a true blue dyed in the Lambs Wool Tory wouldn't touch the damned stuff. Claret was also a Tory drink and Port the Whig tipple in which each side drank damnation to the other.

But these were slow changes and were developments of already known things. The greatest change in our drinking habits was due to three hitherto unknown drinks—all non-alcoholic—and all probably introduced within ten years of each other. These were Coffee, Tea, and Chocolate. Perhaps the first reference to tea occurs in a letter dated June 17th, 1615, written by an agent of the East India Company, Mr. Wickham, stationed at Firando (Japan) to another agent, a Mr. Eaton, who operated in Macão. In this letter Mr. Wickham asks Mr. Eaton for "a pot of the best sort of chaw". But it was certainly not until mid-century that we began to use tea in England. In the *Mercurius Politicus*, No. 435, Sept. 1658, the month and year in which Cromwell died, this advertisement appeared: "That excellent and by all Physitians approved China Drink called by the Chinese Tcha, by other Nations Tay, alias Tea, is sold at the Sultaness Head, a cophee-house in Sweetings Rents by the Royal Exchange, London." Later, in 1659 or 60, Thomas Garroway, or Garway, the first English tea dealer, in a broadsheet called *An exact Description of the growth, quality and vertues of the Leaf TEA*, writes, "in respect of its former scarceness and dearness* it hath been only used as a Regalia in high Treatments and Entertainments and Presents made thereof to Princes and Grandees till the year 1657". Mr. Garroway, the founder of the well-known coffee house, made his tea "according to the directions of the most knowing Merchants and Travellers in those Eastern Countries" and willingly instructed his customers in this art.

*It had previously sold for £6 or £10 per lb. Mr. Garroway offered his plus instructions for 16/- and 50/- per lb. The variation in tea prices depended on the kind of tea.

The Pageant of Stuart England

Pepys had his first taste of tea on Sept. 25th, 1660—and notes "I did send for a cup of tee (a China drink) of which I never had drank before". He does not, unfortunately, tell us what he thought of it. Possibly not much, as he was a great wine drinker, a "vice" he felt almost as remorseful about as he did about his penchant for women and the theatre. Happily for us Pepys, although he tried very hard, never quite overcame these "vices".

Tea was expensive. When first introduced it was a fabulous price. But by 1678 when the East India Company began importing it as a branch of its own trade the price had already fallen: 4,713 lbs. were imported in that year. By 1700 when 20,000 lbs. of tea was imported (roughly $\frac{1}{16}$ oz. per head of population) the average price was around 16/-. The favourite Bohea cost 30/- per lb. and green tea 20/- which was still a great price.

Some believed tea a bad thing. Others, like Mr. Lawrence who kept a Toy Shop (and all sorts of unlikely things were sold in toy shops) at the sign of the Griffin in Poultry, believed or pretended to believe that, since tea was a herb, it had wonderful medicinal properties. He even went so far as to advertise it as a patent medicine. "A Chimical Quintessence" he calls it, made of tea and cocoa nuts "wherein volatile salt, oil and spirit of them both are chymically extracted and united".[13] How Mr. Lawrence managed to extract and combine these seemingly irreconcilable elements is a mystery we shall never solve. But he was obviously one of the fathers of patent medicine advertising and must have made a packet purveying his Quintessence to a public no less gullible than we are today.

Coffee became popular even earlier than tea. Although Robert Burton says "The Turks have a drink‚called coffa (for they use no wine) so named for a berry as black as soot and bitter (like that black drink which was in use among the Lacedaemonians and perhaps the same)," we have no evidence that he had ever tasted coffee himself even though he notes that, for the Turks, "it helpeth‘ digestion and procureth alacrity"[14] although it appears, perhaps strangely to us, that some Turks took opium for the same purpose. Coffee, according to Burton, was "among

Chocolate pot, 1690. Coffee pot, 1680. Cream jug, 1700.

the Alteratives and Cordials corroborating, resolving the Relics, and mending the Temperament'' (Relics, always plural, was what was left of one after a wasting illness). Coffee was also useful to ''strengthen the heart and brain'' which—and how right he is—''mutually misaffect one another''.

Hearts and brains were first strengthened in 1652 at the coffee-house in St. Michael's Alley opened by a Turkey Merchant who, it seems, was tired of people turning up to taste the stuff free and so hired an attendant to sell it. Within a few years coffee-houses multiplied with the same rapidity as Espresso bars have in this decade. If we can believe that singular man Anthony à Wood, London was not the first place to have a coffee-house, Oxford claims this distinction. Wood tells us that a coffee-house was opened there in 1650 ''at the Angel in the parish of St. Peter's in the East''[15] by Jacob, a Jew, and that the beverage was bravely "drank . . . by some who delighted in Novelties".*

Some thirty-five years later M. Misson expressed himself as being very pleased with English coffee-houses and as it is never very easy for the English to please the French, particularly in the matter of food and drink, we may be suitably gratified by his comments. He recommends coffee-houses as good places for idling away an hour or so and says—and this is probably what he liked best—"you have all manner of news there; you have a good Fire which you may sit by as long as you please; you have a dish of Coffee; you meet your Friends for the Transaction of Business *and all for a penny if you don't care to spend more*" (my italics).

Chocolate was introduced earlier than either coffee or tea. It had been drunk in Spain from about 1600, but as we weren't on speaking terms with Spain at that time we didn't get around to Chocolate until we began to import it ourselves from the West Indies. In 1657 a Frenchman opened a chocolate shop—for the sale of solid chocolate—in Queen's Head Alley, Bishopsgate, but as it sold from 10/- to 15/- per pound it did not become a drink for all. Originally chocolate, a Mexican drink, had been made from the roasted and ground cacao bean with peppers and other spices added. It was bitter and pungent and drunk cold by the Mexicans. The Spanish improved on it by adding sugar. By 1700 England had her own improvement in the form of milk. Chocolate however didn't become a really popular drink here until the mid-nineteenth century, due to the high duty imposed upon it, so in the seventeenth century it was a drink only for the rich and the fashionable (Queen Anne loved both chocolate and brandy). It thus must have added considerably to the layers of fat in which the rich and fashionable in that century embedded themselves.

Food in those days was often "sophisticated" in a thoroughly brazen fashion and tea was particularly easy to tamper with. It

*Especially, he says, those self-esteeming "virtuosi or wits" of All Souls. But coffee had been drunk at Oxford thirteen years earlier by "one Nathaniel Conopois", a Greek (later, perhaps, Bishop of Smyrna) or so John Evelyn records on May 10th, 1637.

Of Eating and Drinking

was mixed with dust, fine sand, floor sweepings—and heaven knows what else—all of which added to the weight of the tea and contributed handsome profits to the vendor. The more sophisticated sophisticators brought adulteration to a fine art by adding dried leaves and herbs to tea. It was less easy to catch these fellows out and as tea was a new drink probably no one could tell the difference between the sophisticated and the pure anyway.

There were, of course, two other liquids, far from new, which could have been drunk but weren't in any quantity. One was water—and it is just as well in view of the polluted state of most water that it was considered to be "cold, heavy and slack of digestion"[16] and was eschewed on dietary grounds. The other was milk—and few had a good word to say for it. Indeed the dangers of milk being drunk in any quantity were perfectly appalling. Lady Penruddock, according to Dr. Muffet, died a horrible death of drinking too much goat's milk, so horrible and so fresh in everyone's mind that the doctor out of kindness, forbears to give us the gruesome details—which is perhaps just as well since details were apt to be very gruesome indeed.

Milk was suitable only for children and the aged. Young men were particularly warned to avoid it. It was full of vapours, caused sore eyes, headaches, agues and rheums; indulgence also invited convulsions and cramps. Being over moist it brought on palsy and "as the cheesy part of it is very great" (Muffet) it engendered the stone and other obstructions.

And even for children, where milk was concerned, there were grave reservations for character could be affected by the type of milk drunk.* A lamb suckled by a she goat produced coarse hair, while a kid suckled by a ewe produced beautiful soft wool. James I had a drunkard for a wet-nurse, which on that theory

---

*"Everything takes after the dam that gave it suck. Where had'st thou thy milk?" Rhetias asks Cuculus and Pelias. Pelias, a "singular coxcomb", had a "woman-surgeon" as a wet-nurse—meaning someone who dealt in or sold cosmetics and paint! (*The Lover's Melancholy*, Act I, Sc. 2: John Ford, 1628).

accounts for much—even his weak legs—or so his doctor thought. Thus, it was argued, and had been argued for centuries, that children imbibe the vices and virtues of their wet-nurses. So wet-nurses were chosen when possible for their moral qualities rather than for their milk. If, indeed, a baby were allowed a wet-nurse at all. James Francis Edward Stuart (1688-1766) son of James II and Mary of Modena, was being fed at eighteen days old on "water gruell" made from barley flour, water, sugar and currants. This made the infant Prince of Wales so ill that his half-sister, Anne, wrote to her sister Mary in Holland on July 9th, 1688, "I believe it will not be long before he is an Angel in Heaven". Had the doctors had their way Anne's hopes that the child would ascend to heaven rather than to the throne of England would have been fulfilled. As the baby grew sicker with dysentery, colic and convulsions they persisted in giving him every remedy they could think of (with **sweetmeats** to make them go down) including Canary wine and Dr. **Goddard's** drops. These famous drops were so strong that if one fell upon a piece of woollen cloth it burned a hole in it within half an hour. The doctors would not allow the baby milk. It would kill him within half an hour they said. Fortunately his mother and father over-rode these objections, sent for the wife of a brickmaker as a suitable wet-nurse and the baby did not, after all, join the angelic hosts—nor did he ascend the throne of England. He lived to become known as the Old Pretender. But that story belongs to a standard not a domestic history.

Failing suitable human milk for children, the aged, and the sick, asses' milk was believed best. In view of the well-known personality defects of the ass it is a little unnerving to find that this theory should have been so generally accepted. Perhaps it was felt, better a stupid and stubborn child than one given to loose morals. Although certainly one is tempted to believe on the evidence that many an adult in Restoration court circles had been suckled by some local crypto-Messalina.

And what of our modern standbys, vegetables and fruit? Here, as in previous centuries, there are conflicting accounts

Of Eating and Drinking

of the kind and quantities of vegetables consumed. Lettuce and sallets were eaten, but vegetables, as such, seem to have been rather despised by town dwellers at any rate. Even English maidservants who travelled on the continent with their mistresses were contemptuous of the potages and legumes of France. This was a piece of pure urban snobbery. Cottagers in England grew vegetables, therefore vegetables were fit only for cottagers. They were rather low class, as winkles and eels are today—despite the fact that eels were once the food of royalty and a king had even died of a surfeit of them. Yet we know that beetroot, endive, spinach, asparagus, cabbage, carrots, turnips, parsnips, beans, peas, and artichokes were eaten and that the century also saw a great increase in market gardening, particularly from 1650 on.

M. Misson was not favourably impressed by what we did to vegetables even then. The middling sort of people when they eat a bit of boiled beef, he says, "besiege it with five or six heaps of cabbage, carrots, turnips or some herbs or roots well salted and swimming in butter".* We were not, in fact, "delicately served", and our table manners still left much to be desired. Certainly the belief that vegetables like potatoes were "windy meat" was widespread in the first half of the century anyway, and may account for our avoiding them. We seem to have been greatly troubled with wind. Robert Burton lists thirty-one herbs, seventeen spices and twelve compounds useful for expelling "hypochondriacal or windy melancholy", to say nothing of various oils and fomentations for outward application. He recommends cupping glasses too which, when applied to the "hypochrondries without scarification . . . do wonderfully resolve wind".

*Isaac D'Israeli in his *Curiosities of Literature* credits Sir Anthony Ashley (died 1627) with introducing the cabbage into England. Possibly because on his monument he is depicted with a cabbage at his feet "like a bishop's marble hound". The only curiosity here is that Isaac D'Israeli should have believed this. Cabbage has been known in England since Roman times and is, very possibly, indigenous.

The Pageant of Stuart England

We were probably better off for fruit than for vegetables, with our native-grown apples, pears, plums, cherries, gooseberries, raspberries, apricocks, peaches, nectarines and so on. We also imported quantities of oranges, lemons, prunes, raisins of the sun, prunes, figs and, of course, all manner of spices, and olives. Then there were strawberries, to be eaten raw with wine or sugar or made into a tart—although fearful of windy food no one seems to have been put off by the fact that Melchior, Duke of Brunswick "burst asunder" of a surfeit of strawberries at Rostock. Bursting asunder is, admittedly, neither romantic nor heroic which is perhaps why this "fated chieftan" has no poet to record his amazing and untimely death.

A new fruit introduced during the century was the banana. Thomas Johnson, a member of the Apothecaries Society, exhibited in his shop window in Snow Hill the first bunch of bananas ever seen in London. They were sent by his great friend "Dr. Argent, president of the college of Physitions" and came all the way from the still "vex'd Bermoothes". Johnson hung the strange fruit in his window on April 10th, 1633 and records that they lasted until July when they were "soft and tender". He was also brave enough to cut slices off them, eat, and observe

Earthenware wine bottles.

Of Eating and Drinking

they were seedless and pleasant to the taste.* Later in the era, bananas became more common but were rarely eaten raw. They were made into dumplings and tarts. This sets us a problem in trying to decide which species of banana was used. The banana we eat today is of the subspecies "sapientum" and can be eaten raw, whereas the "musa paradisiaca" a native of India and South Asia requires cooking.

Another new fruit, the pineapple, became known but only as a curiosity. John Parkinson notes it in his *Theatrum Botanicum* (1640) as the "fruite of a kind of Thistle" and "the most pleasant and sweete fruite in all the West Indies". It tasted like "Wine, Rosewater and Sugar" but a "surfet" is "dangerous". Four pineapples were presented to Cromwell in 1657, and John Evelyn first tasted the fruit in 1668 when presented with a piece from the King's own plate at the splendid dinner the Government gave to Louis XIV's famous minister Colbert. Evelyn was very disappointed in the flavour even if it had a "grateful acidity". This may account for our disinclination to grow pineapples other than as botanic specimens, although we grew oranges.†

Acidity, grateful or ungrateful, was an entirely cultivated taste. Most people preferred things sweet; the sweeter the better— even if love, love's vows, youth, beauty are deceptive because, like sugar and sweets, they melt or crumble away. "Sweet marmelade of kisses newly gather'd" sings the Duchess of Newcastle sometime in the 1660's,

> "Sugar of beauty, which away melts soon,
> Marchpane of youth, and childish macaroon:
> Sugar-plum words, which fall sweet from the lips,

*Parkinson says the banana tastes like "Orris roote preserved with sugar".

†The famous painting of Charles II (by Henry Danckerts) receiving a pineapple from John Rose, his gardener, is not real evidence that Rose grew the pineapple. Evelyn who knew Rose well would surely have known if Rose grew pineapples and would have mentioned it. For he notes everything curious and indeed one feels sometimes that he almost invents curious happenings.

And wafer-promises, mould'ring like chips;
Biskits of love, which crumble all away,
Jelly of fear, which shake'd and quivering lay".*[17]

One can but hope that young Edmund Verney did not have this sweet verse in mind when he went up to Oxford in 1685 with eighteen seville oranges, six malaga lemons, one lb. of "Pick't Raisons", four "Nuttmegs", three lb. brown sugar, one lb. of white powdered sugar, one lb. of brown sugar candy and $\frac{1}{4}$ lb. of white sugar candy stuffed in his trunk. White sugar was not what we would call white, it was darkish and came in sugar loaves from which pieces were broken off to be used as such or powdered.

But perhaps it was just that the Verneys—or young Edmund at any rate—did not hold with the idea of those few who were already beginning to believe sugar a bad food which rotted the teeth. They may have felt merely

"That which preserves Apples and Plumbs
Will also preserve Liver and Lungs".[18]

as Frederick Slare, who seems to us to have had a faulty ear, puts it.† But sugar needed no defenders, an inordinate love of sweet things was as characteristic of the Stuart era as it is of our own. Small wonder that on the continent Englishmen were now noted for their sheer bulk. For indeed, and a glance at most portraits in the seventeenth-century room of the National Portrait Gallery will confirm this, we were embedded in layers of fat. It may be that we slacked off a bit and thinned down during the Commonwealth and Protectorate. Certainly the Lord Protector's wife,

*Our century has sung the same idea to the words "Oh I left my sugar standing in the rain, and so she melted away".

†He hadn't. He was using the almost obsolete very old assonance rhyme, i.e. accented vowels rhyme but consonants don't. Slare was a contemporary of John Mayow and Richard Lower (see Chapter Six) and was interested in the function of the lung.

Wine jug, 1700. Wine cup, 1623.
Wooden "moliquets" for stirring chocolate.

Elizabeth,* set an example of plainness in dress and manner of living and was despised for it. She ate marrow pudding for breakfast and fed her husband on sausages and hog's liver. And if she suspected any dietary discontent among members of her household she quelled it with the unanswerable quotation "The kingdom of God is not meat and drink, but righteousness and peace".

But if the eleven years between the two halves of the Stuart Century provided a period of moderation in eating and drinking it was comparable to the pause between feast and banquet. People just staggered from Great Hall to white wainscoted dining-room picking up certain things on the way, leaving others behind and rearranging still others.

We picked up an extra meal, breakfast—and slowly pushed the dinner hour from midday to mid-afternoon and supper from about six to eight or nine o'clock. We took to tea, coffee,

*Many pamphlets written in the mellifulous prose of the day were circulated about Mrs. Cromwell. She was charged with adultery and drunkenness and her careful management was regarded as parsimony.

chocolate, champagne, port, ratafia, punch and a perfectly appalling British brandy—leaving for the most part osey and sack behind. New drinks, taken apart from meals, naturally required a little something to go with them, so we had "tea lozenges", ratafia biscuits, macaroons and "prawlins". Iced drinks became possible and popular—and the rich even produced iced cream upon occasion.* The pudding achieved ambivalence —savoury, as in a kid's belly, or sweet as in the recipe for "The Best Orange Pudding Ever Tasted".[19] Country people and the unfashionable (nearly synonymous terms) might still gorge on things like "Hodg-Podg", "smoared" hare, and "Olepotrede"; might still serve fish with the first instead of the second course and continue to boil whatever they liked in really repulsive verjuice—but the post-restoration fashionables knew better. It was all "haute cuisine" for the haut monde, and Frenchified dishes in polite middling circles . . . with a touch of the exotic sometimes, such as "Pickle Lila", that new Indian pickle for which Lord Kilmory had such a good receipt. And if anyone dredged up a great vulgar giant of an oyster it wouldn't go into eight stomachs, it would go straight into "Mrs. Syddall's Oyster Pye"[20]—or, more probably, into a cabinet of curiosities.

Tastes in food and drink had been refined somewhat since those days when a final siege upon a citadel of curious fowl and fish, ramparts of immortal crust and bulwark pies was apt to lead to fatal seizures among attackers. But people ate as much if not more and "not the smallest Fruit or Excresence of the Earth, scarce a Berry or a Mushroom" escaped them.[21]

This "Medley of Intemperance" did not pass unobserved or unremarked at home. And as one famous observer, or rather, spectator, put it: "When I behold a Fashionable Table set out

---

*Ice cream, known in Italy from the thirteenth century—due it is said to Marco Polo's travels—reached Paris two centuries later (1533) when Catherine de Medici, a Florentine, married Henry of Valois. Her cooks produced a different ice cream for every day of the wedding celebrations. It is also said that our own Charles I gave his cook a pension of £20 p.a. to keep his recipe for iced cream a secret.

in all its Magnificence, I fancy that I see Gouts and Dropsies, Feavers and Lethargies, with other innumerable Distempers lying in Ambuscade among the dishes".[22] But the English were not, and never had been, put off food by such nonsensical notions. They knew, "There is more good victuals in England than in seven other kingdoms"[22]—and more good men and women too, if any one dared question it.

There was, also, good Queen Anne. When she died—alas, poor lady—so fat, so afflicted with dropsy, many noted with unfeigned astonishment that her coffin was absolutely square.

CHAPTER SIX

Of Medicine and Mumbo Jumbo

"I RUBBED the skin near my rump whereupon it began to be very sore." This is the sole entry Mr. Elias Ashmole made in his diary on August 6th, 1684.

One might think such a minor mishap hardly merited an exclusive note by a man as well known and as hardy as Mr. Ashmole. His *History of the Order and Institutions of the Garter* had brought him a European reputation; his great collection, accepted by the University of Oxford, had become the first Museum of Natural History in England, now the Ashmolean, while his hardiness had allowed him to survive smallpox, measles, swine pox, tumbling off the roof of a barn, and falling into the fire during childhood; plague throughout his life, and being kicked by a coach horse in the year Cromwell died. He was also quite accustomed to boils, chronic toothache, headaches, frequent cold and gout. So a small abrasion, albeit in a rather awkward spot, sounds a mere nothing.

But perhaps the stars were unpropitious on that hot, dry August day when the accident happened (Mr. Ashmole was an astrologer and a Rosicrucian too), for certainly worse was to follow. The brief entries speak for themselves:

"Aug. 8. I purged.
    9. I took leeches.
  10. I purged again.
  12. I applied a plaister to it.
  15. Mr. Agar applied a balsam.

Of Medicine and Mumbo Jumbo

18. Dr. Plot sent from Oxfordshire to visit me, came to me.*
19. I fell into a looseness, which continued two days.
24. Mr. Agar lanced the sore.
26. Being hard bound I was two hours before I could go to stool, and then with exceeding trouble.
31. I was again lanced, to prevent a fistula.

Sept. 10. By this time the sore near my fundament was healed."†

So two purges, one blood letting, one plaster, one application of ointment, two lancings and thirty days later, Mr. Ashmole was himself again. He was then sixty-nine years old and had another eight years of life left in which to continue to survive not only the diseases to which the flesh was an almost helpless heir, but the remedies and cures propounded and compounded for those diseases. A slight abrasion could lead to death; a cough too often turned to a fatal consumption.

It is all very well for us, at this safe distance, to look back and note that the seventeenth century saw the birth of modern medicine. But to the majority of our ancestors who fell ill, medicine as practiced upon them added a further dimension to whatever ailment they suffered. This is not surprising. Medicine was still based mainly upon the old humoral theory of disease‡ as enunciated by Hippocrates in the fifth century B.C., refined by Galen during the third century A.D.; complicated by a corrupt version of Aristotelian "science" (received via Islam), as expanded and beloved by mediaeval scholastic philosophers for whom theology was the prime, autocratic science which embraced

*Dr. Robert Plot, or Plott, antiquary and author of *The Natural History of Oxfordshire* etc., was first "custos" of the Ashmolean Museum, 1683. Dr. R. T. Gunter who has edited the diary suggests Dr. Plot visited Mr. Ashmole on this occasion to receive the Ashmolean Statutes.

†These are the only entries between August 6th and Sept. 10th. One cannot but be struck by the similarity between this and Argan's first soliloquy in *Le Malade Imaginaire*.

‡See *The Pageant of Elizabethan England*. Chapter VI.

all others. To all this was added belief in the influence of the stars (St. Isidore advised doctors to study astrology), magic, witch-craft and a *materia medica* largely compiled by Roman army doctors or taken from Pliny's *Natural History*. But time is a great improver, so many a once simple herbal medicine was no longer made of herbs, it contained added ingredients more appropriate to a sewer than a stomach. Only we hadn't sewers, although Pliny's Rome had.

Admittedly, the study of anatomy had advanced greatly; an advance begun in the fifteenth and sixteenth centuries and due, first, to the wonderful anatomical drawings of Leonardo da Vinci, then to the brilliance of great anatomists like Vesalius and Fabricius. But internal medicine was stuck fast in the silted-up mud of centuries. At the Universities there was no systematic clinical teaching. The medical student was not required to observe illness or disease by anything as practical or useful as contact with a patient. He just swotted up the old books, attended lectures and obtained his degree by "spoken disputation". Clinical teaching was not introduced until around 1638, first at Leyden,* and from then on this school gained a reputation which exceeded that of famous Padua.

Odd though it sounds to us, a new outlook on medicine and its practice was achieved through the reformation of Philosophy —and reformations are notoriously slow. In England this reform-ation was primarily due to Francis Bacon,† in France to René Descartes. Bacon held that observation and experiment, not the speculation and argument beloved of the "schoolmen", should be the basis of "natural philosophy" (we call it science).

*In 1575 William of Orange, seeking to reward Leyden for its defence against the Spaniards, asked the inhabitants which they'd prefer, a remission of taxes for ten years or the establishment of a University. To their eternal credit they chose the latter. The first medical student to matriculate at Leyden was an Englishman, John James. The central figure in Rembrandt's "The Lesson in Anatomy" is a Leyden anatomist, Nicholas Tulp (1593-1674), who first described beri-beri.

†This is often questioned now, but it was not questioned by the founder members of the Royal Society nor by Charles Darwin.

Of Medicine and Mumbo Jumbo

Scientific truth does not arise from authority, it arises from assembling all the existing instances of the object studied. Reject, said Bacon (although not in these words), the four causes of human error (Idols), accepted authority, received' opinion,

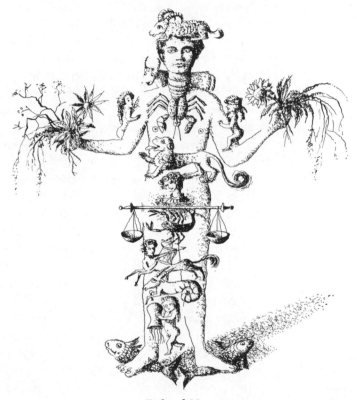

Zodiacal Man

legal bias and personal prejudice. Start afresh. Return to the Platonic way, the true Hippocratic way. Inductive not deductive logic is the tool. Knowledge without works is as barren as words without deeds. One swallow does not make a spring and to jump to general conclusions from one example is folly. Time, Bacon says, is like a river. It brings the refuse down to us but leaves the solid rock behind. Discard the refuse, find the rock and build, stick by stick, stone by stone, fact by fact. The benefit to humanity will be enormous.

Certainly the accumulated refuse of centuries was almost all that remained of medicine, and the Hippocratic rock was a good distance up river. Nevertheless Bacon's own physician, a considerably younger man whose name was William Harvey, thought his eminent patient wrote philosophy "like a Lord Chancellor", but the Lord Chancellor views on medicine would have done credit to the most eminent physicians of the day. He regarded medicine as being "the regulator of a musical instrument of much and exquisite work- manship, easily put out of tune".[1] He seems to have had small use for doctors. They relied, he says, on unco-ordinated individual experience; they were lazy empiricists; they ought to go in for comparative anatomy, dissection and even, if necessary, vivisection; they should build up a corpus of experiments and results which should be readily available to all physicians and they certainly should not go on treating all ailments with the same prescriptions—mostly purges or "restringents".* "Our Physicians", he remarks, "are like Bishops that have the keys of binding and loosing, but no more".

It is doubtful if either bishops or physicians cared much for this statement, more particularly since a bishop (and even an Archdeacon) could license any "quack". So the practice of medicine was by no means limited to those who had a medical degree from either of the two great Universities here or from the great schools of medicine at Padua, Montpellier or Leyden. Doctors were, of course, very much against a bishop's power to license "quacks" and were continually agitating to procure an Act of Parliament to "suppress empirics". Empirics were not suppressed. Nor are they today. Neither was medicine a closed corporation. It could be practised by anyone from the sovereign —and the Stuarts were the last to touch for the King's Evil—to

*"Would you not think that physician mad who having prescribed a purge should immediately order you to take restringents". Dryden. *An Essay of Dramatic Poesy.*

the local wise woman. And the local wise woman was often a better doctor than those who had a medical education. Knowing less, she knew fewer ways to kill.

Here the poor were often better off than the rich, they couldn't afford doctors or the help of those who purported to cure by amulets, charms, astrology as well as by the use of sympathetic magic—although as we know degreed doctors made use of such things, or believed in some of them. Sir Thomas Browne (1605-1682) believed firmly in witches, so did James I, and witches it was well known delighted, among other horrid practices, in making people pine away. Sir Theodore Turquet of Mayerne (1573-1655) a Huguenot refugee who settled in England in 1611 and became the most fashionable physician of his day (he was doctor to Anna of Denmark and other members of the royal family) still used theriac and earthworms in his prescriptions, yet he wrote an historically valuable account of the fever (typhoid) which carried off the young Phoenix, introduced calomel into practice, and was chiefly responsible for the publication of the first London *Pharmacopoeia*. Even the great William Harvey (1578-1657) who was so rude about Bacon's philosophy, believed in telegony, that is, if a woman married more than once, children of subsequent marriages could resemble the first husband. This was a very common belief then (breeders of horses and cattle have only recently discontinued to believe it), and very useful it must have been to a married women engaged in an extra-curricular affair since any tangible result would resemble mama or mama's legal spouse. Of equal validity in those days was a method of determining the sex of an unborn child. If mama's right eye moved more quickly and was clearer than the left, little unwanted was sure to be a boy. It was also believed that girls were begotten if papa were in drink at the time of begetting. It must have been very difficult to disprove this, particularly in court circles. By this token surely James I would have had no sons and Cromwell no daughters.

Such beliefs, if odd, are relatively harmless. When it came to a simple thing like a pin prick all that was necessary was to use the recommended panaceas and treatments of the day and one was as good as dead. Every literate household possessed its own collection of handwritten medical home remedies handed down from generation to generation, and probably one of the now frequent books of collections of recipes produced by a doctor or an enthusiastic layman containing advice on home medicine—and home surgery as well! It was pre-eminently a do-it-yourself age for most people when it came to ailments and cures. It had to be.

Thus we find, in the first part of the century, Sir John Oglander recommending fried horse dung for a bad bruise. Unfried and strained, it was equally soothing for a severe burn or scald. Rather better, one thinks, is the cream and salad oil recommended by Ursula, the pigwoman, in Jonson's *Bartholomew Fair* or the "white of egg, a little honey and hog's grease" favoured by "Jordan" Knockem.

A wound could be staunched by a pad of linen repeatedly dipped in frogs' spawn and dried between each dipping. Failing this, an oyster used as a pad was almost as good. If wounded by any weapon Sir Kenelm Digby, a great dabbler in science, urged the "Powder of Sympathy". This powder was applied to the weapon not the wound. Or if the weapon were unavailable—as it might well be in times of war—the powder worked equally well if applied to that part of the clothing or to the first dressing which touched the wound *after* clothing or dressing was removed. The miraculous substance was copper sulphate which destroys living tissue and granulation. Perhaps it was as well it never came in contact with a wound. Its virtue, if any, resided in the fact that wounds were left alone. The powder was a very ancient idea, but belief in it persisted for a long time.

If, unhappily, one were bitten by "a nadder", hazel nuts, rue, and garlic mashed with treacle and taken in beer would get rid of the venom. The same draught was recommended for the bite of a mad dog. It would also cure a not mad dog if bitten by an adder, but milk rather than beer was to be used as the vehicle.

Of Medicine and Mumbo Jumbo

Certainly the bite of adder or demented dog is not trivial, but it is possible that many dogs were thought mad when they weren't, and many a harmless snake was mistaken for an adder. Hence the remedy suggested may have gained its reputation through the faulty observation—and fear—of those bitten by harmless snakes and dogs. But a broken leg or arm, painful enough but rarely fatal nowadays, could be most malign in the seventeenth century, despite a sovereign remedy "Oil of Swallows" which lived up to its name. Containing twenty-one herbs, neat's-foot oil, cloves, wax, butter and twenty live swallows all beaten together, it was, presumably, rubbed on the break after it had been set—and setting a bone must often have been a rough and ready business. Indeed, if ill set it could kill you no matter how much of the oil you applied. The doctors who set Ned Mullins' ankle as late as 1663 did such a bad job that it festered. They then amputated his leg but "this was so ill done, notwithstanding all the great surgeons about the town at the doing of it"[2] that six days later Ned was dead.

When we think of the century in terms of disease—possibly not a very cheerful way of thinking—we immediately think of the Great Plague of 1665, or "the Poore's Plague" as it was called because it began in the squalid, overcrowded tenements by London's docks. Yet this was only the worst epidemic in a century in which plague was endemic. The accessions of James I and Charles I were both marked by terrible visitations; 1636 was also a dreadful year. In fact in the seventy-six years from 1603, when more than thirty thousand died, to 1679,* when only two plague deaths are recorded, there were but five plague-free years. The point about the 1665 Plague is, that terrible and terrifying as it was, it was the last epidemic. This century saw the end of the Plague in England, as the previous century had seen

*Plague free years, no deaths recorded, as given in Bills of Mortality were 1624, 1629, 1633, 1635 and 1670. The year 1679 is the last year in which any deaths from Plague are recorded in the Bills. By 1704 all mention of the disease is omitted.

the end of the Sweating Sickness . . . or "the English Sweat" as it was called.*

But as no one knew this was the last great Plague epidemic everyone went on fearing another, and the memory of that "inveterate mortal Contagion"[3] which had carried off perhaps half of London's population—and 259 out of the 300 inhabitants of the village of Eyam, Derbyshire—lived on unforgettably for years. For in 1665 great, busy London became a city of the dead, the dying, the courageous and the criminal. All who could, fled, and as the terrible weeks of the summer passed grass grew in Whitehall and there were not enough bells or hands to toll them to mark the "passing". Private funerals ceased. The dead were piled in carts at night and thrown into great pits. On the doors of sealed, plague-stricken houses a cross and the words "God have mercy upon us" was chalked. Plague, many believed, was a sure sign of God's wrath. Thousands must have perished needlessly in houses which the law turned into prisons and which often became tombs for whole families. By the thirty-ninth week of the plague there were 8,287 burials as against 176 christenings, roughly 47 deaths to one live birth. All trade stopped. Exports ceased, so did manufacturing, and there was great unemployment, not only in London but all over England. The authorities did what they could to relieve want, and to stay pestilence. Great fires of "Sea coal or any other combustible matter"† were lit in the streets to kill infection in the air. All letters passing through the post office were disinfected with the steam of boiling, aromatic vinegar. All infected homes were, by order, fumed with saltpetre and nearly everyone had his own fume as well. The Deanery of St. Paul, as a precaution, was smoked twice a week with pepper, sulphur, hops and frankincense, and a certain Dr. Angier made a fortune (as did

---

*The last epidemic was in 1551. The first in 1485 delayed the coronation of the first Tudor, Henry VII (just as the first plague epidemic delayed that of the first Stuart). Other epidemic years were 1508, 1517 and 1528. The final epidemic began in Shrewsbury (1551).

†Lord Mayor's Proclamation, Sept. 2nd, 1665.

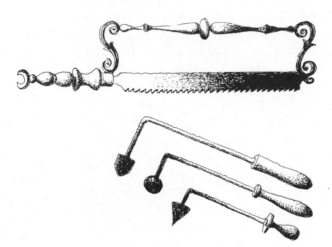

Amputating saw and cauterizing instruments.

many quacks and astrologers) with a fume which he claimed had stopped the plague in Paris, Lyons and Toulouse. "Angier's Fume" was famous, and London's Lord Mayor and Aldermen were ordered to see that the doctor's fume was widely distributed. As its ingredients were saltpetre, sulphur and ambergris, it was as useless as another favourite, "Dr. Atkinson's Fume", made of angelic roots steeped in white vinegar, heated and inhaled. Only cleanliness, flea powder and rat traps could have helped—but no one knew that.

What everyone did know was a "cure". Cures are uncountable—and unaccountable. Every doctor, wise woman, charlatan, quack, astrologer, and head of household had his own specific. Every household book, every herbal of the day is packed with cures for plague. For the most part they make horrifying reading. Even late in the century one finds cures which had remained virtually unchanged since the first great plague of the Stuart era and which, knowing what we know, cannot possibly have helped anyone.

Less revolting than many was the Countess of Arundel's "recepit" against the plague of 1603 which was still being recommended eighty years later and is mostly wine, treacle* and pepper which if the patient were badly infected he would vomit up. One had to persevere in forcing it down for if it could be kept down "there is no doubt of his recovery by the Grace of God".[4] This cure had survived three great plagues and no doubt some survived the cure.

One of the most distressing of the many repulsive preventives and cures called for four ounces of "mummie" (man's flesh dried) cut small and put into a glazed vessel with ten ounces of spirits of wine. The glass was set in horses' dung to "digest" for a month. Another required the brains of a young man who had died a violent death (not too difficult to procure in those days) together with arteries, nerves, and all the pith of the backbone digested for six months in spirits of wine. Two drops in water once a day and one needn't fear contagion. These were amateur or home remedies. The professional doctors did little better. The College of Physicians prescribed a large onion hollowed out and filled with fig, rue and Venice treacle.

That world-famous recipe invented *circa* 1606 which calls for, among its twenty-three ingredients, eye of newt, toe of frog, adder's fork, blind worm's sting, witches' mummy, the liver of a Jew and the whole mess to be cooled with baboon's blood, is not, although it might well have been, a plague cure or preventive. But does it perhaps, satirize the cures of the day?[5] Even worse were the harsh caustics applied to break buboes. Death must have been welcome. One cannot even begin to imagine how, or why, the medical treatment for Plague—or almost anything else for that matter—originated.

What really strikes one most forcefully about the century's

*Treacle was neither molasses nor golden syrup. It was, as the name implies (Gk. thérion = wild beast), originally an antidote for the bite of wild beasts which is why it is also known as theriac. Anciently the name was given to various antidotes but by the seventeenth century it contained sixty-four "drugs" among which was viper's fat, mixed with honey. The Bishop's Bible is commonly known as the Treacle Bible "is there no tryacle in Gilead, is there no physition there" it asks. (Jer. 8, v. 22.)

Of Medicine and Mumbo Jumbo

remedies is the enormous use made throughout the whole period of live animals, excrement, and various insects. When Queen Mary II died of smallpox in 1694—and smallpox like plague was endemic and epidemic—the common treatment for the disease seems to have been a black powder made from thirty or forty live toads burned to a crisp. A popular asthma cure—William III was asthmatic—was a glass of wine in which woodlice had been steeped. Sore eyes were benefited by having dried, powdered hen's dung blown into them. A "present" remedy for Haemorrhoids called for a spoonful of white dog's turd (was the dog white one wonders?), white frankincense, aloes, yolk of egg, oil of roses made into an ointment. A household remedy which claimed instant success in curing consumption and jaundice, published as late as 1714, calls for a peck of large snails roasted, broken up and beaten together with earthworms, slit and scoured in salt water. To this was added various herbs, strong ale and white wine. Another powder for consumption calls for twelve dozen of the smallest grigs, baked dry enough to powder, and taken three times a day with Canary or old Malaga. Just what a grig means in this context I am unable to state positively; it might have been a dwarf hen, a grasshopper or a small eel—but the quantity required suggests that it was the latter.

Again we find woodlice cropping up as an ingredient in "The Rickety Drink"; and snails in an ointment for the back of a "weak Rickety Child"[6]—both recommended during Queen Anne's reign—and all through the century one is painfully aware that Rickets was a common complaint from which innumerable children suffered. This appalling condition, which reached its peak in the mid-nineteenth century, was known and identified in the seventeenth. Strangely enough, it does not seem to have been known or at least wasn't defined as such in previous eras. Rickets was called "The English Disease" on the continent, either because we were most subject to it or because we first identified and named it. Daniel Whistler (1619-1684) got his medical degree from the University of Leyden in 1645 for his treatise on Rickets (*De Morbo puerili Anglorum quam patrio idumate indigenae vocant* "*The Rickets*"). Five years later Francis Glisson, who took his degree at Cambridge in 1634, wrote the classic work on the subject (*De Rachitide sive Morbo Puerili qui vulgo* "*The Rickets*" *dictur*). Eight other doctors were associated with the book but Glisson did most of the work.

It is one thing to describe a condition, it is another to find cause and cure (the first mention of a death from rickets appears to have been in 1634). Thomas Fuller in 1649 describes this "disease of Infants . . . Called Rickets"[7] and reports that a woman in the West Country healed many "by Cauterizing the Vein behind the Ear". This would have been even less useful and more painful than the Rickety Drink or the Cotton Thistledown advocated by Nicholas Culpepper (1616-1654) an astrologer physician who enraged orthodox doctors by translating the *Pharmacopoeia* used by the Royal College of Physicians into English, thereby making it available to all. This must have proved fatal to many, hitherto protected by their ignorance of Latin.

Why, we wonder, did rickets appear so suddenly in this century? The answer is neither simple nor easy. It has been suggested that the great dearth during the last decade of Elizabeth's reign was largely responsible—certainly the poor went hungry—but the rich didn't, and the children of the rich seem to have suffered equally with those of the poor . . . particularly in cities and towns. So it may be the belief that milk was a highly dangerous food for infants and children was a factor in seventeenth-century rickets.* Rich children were fed at weaning on a pap of flour and diluted cow's milk or whey, thus the poor country child was perhaps better off than the rich city child. He was always breast-fed and his unsophisticated parents, if they had a cow, probably didn't realize how dangerous milk was supposed to be. Then, too, the country child scantily dressed got more sunshine than the rich child, whose expensive clothing imitated the gorgeous bulky and all enveloping attire of his parents.

Other deficiency diseases were common and the lack of

*Elizabethan children and old people were allowed milk.

Of Medicine and Mumbo Jumbo

Vitamin A shows up clearly in herbals and household remedy books because so many different things are recommended as a cure for sore eyes, mists and films. This suggests that mild forms of xeropthalmia must have been usual. Poor Peg Verney (Lady Gardnier) went to "Crick Kerne" to consult the famous oculist Daubney Turberville* because of "ill Eyelids, and falling away of the hair, a spot on the pupill and a corrupt fistula in the Corner of the Eye toward her Nose".[8] The latter was perhaps due to a blocked tear duct.

Queen Anne had weak eyes too, and entrusted their care to Sir William Read and "Dr." Roger Grant. Grant, an erstwhile tinker and Anabaptist preacher, had no qualifications whatsoever but he did have absolutely superb testimonials from grateful patients. The grateful patients were usually very poor, or mentally deficient, weak-sighted people attracted by a large sum offered by Grant to sign a statement saying they'd once been stone blind but that his treatment had improved or cured them. Local clergymen were asked to attest such documents and if unpersuaded by an offer of a large contribution to the funds, Grant merely forged their signatures, since he could read and write—qualifications unknown to Sir William Read, albeit he was a cut above Grant, having started life as a tailor.

Read deserted tailoring, became first an itinerant quack, then came to London in 1694, settled in York Buildings, Strand, and began advertising, with a joyous disregard for truth† that he was an eye specialist and also cured deafness, wens, cancer and wry-neck. He also treated, free, soldiers and sailors and cured their blindness. It was for this public service that Queen Anne knighted him in 1705 and appointed him Oculist in Ordinary.

*Turberville was Pepys' "physician for the eyes". Pepys thought it strange that Turberville was so famous yet "to this day had seen no eyes dissected". This day was July 3rd, 1688 when the oculist, Pepys, and various medical men met in an alehouse to watch the famous Richard Lower dissect several oxen and sheep's eyes.

†Both Read and Grant advertised in the *Tatler* and the *Spectator* and editorial comment on their advertising and methods can be found in *Tatler* No. 224, *Spectator* Nos. 472 and 547.

The Pageant of Stuart England

Sir William hired a hack to celebrate the event in a laudatory poem:

"Whilst Britain's sovereign scales such worth has weighed
And Anne herself her smiling favours paid,
That sacred hand does your fair chaplet twist
Great Read, her own entitled oculist".

Not, perhaps, poetry of the highest order, and even a trifle obscure, but one does so admire the felicitious rhyme for oculist. Mist or cyst must have been strong temptations, stoutly resisted.

Eye afflictions might possibly have been less common if more butter had been eaten. Again, working people were probably better off than the rich . . . they ate butter as we do, the rich used it only for cooking. And if Dr. Muffet suggests that liver is of use for sore eyes, he is perfectly contemptuous of butter, wondering with Pliny that "Africa and other Barbarous Countries esteem it as a Gentleman's dish, where here and in Holland and in all Northern Regions, it is the chief food of the poorer sort". This piece of snobbery, or Pliny worship, was paid for in deficiency diseases right up until after the Restoration when people began to eat bread and butter. Pepys mentions eating it. It did his eyes no good. Nor did Dr. Turberville's pills.

Then there was scurvy, a well-known scourge, with well recognized signs . . . swollen gums, oedema, laziness and so on. Furthermore, the cure was well known too! Sir Richard Hawkins, son of the great Elizabethan Sir John Hawkins, knew the curative powers of "sowre Oranges and Lemons" and had written as early as 1593 "This is a wonderful secret of the power and wisdom of God, that hath hidden so great and unknown vertue in this fruit, to be a certain remedy for this infirmity". And the advanced inhabitants of Bensalem prescribed oranges for "the sickness taken at sea".[9]

But England did not produce citrus fruits and it took us another 300 years to discover that God had hidden even larger quantities of Vitamin C in the hips of that most prolific of English flowers, the wild rose. Even so, and failing citrus fruits, there was scurvy grass which in the first quarter of the century constantly crops up as an item in household accounts at 2/- per pound. And, early in the century, the East India Company arranged supplies of lemon water to all ships. But once again the poorer folk may have been better off than the rich, they ate turnips . . . and the very poor in Wales ate them raw; "Windy meat" . . . but rich in Vitamin C.

So scurvy remained. It even increased, because our Stuart ancestors, not content with a cure known to the Elizabethans and fiendishly determined to be "scientific" at any price, jumped to the absurd conclusion that the cure lay in the sour taste of the fruit! Arguing from this false premise they concluded—the sourer the taste the more efficacious the cure. As fruit juices were hard to keep, particularly in hot climates, and scurvy grass was hardly sour at all, they decided that strong acid drinks were the answer. So orange and lemon water was supplanted by vinegar, which if useless, can have done little harm save to the digestion. But oil of vitriol became a very popular remedy and remained so throughout the century. Two drops a day was the recommended dose. It can have cured no one, but if insufficiently diluted could have ulcerated many a stomach. Why no one observed that such acid drinks had no effect upon scurvy and, therefore, recommended a return to the old-fashioned lemon water and scurvy

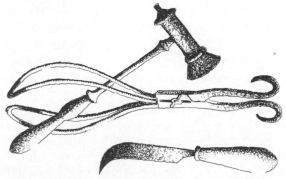

Chamberlen's forceps and other surgical instruments.

grass is impossible to say. Perhaps people had forgotten, as people do, but it seems terrible that our wretched ancestors should have known the cure and abandoned it.*

Yet they did recognize the "cure" for tertian and quartan fevers and agues when it came along, although the remedy was so difficult to procure, so hedged around with mystery, so muddled and expensive that it can have done little good to the ordinary person when it was first introduced. Malaria had been endemic in Europe for centuries and the romantic story of the Countess of Chinchon, wife of the Viceroy of Peru, who was cured of the fever and brought the cure back to Spain in 1639 is too well known to need retelling. The only thing which perhaps needs to be said is that the story now appears to be but a charming fable. But Peruvian or Jesuit's Bark was certainly not a fable, although just to bedevil things there seem to have been two different kinds. One came from the leguminous Myroxylon tree which yielded Balsam of Peru, and its Indian name was Quina-quina (bark of barks). It was scarce and had no curative power whatsoever. The second came from the cinchona —of which there are about forty different species. It was, there-fore, plentiful and it was also the real cure.

As both these were called Jesuit's bark they were administered with very different results. Sometimes a dose cured, sometimes it didn't—depending upon which of the two barks was used—but the fact that it was sometimes effective led to its popularity. Fortunately, the useless Myroxylon bark was scarce and was often cunningly sophisticated with the more plentiful cinchona by those who wished to make a fortune out of supplying an ever-growing demand. Dishonesty was undoubtedly the best policy. Everyone benefited. Or rather those who could pay did,

*As far back as 1535 when Jacques Cartier wintered at Stadacona (now Quebec) twenty-five men died of scurvy and the remainder of the expedition would have perished too if a Mohawk Indian had not saved their lives with an infusion brewed from pine needles and boughs. This gift from the new world was repaid by the old with its usual courtesy—war, pillage, destruction, and tuberculosis.

Of Medicine and Mumbo Jumbo

although in England many Protestants would have died of malaria rather than take a medicine which bore the name of the hated Jesuits. Clever "quacks" were among the first to use cinchona as a "secret remedy" in fever mixtures.

It ceased to be a secret when a certain apothecary, known variously as Robert Tabor, or Talbor, Talbot, who successfully cured Lady Mordaunt's daughter of malaria by his advertised "secret" remedy, also cured Charles II. Charles rewarded him with an annuity, which was unusual; and a knighthood, which wasn't.

Shortly after the King was cured "Tabor" set off for France, altered his surname to Talbot—a name well known in France —and made another fortune. According to Mme. de Sévigné "Nothing is talked of here . . . but the Englishman and his cures". Even so, poor M. de Hautefort found death, if not preferable, at least less painful than paying forty pistoles for Sir Robert's medicine (a pistole was worth around seventeen shillings). A funeral might cost more but it was the last expense M. de Hautefort incurred and he was, one hopes, blissfully unaware of the cost of his last journey. Sir Robert also cured the Dauphin and the "Dauphiness" which, since French doctors were just as given to envy, fear and stupidity as their English colleagues, so enraged Louis·XIV's physician (D'Aquin) that he said, splenetically, the Dauphin had merely been suffering from biliousness! Louis was not deceived. He bought Talbot's secret for a large sum, but promised not to reveal it until after Sir Robert's death. Happily, Talbot died soon after, in 1681, and *The Wonderful Secret for Cureing of Agues and Feavers* became generally known. It was a mixture of rose leaves soaked in water and lemon, to which was added a robust dose of cinchona. Very much later, in the next century, a bottle of fever cure containing cinchona or "quinaquina", as it was commonly called then, became popularly known as "Queen Anne's Mixture", possibly because by Anne's time it had come into more general use or perhaps— and here I hazard a guess—because "quina" sounds very like Queen Anne if carelessly pronounced—and pronunciation was as slovenly then as it is today. It is, reputedly, seventeenth-century seamen who mispronouncing "neger" (EE for Negro) gave us the word "nigger" which in those days had no derogatory implications. "The Negro", says Thomas Fuller, "is the image of God cut in ebony".

Next to the innumerable big killers of the day—plague, typhus, ever-present smallpox, typhoid and measles in children (measles was as serious then as it is in parts of Africa today)—childbirth led the field. Midwifery had made some progress since 1522 when Dr. Wertt of Hamburg was burned at the stake for attending confinements dressed as a woman, in a desperate effort to study the processes of birth and labour; and as early as 1610 in England the Barber Surgeons Company was licensing surgeons to assist at dangerous and difficult confinements, so although midwives were still usual, surgeons could now be present if necessary. Peter Chamberlen, elder of two doctor sons of a Huguenot refugee doctor, invented midwifery forceps early in the century, but the Chamberlens—a family of doctors—kept the secret in the family for 125 years! This, by our standards, is inexcusable, nevertheless, the Chamberlens did attempt to raise midwifery standards. And if Dr. Harvey believed in telegony, his chapter on Midwifery in *De Generatione*—the first original work on the subject by an English author—is mainly devoted to advising patience, observation, and gentle assistance rather than the usual violent methods commonly used in difficult labours, methods which killed the child, if not already dead, and often mutilated or killed the mother too. Due to Harvey's advice, death from haemorrhage became less frequent, but death from infected wounds increased.

Caesarean sections were rarely performed except on the already moribund, as every woman died after this method of delivery.* In addition, puerperal fever was common and the mortality rate among mothers was shocking. As for the children, if born in a large town or city like London an infant had about

*In 1795 Dr. Barlow of Chorley performed the first Caesarian section in England which the mother, but not the child, survived.

Of Medicine and Mumbo Jumbo

one chance in three of reaching the age of one, and about the same one in three chance of reaching the age of five.* Roughly this means that for every 100 live births the survival rate to the fifth year was only eleven per cent.

Children who died very young were referred to as chrism children, because they were buried in the Chrism cloth used at baptism.† Carved in endless procession on tombs they look for all the world like giant cocoons. Adults were buried in a shroud or in their own clothes until after the Restoration when to help the wool trade a woollen winding sheet became compulsory.‡ This was unpopular. Not, I think, because it is as absurd as burying gold at Fort Knox, but because wool was not a fashionable fabric for intimate apparel (there were no woollen underdrawers for example, there weren't any underdrawers at all) and the fashionable did not fancy answering the last trump looking, literally, like nothing on earth. As Nerissa says crossly on her death bed "Odious! . . . in woollen! 'twould a saint provoke".§

All the more provoking because fashionable funerals were elaborate and costly affairs which quite put in the shade the curious burial customs observed in North America today.

*Queen Anne had fourteen children, only one, the Duke of Gloucester, reached the age of eleven. The others died young or were still born. Various reasons are suggested for this; Anne's dropsical condition or congenital syphilis. But we have no evidence that Anne's father, James I, or her mother, Anne Hyde, were syphiletic. Is it at all possible that a rhesus factor was responsible? To the lay mind (mine) the pattern of live births and deaths suggests this might be so. But I am jumping to a conclusion in a most un-Baconian manner here.

†Baptism was very early. John Aubrey was so sickly that he was baptised before morning prayer on the day of his nativity.

‡In 1666. By 1678 any failure to comply with this brought on a fine of £5. Many paid the fine as they preferred linen to wool.

§Pope—*Moral Essays*, Epistle I. Nerissa is reputedly the celebrated actress Mrs. Oldfield (1683-1730) who played Mrs. Sullen in *The Beaux-Stratagem* and is said to have spoken thus with her dying breath. She is buried in Westminster, in woollen one fears, beneath Congreve's monument.

Sometime, early in the era, burial at night with a torch light procession became *de rigueur*. Lady Cheeke (Cheke) who had the misfortune to die of a blood letting performed by the Queen's surgeon who "prickt her too deepe and cut an arterie which fell to ranckle", had a very grand nocturnal funeral with above thirty coaches and "much torch light . . . which is of late come into fashion".[10]

Funerals were an enormously expensive "status symbol". Leaving aside State funerals where mourning garments were supplied to the whole cortège (so many yards of black cloth according to rank), and the effigy of the sovereign fully dressed rested on the coffin within an elaborate architectural "hearse", a rich funeral could easily run into thousands of pounds. The rich were "chested", the poor more happily went straight into the earth. Mourning was, we might think, carried to extremes. Parents were mourned for three or four years. Widows or widowers, unless they re-married, mourned for life. Widows weeds were dreadfully heavy and enveloping during the first half of the era but by 1650* a close-fitting widow's cap with a small flat forehead peak replaced the nun-like veil . . . which is why hair growing from a small peak in the centre of the forehead is called a "widow's peak", a hairline much admired by Victorians.

Rooms in a bereaved house were hung with black. Mirrors were covered or turned to the wall. Heraldic flags were displayed and hatchments over the front door. Food and drink were supplied to mourners and, sometimes, a pot of wine was stood upon the chest so that those who came to pay last respects could drink the health of the deceased on his long journey. Funerals, after the Restoration, were by invitation. Cards engraved with all the insignia of death were sent out. It was uncommon for a woman to attend a man's funeral and vice versa. Presents were given to those who bore the pall (coffin cloth), a scarf or gloves were usual (Walter Calverley is always noting these in his diary),

---

*The earliest one I know is in a portrait at Rousham House, dated 1642, but they were probably earlier as they certainly show in Dutch portraits of earlier date.

Anatomical composition for students.

and Mourning rings, a gift of the deceased, figure largely in post-Restoration wills. A bereaved wife or husband slept in a mourning bed, all costly black draperies and, as this was very expensive, the bed was often loaned around in families. Mourning was also extremely detailed and extended to black saddles and bridles on horses, the family coach was painted black too. When Sir Ralph Verney became a widower he even wore black "taffety" night clothes, black nightcaps and had a black comb and brush. With the death rate as it was many families must never have gone out of mourning at all.

But if a child survived it now often found itself the possessor of two Christian names. This custom, hitherto uncommon in England,* probably first became fashionable in court circles.

*After the publication of the Geneva Bible in the previous century Biblical names had been very fashionable. This fashion was taken to America in the seventeenth century.

231

The Pageant of Stuart England

The new Stuart king had been baptised James Charles (certainly he seems to be the first occupant of the English throne to have two names) and his elder boy was given two names also, Henry Frederick, after his paternal and maternal grandfathers, one imagines. By the end of the era, two names had become quite common and often the second of the given names was descriptive of an event connected with the child or its parents, and often a surname was included, mostly by the landed gentry. But this was considered very new-fangled and was not approved of by traditionalists.

Traditionalists cannot have approved of the new-fangled names extreme Puritans were giving their children either. Names which suggested the virtues, aspirations, or religious sentiments of a particular sect (there were perhaps 200 sects). The custom probably reached its peak by mid-century but it began much earlier. There is more truth than fiction in the names Ben Jonson (1572-1637) gave to his Banbury baker, "Zeal-of-the-Land" Busy and to Mistress "Win-the-Fight" Littlewit.* To certain Puritans only the surnames would sound satirical. Little girls, really, came off rather well with Grace, Prudence, Faith, Hope, Charity. But hapless male infants were saddled with names like Helpless, Sorry-for-Sin, Lament, and Flie-Fornication. The brothers Frewen were baptised Accepted and Thankful by their nonconformist father, but Accepted turned out to be Anglican and Royalist and ended up in 1660 as Archbishop of York. Praise-God Barebones it is said had a brother whose given name was, If-Christ-had-not-died-thou-hadst-been-damned. Although, perhaps, preferable to Flie-Fornication, it must have been rather a bore when it came to signing letters or documents.

Childbed and countless pregnancies were to women what war was to men—though wars do end if only for brief periods—but obviously not all women and children died. Some women even lived to break records for the number of living descendants. Dame Hester Temple, wife of Sir Thomas Temple, had nine sons

Bartholomew Fair first acted in 1614. Shakespeare, more brutally, calls his Puritan "Malvolio".

Of Medicine and Mumbo Jumbo

and four daughters who lived and kept the race going. When Dame Hester died, in the year Cromwell became Lord Protector, her children "had so exceedingly multiplied that this lady saw seven hundred extracted from her body". Thus "God bestoweth personal felicity on some far above the proportion of others".[11] Earlier and less felicitous if one likes crowds, was Mary Honeywood (née Waters or Attwaters). When she died at ninety-three in 1620 she left sixteen children, 114 grandchildren and 288 great-grandchildren—a total of only 367 descendants. One wonders if this new idea of counting descendants (and calculating population) was perhaps the inspiration for Henry Neville's novella *The Isle of Pines*, where one male and three females cast away on a desert island produce forty-seven children. After fifty-nine years the descendants of the four original parents numbered 1,789.

A more famous occupant of a desert island was Alexander Selkirk, the "onlie begetter", it is sometimes claimed, of Defoe's *Robinson Crusoe*. Selkirk was rescued by Dr. Thomas Dover (1660-1742) of Warwickshire. Dover had decided it was more profitable to be a privateer than a physician and on a voyage round the world (1709) he rescued Selkirk from Juan Fernandez, plundered the city of Guayaquil, Equador, fed his sailors on dilute sulphuric acid as an anti-scorbutic, sailed by the Cape of Good Hope, and returned home loaded with Spanish loot. When he retired from profitable piracy he practised medicine and invented Dover's powder—ipecac and opium—which we still use today.

Dover at one time was a pupil of Dr. Thomas Sydenham, and Sydenham (b. 1624) is one of the reasons we can truthfully say that—despite the horrors of diseases and cures—the seventeenth century saw the birth of modern medicine in this country. Sydenham, Puritan and Parliamentarian, friend of Boyle and John Locke, went to Oxford and Montpellier and had not the smallest patience with book learning or medical books. "Young man, go to the bedside; there alone can you learn disease" was his advice to another pupil, Hans Sloane.

The Pageant of Stuart England

This was one of the precepts of Hippocrates and it was this which Sydenham followed and so, although he never knew it, he became the father of clinical medicine. His bedside observations were wide in scope and character, his descriptions of diseases clear and concise. He gave the first description of acute rheumatism, hitherto lumped in with gout; of scarlatina, hitherto confused with measles. He studied epidemics, noted their seasonal variation and left extraordinarily clear and detailed accounts of malaria, smallpox, plague and hysteria. He was among the first to prescribe iron for anemia, fresh air and exercise for consumption, and he did much to popularize the use of cinchona. He also treated syphilis with mercury until excessive salivation occurred, but believed it was the saliva and not the mercury which effected the cure.*

All this careful work had to come first before any real attempt at preventive or cure could be made. Ailments had to be recognized for what they were, identified, separated out from each other, their courses and symptoms charted. Sydenham did this, sitting beside the bedside of his patients, observing and recording as Hippocrates had done and as Francis Bacon had recommended. Sydenham was never elected a Fellow of the Royal Society, nor of the Royal College of Physicians, which seems to indicate that neither of these august bodies can have been aware of the value of his work. Nor did his books become popular until after his death. Posterity has rectified the error of Sydenham's contemporaries for he is known as "the English Hippocrates". Yet the English Hippocrates could define but not cure his own gout, and when his pupil, Thomas Dover, contracted smallpox "honest and good Dr. Sydenham" as Dover calls him, bled him, gave him

*The discovery made by W. von Jauregg, Vienna in the nineteenth century that the high fever in malaria was of value in curing G.P.I. suggests that possibly malaria cured some cases in the seventeenth century. But in this century, as today in a different context, the sophisticated when visiting easy morts, punks, bang-tails, blowza-bellas, doxies or trug-moldies—the more printable names for harlots—took precautions against VD by using a device invented by a Colonel Condom.

an emetic, put him in a cold room, kept all windows open, refused to allow bedclothes higher than the navel, and made the patient drink twelve bottles of small beer "acidulated" with vitriol, every twenty-four hours.

Sydenham died in 1689; the year in which Lords and Commons acting as a revolutionary Convention (they couldn't be a parliament without a sovereign and James II had fled) elected William and Mary to the vacant throne—and so constitutional monarchy began. In this year too, Mrs. Aphra Behn died, Mr. Ashmole in a codicil to his will left his sister £100; Mr. Evelyn at Mr. Pepys request was painted by the famous Gottfried Kniller*— better known to us as Godfrey Kneller—and Mr. Evelyn's cousin, Evelyn Pierpont,† became the father of a daughter, Mary.

Sydenham was a Parliamentarian and it is unlikely, due to difference of age rather than of politics, that he ever met the Royalist, William Harvey (1578-1657), who gave an imperishable lustre to the age with his discovery of the circulation of the blood. Harvey took his degree at Padua, the great anatomical school, and at Cambridge. He began practising in 1602, was physician to the first two Stuarts but his great book‡ was not published until 1628 —in Frankfort, and in England twenty-one years later! It was finally translated into English in 1653, four years before Harvey died.

It seems odd, ridiculous, and absurd to us now that before Harvey it was believed that the liver, the seat of all "humours" was also considered the central blood organ, and that it was thought the blood moved backwards and forwards, passing from right to left ventricle of the heart, where necessary through pores

---

*Now in Christ Church.

†Or Pierrepont. He unexpectedly became fifth Earl of Kingston in 1690 owing to the deaths of the third and fourth Earl, his elder brothers. Henry, second Earl, studied law and medicine and was a F.R.C.P. and a F.R.S. It is said he hastened his end by taking his own medicines.

‡*Exercitatio Anatomica de Motu Cordis et Sanguinis in Animalibus.*

in the septum. Harvey's work entirely changed this conception, although certainly not rapidly, for most Professors of Physic everywhere probably agreed with the French anatomist Riolan, who with savage sarcasm said that if Harvey's discoveries went against the teaching of Galen, it could only mean that Nature must have changed almost entirely since Galen's day! In England it was "an opinion which entered the world with great disadvantages"[12] because it was strange and because "the grandees of the profession were of the opposite judgment, heavy enough to overlay (and so stifle) any infant opinion by their authority".[13] But the grandees were as wrong about Harvey as the papal authorities were about Galileo. Both men drew conclusions from observation of the particular or a class of particulars and not from specious generalities.

Harvey built up his case step by step. He proved the heart a hollow muscle which impelled the blood into the arteries and gave rise to the pulse. But where does the blood come from and where does it go? he asked as he ligated veins and arteries at various points. And calculating that, as neither arteries nor veins were either ruptured or emptied, and so the entire volume of blood would be used up in a very short time, he began, he says, "to think whether there might not be a motion, as it were, in a circle". So the great new conception of the circulation of the blood was born and the greatest book in medical literature was written.

Yet Harvey did not gain much reputation among his contempories as a physician and his practice was not very great "towards his later end".[14] Doctors agreed he was a great anatomist, but none admired his "Theraputic way" and "several practicers . . . would not give 3d. for his bills".*[15] Harvey, like Sydenham, suffered from gout. Sydenham drank wine to cure his, but Harvey would sit on the roof of Cockaine House if it were frosty and put his legs into a bucket of cold water, then "when almost dead with cold" he would "betake himself to his Stove and so 'twas gone". Harvey, short, dark, with a lively black

*Doctors often bought other doctors, prescriptions from apothecaries.

and "little Eie" was "Cholerique" when young and quick on the draw (dagger) but also given to contemplation. He sat under a hedge at the battle of Edgehill reading a book and, later, had caves dug at his home in Surrey where he could sit and contemplate in summer. The minor fruits of contemplation led Harvey to conclude that man was but "a great, mischevious Baboon"[16] and that the Turks alone knew how to órder and govern women. Perhaps for this reason he remained a bachelor, yet he kept a

Surgical scissors and instruments.

pretty wench to wait on him which John Aubrey opines "he made use of for warmeth sake as King David did". Odd this, because the doctor always felt the heat terribly. It is even odder to think that when his great work came out his practice fell off and that the "vulgar" believed him "Crack-brained" while all physicians were against him. Fortunately Harvey lived to be seventy-nine and some twenty to thirty years after the publication (in Germany) of his book had the satisfaction of seeing it accepted. Considering the native slowness to accept the unorthodox and general suspicion of anything new or "outlandish", this was really no time at all.

Once Harvey's discovery was accepted it opened other fields of experiment. Curiously enough, it was young Dr. Christopher Wren who suggested one of them. He first had the idea of intravenous medication, suggested it to Robert Boyle and the pair carried out the experiment by injecting opium and crocus mettalorum into dogs. Wren also illustrated the book of the fashionable Royalist physician, Thomas Willis (1621-1675), *Cerebri Anatome*, one of the first descriptions of the brain. Willis's name lives today in "the circle of Willis" (the arteries at the base of the brain) named for him.

Knowledge of circulation led also to the first attempt at blood transfusion, an experiment performed by Dr. Richard Lower (1631-1691). It was not particularly successful but the idea so excited a Berlin "scientist" that, in a thoroughly Germanic way, he jumped to the conclusion that incompatible marriages could be made happy by reciprocal transference of blood of the miserable consorts. Even so, this idea isn't a patch on the astounding transformation which took place when Sir Nicholas Gimcrack transfused "64 ounces, Haver-du-pois"* of Sheep's blood into the veins of a madman. The sheep, incidentally, died. But the madman . . . !

More successful was the solution of the problem of the interaction of air and blood by Dr. Lower and Dr. Robert Mayow (1643-79). Both were Cornishmen and based their work on the experiments first performed by Robert Boyle with his air pump, and by Robert Boyle's assistant, Robert Hooke. Hooke gave what is tantamount to the first demonstration of artificial respiration, using a dog as subject. Dr. Lower also proved that the dripping accompaniment of a cold arose from the mucous membranes of the nose. Hitherto, it had been regarded as a "purging of the brain". None the less, people continued to purge their

---

*Most of the experiments being carried out in medicine and science are ridiculed by Thomas Shadwell in *The Virtuoso* through the character Sir Nicholas who also had "Microscopes, Telescopes, Thermometers, Barometers, Pneumatick-Engines, Stentorophonical Tubes and the like", to aid him in his experiments.

Of Medicine and Mumbo Jumbo

brains by artificial means (pepper, snuff, etc.) for all sorts of ailments and also to sharpen their wits. There was nothing like a good purge for brain or bowel. This, too, was part of the Englishness of the English. It still is. Although we no longer artificially purge our brains we do believe firmly in a "good blow".* As for our bowels, we are still positively obsessive about them.

Richard Wiseman (1622-1676) is another distinguished name. He made surgery a profession equal to that of medicine and, inevitably, is known as "the Father of English surgery". English physicians may not have felt that surgeons were "a race of evil, extravagant coxcombs who wear moustaches and flourish razors" as did Guy Patin, head of the Paris Faculty (Patin also thought Harvey mad) but surgeons, being tied, rather, to barbers, were pretty much despised. Wiseman'a book *Severall Chirugicall Treatises* was the most important work on surgery to appear in this country up to that time. His treatise on the King's Evil showed where surgery could help when the Royal Touch was not available, although he himself believed implicitly in the efficacy of the Royal Touch. Queen Anne, as we know, was the last Sovereign to touch for the King's Evil, among the touched being a two-year-old boy who remained uncured but achieved great fame later in the eighteenth century. His name was Samuel Johnson.

These and others have left us greatly in debt to the century. They accumulated facts, defined and described certain diseases and conditions, experimented with new ideas and new tools— for new ideas need new tools. They were, in fact, laying the foundation for methodical research into science, medicine and natural phenomena and leaving behind a corpus of material to be used, added to, refined by those who came after. Nevertheless, it takes a very long time to learn what to do with the

*For the benefit of any non-English readers, this does not necessarily refer to the use of a pocket handkerchief or to a clout on the head. It means going for a long walk—preferably in wet and windy weather.

undeniable facts so accumulated. Hence, for the average person, the chance discovery of the cure for malaria was far more immediately useful than the meticulous work of a Harvey or a Sydenham.

In the meantime, while waiting for new discoveries to be translated into terms of benefit to humanity there was that admirable panacea for all ills "the Bishop of Worcester's Curing Powder" which was recommended as a sovereign remedy as late as 1683 in that indispensable book *The Queen's Closet Opened.* It required the powdered black tips of crab claws—crabs to be caught when the sun enters Cancer; musk, civet, ambergris and magister of Pearl, plus the skins of "Adders or Snakes or Slow worms" reduced to a jelly in spring water. If one boggled at adders and the like, hartshorn could be substituted but it had to be hartshorn from a red deer killed when the moon was in Leo (August). Just which of Worcester's Bishops is responsible for this curing powder I am unable to say (it sounds a very old recipe) but the good Bishop must have been part astrologer, part witch-doctor as well as a Doctor of Divinity. Dr. Richard Napier, astrologer and rector of Great Lindford, Bucks., on the other hand, claimed the direct assistance of the angel Raphael as a diagnostician.

In addition to the usual diseases, there seems always to have been some risk of poisoning, by enemies, friends, food or even medicine. Rumour was never slow to attribute sudden death— or even unsudden death if it happened to an important person— to poison. King James I was rumoured to have poisoned the young Phoenix, and certainly Frances Howard poisoned Sir Thomas Overbury. James's favourite, Buckingham, or his mother were thought to have poisoned James. Lady Denham and the beautiful Venetia Digby, Sir Kenelm's wife, were believed to have been handed a Borgia cup by their cuckolded husbands, and there is said to have been a poison plot against Charles II.

It was, therefore, best to keep a sure antidote in the house. Unicorn's horn, an early-century favourite, was terribly scarce

and fabulously expensive so Mithridate and bezoar stone*
though not cheap appear in contemporary account books. East
Indian bezoar cost £3.10.0 the ounce; grey bezoar around
£1.8.0 but Mithridate was much cheaper at 2/-. Both were used
as preventives for disease as well and the bezoar stone was
thought to have a special virtue against "all melancholy affections".[17] It was also thought to be efficacious against plague,
a belief exploded by Dr. Nathaniel Hodges during the Great
Plague of 1665. Saffron, too, was another and more easily
procured antidote, it grew plentifully at Saffron Walden and
Thomas Fuller† says he owed his life to it when afflicted with
smallpox, which regularly carried off thousands and scarred
millions. No antidote saved the Exeter apothecary Humphrey
Bidgood, however. Poor Mr. Bidgood came to an untimely end
in the 1640's when his apprentice, Peter Moore, mixed powdered white mercury in his master's pottage. As soon as the
unfortunate man tasted it he began to swell and shortly afterwards
died. But perhaps the poison acted so rapidly that Mr. Bidgood
didn't have a chance to get at the remedies which, being an
apothecary, he must have had in stock.

During this century it became popular to take the waters at
various newly discovered spas. Bath, known from Roman times,
became fashionable after Anna of Denmark's visit, but we hear
less of Buxton than in the previous century. As it was believed
that England afforded the "most sanative waters for English

---

*Bezoar, a stony mass found in the stomachs of goats, antelopes,
llama, etc., was a greatly esteemed antidote. Presumably the East
Indian variety was the surer remedy. Grey bezoar was perhaps native
or of European origin and therefore considered less good. Mithridate
contained seventy-two ingredients. Named for Mithridates VI of
Pontus, the recipe was well tried as the King had died around 63 B.C.
Probably the ingredients varied as the centuries rolled on.

†He also says a crocodile's tears are never genuine unless he is forced
to come near saffron. The reason, a little illogically, is that a crocodile
is all poison and saffron is the antidote for all poison. The crocodile's
name he says is from krokodeilos, i.e. saffron fearer. A charming but
bogus derivation.

bodies"[18] new wonder-working wells and springs became the rage. There was Tunbridge, so good for splenetic distempers; Knaresborough (discovered in 1620 by Master Slingsby) with waters of a "vitrioline" taste and odour, splendid for stomach, bowels, liver, spleen, blood, veins, nerves and for consuming "crudities" . . . one could hold one's nose as one dipped or drank. The twin springs at Leamington were much admired, though as different as Jacob and Esau "one salt one fresh".[19] At Newnham Regis there was a dual purpose spring; if salt were added the water acted as a purge; if sugar, its effect was the exact opposite. This spring was also said to be good for the stone (a constant affliction) which sounds a little improbable as the waters also had the faculty of petrifying wood.

The medicinal waters of Epsom were discovered by a Mr. Wicker, possibly as early as 1618. He observed, during a severe drought, a pocket of water in the hoof-print of an animal. At first he thought it the stale of some beast, but seeing the water was clear he promptly dug a hole nearby. Next morning the hole was filled and running over. This did not solve the problem of watering stock—animals wouldn't touch the stuff—but humans were soon flocking to Epsom and by Pepys' day it was a very popular resort.

Late in the era, we are relieved to find a slight improvement in medicines which could be run up at home; also some doctors were now being a bit less nauseating with their brews. For home manufacture, Cousin Botry's receipt for dropsy is a sort of herbal beer which was taken by the barrelful until one was cured. Lady Gage's remedy for the same complaint is even more simple—a teaspoonful of mustard seed with a draught of broom water, night and morning, had cured Lady Betty's thirst in three days. Who Lady Betty was, we are not told, but we *are* told that "she is neither swelled in the body nor Legs, nor more than she was five years ago". One doesn't much like the implications of "no more than she was". Broom was believed to be a diuretic too, and Mrs. Blencowe and others give a description of its efficacy, as such, which is little short of astounding.

Microscope, 1665.

If low in the mind or lacking energy due to disease, "dumps" or any other cause, the late seventeenth-century equivalent of modern pep pills was "High Spirrited Pills". These could be run up at home and contained "salt of Steel" galbanum, castor (probably refined sugar, not unrefined beaver) assafoetida, amber and camphire, and were guaranteed to lift the dispirited to the heights. Dr. Lower's drops, although his name does not suggest it, were even better. They cured not only the dumps, but giddiness in the head and "Hysterical or Convulsive fits". As the basis of this tonic was a pint of the best brandy it would certainly lift the spirits and might even be useful in fits but can it have cured giddiness in the head? Or, more simply, one could "refocillate" one's wasted spirits with "a roll and a pot of Ale" as Aubrey tells us William Prynne did, although it is doubtful if this was sufficient to overcome the dejection of having one's ears cropped . . . as poor Prynne had.

Such remedies could be augmented by advertised cures. Susannah Kirleus, daughter of "that eminent doctor Thomas Kirleus", like Shakespeare's Helena a century before, was busy advertising her father's famous pills and drink for the cure of "The Secret Disease" and various other things without—and one is vastly relieved at this—"without the use of Mummie, which destroys many".[20] There was a "Cephalick Tincture" which instantly cured diseases of the nerves[21] while for those whose nerves had gone too far, there was Robert Norris recently moved to the Pestle and Mortar "near the middle of Hatton Garden", who had a large airy house "fit to receive persons of the best rank of Either Sex with suitable Attendance". Mr. Norris was successful, he claimed, in curing "Lunaticks" and if unsuccessful would board the "incurable" on "Reasonable Terms".[22]

Those unable to avail themselves of Mr. Norris's private lunatic asylum went to Bedlam, or Bethleham (rebuilt in 1675 at a cost of £18,000). James Harrington (d. 1677) the author of *The Commonwealth of Oceana* was in neither place. He sat in a little summer-house at home with fox tails in one hand and a fly swatter in the other. Ever since his shameful imprisonment he had been mildly demented, believed his own sweat produced flies and bees and was at great pains to prove it to his friends. Nor had Lady Ralegh been put under restraint, although she was, reputedly, seen everywhere after 1618 carrying a red leather bag of unusual shape and size. It was believed to contain Sir Walter's head.* "All the arts of the best physicians" could not cure the wife of the younger son of Sir John Byron who went mad after the birth of twins. "She was not frantic but had such pretty delirations that her ravings were more delightful than other

*But Elias Ashmole told John Aubrey that Carew Ralegh (Sir Walter's son) had told him (Elias) that when his father's grave was dug up skull and neck were intact, proving Ralegh hadn't been hanged. Only lower classes and women were hanged. Upper classes were beheaded and so hanging was a shameful death for the upper classes.

Of Medicine and Mumbo Jumbo

women's rational conversation". Or so says Lucy Hutchinson and I've a mind to believe her.

In addition to advertised remedies and home remedies, there were by the end of the Stuart era many more medical prescriptions being published in book form, such as "the genuine receipts of the famous Dr. Radcliffe, who amassed so vast an Estate by his Practice, that future ages will hardly credit it". Future ages, at least in Oxford* and London have indeed credited it and blessed this most fashionable physician who earned twenty guineas a day, and used a simple pharmacopoeia. The publisher of "Dr. Radcliffe's prescriptions" (*Pharmacopoeia Radcliffiana*), Charles Rivington, who also appears to be its editor, urges every one to do likewise and to use as few remedies as possible "Jumbles" says he "affect our Blood and Vessels as they do our Stomachs; nor can we easily bear 'em so that the Remedy becomes as troublesome as the Disease".

Dr. Radcliffe, eschewing Jumbles, made a number of remarkable cures and kept his prescriptions admirably simple. He relied more on herbs than on metals or gruesome ingredients and, in a way, was returning to the much earlier idea of simples, before compounds became the rage . . . and the more compounded and involved the better. His "Alexipharmack Bolus", a "mighty recruiter of spirits" was merely clove gilly-flower syrup, virginia snake-weed root, and Gascoign's powder. This pill "pushed the anamalous gout to the extremities" and so expelled it from the "Internal parts". It was, unfortunately, of no use in "polypi of the heart". The "Encoprotick Pills" were excellent for the usual English complaint—costiveness, and one cannot but admire Dr. Radcliffe's candour in admitting that his "Navel Plaisters" for the vapours weren't much good but that "they make a shew". His strengthening plaster, to help in childbirth was also of small use, he says, but he felt it good policy to let a woman in childbed feel that everything was being done to relieve

*He left money, later used by the trustees, to found the Radcliffe Infirmary, Oxford, one of the finest hospitals in the country, he also left bequests to St. Bartholomew's.

her suffering. Here we begin to understand his secret, his medicines were harmless, they even helped; but it was probably in supportive therapy that Dr. Radcliffe excelled.* His "Paregorick Draught" was doubtless of very great value in combating pain and insomnia, convulsions and "Hysterical Hurries in Women", but he does not recommend it as being good for "Languid" people—not surprisingly as opium seldom is —"chronical pains in the head" or "satyrriasis". His febrifuge julep contained Peruvian bark but, the editor warns, the bark should be chosen by a physician to avoid being swindled.

Rivington, in his observations upon Radcliffe, gives us an amusing sidelight into his own pet theories. He believed—if I have read him aright, not always easy as his "technical jargon" (used to impress) is often so obscure as to make little sense— that in England the "most rebellious Distempers . . . are from stubborn mineral salts" which, among other things, "dilaniate the Fibres into Ulcers" or at best make them "Osscilate" too briskly, causing "a quicker Circulation and an Hectick". One doesn't understand it, but it sounds positively dire . . . and there seems small hope of escape as England "abounds in vitriolic salts in its soil which cause so many ills". Hence, he favours the use of Dr. Radcliffe's "Smooth Electuary" (conserve of violets, mallow, gum arabic, red coral and syrup of "comphry") as it absorbed "Acidities" and was excellent if the "serum of the blood" was overloaded with "an acrimonious salt". The Electuary was good for a hangover too, although those who drink spirituous liquors are warned to "expect the Dismal Consequences" for the fibres became inflamed, the humours "sharp

*Yet he refused to attend Queen Anne, when a Princess, saying her illnesses were merely the vapours and so he and the Queen were not on friendly terms. When the little Duke of Gloucester was dying, she finally sent for Radcliffe. He came, unwillingly, diagnosed scarlet fever and learning that the boy's doctors had bled him said bluntly "then you have destroyed him; and you may finish him for I will not prescribe". Radcliffe also refused to attend Queen Anne in her last illness when Lady Masham sent for him, privately, so it was Dr. Arbuthnot who gave the signal that Queen Anne was dead.

and corrosive" and the "Circulation too hastened". Which really isn't an inaccurate description at all.

Rather more useful than the Electuary was tapping for dropsy, a treatment introduced then and still used today. Many doctors, including Dr. Radcliffe, did not hold with it. Dr. Radcliffe none the less, sounds as if he were candid, conservative (in the best sense of the word) and kind. In fact Rivington tells us "to say the Truth, the Doctor seem'd always to have one maxim in view which was to do no Harm to the Patient". This seems a clear enough enunciation of an admirable and all too rare policy. But it does not quite satisfy Rivington who makes this rather cryptic comment, "In my opinion a little more would but do and have answer'd his end very well too". We are left asking . . . a little more what? . . . medicine or harm?

This book, published two years after Dr. Radcliffe's death, is not important, although it makes interesting reading and is certainly less alarming than many other such books of the period. It was, I think, designed to cash in on Dr. Radcliffe's reputation and make money for the publisher and editor who ends his preface with the candid comment that he would have offered more receipts "but the Humour of writing is wore off nor shall it be easily assumed until further Encouragement".

Dr. Radcliffe, Sophia, Electress of Hanover, and Queen Anne all died in 1714. That year Laurence Sterne had survived the dreadful infant mortality rate and reached the age of one, Richard Wilson and William Shenstone were safely born, and Sir Isaac Newton was President of the Royal Society. In its transactions for this year there appeared a paper based on the observations of, and written by, a Fellow, Dr. Emanuel Timori, the best physician in Constantinople. It concerned the method of inoculation against smallpox in use among the Turks. Two years later Evelyn Pierrepont's daughter—now Lady Mary Wortley Montagu—had herself and her small son inoculated and began a campaign—much opposed by many—for inoculation. But that is a later story, although it has its real beginning in this last year of the last Stuart. Or should one say its true beginning lay in the time of the first Stuart, with a fallen and long-dead Lord Chancellor?

For it was now eighty-eight years since that icy March day when the man who urged a return to true Hippocratic ideals, who believed only experiment and observation could lead to correct conclusions, stopped his coach at the foot of Highgate Hill and together with a friend, Dr. Witherborne, went into the house of a poor woman, bought a chicken, made her eviscerate it on the spot and then went out and stuffed the chicken with snow. While driving he had been seized with the intense desire to know if snow, like salt, would retard the process of putrefaction.

Climbing back into his coach with the doctor and the snow-stuffed chicken he was suddenly taken with so great a chill that he could not return to his lodgings and had to be taken to the Earl of Arundel's house nearby. Here he was put into a great guest bed which was freshly warmed with a pan. But the pan could not drive the damp from a bed, unused for a year, nor could it drive the chill from the bones of a man of sixty-five. Bit by bit, his breathing became more laboured and the delicate, lively, hazel eyes which Dr. Harvey thought were like those of a viper, brightened with fever as the magnificent brain dulled and sank into sleep and oblivion.

"Man," he had once written—and the statement slowly echoing throughout England and the world, began to unlock the tight little boxes of men's minds—"Man, who is the servant and interpreter of nature, can act and understand no further than he has observed, either in operation or in contemplation, of the method and order of nature".[23]

And so, out of a desire to observe, know, understand for himself the preserving effects of snow upon a dead chicken, Francis Bacon, Lord Verulam and Viscount St. Albans, died.

CHAPTER SEVEN

Of Innovations and Knacks

THE "New Digestor or Engine for Softening Bones" was a great success; and if for some the name has a slightly ghoulish ring, while for others it may suggest a method of producing an excellent fertilizer for roses, we are left in no doubt of the "Engine's" real purpose by an entry in John Evelyn's diary dated April 12th, 1682. "I went this afternoon", he writes, "with several of the Royal Society to a supper which was all dressed, both fish and flesh, in Monsieur Papin's* digestors, by which the hardest bones of beef itself, and mutton, were made as soft as cheese, without water or other liquor, and with less than eight ounces of coals, producing an incredible quantity of gravy."

These distinguished gentlemen, under the presidency of Dr. Wren, ate pike and other fish bones "without impediment", and a jelly made of beef bones "the most delicious I have ever seen, or tasted". But in Evelyn's opinion "nothing exceeded the pigeons, which tasted just as if baked in a pie, all these being stewed in their own juice, without any addition of water save what swam about the digestor as *in balneo*". This "philosophical supper" was greatly and merrily enjoyed by the company and Mr. Evelyn even went so far as to send a glass of the delicious jelly to his wife as a reproach to "all that the ladies ever made of their best hartshorn".

*Denys Papin, F.R.S., physician, philosopher and wonderful "mechanic" was curator of the Royal Society. He also invented a boat with paddle wheels.

This was really rather mean, considering how very difficult it was in those days to grate hartshorn and to soften it by boiling. Neither history nor Mr. Evelyn record the thoughts of Mrs. Evelyn on receipt of this superior, if reproachful, jelly. Nor have we any evidence that this obvious ancestress of the pressure cooker* ever found its way into the seventeenth-century kitchen to be used for preserving or stewing fruit, extracting "tinctures", or saving fuel—all of which were its other named advantages. By this time, and indeed ever since the beginning of the century, there had been an increasingly urgent need, due to depletion of forests, to find alternatives to wood for heating and cooking. Sea coal, difficult to get and expensive, was being more and more used for heating, but its smoke and tar rendered it virtually useless when it came to roasting meat on a spit—the usual method of roasting. Smoke, it was thought, was useful in turning a wooden "jack" in the chimney which in turn rotated the spit but of course it was heat not smoke which did this and a great roaring fire was needed to produce sufficient heat. As early as 1605, Hugh Platt gave his inventive mind to the problem of how to overcome the known disadvantages of coal and was knighted for suggesting—among other inventions—how to make "a new, cheaper and delicate fire of coal balls" and we find this a subject which engaged the interest of a good many people—without much evidence of success—throughout the whole of the era. Indeed, even Mr. Evelyn tried his hand at making what we call briquettes by mixing charcoal dust and loam together and, on July 8th, 1667, he shewed my Lord Brereton and others who dined with him "my new fuel, which was very glowing, and without smoke or ill smells".

*This "Machine pour Amolir les Os" consisted of two metal cylinders, one of which fitted into the other. The top cylinder had a vent covered by a weighted piece of metal and, presumably, when the pressure inside grew too great this acted as a safety valve. The bottom cylinder, very much deeper than the top one, must have held the water. Thus the engine seems to have been bain marie and pressure cooker combined.

Of Innovations and Knacks

Accustomed as we now are to professional scientists and scientific societies whose interests, unavoidably, lie in highly specialized and esoteric fields far beyond the understanding of most of us, it is a little difficult to realize that the first "scientists" were nearly all amateurs in the true sense of that word, and that members of the Royal Society* were almost as interested in a pressure cooker as they were in Newton's discovery of the refrangibility of light of different colours; as eager to find out why French bread was allegedly better than English as to understand why a flame went out in the vacuum produced by using Robert Boyle's "Pneumatic Engine" or air pump. It is understandable only when we know that the avowed purpose of the new philosophy was to improve the lot of mankind. Bacon believed that "the roads to human power and the roads to human knowledge lie close together". He saw science as the great civilizer which would bind man to man and ultimately lead to a greater understanding and to a greater love of God. And for ordinary mortals unable perhaps to tackle or to understand either his *Advancement of Learning* which, in 1605, reviewed the present state of knowledge; or his *Novum Organum* which, in 1620, described the new method of experimental philosophy—and if John Chamberlain wasn't "encouraged" by its title Master Cuffe was positively rude about its contents—Bacon wrote *The New Atlantis*. This was one of the great pieces of what we would call science fiction, and the purpose and fruits of science as explained by a master of Salomon's House must have sounded as fascinating and fantastic in 1629† as *Around the World in 80 Days* sounded in 1872.

Robert Boyle summed up the aspirations of science in those days in a letter he wrote, dated October 22nd, 1646, to his ex-tutor Mr. Marcombe, explaining the "invisible" college.

*The original ninety-eight Fellows at the Royal Society for the promoting of "Physico-Mathematicall Experimentall Learning", were chosen for their interest in science not for any special skills.

†Written between 1611–1618 but not published until three years after the ex-Lord Chancellor's death.

"Our new philosophical colledge" he wrote, "values no knowledge but as it hath a tendency to use." Britain could become—in time and in fact—the Bensalem of Bacon's imagination. But the new Experimental philosophy was not confined to those who made it their sole interest in life, or even to members of the invisible college. It became fashionable. Gentlemen of birth and education, no less than those we now think of as "great name" scientists, dabbled and discovered in their own "Elaboratories"; attended meetings; exchanged letters, papers, and views, as in the previous century (and in this one too) they had exchanged verses and "Englished" the classics. To be interested in natural philosophy, to know something about it was considered to be as necessary an accomplishment as playing a musical instrument.

King Charles II was always deeply interested in science, even if he did laugh at those who met at Gresham College for spending their time "weighing air".[*1] He had his own Elaboratory in St. James's Park and both he and his aunt Elizabeth's third son, Prince Rupert, were accounted "illustrious spagyrists (alchemists) and operators"[2] and not only by their own countrymen. M. Misson remarks that Charles was "curious in Physical and Mechanical Experiments" and there is a wealth of evidence in letters and diaries of the time to support this statement. Prince Rupert who, richly clad in scarlet and silver lace and mounted on a black Barbary horse, had gained and lost Bristol for his uncle Charles I (1645), was the inventor of "Prince Rupert's Drops" —those tadpoles made by dropping molten glass into cold water which explode if you break off the tail. But this enormously tall prince probably only introduced them into England. Ruprecht was also once credited with inventing the process of mezzo-tinting, a secret which he perhaps got from Ludwig von Siegen, but certainly he and the painter Vaillant carried out a series of successful experiments in this new art-science.

But it was really the King's interest and faith in science which did so much to make it fashionable. The court still led the way

*Aristotle rejected the idea that air could have weight.

and set the fashion in matters of taste and in the patronage of the arts. It continued to do so, though in a rather diminishing way, after Charles's death and until the Hanoverians took over. Charles's foreign policy may have been disastrous. His private life, which he lived so publicly, may have given—and often did give—great offence to many, and the reputed siring of

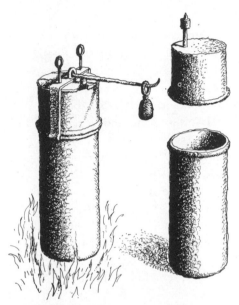

Parent of the pressure-cooker.

fifty-eight bastards was undoubtedly counted as one of his lesser extravagances. But his active interest in, and encouragement of, science made "The Invisible College"* visible as the Royal Society to which, in 1662, he granted his charter. This is the great landmark in the history of science.

Charles, himself, was a member of the Society and in the year

*The Invisible College members met in London and also in Oxford in the rooms of Dr. Wilkins, Warden of Wadham (1658-9); Master of Trinity College, Cambridge (1659); Bishop of Chester (1668)—and Cromwell's brother-in-law.

before the Charter was granted he visited it in Oxford. This caused some anxiety to a number of the members since they weren't quite sure what sort of entertainment would please or interest the recently restored monarch. Dr. Wren thought there should be something of "Pomp" in whatever was presented because to produce "Knacks only", as jugglers do, would "scarce become the Gravity of the Occasion". He suggests, in a letter to Lord Brouncker in 1661 a half-dozen experiments lying between Pomp and Knacks, "luciferous in Philosophy, and yet whose Use and Advantage is Obvious, and without a Lecture; and besides may surprise with some unexpected Effects". This, he felt, should be enough for one hour's entertainment of the Royal Patron. "The Key that opens Treasures" he observes sagely "is often plain and rusty, but unless it be gilt 'twill make no Show at Court."[3] Or as Thomas Powell put it in a slightly different connexion and even more strongly, "As nature hath her ludicra so art hath hers too".[4]

Ludicra and knacks are not to be scorned even by the most serious minded. The kite*—so named in the Stuart Century because it was two-tailed and resembled the bird—was only a toy; kite flying remained a game until well on in the eighteenth century when the toy first became useful for meteorological purposes. The rocket, chiefly a grand ornament of fireworks displays, remained so until the battle of Waterloo. On the other hand, the camera obscura† used for centuries by astronomers wanting to observe solar eclipses without damaging their eyes,

---

*But known in China as early as 1,000 B.C. The fork-tailed bird for which we named the toy is now very rare: it was so common in the seventeenth century that it scavenged in London's streets.

†The early camera obscura, as the name implies, was a dark room or vault with a tiny hole in wall or window shutter through which the outside view was projected on to the opposite wall or on to a white screen—upside down. Three improvements took place in the sixteenth century. 1, a convex lens was inserted into the hole and gave a larger, brighter picture; 2, a diaphragm sharpened the image; 3, a mirror turned it right side up. These separate discoveries were all made by Italians.

was improved and put to other purposes. Artists used it as a quick and easy way of making sketches, non artists and peeping Toms and Tomasinas just sat and watched, unobserved, what went on in the streets. In the seventeenth century the camera obscura became portable, first clumsily like a sedan chair, then rapidly reduced to box size and even smaller so that it could be carried under the arm. This small, portable box-camera, dating from the middle of the century, was the direct ancestor of our photographic camera.

But there were other tools of science which could be used for public and private amusement. In England in 1600, if one wanted to see the heads of malefactors embossing Temple Bar, one had to depend on one's eyesight, but by 1700 a really staggeringly clear close-up could be had by having a good look through a telescope at a ha'penny a look.* Private individuals, not necessarily rich ones, often had their own telescopes and invited friends in for an evening of viewing the night sky from roof or garden or even, it is feared, for a day-time peep into the houses or gardens of neighbours.† Then there was that innovation based probably on the thermoscope "a very pretty weather-glass for heat or cold".[5] Such toys and innovations could be bought from various makers in London. Mr. Ralph Greatorex, the mathematical instruments maker, could run one up in no time. He was something of an inventor too. His engine for drawing up water (Pepys, Oct. 11th, 1660) sounds uncommonly

*Temple Bar was new too. Re-erected in 1672 to the design of Sir Christopher Wren, it was removed in 1878 and erected a year later near Cheshunt. A pillar surmounted by a griffin now marks its original site.

†Readers will remember that in Thomas Tomkis's comedy *Albumazar the Astrologer* which so entertained James I in 1614 on his visit to Cambridge, a "perspical" or telescope is used. Through it Pandolfo observes the Court at Cambridge (from London!) and sees Tom Coryat land at Dover: Pandolfo also used an "autocousticon" for long distance hearing. The play was revived in 1688 and Dryden wrote a prologue for it. A "vulgar" telescope and "perplexive" glasses also appear in Jonson's "*Masque of News from the Moon*".

like a development of the screw of Archimedes, which is not to say that Mr. Greatorex hadn't worked out a better one. His "quench fire" may or may not have proved useful during the Great Fire, but his varnish for paper was definitely not a success. It sank in.

Again, if in the time of James I many were intrigued by the attractive power of amber (elektron) and jet—the "vis electrica" of William Gilbert—by mid-century they were using the word electricity to describe it, a word first coined by Walter Charleton* in 1650, and by Queen Anne's day the great wonder was Francis Hauksbee's machine for producing frictional electricity. He called his device Autila. It served no known purpose but it did emit electric sparks and a crackling sound which, some thought, resembled thunder and lightning in miniature. Incidentally—or perhaps co-incidentally—in the very year the elder Hauksbee first demonstrated his machine a child, who was to grow up, fly a kite and by this discover the identity of lightning and electricity, was born to Josiah Franklin, a Banbury dyer who had emigrated to Boston probably in 1685. So the ludicra of art and science—the small toys, the tiny automata, the odd machines, great and small, which produced strange phenomena, or magic tricks far better than any conjuror's—served many useful purposes and, no doubt many useless ones too. They also attracted, as they always do, the crowds of the day.

Thus, even at the beginning of the Stuart era, fifty years before the foundation of the Royal Society, there was a steady stream of visitors of high and low degree who went to Eltham to see Cornelis Drebble's Perpetual Motion machine and on Thursday, May 1st, 1610, the twenty-four-year-old Lewis Frederick, Prince of Wirtemberg (we now spell it Württemberg) went to see it. Unfortunately he, or rather his secretary Jacob Würmsser, tells us nothing whatsoever about the Perpetual Motion. Perhaps

---

*Charleton, a physician interested in philosophical and antiquarian matters, wrote a number of pamphlets. One of them proved that Stonehenge was built by the Danes.

it was too difficult and baffling to describe or perhaps they were
both tired after seeing a performance of Shakespeare's *Othello* the
previous evening, but it was remarked with some surprise that
Drebble was handsome and had "gentle manners, altogether
different from such like characters".[6] Which suggests that
hitherto inventors had been more noted for their ugliness and
rudeness than for their ingenuity—or at any rate upon the
Continent. We are indebted to Thomas Tymme for a rather
muddled description of this famous machine which attracted so
much attention (Drebble presented one to James I, probably as
early as 1607). The description would be far less muddled had
Mr. Tymme not put it in the form of a dialogue, a favourite
literary device, between two imaginary characters "Theophrast".
and "Philadelp". Poor Philadelphus, a positively clay-brained
character, isn't very bright and acts as the interlocutor or end
man, yet it is possible to discover that this machine (maugre
Copernicus) "represented the motions of the heaven about the
fixed earth".

Standing in a temple-like structure of four columns surmounted
by a cupola was a hollow globe fitted with brass wheels and
supported by winged beasts. Pointers, seemingly held by the
figure of a man, indicated on the globe the month and year, like
a perpetual almanac. But more, the contrivance showed celestial
motion too—no matter how erroneously. A small globe perched
on top of the larger one showed the moon's aspects. A glass
tube filled with salt water described the circumference of the
larger, earthly globe, and the salt water, we are assured, rose
and fell with the tides. Philadelphus was so impressed with
Theophrastus's description of this that he felt the machine quite
effectively disproved Copernicus, and that the earth was indeed
stable and fixed. One cannot say just what led Philadelphus to
this astonishing conclusion from such "proof" but doubtless
Mr. Tymme, "Proffesour of Divinitie", felt the same way.
He was obviously a schoolman.

How did such a machine work without springs or weights?
—for we are told they weren't used. Theophrastus, ever helpful

and bent on displaying his scientific knowledge, tells the awed Philadelphus that the wheels were moved by "extracting a fiery spirit from mineral matter", this combined with air moved an axel tree which, in turn, moved the wheels. We are at liberty to doubt this "fiery spirit", but "mineral matter" suggests the secret may have been some form of magnetism. Drebble must have been familiar with Gilbert's* work and although he was often called sorcerer, magician, alchemist and even "ein charlatan" he was an able, intelligent Dutchman and an extremely good mathematician and mechanic. As to why the machine was called Perpetual Motion, since our idea of perpetual motion is rather different, it is probably because the movement of celestial bodies was "perpetual" and also because the movement of the wheels was so slow it was believed they would never wear out. They wouldn't rust out either, being doubly plated with gold. Alas, years later, when Dr. Wilkins wrote about Drebble's machine, the perpetual motion had long since ceased. But what a furore it once caused: "My very house turns round with the tumult! I dwell in a windmill! The Perpetual Motion is here and not at Eltham"[7] Morose cries, a topical reference which delighted contemporary theatre audiences. And certainly perpetual motion in another sense *was* here. The whole century is full of movement of one kind and another . . . political, religious, scientific.

In a narrower sphere, but one which was to have enormously

---

*William Gilbert, 1544-1603, the outstanding man of science in Elizabeth's reign, was a doctor, member of the Royal College of Physicians and, in 1601, personal physician to the Queen (salary of £100 per annum). He left his books, mss., instruments and minerals to the Royal College—all were destroyed in the Great Fire. His treatise on magnetism, *De magnete,* the first great scientific book published in England, opened the century. It contained an account of all his experiments on magnets, magnetic bodies and electrical attraction. He was the first to conceive of the earth as nothing but an enormous magnet and also first to advocate the views of Copernicus in England. Drebble, obviously, didn't hold with such views.

Isaac Newton's telescope, 1668.

important results later on, men were simply fascinated by what fire applied to water could do in moving things and in creating sounds. They were excited by the prospect of a boat which could move against tide or wind without the aid of oars or sail. They attempted—some say successfully—to fly. Francis Godwin wrote a wildly popular book, *The Man in the Moone.** Dr. Wilkins followed with one about the world in the moon and people reached it in imagination, as we seem about to in fact. They

*Probably the first book on space travel since Lucan, it was published posthumously in 1638. Dr. Wilkins is thought to have derived much of his material from it. Godwin's hero who reached the moon was a Spaniard, Domingo Gonsales. The book was so popular that it went on selling for a century or more and by 1768 had gone into twenty-five editions. There was also Jonson's *News from the Moon* (1620-21), but this was a court entertainment with a much more limited audience.

were vastly intrigued, too, by a ship which could be rowed and navigated under water (the diving bell was known but was rather unsafe). Drebble had fashioned one of these and he was "a very cunning man in nature's secrets" according to the Dutch Ambassador. The ship, which seems to have been a submersible rowing boat covered with well-greased leather, had oars protruding from leather valves and was tried out in the Thames between Greenwich and Westminster in 1620. It also appears to have been abandoned there. But, like Drebble's perpetual motion machine it caused much excitement:

> "It is an Automa, runnes under water,
> With a snug nose, and has a nimble taile
> Made like an auger, with which taile she wrigles
> Betwixt the coasts of a ship and sinkes it straight."[8]

This description is probably exaggerated, ironic and used for comic effect, but it leaves us in little doubt as to the purpose of the underwater ship. Robert Boyle writing in 1660, believed this submarine had functioned quite effectively. Although he had no first-hand knowledge of it (as he wasn't born when the trials took place) he investigated by talking to Drebble's daughter and son-in-law, Dr. Kuffler,* and received further information from a passenger who was still alive. What interested Boyle most was that Drebble was alleged to have invented a method of purifying air within the ship so that the passengers and the twelve rowers were not suffocated.

*Dr. Kuffler (Keffeler or Keifer or Knuffler) either inherited his father-in-law's secret for making red dye, or invented it himself. It was known as "Kuffeler's colour" also as "Bow dye" as the first dye house for that particular colour was set up at Bow. Evelyn and Pepys both visited him, the latter on several occasions in '62 and '63 and wasn't very impressed with his engine for blowing up ships. Evelyn saw him later in 1666 when he examined portable iron ovens Kuffler had made for the Prince of Orange's Army. At the time of this visit we were at war with the Dutch.

Of Innovations and Knacks

A submarine, however, can hardly be called a knack, although it may have seemed like a conjuring trick or an invention of the devil. Nor do contrivances whereby Drebble could make it rain to the accompaniment of thunder and lightning or, in summer, refrigerate the atmosphere, sound particularly knack-like. The refrigerating trick was exhibited to King James in Westminster Hall and it became so cold that James and his party hastily fled . . . or so we are told. Yet no one seems to have thought of applying this machine, or whatever it was, to the preservation of food during summer.

More of a knack was an instrument which sounds suspiciously like a T.V. set whereby one could see pictures and portraits of anyone anywhere in the world. This may just possibly have been a magic lantern (of which more later) or it may have been a camera obscura making use of reflected pictures and drawings. But as far as I know no one had the magic looking-glass which Henry VII is said to have owned wherein he could see what was happening anywhere at any time. This must have been of supreme value to him both before and after he defeated Richard III. Unfortunately, on the day Henry died the glass shattered to bits "of itself". Subsequent Tudors had to rule blind, as it were, until Walsingham invented the secret service.

A more widely known and accessible if less useful knack must have been "a conceited lamp for forcing water through the figure of a bird".[9] Here a tiny boiler concealed within a crown on which the bird sat, was filled with water and set over a multi-wick lamp. The water was "converted into air" (steam) which was forced out through very small tubes and valves inside the bird. It wasn't a very new knack though, Heron of Alexandria had shown how to make the same thing nineteen centuries before. But that remarkable man the second Marquis of Worcester claims that he could make an artificial bird fly and there is no reason to disbelieve him as an automatic peacock which walked, ate corn, and excreted it was invented by a French general in the 1680's. Regiomontanus, whose real name was Johann Müller, much earlier made an artificial eagle and had also constructed an iron fly which would buzz about a table—or so it was believed. These were but his knacks, his ludicra. More importantly, and with the aid of his rich patron, Regiomontanus is said to have equipped the first Observatory in Europe where in 1472 he had observed Halley's comet,* without benefit of telescope. Drebble claimed—or it was claimed for him—to have invented the telescope too. He didn't. But it *was* invented by a Dutchman or several Dutchmen perhaps, around the turn of the century. Prince Maurice of Nassau was quick to realize its military uses and fervently hoped that the new invention could be kept from his enemies, as it gave him a tactical advantage. It was a vain hope as all such hopes are.

In Italy a professor of mathematics heard or read of the invention, constructed a telescope for himself, pointed it skywards and gave the schoolmen a monstrous shock by discovering the Pleiades numbered not seven but forty. He also saw four moons circling Jupiter and worse, claimed that the sun had spots! This, in particular, agitated his contemporaries greatly. The sun, as everyone knew, was, like God, perfect: without spot or blemish. To suggest it was maculate verged on madness or heresy. Galileo Galilei was obviously a dangerous man. what would he say next? What he said next was published in 1632 under the title *Dialogo dei due massimi sistemi del mondo*. This threw theologians and ecclesiastical authorities into a panic. It threatened to shatter their world to bits.

Christopher Wren was born in the year Galileo's book was published. Wren improved the apertures of the telescope so that it could let in more or less light "as the observer pleases" by opening and shutting "like the pupil of an eye".[10] But it was Halley's friend, Isaac Newton, born in the year Galileo died who,

---

*Edmund Halley observed it in 1682. It has been seen twenty-six times since 12 B.C., is depicted in the Bayeux Tapestry and is due next in 1986. Halley paid for the publication of Newton's "*Principia*", climbed Snowdon, explored the Atlantic, described the Trade Winds, is the "father" of physical geography, and originator of the science of life statistics.

Of Innovations and Knacks

in 1688, designed the first telescope where a concave mirror replaced the object glass. Newton's improvement is the remote parent of the giant astronomic telescope at Palomar, just as in Newton's laws of motion lie the seeds of Einstein's theory of the space-time continuum. "I do not know", said Newton shortly before his death, "what I may appear to the world, but to myself I seem to have been only like a boy playing on the sea-shore, and diverting myself in now and then, finding a smoother pebble or a prettier shell than ordinary, while the great ocean of truth lay all undiscovered before me".*[11]

But to return to that man of bewilderingly many parts, Christopher Wren. As a member of the singular circle at Wadham which during the Civil Wars concerned itself with the New Philosophy rather than with the New Government, Wren developed a number of theories and inventions,† "some of which on the return of the Publick Tranquility, were improved and perfected".[12] The fifty-three "Theories, Inventions, Experiments and Mechanick Improvements" catalogued by his son, range very widely from a "Hypothesis of the Moon's Libation, in Solid" to "A Way of Imbroidery for Beds, Hangings, cheap and fair"—which seems rather a far cry from St. Paul's Cathedral. But certainly cheap and fair curtains and hangings had more than a "tendency toward use". By their very cheapness they would benefit and improve trade in domestic and foreign markets, and it was Robert Boyle who pointed out that "the Goods of Mankind may be much increased by the Naturalist's (scientist's) Insight into Trade". The experimental or natural philosophers of the Royal Society were "economists as well as

*Newton, born on Christmas Day 1642 died on March 20th, 1727. His eighty-five years begin in the reign of Charles I and end three months before George II succeeded his father.

†It is said Henry Oldenburg, first Secretary of the Royal Society, "with Disingenuity and Breach of Trust" communicated secretly with friends in Germany and France many of Wren's experiments and inventions and that these were unfairly claimed by others and published abroad under other names. In 1667 Oldenburg was imprisoned for political correspondence.

scientists'' and so were concerned with the means of ''increasing the output of various commodities, or of heightening the efficiency of technical processes''.[13]

Wren, like Drebble, also invented a ''Perpetual Motion or weather wheel and weather clock compounded''. He worked out the correct temperature for hatching eggs, insects and ''plants'' by means of ''long lived lamps'', as did others, and he, too, was interested in ''Ways of Submarine Navigation''. We also find in the catalogue a way ''To stay long under water'' and a ''Strainer of the Breath, to make the same Aire serve in Respiration''. But in view of a letter which Wren received in 1658 from the versatile Thomas Sprat D.D. (later Bishop of Rochester) the strainer may not have had anything whatsoever to do with submarine navigation.

Dr. Sprat wrote to tell his colleague of the sad condition of Gresham College. Due to its use as a barracks by Parliamentary soldiers, it was ''in such a nasty condition, so defil'd and the Smells so infernal'' that only Dr. Goddard* still stayed on which, says Dr. Sprat ''he could never be able to do, had he not before prepar'd his nose for Camp Perfumes, by his voyage into Scotland'' and, he adds with a touch of negligent malice ''had he not such excellent Restoratives in his Cellar''. Wren quite undaunted by the evil odours—even though it was still believed they bred diseases—returned as soon as possible to Gresham College and his ''Tube''.

But while astronomers scanned the heavens others were busy with the minutiae of the micro-cosmic world, for the development of the compound, as opposed to the simple, microscope took place in this century. Invented, perhaps, by Hans or Zach-

*Dr. Jonathan Goddard, F.R.C.P., inventor of the famous or infamous drops which nearly killed the infant son of James II, was appointed Gresham professor of physics in 1655. He had earlier accompanied Cromwell to Scotland and to Ireland. As he had been a member of the Barebones Parliament and of the council of state he, presumably, might have been able to prevent Gresham College being used as barracks and stable. Goddard also defended those physicians who left London during the plague.

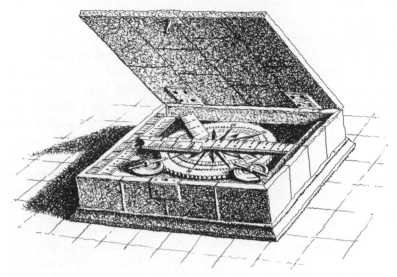

Early calculating machine, 1663.

arias Janssen sometime in the last decade of the previous century, it wasn't much used here until after the Restoration. Then the new science of micrology really got under way in England. With the microscope, as Henry Power (1623-68), physician, naturalist and one time practitioner in Halifax put it:

"In the wood-mite or -louse you may behold
An eye of trellice work in burnisht gold."

It may not be a very good couplet for an age which perfected the couplet but it has a fresh wonder, delight and excitement which most of us felt when, as children, we looked into a microscope for the very first time. And this is precisely what the seventeenth century was doing.* The "disregarded pieces and

*On Aug. 13th, 1664 Pepys notes "home to read a little in Dr. Power's book of discovery by the microscope to enable me a little how to use and what to expect of my glass". He had bought this "most curious bauble" only that afternoon. It was "the best in England" but cost "a great price"—£5.10.0.

huslement of Creation''[14] became a new, miraculous, undreamed of world.

Of the five great microscopists of the time, two were English —Nehemiah Grew who recognized the sexuality of plants, and Robert Hooke who, to the vast amusement of Samuel Butler, examined a louse and quite plainly perceived "a small current of blood, which came directly from its snout and passed into its belly". Hooke's microscope gave a magnification of about 100 diameters. Today the electron microscope, which doesn't work on an optical system at all, magnifies by 30,000 diameters and is so much beyond the understanding and pocket and house-room of most of us that it cannot be left carelessly about to entertain our guests, ourselves and our children. But in the late seventeenth century microscopes became almost as popular, among those who could afford them, as Kaleidoscopes and Stereoscopes were in Victorian times. Who could resist that beautiful and hitherto unsuspected jewel with which the Lord had so distinguished the common wood-louse?

The microscope cannot be classed as a "knack" yet even when used by amateurs solely, and in that sense, for amusement it must have contributed to the general knowledge of the day. In the more obviously knackish line, if less likely to advance learning (and of this we can never be sure), was an imprisoning chair made "à la mode" which, when an unsuspecting visitor sat down in it, immediately locked the sitter in a strong un-breakable embrace . . . to the great merriment of all present. It was even funnier when the apparatus couldn't be made to go into reverse. Such chairs had been known in Italy for some time and one cannot but feel that there is a slightly Borgia touch about the whole idea. Sir William Batten, Surveyor of the Navy, who lived "like a prince" at Walthamstow had such a chair among his "great store of rareties". He called it King Harry's chair—for reasons unknown to me—and Pepys thought it very good sport to be "catched with two irons".[15]

Then there was the "Untoothsome Pear", invented by that strange genius Edward Somerset, second Marquis of Worcester

(who, surprising as it may seem, invented the steam engine*
and also a "semi-omnipotent engine" which he so loved he
wanted it buried with him). This was a metal ball shaped like a
plum or pear which "being dexterously conveyed or forced
into a bodies mouth" shot out innumerable bolts all round.
Nothing could remove the pear but a key. The ball couldn't be
filed off or extracted unless, possibly, the victim's teeth were
extracted too—if any remained after dexterously conveying
or forcing the strange fruit into the victim's mouth. I am at a
loss to know what purpose such a prankish invention served.
It cannot have been much of a weapon and certainly as a practical
joke it must have been excruciatingly un-funny.

More useful was a pocket engine which placed on any door
would open it noiselessly save for one "crack". Had it not
been for that one sharp sound the noble innovator could have
become the patron saint of house-breakers. He also made a key
which would turn into a pistol; and "a most conceited tinder
box" with which one could light a candle or fire at any time of
night without even putting a hand out of bed. This too, could
be turned into a "serviceable pistol" at pleasure. And here we
can perhaps see the beginning of the modern cigarette lighter.

The tinder box pistol was not quite so wonderful as an alarm
clock invented by an Italian, which would waken one at any
hour of the night and, as it struck the predetermined hour,
it also struck fire from a flint which fell into a tinder box,
enabling one to light a candle at once. This doesn't seem so very
far removed from our useful if hideous modern clocks which
boil water, make tea and waken us when it is ready.

But the less sophisticated probably still contented themselves

*This Fire Water-Work was seen by many at Vauxhall in 1670 and
possibly earlier—"one vessel of water rarefied by fire driveth up forty
(feet) of cold water" (see Henry Dircks' biography of the Marquis
published 1865). The steam engine exhibited by Savery in 1699 and
described in "Philosophical Transactions" (1702) seems to have been
an exact counterpart of Worcester's invention. Savery's engine was in
use by the first decade of the eighteenth century. It pumped water out
of coal pits.

with such simple knacks as "engraving" pictures and messages on eggs, an idea suggested by Sir Hugh Platt in 1594 but which continued to be popular for another fifty or sixty years. Dip an egg in melted suet, allow it to harden, then, with a needle make the drawing, or if not talented in that way write a message or motto upon the coated egg "leaving the shell bare at the bottom of the work". Then place the egg in good wine vinegar for six or eight hours; next, dip in warm water to get rid of the congealed suet and there to the astonishment and amazement of your friends, is your handiwork looking for all the world as if it had been "graven" on the delicate shell. This knack, admittedly, is neither quick nor surprising but at least it has the merit of being inoffensive and inexpensive and it will still amuse the not too sophisticated child. A quick trick was to make an egg stand on end, a trick which it is said, Columbus showed Ferdinand and Isabella and which proved to their satisfaction that the world was round, just as Drebble's Perpetual Motion proved to poor, idiotic Philadelphus that it was firmly fixed. The knack is to shake the egg so violently that the yolk breaks and becomes mixed with the white within and the egg miraculously will stand on its big end.

Far more astounding, although probably not to be recommended as a party game, was to stir a cauldron of boiling lead with the hand, a knack known principally to conjurors and the like. At that time it required a protective ointment made of "bole armoniack", camphire, aqua vitae and quicksilver. Platt once saw a Dutchman called "Hance" perform this feat in a garden in Southwark. He was "a pretty nimble chymist" but all he charged for obliging was a pot of the best beer. This is still one of the experiments which children like most when they attend the Christmas lectures at the Royal Institution in Albemarle Street (or at least it was a favourite twenty years ago).

But probably the best scientific knack of all, from the point of entertainment, was the magic lantern. Who first invented it we cannot say with any certainty. Like so many things it just grew over the centuries and appeared simultaneously in various countries. A German Jesuit, Kircher, seems to have laid a claim to its discovery in 1646 and found it necessary to explain that it was not the work of the devil, but the result of contemplation. But the principle was known long before this and may even have been the means whereby Drebble showed princes and people of foreign lands to his wide-eyed visitors.

It may be that such things were disapproved of as devilish works under the Commonwealth; in any event, magic lanterns don't appear to be very general until after the Restoration. Pictures painted on long strips of glass could be shown sequentially and in next to no time the lantern was being used for plays. By the early eighteenth century the mechanically-moved slide was invented and this by producing quick movement, gave life to the picture. The principal is basically the same as that of the cinematograph, but in the seventeenth century the magic lantern must have been the equivalent of TV in the homes of the well-to-do.

Outside the home it may even have been the equivalent of the cinema—at least for those who subscribed to the *Daily Courant*. For on Monday, February 20th, 1709/10 readers of our first daily were drawn by an advertisement inviting them to "A Moving-Picture" which was to be seen daily at the Duke of Marlborough's Head, a tavern in Salisbury Court, Fleet Street. It must have been very gratifying to know that this "MOVING-PICTURE, intirely new" far exceeded "the German Picture formerly shewn at the same House in the Opinion of all who have yet seen it". Obviously, anything the Germans could do we could do better, and people flocked to see the advertised programme which included "a most noble Landskip finely painted by the best Hand, it contains the prospect of a City with a Harbour; a large extent of Land with a River winding and running into the Sea; a Bridge leading to the City; and near 70 figures in lively Motion: viz. Several stately Ships and Vessels sailing; a Coach and 4 Horses; a Gentleman in a Chair saluting the Company; a Cart; a Windmill; Swans whose motions are to the Life; a Man diging [sic] Gravel; Gentlemen on Horseback; Huntsmen and Dogs; Shepherds and Cattle; Milkmaids, &c. Nothing but the Sight can give a right Notion of this curious Piece of Art". This, of course, may not have been a magic lantern show, it may have been produced by a camera obscura; it is difficult to say which was responsible. But "going to the Pictures" is not new to our century.

Mr. Reeves, the perspective glass-maker, must have done very well out of this new craze for magic lanterns. As far back as Sunday, August 19th, 1666 he and Mr. Spong spent the afternoon and evening with Sam Pepys. Reeves had brought with him "a lanthorn, with pictures in glass, to make strange things appear on a wall, very pretty". They spent the afternoon talking about optics and the evening observing Jupiter—girdle, satellites and all—with Pepys' twelve-foot telescope. By August 22nd, Pepys, unable to resist the temptation of a "lanthorn that shows tricks", had bought it, a little perspective and a telescope for a total cost of £9.5.0. Pepys himself seems to have invented the pocket slide rule which he had specially made in 1663 by Mr. Browne the mathematical instrument maker or, as he says, "I have myself the honour of being the inventor of the form of of it", meaning its small size. But instruments were getting smaller anyway and, for the benefit of those whose interest was chronic and genuine or perhaps for the rich, fashionable show-off, telescopes and microscopes were sometimes combined with walking sticks; quadrants with tobacco boxes, and slide rules with snuff boxes.

The slide rule seems to have been invented in England by Edmund Gunter, perhaps in 1620, or by William Oughtred who claims he showed the idea to Gunther in 1618. Oughtred (1574-1660), "that was an Honour to the English Nation"[16] was Vicar of Albury, Surrey for fifty years, father of nine sons and four daughters, neighbour of Elias Ashmole and teacher of Christopher Wren, Charles Scarborough and John Wallis (Anne Blencowe's father). He was also an Astrologer, and from the "calculation of coincidence with the diluvian period"[17] anticipated some extraordinary event in 1656, such as the conversion of the Jews. He was wrong about the conversion but, in 1656 Cromwell, always more liberal than this Council, at last managed to persuade his Councillors to allow Jews to settle in England (this was his fourth try), permit them to hold private services, and to buy a cemetery outside London.

Oughtred, country people believed, could "conjure" (i.e. raise spirits), but this was perhaps due to his strange habits as well as to his reputation as an astrologer and mathematician. He was so entirely devoted to mathematics that he kept an ink horn on his bed staff and often stayed up night after night working out some problem, forgetting, even, to appear for meals. Clearly this lack of interest in food was so abnormal and impossible that Oughtred must have had supernatural sources of sustenance. His reputation as mathematician was far greater abroad than at home, and when learned foreigners came to see him they were horrified that so famous a man should live in near penury and appear in an extremely ancient cloth cassock and an old-fashioned russet hat which had been a Beaver* in Elizabeth's day, but which had long since lost its "fur".

Foreigners were, of course, foreigners and quite incapable of understanding that this was—and is—all part of the English-ness of the English. Oughtred did not live long enough to discover the Philosopher's elixir in which he became interested, rather too late in life. He died of joy—aged eighty-six—at the return of Charles II—or so his great friend Mr. Ralph Greatorex said. Oughtred invented trigonometrical abbreviations and introduced the signs for multiplication and proportion which we still use.

Mathematics were then a great source of pleasure and re-creation and all sorts of people devoted themselves to the subject

---

*Beavers were made of real or imitation beaver fur. A peach-coloured beaver (obviously imitation) cost £2 in Elizabeth's day. Pepys' Beaver cost £4.5.0. My navy school beaver cost $1.75 (7/-) (£ = $5 then). I remember the price only because it was eaten by a bear at a circus in Chicago and my grandmother had to buy me a new one. It seemed a fantastic price for so horrid a hat. School beavers now cost around 30/-.

with the zest we now reserve for crossword puzzles. But terrible quarrels arose over "Arithmeticall Problems". Thomas Hobbes, who fell in love with Geometry at the age of forty, was sure he had squared the circle. Dr. Wallis "that egregious lyer and backbiter"[18] was equally sure he hadn't. The acrimonious dispute between them rose to such a pitch that the only thing John Aubrey was sure of, was that their "Mercuries" were in "opposition". Astronomers, in particular, were wildly keen

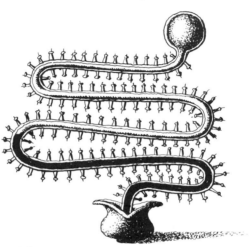

Thermoscope, parent of the thermometer.

to find some mechanical means of coping with figures. The first "counter" outside of that quinary system kindly provided by nature in the shape of fingers and toes, was the abacus, which in its later frame form is still used in many parts of the world today with great speed and accuracy. Counting by pebbles or stones (Latin *calculi*, hence our calculus) cast upon a lined board or table was nothing new—we still "cast accounts", "borrow" and "carry"—but the idea of counting by means of little numbered "rods" was very new. Credit for this goes to John Napier (1550-1617) laird of Merchiston who, as even the most tiresome of schoolboys knows, invented a new method of calculation, in 1614, called logarithms and "by them all troublesome

multiplications and divisions are avoided".* Napier also introduced or developed a notation for decimal fractions but Napier's
rods or "Napier's bones" as they were commonly called (still to
be seen in the Science Museum) provided a mechanical way of
dealing with large numbers. Without logarithms the slide
rule would not have been possible, while Napier's "artificial
numbers", as logarithms were first called, were a great boon to
astronomers. Napier was a brilliant mathematician and a most
zealous Calvinist but he, too, was thought to be a magician and this
seems to have had nothing to do with mathematical magic. He was
credited with having a black cock (his family were hereditary
Poulterers to the King) which possessed the faculty of being
able to keep him informed of the thoughts of his servants.
This must have been even handier than knowing about logarithms
since in those days servants, and lots of them, were the rule
rather than the exception—for the rich.

Napier, like Drebble and others, was also interested in
"devises for sayling under water". But his greatest success was
a book on the Revelations of St. John. It was a best seller and,
not surprisingly, was far more popular than his mathematical
works. In this revealing book which went through twenty
editions, he "calculated" that the "day of God's judgment"
would probably fall between the years 1688 and 1700. There must
have been many people who in 1688 believed this prediction
had come true.

But the end of the world—or the landing of William of
Orange—was still a dozen years ahead when Sir Samuel Morland
(1625-95) produced the first English calculating machine,
worked by wheels or dials, and presented it to Charles II. In
fairness, it must be said that Morland was not the first inventor,
Blaise Pascal—at nineteen—had produced one (in 1642) to
help his father, who as Steward of Rouen was greatly concerned
with the collection of taxes and patently needed help. But

*So says Henry Briggs in his *Arithmetica Logarithmica*, the fundamental
book on logarithms first published 1624. Later edition 1631 in
English.

Morland's "arithmetical wheels" were the first of their kind in England.* Evelyn saw them when he was visiting Moreland in July together with his new harp and his "quench fires".

Morland was a typical product of the century. Diplomat, mathematician, assistant to Cromwell's Secretary Thurloe and, later, firm promoter of the Restoration, he wrote on mathematics and hydrostatics, invented a "speaking trumpet", a plunger pump which raised water to the top of Windsor Castle, and a handy screw bridge for Lord Arlington's gardens at Euston house. He also experimented with high-pressed steam which he even suggested as a means of propelling vessels. In 1692 he went blind and this led him to invent a method of writing and a wooden calendar "which instructed him all by feeling".[19] Just before his death, poor man, he was afflicted with such melancholy that he buried £200 worth of love songs six feet underground in his garden at Lambeth because they were "vanity", and thereafter consoled himself with psalms and hymns which he played upon the theorbo (a sort of bass lute).

Because there was a great surge of interest in calculation and measuring by mechanical means, sooner or later the mileometer or "Way Wiser", as Wren called the one he devised, became inevitable. Wren's Way Wiser, presented to the Royal Society by Dr. Wilkins, had five indexes and measured in perches, furlongs, miles, tens of miles and hundreds of miles. It was fitted into a space cut into the axel tree, which was "made hollow". Through this ran a hollow rod fastened at one end to the nave of the wheel so that it turned with the wheel. At the other end a "worm" was fixed and this turned the perch cog, which turned the other wheels. The idea was not new— few things are. Vitruvius mentions something very similar† and Commodus, one of the viler of the Roman Emperors, reputedly had several carriages which measured the road and pointed out the hours. There is also a device which appears to

---

*Also in the Science Museum: South Kensington.

†The Hodometer—to calculate distance by land or sea (Book X: Chapter 9).

be a way wiser carved among the warlike trophies in the Ducal
Palace at Urbino, built in the fifteenth century. But way wisers
of various sorts began to appear in the sixteenth century and became less rare in the seventeenth. Colonel Blount, in 1657,
had a "very pretty and useful"[20] way wiser attached to his
coach and may have invented it himself, as he was an ingenious
innovator. This innovation must have proved ultimately useful
to everyone because mechanical measuring of miles must have
helped to do away with local variations which so annoyed
Celia Fiennes when she made her northern journey on horseback
somewhere around 1697. Having visited the sixth of the seven
wonders of Derbyshire, known to the robust—and the Puritan
Celia was certainly not squeamish—as the "Devil's Arse"*
Celia notes, "From Castleton to Buxton is 6 miles, but they are
very long, you might go ten miles near London as soon as you
are going halfe so many here". Much of the north country still
favoured the "old British" mile or long mile of 2,428 yards
although the statute mile had been fixed more than a hundred
years before Celia decided to "do" England on horseback. This
was no mean feat with roads as they were; and unorthodox too
—gentlewomen almost invariably travelled long distances by
coach. But coaches and carriages were in dire need of improvement and there were many who attempted this. Some tried new
ways of braking, others means of releasing the horses quickly
when they bolted as they so often did, while others tried their
hand at improving springs. But the greatest innovation was
probably the use of glass to replace leather curtains, though if
a glass coach or carriage overturned—by no means an infrequent
occurrence—one might be sliced to ribbons. This cannot have

*This famous peak is topped by Peveril Castle below which a narrow
cleft leads into a cave. Here, Miss Fiennes noted "were several poor
little houses in it built of stone and thatched like little Styes". Defoe
gives a fuller description of the cave and its inhabitants in Letter VIII
of his "Circuits". He seems to have thought our ancestors rather
coarse for having thought of "so homely a sirname" for the sixth
wonder, while the Victorians thought Defoe worse than coarse for
having thought up Moll Flanders.

been so very much worse than being sliced to bits by a winter wind and rain—still, in winter, one could have a foot-warmer. Foot-warmers more often than not were metal-lined wooden boxes into which very hot pieces of iron were inserted. They must have weighed a figurative ton. Nevertheless, a foot-warmer was also useful when working away in a quiet and bitterly cold study or library in the country house you'd happily built or unfortunately inherited; or in London where the smoke from a sea-coal fire ruined books, papers, eyesight and bronchial tubes.

Men were interested in measuring and calculating things other than distance. Heat, cold, rainfall, barometric pressure, the age of the earth, body weight in varying circumstances, population and even the volume of trade came under the inquiring mind and the inquisitive eye of the century. All this measuring, however, required new tools of one kind or another and the seventeenth century gave us many of the basic tools—or improved upon existing ones—with which we are, for better or for worse, continuing the job.

More often than not, these new or improved tools and instruments had very little immediate use in ordinary, domestic life "for Time is the greatest Innovatour" and "Innovateth greatly but quietly, and by degrees scarce to be perceived".[21] For example, in the previous century the table fork was introduced into England, but forks were an extra-corporeal tool of the rich and not of the poor or even of the middling sort. If we examine farm and cottage inventories forks are scarcely ever mentioned even by the end of the seventeenth century—the first mention among the less well-to-do in mid-Essex comes as late as 1725. Similarly, the thermometer—which made its first appearance around the same time as the table fork—played no part in hospital routine until mid-Victorian times. This is not really surprising. Small thermometers were then about a foot long and were "small" only because they had been even longer and often strangely curved when first introduced. These were hardly thermometers as we know them. They were air thermoscopes; a hollow glass globe or bulb drawn out into a straight or curly

Early hearing trumpets of glass.

open-ended tube. When the bulb was heated and the tube's open end was thrust into a small basin of water, the water rose in the tube as the bulb cooled. By repeated heatings and coolings, alterations in water level could be measured. This was a not very accurate way of noting temperature changes; such thermometers were affected by atmospheric pressure as well as by temperature. That very great "Sceptical Chymist" Robert Boyle* made this quite clear with what we call "Boyle's Law" —the law which stated the relationship between the pressure and volume of gas. Liquids were not so affected and in time the liquid thermometer came into being. Ferdinand II, Grand Duke of Tuscany and father of Cosimo III, is believed to have been the first scientist to seal the end of the tube. He also had a unique thermometer small enough to fit into his pocket, so that particular tube must have been sealed. Even more daringly he

*Boyle who invented the word barometer was sceptical only about the old methods of the alchemists; divorce proceedings between science and religion had not then started and Boyle, one of the greatest of our natural philosophers, was also deeply interested in theology. Through his will he founded the Boyle lectures for the proving the Christian religion against "notorious infidels"—with the wise proviso that controversies between Christians were not to be mentioned.

substituted coloured alcohol for water. By the second half of the seventeenth century the Florentines—who were certainly among the most notable spagyrists and operators of the day—were using mercury. In England, Isaac Newton took to using linseed oil in his thermometers and seems to have been the first to construct a scale of degrees. It is almost impossible for us to imagine a time when there was no agreement as to scale, and when degree itself meant steps in a ladder, or position in the social scale. But, probably in the year of Queen Anne's death, G. D. Fahrenheit solved the problem when he devised his scale based on zero (taken to be $32°$ below the freezing point of water) and $96°$ (three times that of the freezing point) as the blood heat of the body. This is $2·4°$ less than our standard of normal, which doesn't mean we are more hot blooded but merely that measurements have become more accurate. Still, few physicians could have used these early thermometers as diagnostic instruments even if they'd seen the possibilities.* If a person had one of the fevers so common to the times the physician could tell by look and feel, provided the fever was severe enough. But the small daily rise in temperature indicative perhaps of a low grade infection or T.B. would have escaped him. Even if it hadn't there was little to be done about it.

Two other inventions, which must have seemed little more than "knacks" at the time, made their appearance in the last half of the century. Robert Hooke, a disagreeable but very great scientist who invented among other things the hair spring and marine barometer, demonstrated in 1667 that a string stretched taut between two diaphragms would carry the voice privately—a demonstration which most certainly gave this twentieth-century child much joy when it turned up as a toy one Christmas. But this demonstration of Hooke's also demon-

*In France, the physician Jean Rey used the thermometer for clinical purposes in 1633 but as bulb and stem were partly filled with water and the end unsealed, evaporation must have led to very partial and inaccurate conclusions. There was also no constriction just above the bulb to prevent a too rapid drop of the water.

strated the principle of the telephone, although it was not until 209 years later that time and Alexander Graham Bell made full use of Hooke's idea.

The invention of the typewriter, or rather an attempt to invent one, belongs to the last year of Queen Anne's reign. On January 7th, 1714, she granted a patent to one Henry Mill, later engineer to the New River Water Company—the company which Anne's great-grandfather had helped found—for "An Artificial Machine or Method for Impressing or Transcribing Letters Single or Progressively one after another, as in Writing, whereby all Writing whatever may be Engrossed in Paper or Parchment so Neat and Exact as not to be distinguished from print". As far as I know this machine was never manufactured but the patent provides a very accurate description of just what a typewriter does.

A typewriter would have been a boon to a century in which people wrote letters, kept diaries, household accounts and recipe books in far greater quantity than in any previous century, and when women added to literary output with biographies of their husbands, plays, and reams of indifferent poetry. Paper and ink are recurring items in every account book and fortunately both were improved. Ink could now be prevented from freezing in winter by the addition of aqua vitae and from going rancid in summer by adding salt or salt water—in passing it is interesting to note that in 1684 Narcissus Luttrell says a patent was granted a person who "invented a way to make salt sea water fresh in great quantity". When ink silted up in inkhorn or standish it was thinned down with gall water—much better than plain, old-fashioned water, beer, vinegar or wine. There was even powdered ink made of copperas, gum arabic and gall finely sifted. This was kept in a box in a warm dry place and when liquid ink was needed whatever liquid one fancied was added. Pencils, as we know them, had been known since the previous century when black graphite was discovered in the northern counties, although few seem to have used a pencil for writing. Pens were still quill pens—metal pens were known and had been known for a long time, but they were rare and so inflexible that it must have been like trying to write with the point of a dagger. It is just possible that some sort of fountain pen was known. Pepys, who wrote a prodigious amount, records a reservoir pen. He also had a silver pen, but it may have been a quill with a silver band or perhaps he means a "penner"—a silver carrier for several quills with ink pot attached. Since quills are hollow it must have been fairly easy to fill the hollow with ink. But quills are also very perishable and leaky so we haven't an example of a reservoir pen left (at least I can't find one) to show us how the flow was controlled. Possibly a wax plug pierced with a small hole was inserted into the open end of the quill or perhaps the whole reservoir pen was of hollow metal—but here I am quite frankly, guessing.

With so much writing going on there was a great interest too in ways of making extra copies of things written, or drawn, and the century is full of ideas for "double writing". It is also full of ideas on how to communicate by cyphers, shorthand, colours, sound, and light. John Aubrey, one of the original Fellows of the Royal Society and the discoverer of Avebury, worked with Andrew Paschall, Rector of Chedzoy, Somerset, on a phonetic alphabet, although he feared some might "looke upon it as a Whim-wham". Sir Hugh Platt (who invented alphabet blocks) suggested an alphabet for secret communication which could be used in a roomful of people. Vowels were indicated by pointing to thumb and finger of the left hand, consonants by "gestures, countenances or actions". One could make up one's own, but to illustrate the sort of thing he means, Platt suggests "an hem for a B", a cross on the forehead for a "C" and a "fillip" for a "D". The flaw here would appear to be that those who indulged in this method of secret communication in a roomful of people must have looked to the uninitiated very much as if they were suffering from some mild mania or a nervous affliction closely allied to St. Vitus's dance. Platt, however, did suggest that this means of communicating was necessary for "such as lack their speech".

Of Innovations and Knacks

Finger speech or "Arthrology", as it was called, was more usefully served by George Dalgarno in his *Deaf and Dumb Man's Tutor* published in 1680. Earlier, this Aberdonian had published a treatise *Ars Signorum* or *A Universal Character or Philosophic Language* and a philosophic language was the great dream of Bishop Wilkins's life. He wanted to invent a scientific esperanto of symbols *A Real Character and a Philosophical Language*.

Even the Royal Society was interested in the possibilities of improving English or in creating a flexible picture-word language for philosophical purposes. The century had been struck absolutely voluble with amazement at the discovery of the Chinese script which substituted word symbols for sounds. This meant that the Chinese, whose spoken language varied greatly from district to district, could nevertheless read the same texts. Two Chinese, neither of whom could understand a single word the other said could yet communicate by writing. The written work of the whole of China was available to every educated Chinese. The utility (or propaganda value) of such symbol or pictograph "language" was readily seen. It would facilitate intercourse with various nations and be of immense benefit to trade and commerce. It would help in civilizing barbarous countries and would enormously facilitate the propagation of the Gospel. (The SPCK and SPG were both founded in the seventeenth century.) Already there was a common language not only of algebraic symbols but of simple arithmetic. Two plus two equals four and when written thus, $2+2=4$, was a system of notation understood by all of any education whether two was pronounced "deux", "due", "zwei" or "twa"—as in the sisters of Binnorie. It had its limitations however. You cannot use the system to ask the way to Rome or Canterbury if you happen to be a stranger in Italy or England, or to request a room at the inn and a cut off the joint. Though of course, really well-educated people were rarely lost abroad. Provided they could find an equally well-educated person they could converse in Latin.

But with new ideas, new experiments, new discoveries,

Latin was not a sufficiently flexible medium of universal communication. It was not very useful in civilizing barbarians. Besides, to spread the gospels in Latin no doubt smacked of popery. In addition, there were so many different flexions for one and the same functions, so many ambiguous prefixes to say nothing of declensions, sex, and conjugations that Latin posed problems for savages who for some quite obscure reason found even English difficult. But Wilkins was less interested in helping trade, and propagating the gospel by his new logographic language, than in making all scientific and philosophical knowledge available to all men everywhere through an "algebra of thought". He failed. His system of translating "notions" into symbols rather than sounds was too involved, too rigid (he attempted to put all branches of human knowledge into forty pigeon-holes). But if he failed he failed nobly, and he, together with Dalgarno (and Leibnitz), triggered off the movement which, early in the eighteenth century led to the *Systema Naturae* of Linnaeus. This, in the end, led to the creation of an international vocabulary of classification and finally to a revision of chemical terminology which made scientific discoveries, no matter who discovered them or where, as immediately and universally understandable to scientists as $2+2=4$ is to us. Scientists thereafter could and did speak to each other by such symbols. The "secrets of nature", when discovered, were communicated freely and in this sense the natural philosopher or scientist was a Universalist. It must be bewildering in our changed world for scientists to find themselves gaoled for doing what their ancestors had done for centuries. To explore nature's secrets to add to the sum total of knowledge, this was once the true aim of free scientists and natural philosophers.

Francis Godwin (1562-1633) was not an experimental philosopher. He was Bishop of Llandaff and Hereford* and the son of a Bishop. Possibly this provided the inspiration for his *Catalogue*

*His grandson Morgan was a minister in Virginia and in 1680 he published "*The Negro's and Indian's Advocate suing for their Admission into the Church*".

Of Innovations and Knacks

of the Bishops of England, and his *Historie from the Beginning of Henry VIII to Quene Elizabeth* of which John Chamberlain says, "I heare not much of yt either en bien nor en mal".[22] But the new wonders of the new century, the innovations and knacks, the perpetual motion machines, the *vis electrica* of the early years of the Stuart era must have fired his imagination in a way that

Nocturnal astronomical instrument for finding the time at night.

the lives of the three middle Tudors and of long dead English Bishops—no matter how splendid or sordid—never could. And so he wrote his famous book, *The Man in the Moone*.

Avidly read for a century, the opening pages of this book must have astonished our Stuart ancestors as much as 300 very odd years later they astonish us—but for other reasons; "You shall then see men flie from place to place in the ayre;" he writes, "you shall be able (without moving or travailing of any creature) to send messages in an instant many Miles off, and receive answer again immediately; you shall be able to declare your minde

283

presently unto your friend, being in some private and remote place of a populous Citie, with a number of such like things: but that which far surpasseth all the rest, you shall have notice of a new World of many most rare and incredible secrets of Nature, that all the Philosophers of former ages could never so much as dreame off.''[23].

Or again listen to young Dr. Wren as he addresses his audience upon being appointed professor of astronomy at the long-vanished Gresham College. ''He that looks upon that little Parcel of the World'', he says, ''which the Ancients contented themselves with, and sees now, how we furrow the great Ocean, and gather our aromatick Harvests from the remotest Parts of the Globe, and can enjoy in our own Europe, whatever Thule or Aetheopia, the rising or setting Sun can produce must needs rejoice, that so much larger an Inheritance is fallen to Mankind, by the Favour of Astronomy.''

CHAPTER EIGHT

Of Recreations—Simple or Sinful

THOMAS TYNDALE was born in Armada year. Now in his eighties he lived quietly in the parish of Kington St. Michael and in the past, remembering for the benefit of his Wiltshire neighbour, John Aubrey,* the "true Gravity and prudence" of the old Queen's court. "Alas, O God's will!" things were not as they had been, what with coaches for everyone and gentlemen so "effeminated"† that they couldn't even ride a hunting nag, England was in a sad pickle. Even in the time of the first Charles young men had known how to handle horses and arms. Now, in the time of his son! Well—"God save the King".

In the golden age of Elizabeth the gentry, "robust and hardy and fitt for service", met in the open fields with hounds and hawks and not in a sordid alehouse to drink for days and "fall together by the eares". The old gentry kept open house, a good

---

*Thomas Tyndale appears very thinly disguised as "Curtoise, a Knight of the Bath and Protector of distressed Ladies" in Aubrey's play *The Countrey Revell*.

†This was no new accusation, the rot had set in six centuries before. William of Malmesbury says that just prior to the Conquest, Englishmen of the upper classes had transformed themselves by copying French manners. They went about "fantastically appointed" with garments about the knee, heads and beards shorn and upper lips festooned with long flaxen mustachios. Worse, they wore heavy gold bracelets, tattooed themselves and drank to excess. On the eve of Hastings while the English caroused, danced, gambled and drank, the Normans (whom we were supposed to have copied) piously confessed their sins and, presumably, slept soundly.

table, a fine retinue of servants, their tenants' respect and consequently there was "no depopulacion in those dayes". Those were the days when the elders and betters of a parish "sate and beheld the pastimes of the young men" such as "wrastling, shooting at Butts, bowling and dancing". Today, all was changed. There was nothing but "pride, whoreing, wantonnesses, and drunkennesses". Even servants looked and behaved like "clownes" with "Breeches of one sort, Doublet of another", bespotted and greasy.

"You see in me", the old man said with a mixture of choler and sorrow, "the Ruines of Time. The day is almost at an end with me, and truly I am glad of it; I desire not to live in this corrupt age."[1] The day which began so gloriously in 1588 ended for Thomas Tyndale in 1672.

Yet the pleasures of whoring, wantoness and drink, contrary to popular belief, do not cause nations to fall. And if young men in post-Cromwellian England no longer practised at Butts, it was not necessarily a sign of effeminacy nor of an incapacity to bear arms. Agincourt and Crècy had been won by English bowmen but gunpowder had long since come in and, as destructive weapons in those days could be used equally for sport or war, archery was "quite laid aside by Englishmen for fighting, there being found out more dextrous and speedy ways to kill and destroy one another".[2]

Thus, after the Civil Wars, young men took their guns, as they had once taken their cross bows and instead of shooting each other, shot birds. It was a span new idea then and, unbelievable as it seems to us, they shot sitting birds. True, they often shot from horseback which is difficult, particularly as English birds are a good deal smaller than Englishmen (perhaps this is why the ostrich always surprises us so) but in time they became skilful enough to shoot birds on the wing and, also in time, it became unsporting not to do so. But they did other dreadfully unsporting things as well. They cheated, whenever possible, at cards, dice and other games. No fashionable gentleman—or gentlewoman for that matter—could afford to be

Of Recreations—Simple or Sinful

without that comprehensive compendium of 1674, *The Compleat Gamester or, Instructions how to play at Billiards, Trucks, Bowls, and Chess. Together with all manner of most usual and most Gentile Games either on Cards or Dice*, etc. Gentile games were not those forbidden to Jews, they were "genteel" as opposed to the coarser recreations of country folk, the lower orders and riotous apprentices. These still indulged in wrastling, football, cudgel play and the like, thereby either gaining broken heads, limbs and necks or losing eyes, teeth, blood and sometimes even life.

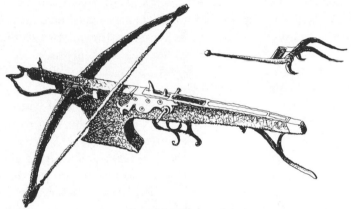

Late century lever crossbow.

The Genteel preferred to gain or lose a fortune gaming—either at home, at the houses of friends, at the Groom Porter's* and, less genteelly, at various ordinaries and gaming houses. Gambling, that part of the Englishness of the English often overlooked by foreigners, was a passion which grew in intensity with the century. The Duke of Ormonde was a great gamester but "decent even in his vices".[3] The Dukes of Monmouth, Lauder-

*The Groom Porter was a court official who saw to the furniture in the Royal rooms and that there were enough chairs for state occasions. As a perquisite of office he was allowed to keep gaming tables and this gave him and his deputies (chosen by him) great power to "supervise, regulate and authorise" all kinds of gaming within the kingdom. It sounds a lucrative office and was not abolished until the time of George III.

dale, and Buckingham were no less addicted, if perhaps a thought less decent; and even our glummest King, William III, lost £4,000 in one sitting. Sir John Denham, ill-fated as poet, architect and husband, was such a gambler when young that his father decided to disinherit him. John reformed, and wrote a treatise against gambling which so pleased his father that he left his fortune to his reformed son after all. Sir John promptly lost it at the card tables. More sensible was Squire Panton's youngest son Tom who, in Restoration year, betook himself to London from Ashby de la Zouche to make his fortune. Commissioned a Captain, he found the pay inadequate and took to cards and dice, soon winning enough to buy his way into the higher ranks until he ended with a regiment of his own, four or five footmen and an extravagant mode of life which included "eating and drinking very high".[4]

The Colonel was skilled in all games, but his chief pastime—and source of income—was Hazard. One night he won so much that he was able to purchase an estate of "above £1,500" per year. He was able to build a whole street near Leicester Fields, which is how Panton Street gets its name. Wiser than most, the Colonel never afterwards touched cards or dice. He lived handsomely on his winnings and died in 1681. Few could have been so skilled, fortunate or sleight-handed as Thomas Panton, yet all hoped to be. To the hopeful *The Compleat Gamester* must have been a boon.

Not only did it teach the popular games of the day, it also warned against sharpers and, in warning, instructed. Putt was the "ordinary rooking game", so cards must be held close "for the least discovery is of the greatest advantage to one's opponent". As the best Putt cards were Trey, Deuce and Ace, followed in "Preheminence" by King, Queen, Knave and ten (the Jack was called the Knave in this century although even today it still bears a "J") sharpers "spurred" or nicked these cards on the back as they turned up so that they could be sure of getting them again when dealing. Or honours were "slicked" —smoothed with a slick stone so that one could always cut an honour as cards were normally rough textured.* Or again the edges of the pack were trimmed, leaving the honours slightly larger so that the dealer could feel and palm them. This was the "breef" and the surest way of winning. Really clever people could, and did, introduce marked packs into gaming houses (and even into private homes). Beware of these tricks, *The Gamester* warns, and also of extra honours held in the pocket or by an onlooker accomplice. Yet when it came to Whist, that game invented in the previous century, the honest player is advised "he that by craft can overlook his adversaries' game hath a great advantage", and a "petty" glance at one's partner's hand was helpful too. Failing this, a simple series of signals is recommended. Marked packs, slicked honours, clever cutting, concealed honours might not be within the mental range or manual dexterity of all, but even the veriest ninny could peek or work out a simple system of signals.

There were other old games, besides Whist, which continued popular. Primero, Gleek, English Ruff or Honours (often called Slam), French Ruff, and One-and-Twenty. The latter developed variations under the names of Costly Colours and Bone Ace.

*Although playing cards had been manufactured for about 200 years there are no known English-made playing cards of the fifteenth and sixteenth centuries. The earliest extant English playing cards belong to the last quarter of the seventeenth century and can be found in the British Museum. (Sloane Coll. and Harleian Coll.) They are unseparated, uncoloured, court cards without pips and may possibly be proofs. The Worshipful Company of Makers of Playing Cards received its charter in 1628 (cards were made at London and Bristol) and the importation of foreign playing cards was forbidden. In view of the enormous popularity of card playing it is astonishing that no cards earlier than about 1675 survive. During the Commonwealth, card playing was out; but educational cards or "Scientalls" were sometimes produced. From then on, fancy cards appeared from time to time; such as fortune-telling cards and those which illustrated the history of the reign of James II and the Glorious Revolution, the fiendishness of the Popish Plot, the destruction of the Armada, or the glories of Queen Anne's reign. These are, obviously, propaganda cards but are certainly the parents of games like "Happy Families".

Rather dull games requiring small ingenuity were Plain Dealing, Queen Nazarine, and Beast. All Fours was much favoured in Kent; and Post and Pair, which required considerable daring was, suitably enough, a West Country favourite. New to the century was Cribbage, reputedly invented by the Cavalier poet Sir John Suckling, one of the greatest gallants of the time, despite a red nose due to an "ill-liver". He was also "the greatest Gamester both for Bowling and Cards"[5] and spent nights studying the best way to manage cards, which was useful. Even more usefully, he managed to get his own private marked packs into all the gaming houses in the country—or so Aubrey says—and by this ruse won some £20,000. But he often lost vast sums too and "his Sisters would come to the Peccadillo bowling-green crying for feare he should loose all their Portions".*

Another new game, at least in England, was L'Ombre or Ombre which had a great vogue late in the century and in Anne's day.† Lanterloo, more commonly "Loo" seems also to have been new, and Picket (Piquet‡), played in a rather desultory fashion since about 1550, suddenly took a new lease of life. Bassett (a game like Faro) was possibly introduced around 1645 but soon made up for lost time by becoming a rage. It was one of Queen Anne's favourites, and a favourite with gamesters too—although as far as one can tell dice games were the real

*Easy natural Suckling "was brave and generous". He came into a fortune at the age of eighteen and in 1639 raised a troop of 100 horse at a cost of £12,000 to accompany Charles I to Scotland. In 1641, he conspired to rescue Strafford from the Tower and to bring in French troops to help the king. The plot discovered, Suckling fled abroad. Unable, it is said, to bear the thought of poverty, he committed suicide (by poison) in 1642 at the age of thirty-three.

†Readers will remember the charming description of this game in Pope's *The Rape of the Lock*.

‡Its early name here was Cent. In France, Lansquenet. The Duchesse de la Ferté used to invite her tradespeople to dine because she found their table manners and gaucheries amusing. Afterwards she would play Lansquenet with them, cheating like mad, because, as she explained to Mme. de Staël, it served them right as they robbed her daily.

Top. Breech loading flintlock gun, c. 1680.
Bottom. Flintlock holster pistol, c. 1680.

way to fortune, a debtor's prison, or exile in Ireland or Virginia.
Leaving aside games played "within the tables" (Backgammon,
Tick Tack, Sice-Ace, Dubblets and Ketch Dolt), In-and-In,
Passage, and Hazard were top dice games and Hazard was by all
odds the most popular. No longer much played here, Hazard
is still the most popular of all dice games in the United States
where it is called "Craps", perhaps because the lowest throw,
two aces, was known as "Crabs". Modern Americans would
doubtless agree with seventeenth-century Englishmen that "it
is the most bewitching game that is plaid on dice, for when a
man begins to play at Hazard he hardly ever after minds anything
else".[6]

Obviously then, if one were to spend one's life at Hazard, it
was as well to remain solvent. But Lambs, Innocents and Colls
stood little chance against the wiles of Huffs, Hectors, Gilts,
Pads, Biters, Divers, Lifters, Filers, Droppers, Rooks and
Budgies. The last two sound like birds but all were cant terms
for professional sharpers, distinguishable only from genteel
cheats simply because they were better at it. Palming or topping
required great dexterity with the nimbles (fingers); slurring
or stabbing meant throwing dice or placing them in a casting
box so that the right face turned up; both methods were done

with great artistry by professionals. Professionals, no doubt, had better false dice too—weighted, or hollowed and filled with mercury, or set with a bristle—and more tricky casting boxes, narrowed inside at the bottom, or shadow painted to look as if they were honestly "screwed".

So if Hazard was your game—or any other ploy with dice—best look out for these tricks. Better still see that your own "bale" of dice was made especially for you. As for the casting box? Why not try that "dextrous dicing box" invented by Edward Somerset, sixth Earl and second Marquis of Worcester, inventor of the steam engine? Few had use for a steam engine in polite society, but a dicing box which held two pairs of dice—one loaded and one "square" (straight) had more advantages than a normal dishonest box or cooked dice. One could play straight for a bit, just for the look of it, then by hitting the box in a certain way against the table, straight dice were imprisoned and fulhams or false teeth released—or so the Marquis claimed—but his book gives no certain indication on how this box is to be made nor is it explicit on "Primero Gloves", where white silk was knotted in the fingers and enabled the player to keep a record of all sixes, sevens and aces "without clogging his memory".[7]

Bowling, too, surprisingly enough, was a great game for cheats who crowded about bowling alleys and greens (our greens were much admired by foreigners even if they thought bowling rather low). The shape of the bowl, flat, "byassed" or absolutely round, was determined by the ground, so choosing the right shape required great cunning. If not clever enough at this, the Marquis helpfully suggests "a deceitful Bowl to play withal". This meant inserting a lead pellet in the right place (wherever that was) to give the bowl a slight undue and necessary curve. Certainly no one thought any the less of the Marquis for suggestions on how to cheat, and his book *A Century of Inventions* (century meaning 100) was dedicated to Charles I. It was written, the author says, at "the instance of a powerful friend". The powerful friend turns out to have been Colonel

Of Recreations—Simple or Sinful

Christopher Copley, a Roundhead. Colonel Copley cannot have been a typical or latter day Puritan* or perhaps he just didn't know about the gayer inventions of his noble friend, for the Puritans had been dead against most pleasures and pastimes ever since the grave and prudent days of the great Queen. Although James I, in 1617, issued his "Declaration of Sports", encouraging people, after divine service, to engage in archery, vaulting, leaping, dancing and other harmless and healthy diversions, he was fighting a losing battle. By 1621 Parliament was strong enough to introduce a dreary bill for the better observance of Sunday and when one outraged member asked what right Parliament had to fly in the teeth of King David, let alone King James, the Commons, equally outraged, replied that such a profane member could not be tolerated and his seat was forfeited. So, bit by bit, Parliament gained the upper hand and by 1642 practically every recreation, no matter how innocent, was forbidden. Theatres were closed, acting prohibited, horse racing banned, as was cock fighting and bear baiting. The latter ban seems to have been less for the sake of the wretched animals than to deny the spectators pleasure, although anyone could see a criminal hanged, drawn and quartered at any time—presumably because this was a horrid warning. Sunday was strictly kept and all were forbidden to engage in or watch such activities as wrestling, bowling and ringing of bells. Games, dancing and masques were out, and nearly everything else one can think of, including football,† which always seemed to put Puritans into ·a particular fret.

*In fairness to Cromwell I note it is said that he was given to practical jokes and horse play such as throwing cushions about, putting coals in the pockets and boots of his officers (he also loved horses) and at the wedding of his daughter Frances to Mr. Rich he threw the sack posset among the ladies "to spoil their clothes" or according to James Heath (1629-64) the historian, he did. But as "Carrion" Heath—as Carlyle with dreary monotony calls him—was a royalist this may not be so. Personally, I hope it is—but see Heath's *Flagellum*.

†In January 1612/13, Lord William Howard bought his children a football. It cost 4d.

The Pageant of Stuart England

Undoubtedly football was rough, noisy and dangerous. Apprentices were given to playing it in the streets, which was often a great nuisance, and solitary, violent, enthusiastic kickers went too far. John Bishop, for one, an apothecary, was a particular trial to certain citizens of Maidstone who lodged a complaint against him because he "with force and arms did willfully and in a boisterous manner run to and fro and kick up and down the Common High Street . . . a ball of leather commonly called a football; unto the great annoyance and incumberance of the said Common Highway and the great disgust and disturbance of others". Although Maidstone had once been "a very profane town" much given over to "morrice dancing, cudgel playing, stool ball and crickets"[8] quite openly on the Lord's Day, it was now reformed and John clearly wasn't or he wouldn't have touched the devil's device, the football.

The reference to "crickets"* is interesting. Although we know it was played in some form or another during the century —and earlier—it does not seem to have become very popular until 1699 but from then on it gathered momentum, and in 1707 is included in a list of people's recreations.[9] If football and other games were wicked, swearing was worse. Any swearer or "prophane curser" was fined, not according to degree of bad language but of social class. Dukes, Earls, Marquises and Viscounts were fined 30/-; Baronets and Knights paid a pound; Esquires' curses fetched 10/- and gentlemen got off with 6/8. Those below the rank of gentlemen paid 3/4. Women were fined according to their husband's rank and those unable to pay (of both sexes) were put in the stocks unless under twelve years of age (the under-twelves were savagely whipped). This must have gone hard on the Cavaliers, known to the Roundheads as

*It is said that in his youth Cromwell indulged in both cricket and football and was a roisterer. This charge, however, is made by the Royalist Sir William Dugdale and may not be true. On the other hand Cromwell in a letter to his cousin Mrs. St. John (Carlyle, Letter 2) seems to have accused himself of having lived a sinful life. This may be, of course, "the dark night of the soul" through which he passed, but it might also include such things as football and cricket.

Of Recreations—Simple or Sinful

"Dammes" from the frequency with which they used the oath. Cromwell's troops were luckier, irrespective of rank, they seem to have been fined 12d. if they cursed.

Swearing, loose behaviour and Sabbath breaking had, however, long been cause for complaint, and complaints were louder in some places than in others, depending upon the religious and political persuasion of the area. In the year when Henry Frederick, the young Phoenix, became Prince of Wales, the citizens of Thaxted were driven to distraction by one, Silvester Rayment (alias Allen), an alehouse keeper, and they besought the King's Justices to bridle and restrain the man. Their complaints, lodged in thirteen telling items, certainly show Silvester in a deplorable light—even by non-Puritan standards. He "usually kepte evell rule in his house (to wit), excessive drinkinge upon Saboth dayes and other tymes and useth much diceinge and cardeing day and nighte".[10] This was bad enough but worse, there was "revellinge all the nighte or the moste parte thereof". drunkeness and "falleing out with noyse" which disturbed the town and even "raysed some out of there beddes". Broken glass was common, cheating was suspected, and Silvester's language was vile—he used the most "filthye termes". There was also that business with Margaret Clerke, poor girl—virtue saved only in the nick of time—furthermore his wife Frances was little better. She beat Marye Cocke over the head for no reason at all and when two months later the constable came to carry Frances off to gaol—having spared her because of her children—Silvester threatened the law with fire, scalding and knife. As he had previously flung a "bason" at the constable, no one doubted he would carry out his threats. Weary of listing such misdemeanours the petitioners ended their complaint by saying there were still others "which wee thinke too tediouse to be rehearsed" and let it go at that.

But how tedious and dismal life must have become during the Commonwealth and Protectorate when "God's privy council", as the Duchess of Newcastle aptly termed the new rulers,[11] prohibited and proscribed, dictated and punished with what seems to us such odious self-righteousness. Christmas was forbidden, mince pies were as abominable as the altar in the east of a church or the sign of the cross at baptism. It was business as usual on Christmas Day with penalties aplenty for those who did not treat it as an ordinary working day. (John Evelyn and others were arrested for attending an "illegal" Anglican service on Christmas Day 1657). Unless, of course, Christmas fell on a Sunday—a day of unmitigated gloom in an already glum enough week. There was nothing to do on a Sunday, even after service. One couldn't visit relatives or friends (a blessing, perhaps) as Sunday travel was forbidden. And as all Puritan "professors" agreed that the Anglican prayer book was "the most abominable idol in the land"[12] the Anglican faith itself had been proscribed as early as 1646 when 2,000 Anglican clergy were expelled from their livings. Hence Anglicans, like Roman Catholics, could not even worship in their own faith on Sunday. Man, at long last, had been made for the Sabbath—a delusion under which we still labour, to a lesser extent, today.

Small wonder, with restrictions, fines, prohibitions, punishment and dreadfully long, dreary sermons and prayers delivered at all times by those whom the spirit moved (and the spirit was terribly over-active), that many must have become so sickened by the rule of the saints (and later the terror tactics of the Fifth Monarchy Men) that it put them off sainthood for life—here and hereafter. So, with the Restoration, the inevitable happened, as it always does. Reaction set in. A reaction which in many instances makes naughty Silvester Rayment look the veriest greenhorn. Which, by sophisticated standards, he was.

It must be admitted, at once, if one reads many of the memoirs, diaries, histories, journals, plays, books and letters of the time, that it is almost impossible not to come to the conclusion that whoring, wantonness and drunkenness were, as old Thomas Tyndale said, the chief recreations of the Restoration monarchy. Undoubtedly such things had existed in Elizabeth's day, but she set no fashion for them. Fond of dancing, cards, music, hunting and a good jest when feeling "dumpish", she expected her maids-of-honour and her courtiers to behave themselves and to avoid scandal. She and her court set the standard for the country. It was a standard which her successor James I and his two grandsons, Charles II and James II, never attempted to follow:

Playing cards, c. 1675.

"He spends all his Days in running to Plays,
  When he should in the Shop be poring:
  And wasts all his Nights in his constant Delights,
  Of Revelling, Drinking and Whoring."[13]

was a view of Charles II which was, and is, by no means uncommon. And where king and court led, others followed. But to relate here Charles's already exhaustively documented amorous adventures is a thing "which wee thinke too tediouse to be rehearsed". Possibly Charles himself became just a trifle bored with such a succession of women but went on hoping he wouldn't be. Yet, in the seventeenth century interpretation of the term, no man could be a true "*honnête homme*" without innumerable love affairs to his credit. Charles had many mistresses, he produced numbers of illegitimate children (when kings produce such children it is more polite to refer to the offspring as "Natural") but in this respect he simply wasn't in the same class with his grandfather, Henri IV of France, who had fifty-six mistresses and was assassinated in his coach while riding out with a brace of them.

Charles was an amiable man (the old sense of Merry is amiable) and although he had so little English blood in him he often seems to us to be the most English of kings—that is he seems more like us than any of the others before, or many since. He loved the sea and the turf. He raced horses and also was the first monarch to race yachts. He was a great walker and could outstride any of his courtiers. He was a good shot, fond of fishing and was quite given over to that peculiarly English characteristic, the love of dogs. His courtiers stumbled over them in his royal apartments which reeked of dog. He was, unlike his contemporaries, not a particularly keen gambler—although some of his mistresses were, he paid their losses but never shared their winnings. He was a most enthusiastic tennis player. Here again, he may have resembled his maternal grandfather. Henri IV was a fierce player although perhaps not a very good one, as, like England's Henry VIII, he lost vast sums in wagers. Tennis—which doesn't mean lawn tennis—had been known for several centuries as a Royal game. Courts were really courtyards and roofed over, and possibly only royalty or the nobility could afford them. James I seems not to have played, due probably to his shambling gait,* but he recommends the game of "caitche or tennise" to his son Prince Henry. The Prince† played well but good sportsmanship was not quite the fetish it now is for the Prince once hit or threatened to hit his father's fancy boy, Robert Ker, with his racket and again, when disputing a point with young Essex, he called the Earl the son of a traitor, whereupon the Earl bashed the prince's head with his racket and drew blood.

*But one of the best players at the court of Louis XIV—the Marquis of Rivarolles—had a wooden leg.

†It was long believed the Prince died of a chill following a game of tennis; but he died of typhoid.

Of Recreations—Simple or Sinful

Henry's brother, the Duke of Albany and York (later Charles I) was also a keen player and in the year when Silvester was so taxing tempers in Thaxted, young Charles, in a tennis suit of "taffety" was being coached by John Webb who received £20 per annum for the job, out of this he had to supply balls and rackets. Balls were leather-covered, hard-cored, and stuffed with wool or hair. Later they were made of cloth scraps pressed tightly together, wound with string and covered with cloth. "Wind balls" were very probably known, and certainly the Spanish must have known rubber ones in New Spain. Rackets were usually diagonally strung and tennis shoes were soft slippers with woollen soles.*

Charles II† also played in taffeta tennis drawers. Pepys watched him on several occasions and remarks "to see how the King's play was extolled without any cause at all was a loathesome sight" and then adds, rather grudgingly, "though sometimes, indeed, he did play very well and deserved to be commended; but such open flattery is beastly".[14] Charles even kept a bed at his new tennis court at Whitehall—rather a grand bed with heavy crimson damask curtains colourfully fringed— and there was a "Portugall mat" under the bed. As Charles started playing around 6 a.m. and Whitehall was positively labyrinthian, a bed at the tennis court saved time.

But tennis in the Stuart century ceased to be a monopoly, confined to King and nobles and played on private courts. As early as 1623 one, Robert Baker, of "Pickadilly Hall"‡

---

*But see that fascinating book *The History of Tennis* by Lord Aberdare.

†It is said he was playing tennis when he received the welcome news of Cromwell's death. The youngest Stuart Brother, Henry, was a champion player—but died young.

‡We have Lord Clarendon's word for it that Pickadilly Hall in the time of Charles I was "a Fair House for Entertainment and Gaming, with Handsome walks with Shade, and where were an upper and a lower Bowling Green whither many of the Nobility and Gentry of the best Quality resorted, both for exercise and Pleasure". (Rebellion. Vol. I.)

was licensed to run a tennis court—licenses were required for "such like places of honest Recreation"—and it may have been here the Suckling sisters sought brother John and cried that he'd lose their portion. But Pickadilly Hall it seems, disturbed the neighbours and set an "ill-example" so during the Civil Wars it was closed and troops were quartered there.

There were other courts in London too and, later in the century in the Provinces,* and although one usually associates philosophers with fishing rather than tennis, Thomas Hobbes (who did indeed produce Leviathan) played tennis until the age of seventy-five—even if from the age of sixty he seems to have suffered from something which sounds uncommonly like Parkinsonism. At Oxford, John Earle says, a trifle sarcastically one fears, the marks of seniority of a young gentleman are "the bare velvet of his gown and his proficiencie at Tennis, where when he can play a Set, he is a Freshman no more".[15] There were two courts at Oxford, five at Cambridge . . . but the Oxford courts were covered. Tennis continued popular until the time of William III—who didn't play although he built a court at Hampton Court—then it began to wane. It is possible that this is when cricket began to replace tennis, at least in London and the Weald.†

Billiards "a gentile cleanly and most ingenious game"[16] now became a popular pastime and by the second half of the century few large towns were without a "publick Billiard-Table". Cues or "sticks" were made of "Brasile" wood or lignum vitae and were bent at one end. This end which was of ivory was used for long "strokes" and the other for short ones. No "lolling, slovenly players"[17] were allowed, and dropping hot ashes from one's pipe on the fine green cloth was definitely not done. It was

*In 1687, Mr. Penn "held forth" at the tennis court in Foregate Street, Chester, which was a Quaker meeting place.

†There was a cricket ground at Smithfield as early as 1668. But the first definite match of which there is a record (*Post Boy*) took place on Clapham Common in 1700. The first "county" match, Londoners versus the Kentish men, did not take place until five years after Anne's death.

Of Recreations—Simple or Sinful

preferable to have a perfectly round ball and an unwarped table too—tables were not then slate-bedded. Trucks, a form of billiards, was "more boisterous", requiring a larger table, cues were iron-tipped at each end, balls were the size of tennis balls.

New to the century was Pall-Mall, the reputed ancestor of croquet, and much favoured by Charles and his brother James. The Mall (much shorter then than now) or near it, was reserved for the use of the King and his court; the surface was prepared by tramping ground cockle shells into the earth. In hot weather, however, this turned to dust and could stop the boxwood ball dead.

Less "gentile" sports, common to town and country were pretty bloody. That old favourite cudgel play, where combatants clobbered each other over the head, was still going strong, although a few weaklings had taken to using light canes instead of the more usual hefty sticks. Wrestling (pace Thomas Tyndale) continued popular particularly in the north. In the south feminine grace was added to the sport by women who wrestled in their shifts and tore out each others' hair by the fistful. There was nothing like a fight for attracting a crowd. Small boys quarrelling in the streets were swiftly surrounded and egged on by adults. Gentlemen often came to fisticuffs with hackney coachmen over the price of a fare, in fact "anything that looks like fighting" was "delicious to an Englishman".[18] Chopping with broadswords or stabbing with daggers was much admired. Combatants were often badly wounded or killed, but no action was taken unless it could be proven that the victor had transgressed the rules or had acted out of malice. Hockley-in-the-Hole was the place to see "sword play" done in style, with a printed list of challenges and the players hacking away at each other on a raised platform. Pepys "saw the prize fought" in September 1667 when one player, a shoemaker, was so badly cut about the wrists he had to give up. The victor undoubtedly had more practice. He was a butcher.

Country sports were no less vicious, but it is a pleasant note that around 1612, near Chipping Camden, Captain Robert Dover, a local lawyer (his grandson invented Dover's powders) instituted the Cotswold "Olimpick Games"* to which "multitudes of people resorted"[19] every Thursday and Friday of Whit week. Here on the high flat plain which curves away in a natural amphitheatre to lower ground, feats of strength such as pitching the bar, throwing the sledge, topping the pike, leaping, wrestling, sword and cudgel play were part of a programme which included head stands, feasting, hunting, coursing and women dancing to bagpipes. As a splendid end-piece, guns from a specially built wooden castle were frequently discharged.

Walking was a recreation no less than a quite usual means of getting from one place to another. In 1631 when the Earl of Banbury "aged four skore and six" was lying on his death-bed, his sister, Lady Leicester, aged ninety-two, was still walking "a mile in a morning".[20] But Katherine Fitzgerald, Countess of Desmond, on the other hand, met an untimely end when she climbed an apple tree to gather fruit and fell out. She was, some say, 120.

Bear and bull baiting returned to popularity after restrictions were lifted and to add piquancy to the fun the bull was sometimes hung with squibs, set off just before the dogs were loosed. A gay interval was provided when a wretched ass with a terrified, screaming monkey as a jockey was baited. Many women kept monkeys as pets, a good one cost as much as £60. Cock fighting was very English. Foreigners could never understand the passion for it, they thought it silly, and a pompous German traveller in Anne's day found it shocking that at cock fights gentlefolk and plebs sat together. Worse, an ostler might win several guineas from a Lord. This was dangerously democratic, English lack of formality, especially at court, was deplorable. King Charles' remarks on the strict formal procedure required when the King

---

*The games did not take place during the Civil Wars but were resumed afterwards and remained a feature of Cotswold life until 1852 when they were stopped by the enclosure of the parish of Weston-sub-Edge. The place is now known as Dover's Hill and is National Trust property. It is still very well worth visiting for a magnificent view of the surrounding countryside.

of Spain heeded a simple call of nature are robust and illuminating.

Racing increased in popularity and although Charles II made Newmarket famous there were racecourses all over the country. In this century a piece of plate as a racing prize began to super-cede the more customary cup. Spectators attended and followed the race on horseback and in late century women again adopted a very masculine riding habit (as they had late in Elizabeth's day). This too astonished foreigners who thought Englishwomen had too much freedom and too little to do.* Hunting remained

Seventeenth century tennis rackets.

a great pastime. The first Stuart was so passionately addicted to it that the Venetian Ambassador reported that the King had entirely abandoned the government of his kingdom and "thinks of nothing but hunting". The last Stuart, too fat and dropsical to sit a horse, hunted in a chaise down avenues and roads especially designed in Windsor Forest and park (a French fashion this) to make "Chaise-riding Fitt for her Majesty's passage". Swift says,

*Béat-Louis Muralt, a Swiss visitor in 1695, quite untouched by the beauty of Englishwomen, admits they had good figures, were tall and richly dressed. On the debit side he says they had bad teeth and when given over to passion were completely carried away. They were also lazy and did little. Women of quality scarcely ever did any sewing or embroidering but all liked walking and being seen "elaborately got up". However, they were not spoiled by men's attention because English men "who are not made for passion" didn't give them much.

The Pageant of Stuart England

"She hunts in a chaise with one horse which she drives herself, and drives furiously like Jehu, and is a mighty hunter like Nimrod".[21] We may doubt the Nimrod bit, but Anne may well have emulated Jehu when one August day she chaised the stag until four in the afternoon and covered forty miles; and William III died of a pneumonia, which brought Anne to the throne, following a hunting accident when his pony, Sorrel (part of the confiscated estate of Sir John Fenwick), stumbled in a molehill.

For those confined indoors by weather, gout, inclination or, if female, by a state of chronic pregnancy there were lots of jolly pastimes to alleviate boredom. Anna of Denmark spent a dreary autumn at Windsor in 1603 playing "Rise pig and go", "One penny follow me", "I pray my lord give me a course in your park", and something called "Fire". None was thought hilarious by Arabella Stuart. But after the Restoration such simple games were supplemented by Acrostics, and drawing Characters—little candid pen portraits of one's self and friends which probably had dire results in many cases. After dinner there was nothing like Crambo, Hunt-the-Slipper, Blind-Man's-Buff, and Hot-Cockles for settling an overburdened stomach and in mixed company the "I-love-my-love-with-an-Apple-because-she-is-Angelic" kind of game became wildly popular. It could be, and was, developed into a game which, if witty, was often of great personal indelicacy.

Reading, too, was a recreation best done indoors, even if Dr. Harvey had sat under a hedge at Edgehill absorbed in a book until disturbed by a cannon ball, and there was a great deal to read. Much more than there had ever been before. Newspapers were new to the century. The first English Newspaper, *The Weekly Newes from Italy Germany, etc.** appeared in 1622, to be

*There was the *Mercurius Gallobelgicus* published in Cologne which circulated in England from *c.* 1587. It gave a weekly chronicle of events in Latin. So the time was ripe for an English newspaper in English. The old Mercurius left a legacy in that innumerable papers during the century took the title Mercurius this, that, or the other. Mercury is still quite a common title for a newspaper in the U.S.A. and also in France.

swiftly followed by a rival *Newes from Most Parts of Christendom*.
The latter was so successful that it devoured, amalgamated, or
married the first paper and the joint production was more
modestly known as *Newes of the Present Week*. So England's first press
combine belongs to the first quarter of this century too. For
newspapers had competition in the now more widely distributed
News Letters. These had originated chiefly in Elizabeth's day as
the work of a paid retainer or "Intelligencer" of some lord or
ambassador who, dwelling remotely, wished to be *au courant*
with events at home or abroad. Written by hand they were, in
a sense, private letters and much freer of censorship than were
newspapers, so a great many people now subscribed to news
letters, paying so much a year for this weekly service.* Newspapers were in the beginning forbidden to touch on domestic
or court news, but news letters escaped this ban.

Newspapers, usually a single sheet printed on one side,
appeared and disappeared with startling rapidity in a century
which also saw the beginning of the great battle for freedom of
the press. Cromwell permitted only two newspapers, both
"official". John Milton, who edited for a year or two the
famous *Mercurius Politicus* (an official paper which lived ten
years, 1650-60) once believed in freedom of speech and
freedom of the press and as early as 1644 said so in his magnificent
Areopagitica. God never meant man to be "under a perpetual
childhood of Prescription" and "he who destroys a good book
kills reason itself" he states, and went on to demonstrate "as
lineally as any pedigree" that only tyrannies went in for censorship. This must have been as unpopular with Parliamentarians
as was his previous pamphlet on *The Doctrine and Discipline of
Divorce* which, published without license, led to trouble and
indeed to the writing of the *Areopagitica* for Milton was outraged by laws which by making adultery the only grounds for
divorce exalted the body above the soul. None the less, Milton
became a press censor himself under the Commonwealth.

*The Staple of News by Ben Jonson gives a neat picture of the Paul
Slickeys of the day.

The Pageant of Stuart England

More newspapers were born with the Restoration; the oldest, the *London Gazette*, today the official government organ, first appeared as the bi-weekly *Oxford Gazette* in 1665. That it was in those days a partisan paper *à l'outrance* is illustrated by its obituary of Mr. Anthony Pearson,† under-sheriff of Durham who, says the Gazette on Monday, February 5th, 1665, "was noted . . . for having passed heretofore through all the degrees of Separation and Phanaticism" but having seen the error of his ways, "died a true son of the Church of England". Edward Lloyd, whose famous coffee house was to become "Lloyd's of London", issued *Lloyds News* in 1696. It was short-lived but appeared thirty years later as *Lloyd's News* and has continued ever since. The Licensing Act was allowed to lapse in 1692; censorship ended in 1693 and from then on newspapers attracted some of the best brains of the time, both in the political and literary world (no such thing as a non-partisan paper then or now). There were of course hacks aplenty—Gervase Markham is said to be the first hack writer—but there were also men like Johnathan Swift who might be called the father of leader writers (he gave up the *Examiner* on becoming Dean of St. Patrick's), and what succeeding century has ever produced a better factual reporter than Daniel Defoe? It is a far cry from the first newspaper which appeared in the last years of the first Stuart to the many newspapers which enlivened the reign of the last Stuart. We read the *News from Italy Germany etc.* out of antiquarian interest, but we still read the *Tatler* and the *Spectator* for pleasure and profit and Addison's prose long remained a model for all such essay writing. In Anne's day, too, the first daily paper *The Daily Courant* appeared (not counting the earlier *Post Boy*, which lasted but four days). It was a single sheet, fourteen by eight inches,

†He was also noted for his tract *The Great Case of Tythes truly stated* (1657). Pearson was born in 1628, became a Quaker *c.* 1653, and, it is suggested, he disavowed the Quaker faith in order to stand in well with the Restoration Government. According to the Dictionary of National Biography he died in "1670?", but I cannot think that any other Anthony Pearson is meant by the *Oxford Gazette*'s notice of 1665.

printed on one side like a handbill and, says the first issue in 1702, it "will be published daily, being designed to give all the Material News as soon as every Post arrives, and is confin'd to half the Compass to save the Publick at least half the Impertinencies of ordinary News Paper". We may, perhaps, doubt that the *Courant* was small out of a selfless regard for the good of its readers, but newspapers, then as now, claimed to do what they did purely in the public interest. Fortunately for us, the claim is sometimes justified. Defoe's paper the *Review* a prodigious one-man effort depending wholly on his own pen appeared in 1704; and England's first evening newspaper the *Evening Post* appeared in 1706.

Although almost from their inception newspapers were distributed to towns and villages by carriers and foot post, to be taken home to lonely cottage or farm in the egg baskets of country women, mass circulation, as we know it, was non-existent, and broadsheets and ballads which snowed down upon the century filled the need now catered for by the popular tabloid. Through broadsheet and ballad our credulous and sensation-loving ancestors were kept informed of horrors, miracles, multiple births, prodigies and the disgraceful goings-on of high society—in prose and verse.

As the seventeenth century was the golden age for street ballads* many a poet turned to ballad writing, often for propaganda purposes. But ballads dealt with wonders and portents too; a strange, miraculous fish washed up near Worwell in Cheshire in 1636 (this ballad is full of amazing details, although the anatomical ones seem highly improbable); the great hailstorm which fell upon London in 1680 and wounded men (in Shoreditch a hemp dresser was "stricken dead" by lightning but happily recovered), killed birds and did much damage with hailstones as big as eggs.† And, even more strange and more terrible, the appearance of the devil himself on October 13th, 1684. His Satanic Majesty presented himself to Thomas Cox,

*More than 250 ballad publishers were known in London alone.

†Narcissus Luttrell says they were as big as "pidgeons eggs".

a Hackney Coachman, first as a gentleman and then as a great bear with glaring eyes which frightened Thomas senseless—but not senseless enough to forget the happening which lost nothing in the re-telling. This tale soon turned up as a marrow-freezing ballad with a moral. The horrid visitation had paralysed all of Tom, save his tongue, and with this unparalysed bit he was able to tell the story and express remorse for his former calling—though one cannot quite see why, unless he cheated his fares. Of course all such things, together with news of comets, unusual weather, and various "prodigies" were but warnings from God—portents of worse to come—for everyone believed in signs, portents and the influence of the stars. But probably the most famous ballad of the time and best known to us, is the revolutionary song "*Lilliburlero*", reputedly written by Thomas, Marquis of Wharton, who boasted that he'd "sung a king (James II) out of three kingdoms" with it. The English read more newspapers and magazines than any other people on earth, and the root of this passion or habit lies deep in the first newspapers, ballads and broadsheets of the Stuart century.

Oddly enough, although the time is rich in poets and playwrights, the English novel was in a very poor way. Those written during the first half of the era merely imitated and developed the florid language and silly conceits which flawed late Elizabethan literature, but they lacked the naïve charm of Elizabethan work. Usually they are set in outlandish countries and are full of absurdities and improbabilities; devoted lovers disguise themselves as foreign waiting women to attend the beloved mistress; beloved mistress is so blind or stupid that she never guesses the sex of the faithful maid (but who knows, foreign women may have had beards) and loves and caresses him/her like a sister which, as may be imagined, puts quite a strain on the maid. Narrow escapes from pirates, bandits, heartless fathers, wicked stepmothers, avaricious uncles, sexy dukes, and distasteful marriages are the stock in trade of English novelle. Even so, not nearly enough were written to fill the demand for them and they were so short that they could be read in a few hours. So

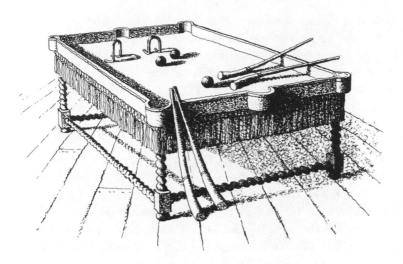

Billiard table and cues.

the upper classes and the bourgeoisie took to French novels.

Henrietta Maria who, with the usual English pig-headedness was called Queen Henry—Henrietta sounded a fancy, made-up name (which it then was)—made the pastoral and chivalric novels of d'Urfé popular and from these sprang the French heroic-romantic school as exemplified by La Calprènede and Mlle. de Scudéry. They were read too. Tome after tome after tome of interminable, improbable, amorous adventure. Mlle. de Scudéry's *Clélie* is a splendid example of the labyrinthian clinch-tease school of writing, for Mlle. is extremely proper. (The Map of Tenderness was much admired). The story opens on the very eve of the marriage of Clélie and Aronce—nine volumes and seven years later the pair finally manage to get to the altar—and on the last pages too. Such novels fascinated the readers from mid-century on. During the civil wars Dorothy Osborne and Sir William Temple, whose· own wedding was nearly as long delayed, constantly exchanged the innumerable volumes of *Cléopâtre* and *Le Grand Cyrus* and King Charles, on the eve of his execution, presented his own copy of Gomberville's Mexican Romance *Polexandre* to the Earl of Lindsay.

But the English genius for prose would out. It expressed itself not in the novel which hardly existed* but in sermons and in religious, political and scientific tracts which could appeal only to the educated minority. There were poets with a somewhat wider appeal. Shakespeare, Ben Jonson and others, born in the sixteenth century were still alive and writing in the early Stuart period. Milton is a great soaring peak in the middle. The metaphysical poets like Donne and Crashaw were more narrowly famous, the ligher veined Cavalier poets more widely so. Dryden, whose output of plays, poems and critical essays was enormous, worked in the decasyllabic couplet which Pope polished and brought to perfection and there was no lack of perfectly dreadful and boring verse too. Equally, the age was well supplied with literary criticism and satirical poetry. Butler's *Hudibras*, Dryden's *Absalom and Achitophel* are the most famous although Butler is probably more quoted than read today . . . which seems a pity. Yet none of these men or his works had any wide effect, or made any great impression, on the daily life or thought of the average person—the farmer, the labourer, the artisan, the beggar, the small, the poor and the humble folk everywhere.

*Emmanuel Ford's *Ornatus and Artesia* which by 1683 had gone into seven editions is an example of the florid late and post-Elizabethan style. Lord Orrey's *Parthenissa* merely imitates the long-winded French novels. Henry Neville's *The Isle of Pines* (1668) is hardly a novel as it runs to barely 3,000 words, but the idea is new and interesting and may have provided, along with the true stories of Selkirk and Pitman, part of the original impetus for Daniel Defoe's *Robinson Crusoe*. Mrs. Aphra Behn's *Oronooko* (1688) is the first long, short story (approx. 30,000 words) or novella of any originality and talent. It was Mrs. Behn and William Congreve—his only novel is the rather silly *Incognita* (1691?) —who revolted against the long, heroic-chivalric French tradition. The first English religious romance *The Martyrdom of Theodore Didymus* belongs to the seventeenth century and was written by the scientist Robert Boyle. Nevertheless Samuel Richardson who was to write the first true English novel was born in 1689 although his famous novel *Pamela* did not appear until 1740.

Of Recreations—Simple or Sinful

Yet they, too, had their literature, their book. It was, and still is, one of the glories of our language. The King James Bible, translation though it is, is still the greatest single book in the English language, and for centuries it had an effect upon our character, our speech, our style of writing. It was not the first Bible in English, of course, and much of its beauty is owed to Tyndale, but it did become the standard Bible and in time superceded all others.* It became known in every home, everywhere. It was bought by those who could afford to buy it, lay open in churches for those who couldn't, and was read out at every service to be heard by rich, poor, lettered and unlettered alike. The lonely shepherd in the Cotswolds had never read the poems of John Donne but he knew the Song of Solomon and that David, too, was a shepherd. The village carpenter in a remote border village had never heard of Mr. Dryden's *Religio Laici* but he, himself, followed Joseph's trade. Mr. Milton's *Paradise Lost* was read by a few thousand† but to the 4½ or 5 million people who were England, Paradise and its loss were to be found in the first chapters of Genesis. The Bible and its stories were an integral part of daily life and speech. "The language of the common people (in Northamptonshire) is generally the best of any shire in England", Thomas Fuller says, though perhaps he was prejudiced as he was a Northants man himself. But he also says that a labouring man told him this was because "the last

*It seems hardly necessary to emphasize that this was not a brand new translation; it is estimated that ninety per cent of Tyndale's Bible appears in the King James Bible. Nor did everyone take to the new Bible immediately. The Bishops' Bible, Tyndale, Mathews, Coverdale and the Genevan Bible were still in use; nevertheless it is still true that the King James Bible has been the most powerful book of all in the daily life of the English. As Dr. A. L. Rowse points out, "It seems hardly less than a miracle that a committee of ecclesiastics should have produced an undying masterpiece of English prose". (*The Spirit of English History*).

†Only 1,300 copies were sold in the eighteen months after publication in 1667. Milton received £10 for it. His widow a further £8 after Milton's death.

translation of the Bible . . . agreeth perfectly with the common speech of our county.''*

Certainly, the common people were not interested in the theological controversies, the differences of interpretation, the logamachy of the day. To them the Bible was the Word of God made manifest in Christ but also operating through men like themselves, and through events which they could understand. It was their favourite book; full of people, beasts, fishes, birds; of war, horror, love, death and miracles. Through its pages kings, princes, soldiers, shepherds, beggars, the rich, the poor, the sick, the healthy, the proud, the humble lived, moved and died. The book told them of splendid feasts and bitter famine; of present joy and perennial sorrow; of the hope of heaven and the horror of hell. It spoke of sowing and reaping, of good and bad harvests, and everywhere there was the countryside. True, it was a strange countryside in certain respects, but if it hadn't been for things like the desert, the Red Sea, cedar and olive trees, plants, people and places with outlandish names, it might well have been England. What happened in the Bible could so easily happen—and did happen—to its readers. They could and did identify themselves with certain characters just as they had once so eagerly watched and identified themselves with the characters in the old Mystery plays now all but dead—and, as later in the century, they identified themselves with the adventures of "a man cloathed in rags . . . a book in his hand and a great burden upon his back" who lamented and cried "What shall I do?"

For we are quite fatally mistaken if we judge the first readers of *The Pilgrim's Progress* by what the book now stands for in the corpus of English literature. At the time of publication (1678), during Bunyan's lifetime, and for a century afterwards it made little if any appeal to the educated minority. They thought it a crude, ill-told fairy tale. Its popularity was confined almost entirely to lower and middle class religious families; even the cheap paper and printing of the early edition tell us that this

*"La lingua Inglese in bocca Northantese" in fact.

312

Fighting cocks.

book was not meant for the rich, the elegant, the sophisticated or the cynical. It was read chiefly in cottages and farmhouses, and in crowded tenements. It was to be found in great houses . . . in the servants' hall or in the kitchens. It was the common people who first saw and recognized the power and purity of this wonderful allegory. They recognized it in their thousands and the book went through edition after edition. Its characters were clearly defined and easily recognizable. It had all the vividness of the drama (and much dialogue too). It was kin to the long-vanished Moralities.

For the stage had long since become a limited, secular art and, as such, had been cried down since Elizabeth's day as a means whereby Satan accomplished his ends. His ends were, as usual, "to bring men and women into his snare of concupiscence and filthie lustes of wicked whoredome".[22] Mr. Prynne . . ."an Utter Barrister" held much the same views. Furthermore he published them just before "the Quene's acting of here Play", George Gresley tells Sir Thomas Puckering in 1632.[23] The Queen was Henrietta Maria who appeared privately at court in Montague's *The Shepherd's Pastoral*—it is said that learning her part helped to improve her English. But "Women actors" said Prynne, are "notorious whores", which was hardly the thing to say about the Queen who certainly wasn't. And he asks, in view of St. Paul's prohibition against women speaking publicly even in churches, "dare any Christian woman be so more then whoreshly impudent as to act, to speak publiquelie on the stage (perchaunce in Man's apparrell and cut haire)". William Prynne* had his ears cut—for the first time—for this. After the second time he had to wear his hair long to hide his mutilated head.

But Satan had to abandon this particular snare for eighteen years between 1642 and 1658, and so did actors and playwrights. Hence there was a great break with the dramatic past, a wonderful past which in the first part of the century contained Shakespeare, Jonson, Field, Beaumont and Fletcher, Dekker, Heywood, Middleton and others. With the Restoration the theatre flourished again and within its physical limitations was wildly popular. The physical limitations were a lack of theatres (only two in London). As long runs were still unknown a great number of plays were needed and were forthcoming from professional and amateur authors alike, and writing plays was an accomplishment of gentlemen too. Neither tragedy nor the heroic play had much success in the reconstituted Stuart England—there had been

*William Prynne (1600-69) wrote 200 pamphlets against Archbishop Laud. His ears were docked first in 1634 and finally quite sliced off in 1637. Fellow Puritans John Bastwick and Henry Burton lost theirs at the same time which greatly inflamed feeling against Laud. All three men were henceforth regarded as living Martyrs by the Puritans who had dipped sponges and handkerchiefs in their blood—which is interesting in view of the Puritan opinion of relics. Prynne was again imprisoned by Cromwell for denying the legality of Army actions against Parliament but was later released by Cromwell and then worked hard to restore the monarchy! He was made Keeper of the Records in the Tower by Charles II who appreciated his good work, and this job, I think, made him very happy. I hope so, for he was, surprisingly enough, a courteous old man and kind to students, though embarrassingly convinced of the immorality of Nuns.

enough real tragedy*—so comedies, and Charles preferred
them, became the rule. Women now publicly played women's
parts (they had done so since 1629 but then they had been
French like the Queen and her ladies of which any immorality
is to be expected, and the plays were court plays). So the long,
vivid history of love affairs between members of the nobility and
actresses begins here. As a matter of protocol one must allow
Charles II to head the list, although Nell Gwyn had had two
well-born lovers, both called Charles—one was Charles Lord
Buckhurst—before the king took her over. So she called the
king Charles the Third.

Immediate post-Restoration plays are, not unnaturally, anti-
Puritan, not to say Tartuffian, in feeling. What we are pleased
to call Restoration Comedy—the works of Etherege,† Wycherley, Vanbrugh, Congreve, Farquhar and Cibber,‡ which are best
known to us, came very much later. Their plays—comedies of
manners as opposed to the earlier Jonsonian comedy of humours—
are remarkable for observation which if not deep is brilliantly
detailed. The phosphorescent scales of a corrupt society are
polished until they glitter, sparkle and reflect in a thousand tiny
mirrors the foibles, the affectations, the manners and morals of

*One does not forget Otway's *Venice Preserv'd* nor *The Orphan* but
these are exceptions to the rule.

†His *Love in a Tub*, 1664 is certainly Restoration period. But all other
plays by the playrights mentioned are late seventeenth century or early
eighteenth century. Etherege's perfect mirror of the times *The Man of
Mode* did not appear until 1676, while Congreve's first play *The Old
Bachelor* was not written until thirty-three years after the Restoration,
in 1693.

‡But Cibber represents a change in taste. His *Love's Last Shift* shows
virtue in distress and the heroine attempting to reform a libertine
husband by appealing to his feelings. Husband and audience were
reduced to tears by this. This was an innovation and *Love's Last Shift*
is our first sentimental comedy. It was left to Richard Steele to exploit
this new vein of sentimentality, not very successfully until *The Conscious
Lovers* in 1722 received the accolade in being thought to be the only
play suitable for a Christian to see. Parts of it were "almost solemn
enough for a sermon", or so George Adams says.

The Pageant of Stuart England

the narrow and shallow fashionable world. Shakespeare too, held the stage (the first folio had been printed in 1623) sometimes as originally written but more often improved, remodelled and modernized to suit "refined" taste. For Shakespeare was now thought a pretty barbarous and crude old fellow—he did not preserve the unities. The French had put this idea into our heads, so had long study of Horace's *Ars Poetica*. Thus *Romeo and Juliet* with the assistance of James Howard, was turned into a Tragi-Comedy. *The Law against Lovers*, highly praised by contemporary critics, emerged from the mangled and amalgamated remains of *Measure for Measure* and *Much Ado*; while *The Tempest* aided by Dryden and with music, happily, by Purcell, became the *My Fair Lady* of the day under the title of *The Inchanted Island*. *Macbeth* was improved by "alterations, additions and new songs" as well as by some sort of flying machine for the witches, and a trap-door for the ghost. *A Midsummer Night's Dream* was transformed into a sort of operetta with music by Purcell and such elaborate scenic effects—including a Chinese garden and lots of monkeys—that the actors failed to make any money. *Richard II* adapted with quite demented freedom by Nahum Tate, was re-titled *The Sicilian Usurper* and clever Mr. Tate also managed —though this must have been fairly easy—to turn *Coriolanus* into *The Ingratitude of a Commonwealth* in which Valeria appears to be a satirical portrait of the woman writer and "philosopher" Margaret (Lucas) Cavendish, Duchess of Newcastle.

For it was in this century that women really took to writing,* although often this important fact is lost amid the voluminous output for which the century is famous. Apart from diaries, letters and journals by women, which cannot be discussed here, four very different women produced four notable biographies or autobiographies; Lucy Hutchinson, the Duchess of Newcastle, Lady Anne Fanshawe and Anne Clifford, once Countess of

*In Elizabethan and early Stuart times one notes Catherine Killigrew, Mary Herbert, Countess of Pembroke, Anne, Countess of Winchelsea to say nothing of Queen Elizabeth herself, but there was no "school" of women writers comparable to that of the late seventeenth century.

Of Recreations—Simple or Sinful

Dorset (who personated the River Aire in *Tethys' Festival*), now Countess of Pembroke. Of these, the Duchess was the only one to write other things as well—poems, plays, "Sociable Letters" and philosophic fantasies. She had no need to write to live—although when in exile with her husband he had been forced to leave her behind in Holland as surety for his debts—and it is quite clear that she had a driving urge to write. It seemed to her that writing was a far better occupation than the loose behaviour with which the court ladies whiled away their time. Was writing a less useful occupation than embroidery or painting? she asks (Mary Beale, our first professional woman painter belongs to this period too) or less useful than "the making of Flowers, Boxes, Baskets with Beads, Shells, Silke and Strawe?" These "gentile" and womenly pastimes, so scorned by the Duchess, are surprising—particularly the bead and shell work—they sound so very Victorian.

But nothing could be less Victorian than the literary efforts of certain other women of the era.* Mrs. Aphra Behn (1640-89) was the first woman to turn to playwriting as a profession (she also wrote novels) and was followed by Mrs. Manley (1663-1742) and Mrs. Mary Pix (1666-1720?). Fat and bibulous Mrs. Pix, a clergyman's daughter, has—or at any rate had until a few years ago—the distinction of writing one of the filthiest plays in the English language (*Spanish Wives*). Mrs. Manley made up for lack of talent by sheer scandal and licentiousness. Mrs. Behn, the most talented of the lot, is a past mistress of the prurient. She wrote fifteen plays, ten novels and other miscellaneous works in sixteen years (she died at forty-eight and is

*Women who achieved a more or less unsullied fame were Katherine Philips the "Matchless Orinda"—a pretentious poseuse; Elizabeth Thomas whose verse was overpraised by Dryden; Mrs. Susanna Centlivre who married one of Queen Anne's cooks; Elizabeth Rowe, whose much praised poetry was written under the pseudonym "Philomela"; Katherine Trotter who wrote plays and philosophical works, and Elizabeth Haywood. The bulk of Mrs. Rowe's works lies in the Hanoverian era as does that of Mrs. Haywood, but all these women were born in the seventeenth century.

Semi-permanent setting for Masque, temps. Charles I.

buried in Westminster Abbey)* and was censured for writing plays which would not have been so censured had they been written by a man. Critics condemned her for dullness on one hand and indecency on the other (but who could be more dull and relatively decent than Thomas Shadwell?). Mrs. Behn had other characteristics permissible in men but not in women; she led an openly immoral life, she was a wit, her conversation was good. Men in their private capacity liked her. Women privately and publicly didn't. But Mrs. Behn and other women playwrights merely reflected their times and must not be viewed out of context. Certainly the Restoration attitude to women was cynical, and in an age thoroughly bored with ordinary, everyday, almost cosy immorality, and where everyday language was so often couched in "the most filthye termes", playwrights, to titillate jaded appetites—for plays were printed and avidly read —turned to jolly themes of incest and perversions of all sorts. We ourselves have added sexual violence and brutality of every

*But see V. Sackville-West's *Mrs. Aphra Behn*.

Of Recreations—Simple or Sinful

kind to this repertoire which would have shocked our late Stuart ancestors, although it probably wouldn't have shocked the late Elizabethans or early Stuarts who seem to have revelled in really gruesome plays like *'Tis Pity She's a Whore*. But at least in those days no playwright ever attempted to justify his work on the grounds that a play dealing with incest and violence was really a moral tract against the subject matter dealt with.

But if dirt was "pay-dirt"—and it was—Mesdames Behn, Manley and Pix were merely following and sometimes exceeding male authors (as women often do) in using such themes. "I made 'em all talk baudry; ha, ha, ha," Bayes tells Johnson "beastly downright baudry upon the stage, i'gad, ha, ha, ha; but with an infinite deal of wit that I must say".[24] Bayes is a satirical portrait of John Dryden in whose play *Secret Love* there is a great deal of bawdry indeed—and wit too. Lamentable though it is, not even the men could excel Mrs. Pix when it came to plain bawdry and no wit at all.*

Theatrical in effect but available to a far larger audience were pageants and shows. People were still mad about them and had been for centuries. But in this century the Lord Mayor's Show—always the greatest of the year—took a slightly different turn, owing to the activities of Sir Thomas Myddelton of the Grocers' Company. Sir Thomas, brother of Sir Hugh whose New River Company brought water to London in James I's day, and of William who made a metrical version of the psalms, decided to try something original in the line of pageants when he became Lord Mayor in 1613. So he put on a water pageant embodying scenic and emblematic representations of his company. This wasn't all that new, the first scenic pageant was, perhaps, that

*There were many who objected to obscenity on the stage and said so. Most notably Jeremy Collier in *A Short View of the Immorality and Profaneness of the English State* (1698). Queen Anne, like her sister Mary, was no theatregoer and ordained that no plays be acted "contrary to religion or good manners" (Luttrell, January 18th, 1704). It had small effect and another proclamation was issued, 1711 to reform "the indecencies and disorders of the stage".

put on by John Wells, also a Grocer, in 1452, fifty years before Columbus, in error, discovered America. But not even old Tom Parr who died in 1635 at the age of 153 could remember that pageant, although he could remember Columbus and the Cabots, Cortez and Champlain, to say nothing of the great Elizabethans, and Ralegh, whose head, metaphorically speaking, was presented to the King of Spain by James I. So the Myddelton pageant with its five islands in the river "artfully garnished with all manner of Indian fruit trees, drugges, spices and the like" was new to the spectators of the day, and seems to have set a fashion in, and a standard for, all subsequent shows which remained splendid up until around 1707 when a decline set in. As the company to which the Lord Mayor belonged always paid for the show, the pageant naturally reflected the exploits of the Lord Mayor's company and now, in this century, poets were hired to create the arrangements of scenes, characters and dialogue and the whole thing was printed like a programme. Music was supplied by the city waits and the king's trumpeters when shows were on land; when on water, music of a different order was supplied by "drummes and pfiffes". At night there were rather saturnalian torch-light processions and fireworks over the Thames—the safest place for them—although time and again all through the century and all over the country firework shows ended in disaster. Right at the beginning of the Stuart century, in 1611, the Mayor of Norwich put on a grand display to thank the good citizens for his election, but something went wrong, as it so often did, and 150 of his faithful citizens were killed or injured. The Mayor's name was Thomas Anguish.*

Coronations were then as now good for a splendid show and the Stuart century saw five of them and might have seen a sixth had Cromwell accepted the crown (his funeral procession made up for it). Charles II's procession from the Tower to Whitehall†

---

*He was also a great benefactor to the city and is remembered for this in Norwich rather than for the unfortunate occurrence cited above.

†The procession in those days took place the day before the Coronation.

was from all accounts the most splendid of the lot. Streets were newly gravelled and strewn with flowers, every house was hung with tapestries—if any—or failing this the best carpets, bed coverlets and tablecloths. Ornate triumphal arches spanned the militia-lined streets, scaffolding held spectators, many of whom had seen the restored king's father step out onto another kind of scaffold—and every window and balcony along the route was crammed with people to see the King, the nobility, officers of state, all splendidly dressed, pass by on horse-back. The procession also contained a company of men dressed as "Turks". Although, like Sam Pepys "I know not what they were for". Turk did not necessarily mean a person from Turkey. Turk and Turkey* more often than not meant foreign. Mr. Samuel Pordage, a poet of no note, who crossed swords with Dryden and also "Englished" Seneca, celebrated the occasion (as did many others) in stultifying verse:

> "How thwacked the galleries and windows be
> With England's pride in all their braverie:
> Clear firmament of stars, from whence
> They shower upon you a kind influence."

Although Mr. Pordage's father, the rector of Bradfield, Berks. (now also happily restored to the living), was a keen astrologer, Mr. Pordage's stars were not stellar bodies: they were women. There is much, much more in this vein.

Among popular recreations of a more vigorous nature was dancing—"the horrible Vice of pestiferous Dancing" as Stubbes (*The Anatomie of Abuses*) once called it, and the balls of Restoration Whitehall were often as spectacular and memorable as the famous Masque *Solomon and the Queen of Sheba* which had been given in 1606 at Theobald's in honour of King Christian of Denmark. On this notable occasion the lady who played the Queen was stumbling drunk and sprayed the guest of honour

*Hence the edible Turkey (Mexico), the name was also used for the Guinea fowl which comes from Africa.

with gifts of wine, cream and jellies. Not to be outdone, the guest of honour himself fell flat on his face when he tried to dance. Faith, Hope and Charity were all drunk and even Victory, vanquished by wine, was laid out cold and had to be carted off and added to the other casualties in an outer chamber. Dancing in.Masques was not the Restoration court idea of fun (Masques were rather out) but fancy dress balls were. At one of these it was rumoured that a lady-in-waiting had dropped a child, a rumour which might well have been true. John Russell, brother of the first Duke of Bedford, was a most "desperate" dancer and had a printed list of some two or three hundred dances to choose from. But the Restoration court found John's dancing like his clothes a good twenty years out of date.

Twenty or so years ago, Charles I had been king, but even then there had been laments that "the court of England is much altered"[25] and that dancing was no longer as solemn and correct as it had been in the days of Elizabeth when "gravity and state" were upheld, or even in the days of the first Stuart when things were still "pretty well". Dances and dancing in the time of the first Charles had greatly deteriorated, those who remembered old times and old manners said; everyone, lord and groom, lady and kitchen maid now danced without "distinction" or cere-mony and there was nothing but "trench-more, the cushion dance, omnium gatherum, tolly-polly, hoyte cum toyte".[26] The Restoration court couldn't bear this sort of thing either, but for other reasons. No one was going to clump about with comic John Russell doing the clownish "Baldines", the tedious old Galliarde or Volta nor the Braule (corrupted to Branle in French and Brawle in English) and, hoyte cum toyte Sir, certainly not that ridiculous old Egg dance! So in the time of Charles II the court, imitating the French, went in for the Pavane, the Courante—a favourite of Louis XIV—and the Sarabande with music played on the guitar which everyone tried to learn "and God alone knows the universal twanging that followed" says the Count de Gramont. The Minuet, just about now, ceased to be a peasant dance (originally it was a branle of Poitou).

Of Recreations—Simple or Sinful

It came to Paris *c.* 1650, turned formal, and was set to music by Lully. The exiled English court learned it there—and its pendant gavotte—and brought it back to England. The gavotte was originally full of kissing and kicking up of heels (kissing dances were the rage) and didn't sober down until the latter end of the eighteenth century. Another desperate dancer was Lord Lanesborough who capered about on gouty legs until a great age. When Prince George of Denmark died in 1708, the ancient corybant sought an audience of the Queen for the sole purpose or urging her, in the strongest possible terms, to preserve her health and dispel her sorrow by dancing.* As poor Anne was so fat, gouty and dropsical she could barely walk, the advice seems just a shade tactless.

But it was in Anne's time that dancing and dances really assumed the elegance which we associate with the eighteenth century. This was largely due to Beau Nash who made the Assemblies and Balls at Bath—a fashionable resort—models of propriety and elegance and issued his famous rules for conduct. No longer were men permitted to dance in boots, nor were women allowed to appear in aprons. Fashionable society was, at last, becoming polite—at least on the surface. The wheel had come full circle.

Polite society apart, there was still much dancing throughout the country at fairs, Whitsun ales, and the like. Fairs were held everywhere, many were famous and infamous. Mayfair, London, was the site of a fair noted for its prostitutes and Bartholomew's Fair was the most famous of all. Here poor Elkanah Settle, the city poet and author of bombastic tragedies, ended his days (before dying in the newly endowed Charterhouse) playing a

---

*Lord Lanesborough isn't quite so demented as he sounds. He was just rather old fashioned or rather eccentric and no doubt believed, as it had once been believed in Germany, that a year's good health rewarded those who danced before the statue of St. Vitus on his feast day, June 15th. This became almost a mania and in Germany was forbidden by the authorities. So St. Vitus's dance has really nothing to do with chorea.

sort of pantomime dragon!—in shows like those once put on by Jonson's "Lanthorn Leatherhead".

In London (and elsewhere) there were also famous gardens or walks such as Mulberry Gardens, St. James's and the old Spring Garden near Charing Cross. The even newer Spring Garden at "Foxhall" (Fulke's Hall), later called Vauxhall, was open until midnight for light suppers of jellies, syllabubs and tarts—of both kinds—as thickets were thoughtfully provided for love making as at "Tatnam's", Tottenham Court (now Fitzroy Square), a nobleman's mansion surrounded by pleasure gardens. Or, after 1684, one could go out to Islington—a large village half a league from London—to gamble, walk, dance, eat or drink the waters of the new wells opened up by Mr. Sadler. But by 1700 Mr. Sadler's Wells (like Cupid's* Garden across from the Savoy) had become the haunt of the less respectable elements of a city which had never been noted for respectability anyway, and which seemed to be getting worse than ever despite the watch and the new street lamps—one to every tenth house (houses were of course not numbered). Young hooligans throughout the whole of the era made the night a time of terror for respectable and non-respectable alike. The most famous or infamous gang were the "Mohocks"†—"A Name borrowed from a Sort of Cannibals in India" the *Spectator* erroneously informs its readers. These toughs had been paralleled in the early century by the Roaring Boys—and that Roaring Girl, Mary Frith—but the Mohocks and other nocturnal gangs of the late seventeenth and early eighteenth century seem to have gone in for a more calculated viciousness—or perhaps their exploits are just better documented. Various forms of beastliness included: slashing with razors, breaking noses, making victims do a sword

---

*Or possibly Cuper's gardens . . . but generally called Cupid's.

†The Mohawks were, of course, one of the most easterly tribes of the Iroquois confederation. In 1666, the year of the Great Fire of London, Sieur de Tracy, Lieut-Governor of French territories in Canada, made a punitive expedition against the Mohawks in what is now the northern part of the State of New York.

dance . . . by slicing at their legs. They robbed, looted, overturned carriages, coaches and sedan chairs. Some Mohocks were hardened criminals, others were "youngsters" who, out of bravado or boredom joined the gangs for fun. Fun to them was "the outrageous ambition of doing all possible Hurt to their Fellow Creatures".[27]

A great deal of pleasure, however, was found in music—England was still considered a very musical nation—particularly

Spinet, second half of seventeenth century.

in singing (it still is, as the number of choirs in England shows). Many noblemen kept professional musicians as members of the household and Aubrey says, with palpable nostalgia, that he can remember a time when each family had its own harper. There were still roving bands of musicians who were welcomed everywhere—strolling musicians and players were the equivalent of very intermittent wireless and television programmes. And the first "opera" in England belongs to this century. *The Siege*

of Rhodes* was performed, privately, due to the ban, in 1656—
although it was more recitative than opera. But once the ban
was off, opera increased in popularity. In Anne's reign one of
the most popular operas was *Hydaspes* in which Nicolini (Nicolino
or Nicolo Grimaldi) was an enormous success as the eponymous
hero. What really seems to have impressed the audience more
than Nicolini's voice was his fight with the lion. There had been
many an inferior lion in the opera, but by 1710 the perfect lion—
in the person of a country gentleman who did it for fun—was
found. He fitted his lion skin costume so well that you couldn't
see his feet; he sprang about on all four seeming paws and hind-
legs with the utmost nimbleness, and, in the lion's part, gave
the naked and singing hero a real fight. What could be more in
keeping with the Englishness of the English than singing combined with lion or man baiting? And if the principals sang their
own language (Italian), how very sensible to have minor characters and slaves sing in English—one could thus understand almost half the words.

Although it seems the orchestra for *Hydaspes*, led by Pepuschi,
was chiefly foreign, every educated person in the country was
able to play one, sometimes two, or even more instruments . . .
and little musical evenings were held among friends everywhere.
Viols, lutes, guitars, were much favoured, but in the Stuart
century the violin began to supercede the viol and soon nearly
every village had its own fiddler, to say nothing of a company of
hand-bell ringers, while most towns had their own bands or
companies of musicians. Virginals were now being ousted by the
spinet and later both were superseded by the wing-shaped
harpsichord with its double keyboard. Dr. Claver Morris,
mad about music, notes sadly in his diary that at one musical
evening Mr. Hill's harpsichord was nearly a "note" below
concert pitch. This was bad enough but, worse, the young ladies
who performed on this underpitched instrument were very

*Only a year behind the first French opera *Triomphe de l'Amour* etc.
How very revealing of the Englishness of the English and the Frenchness
of the French the titles are.

poor when it came to the treble. A painful evening for this West Country Doctor who so loved music that he asks in his Will that there be no "Grief or Concernment" at his death, but if possible "there might be a Consort of music of three Sonatas at least in the Room where my Body is placed".*

Concert was invariably spelled Consort in .those days. Ladies who did not play the harpsichord—due perhaps to an inability to master the treble—presumably left off bead, silk, straw and basket work to perform, upon request, upon dulcimer, cithern and guitar. Ladies had taken to the latter almost to a woman as it was the favourite instrument of Charles II, and indeed Mary Davis, the actress and singer, had played so well that she won the King's heart for long enough at least to produce a daughter. The daughter—and I confess this does sound odd to me—was given the name and title of Lady Mary Tudor by her music—and mutton†-loving—father. Gentlemen—in despite, or perhaps because of Aristotle's dictum—played the flute,‡ the lute or blew into the more moral trumpet, horn or snake—that long curly instrument invented in the previous century. But any excuse was good enough to set most of us beating drums and ringing church bells with enormous gusto—John Bunyan's worst vices were "bell-ringing and playing at hockey"§ according to Macaulay. Foreigners might, and did, think us absolutely clay-pated for this love of "noise". We didn't give a Spanish fig for what foreigners thought about our noisy ways or anything else for that matter. And we readily added to the noise when possible and showed foreigners what we thought of them by hurling im-

*The Doctor died on March 19th, 1726 aged sixty-seven, and is buried in the East Cloister of Wells Cathedral.

†mutton = a prostitute.

‡"The flute is not an instrument which has a good moral effect; it is too exciting", *Politics* Bk. VIII: 6: trans. Benjamin Jowett, 1908.

§Hockey, a very old game, was, in its early form, called "cambuck". In Gloucester Cathedral there is a fourteenth century window showing a boy with a hockey stick and ball. I am told there is a similar window at Canterbury.

precations and stones at them and cheerfully overturning ambassadors' coaches. When it came to foreigners there was a touch of the Mohock about us all. But gentry and non-gentry alike took to bell ringing with enormous enthusiasm. Ringing the changes was a very popular recreation indeed—both literally and figuratively speaking—in the Stuart century. But since every human being has a built-in musical instrument which costs nothing (admittedly some are better than others) singing was the really popular art of the day. People got together to sing catches and glees at home, at the houses of friends, in taverns and coffee-houses; in addition, various musical societies sprang up. As early as 1670 there was one which met in rooms in Old Jewry which published a song book called *The Catch-as-Catch-Can or the Metrical Companion*. Another society met at the Bishopsgate post office, and neither this nor others can have been an all male choir, for to our surprise we learn that by Anne's day gentlemen were being warned that "Vocal Musick" was "Lewd to Scandal". It was "Arsenick upon Ratsbane", "Poison upon Poison" at best but when performed by women it was sheer "Gunpowder" and "blew up Virtue in a Moment".[28] This leaves us wondering what actually did go on at those musical evenings in the old post office.

One of the strangest and most passionate addicts of music was Thomas Britton who hawked small coals through London's streets. As early as 1678* Britton, then aged twenty-four, started to hold subscription concerts every Thursday evening in the loft above his coal store at Jerusalem Passage, Clerkenwell. Coal was his living. Music was his love. With the proceeds of one he supported the other. His concerts became famous and continued so for forty years. The music was said to be the best in London and every distinguished foreigner was taken to a Britton concert as a matter of course (and perhaps to show that it was not all drums and bells with us). Britton collected musical instruments, books, dabbled in the occult, and was

*Some six years earlier John Banister held subscription concerts at the "Musick School"—"over against the George Tavern, Whitefriars".

Of Recreations—Simple or Sinful

"so bright a genius in so dark a sphere" (Matthew Prior) that he was sought out by scholars and musicians—Händel* and Pepuschi played at his later concerts. Unhappily it was his interest in the occult which brought about his death. Some fool brought a ventriloquist† to a concert so when a voice speaking out of the ether—as Britton thought—told him his end was near and that he must fall upon his knees and prepare to meet his God, the Musical Small Coals Man thought this a genuine supramundane phenomenon, did as he was told, took to his bed and two days later, on September 27th, 1714, died.

If Britton was one of the attractions of London, teeming, restless London itself was a great magnet which attracted all visitors. Natives and foreigners took to sight-seeing with such avidity that as early as 1611 a critic peevishly asks

> "Why do the rude vulgar so hastily post in a madness
> To gaze at trifles and toys not worthy the viewing?" [29]

Among the trifles and toys which attracted early Stuart sightseers he lists, rather surprisingly we may think, the monuments at Westminster and Drake's ship at Deptford (one could eat on board but the ship was soon devoured piecemeal by souvenir hunters). The "slip shoes" of King Henry (VIII?), a whale bone at Whitehall, the Mummied Princes—whoever they were— and the unicorn's horn at Windsor may possibly be more trifling, but who can blame our ancestors for wanting to see the "Cassawarway" and the "Beauer i' the Parke" or "Harry the Lyon" at the Tower Zoo or any other member of the wild animal kingdom—man, woman or beast (like poor Pocahontas) brought into the country by travellers or collected by sea captains abroad either in their own or in others' interests?

---

*Händel produced his opera "Rinaldo" here in 1711 and returned to England for good in 1712.

†The famous Clinch or Clench of Barnet, who could also imitate all sorts of birds and beasts and who gave performances at various taverns.

The Pageant of Stuart England

In England the mania for collecting grew slowly during the first half of the era but with bewildering rapidity after the Restoration. Collecting, which had taken a firm grip on Europe in the sixteenth century, did not really get under weigh here until the seventeenth century, and it is in this century that England's first public museum appears—not in London but in Oxford. The nucleus of the British Museum lies in this century too (although the Museum, as such, didn't come into being until 1753), in the great collection made by Doctor (later Sir) Hans Sloane. Men like Sir Robert Cotton and Sir Thomas Bodley at the beginning of the Stuart period, and Robert Harley (Earl of Oxford) at the end—to name but three—collected books and manuscripts which have enriched us ever since.

The rude and vulgar may not have been interested in looking at books. But, they were as interested in looking at other things as collectors were in collecting them. It is true that almost anything interested both collector and viewer. People flocked to see,

>   ". . . a strange outlandish Fowle
>   A quaint baboon, an Ape, an Owle,
>   A dancing Beare, a Gyants bone,
>   A foolish Ingin move alone,
>   A morris dance, a Puppit play
>   Mad Tom* to sing a Roundelay
>   A woman dancing on a Rope . . ."†

and so on. But this avid curiosity was surely a part of the great spirit of inquiry of the time, mirroring it on an ordinary, more

---

*Tom of Bedlam. Bedlam too was one of the sights . . . the insane were strange and amusing animals.

†Fire-eating, tumbling, hocus pocus (conjuring), and rope dancing were popular throughout the era. Jacob Hall, a famous rope dancer, was one of the numerous lovers of Barbara Villiers. This affair really annoyed Charles. He thought she'd rather let the side down with a rope dancer.

everyday, level. All sorts of people collected all sorts of things, in a joyful, haphazard, glory-hole sort of way. Even connoisseurs could be caught by crafty European dealers who prospered wonderfully by palming off fakes and worthless objects on even the most knowing collectors—who were really not awfully knowing when it came to the more portable antiquities of Greece

Maple and pinewood Viol, *c.* 1700.

and Rome. Not a few antiquaries, for example, collected headless marble torsi and, having not the smallest idea who the headless ones were, gave them the names of Homer, Pindar, Apollo and so on. Elsewhere, we find that many collections were in a rare old muddle, as that Frankfort-born, fault-finding visitor, von Uffenbach, tells us. He was a great one for seeing the sights, visiting libraries and collections, but was quite disgusted by the un-Germanic lack of order and method. James Petiver's collection of botanical specimens and natural curiosities were kept, he says, "in true English fashion"—meaning in utmost confusion. Petiver, shockingly, could scarce speak Latin! Collections at Oxford and Cambridge were no better (the music was bad there too), but he rather admired a "petrified" English cheese on view at St. Johns (Cambridge) while at St. Johns (Oxford) a sheep with two heads, and a bladder stone the size of a hen's egg quite caught his imagination.*

At the Anatomical School he was shown two worm-eaten loaves from the Siege of Oxford, a heelless shoe of Queen Elizabeth's, the sword with which James I had knighted Sir Line (Loin) Beef, the hand of a siren, dried; Joseph's coat—and suitably—the anatomy (skeleton) of a pigmy. At the Ashmolean he viewed a stuffed reindeer, an Indian ass and a Turkish goat; Indian plants, precious stones, the tooth of a Danish giant found near Pontefract; ivory carvings, a runic calendar, and spiders in amber; a horn from the head of Mary Davies who died in 1688, and various other marvels all shown by the under-custodian "a silly fellow", but the chief custodian, Mr. Parry, was "too busy guttling and guzzling to show it to strangers". Nevertheless, von Uffenbach is surprised that the treasures are as well preserved as they are "as everyone in true English fashion handles them roughly and all persons—even women—are admitted on payment of 6d., who run about and will not be hindered by the sub-custos".[30] Obviously, no good could come of letting women run about in the Ashmolean. Doubtless they had driven Mr. Parry to drink.

More to the visitor's liking was the collection of one, Claudius de Puy, but he wasn't English. He was a French-Swiss calico printer who had settled in London. His Swiss blood, no doubt, accounted for the order in which he kept his collection and he had, with admirable thoroughness, ticketed his objects with written explanations of what they were. It was as well, for he had an unselective lot of things to show, including a small zoo. But here one could see, amongst hundreds of other fascinating items, Indian birds' nests, a fine mandragora, sea-beasts, mother-of-pearl shells carved with the story of Lot, an elegant rush hat lined with palm leaves (great interest was shown in outlandish apparel in those days) a piece of thorn bush with huge thorns said to be of the kind with which Christ was crowned, and a

*But von Uffenbach was, none the less, a true bibliophile—he also played the flute and the violin—though he thought the English rude and not very cultured.

picture of Christ made of feathers. There were musical instruments, a snake's skin sixteen ells long, a hollow walking stick containing both a sword and a gun; various idols—one with an ass's head was reputedly Moloch—and a notable marble Priapus, more curious in attributes than even the most ancient of Greeks could have suspected (replicas of this statue also appeared in other collections, one wonders where they were made). Upstairs, there were waxworks where Cleopatra lay "with the cure of all our ills"[31], her red-eyed maid weeping beside her while, nearby, Anthony busily stabbed himself. Here too, Rosamund, fair but quite demented, knelt before Queen Eleanor who handsomely offered her a choice between a dagger and a cup of poison (Rosamund, however, refused and hied herself to a nunnery at Godstow). Not far away Sophia of Hanover, "heiress of England", slept by a table. Queen Anne, who detested Sophia, was wide awake "a well-made but flattering figure". But undoubtedly the *capolavoro* of de Puy's collection was to be found in Room 2. It was Cromwell's head "just as it fell down with the spike broke off". Or at least that's who or what de Puy said it was, and told von Uffenbach he could get sixty guineas for it. Von Uffenbach was not very interested. He much preferred the head of a mummy. It was, after all, of much greater antiquity.

Infinitely less well displayed but probably more fun was the collection of James Salter on show at his Coffee-house in the nearby village of Chelsea. James, who called himself Don Saltero, had had various jobs—tooth drawer, trimmer, scraper—before settling down as "a gim crack whim collector" (the words are his own) in his "Chelsea Knackatory" in 1695. Here, as his advertisement tells us

"Monsters of all sorts are seen,
　　Strange things in nature as they grew so:
Some relicks of the Sheba Queen
　　And fragments of the famed Bob Crusoe.
Knick knacks, too, dangle round the wall,
　　Some in glass cases, some on shelf;

The Pageant of Stuart England

But what's the rarest sight of all,
  Your humble servant shows himself . . .''

He then begs readers to direct friends to his Museum and coffee-house where, in addition to drinking coffee and seeing the collection, he will gladly bleed them, shave them or draw their teeth! Truly a man of many parts, this Don Saltero, and in this too he mirrors the age.

For on one level there is Dr. Hans Sloane, on another James Salter. The rich fashionable physician with his cabinet of curiosities and the unfashionable tooth drawer with his Knacka-tory expressed and fostered a love of "curiosities" each in a personal and individual way. Those who had not the entrée to Dr. Sloane's collection in Bloomsbury or at his country place at Chelsea, could enjoy the pleasure of Don Saltero's not so far away in Cheyne Walk*—even if the relicks of Sheba's queen do sound a trifle dubious. For the fresh spirit of wonder was still alive in those days. That childlike ability to be astonished, de-lighted, and amazed at the world and all the ordinary and extra-ordinary things it contains is a prime characteristic of the Stuart century.

---

*I am indebted to Professor Donald F. Bond for drawing my attention to the fact that James Salter owed his success to Dr. Sloane. Dr. Sloane let Salter have the house in Cheyne Walk, and also started him off by giving him items from his own collection. Thus, the Sloane collection was the nucleus of the long-vanished Chelsea Knackatory no less than of the British Museum.

CHAPTER NINE

Of Cosmetics and Perfumes

ARAMANTHA was fortunate. She had a "glad eye" (the phrase had not its present-day meaning), graceful figure, sweet voice, snowy hands, and curly hair. In short, she was a Provence rose "flower'd with blush" and had no need of

> ". . . cabinets with curious washes
> Bladders, and perfumed plashes."

Nor did she rise late and spend hours dressing. "Up with the jolly bird of light" was Aramantha and, slipping into some filmy nymph-like garment, she wasted no time on beauty aid or looking-glass.

> "No venom-tempr'd water's here
> Mercury is banished this sphere":

because

> "Her pail's all this, in which wet glass
> She both doth cleanse and view her face."

Then, ready for breakfast, the lucky girl proceeds to a nearby meadow—envied by every flower as she passes—where, obligingly

> "A rev'rend lady cow draws near,
> Bids Aramantha welcome here;
> And from her privy purse lets fall
> A pearl or two . . ."

The Pageant of Stuart England

After a "breakfast on her teat",[1] Aramantha is ready for the exciting and idyllic day wherein she and Alexis are, at last, re-united.*

The rev'rend cow and the manner of breakfasting may sound a trifle unpoetic not to say distasteful to us, and we have no evidence that fashionable women of the time found it palatable either. Nor indeed would any woman during the whole of the Stuart century have approved of a wafty garment. If men and poets went on, as they had since Tasso first sang of Aminta,† depicting ideal women as a nymph cum goddess, mundane or mondaine woman, as usual, paid not the smallest attention. She had quite other ideas. She did not object to being addressed or thinking of herself as Chloris, Althea, Chloe, Flora, Delia, Lesbia, Celia, Saccharissa, Lucinda, Corinna or any bogus golden-age name which conjured up love, innocence, beauty and a warm climate. She liked the idea of a passionate shepherd or a noble savage, like Mrs. Behn's Oroonoka-Caesar, as a lover. She was not in the least averse to having her beauty sung in pastoral or minor lyric full of glades, streams, mossy banks, chorister birds, fruit, nuts, and flower-emboss'd carpets of green, provided no fool husband or lover really expected her to live in rural England. Rural England, she well knew, was full of mud, bumpkins, grass, trees, rain, animals, and small squires who possessed old houses, frumpish wives, lumpy daughters—"O such Out-landish Creatures! Such Tramontanae and Foreigners to the Fashion"[2]— and red-faced sons in boots. The country, with the possible exception of Tunbridge Wells and Bath, lacked such amenities as sparks, wits, beaux, fops, theatres, shops, promenades, gossip, scandal, crowds. It just wasn't London. No woman could be truly fashionable and live out of

---

*Armantha turns out to be none other than the more famous Lucasta under a nom de guerre as it were. The name Lucasta derives from lux casta, "chaste light" and the original nymph, according to Anthony à Wood, was Lucy Sacheverell who, upon Lovelace going to the wars, married another.

†Or since Theocritus and Virgil.

Type of patches in use during the century.

London. Even the larger and less deadly provincial towns were twenty-five years out of date when it came to such important things as the cut of a sleeve, the colour of one's hair, the shape of an eyebrow.

Yet even in darkest England there was no lack of beauty hints. The difference lay in that country hints were apt to be "hereditary Receipts", handed down and recorded in the same book which held recipes for cookery, physic and minor surgery, whereas in London new ideas were always coming in from the despised Continent—particularly from France and Italy. Nevertheless, many a hoary hereditary Receipt was refurbished, newly printed in London, and passed off as the *dernier cri*. The result was a great mass of wild and unco-ordinated information on how to make one's self lovelier even if one weren't all that lovely to begin with. And if, occasionally, the end product of beauty aids and cosmetics was disastrous—a most inconvenient poisoning from an excess of white lead, or a permanent scarring because of slight carelessness with the stone lime—well, one was frequently poisoned by bad food, or scarred for life by smallpox anyway. It was worth the risk.

And risk it often was. There were innumerable "venom-tempr'd waters" to turn even the most indifferent skin into no skin at all. That popular Elizabethan skin clearer, "Soliman", largely oil of vitriol, was only gradually superseded by more gentle washes made of powdered white mercury, lemon juice, pulverized egg shells and white wine. May-dew was still a favourite in town and country, but in town one no longer rose with the "jolly bird" to sop it up, it could be bought in shops and it was guaranteed genuine, although it might have come from the nearest conduit. Less attractive, but available all year round, was puppy dog urine.* This reputed skin beautifier was used by Mrs. Pepys who also supplied some of it to Pepys' Aunt Wight. This caused Sam "some little discontent".[3] Rather unreasonably, one feels, in view of the loathsome and repulsive ingredients used in many medicines. Sweat from behind the ears was useful for chapped lips and powdered myrrh sprinkled with white wine and placed on a heated iron plate gave off fumes which "filled up empty pores" (wrinkles) and smoothed the skin.

The removal of blemishes required more stringent measures. The rather eccentric William Butler—one-time doctor to Prince Henry—cured early century spots by hanging his patients until they were blue in the face, he then cut the vein which fed the "pimples" to let out the "black, ugly blood". This sounds a little drastic, and a more popular cure was May-dew and "Oyl of Tartar" mixed, which took away "all foul spots" and was particularly efficacious in banishing morphew and freckles. This recipe, in use for many years, appeared together with much other startling information in *The Queen's Closet Opened*, a compendium of old and new recipes from many sources (some date back to King Edward, presumably the sixth, not the first) which was selling very well in 1683. A red or pimpled face responded to liverwort and cream, or to the juice of the same plant taken in beer. A "Shining or Redness of the Nose" was reduced by dew sopped up in a cloth, wrung into a "fair dish" and used as a wash. In more obstinate cases an

*Urea *is* a disinfectant, still used in the Middle East.

Of Cosmetics and Perfumes

unguent of peeled gourd seeds and bitter almonds was recommended.

Although Mary Bagot's nose was not red, she had "large red ears and flat feet", or so Miss Hobart, a fellow maid-of-honour to the Duchess of York, said.[4] But these defects proved no handicap to Mary who married well, twice. Her first marriage made her Countess of Falmouth, her second to Charles Sackville—once the gay, witty and debauched Lord Buckhurst—made her Countess of Dorset and mistress of Knole. Lely's three-quarter length portrait of Mary, dressed rather *à la bergère* (a bosom roped off with pearls, drop earrings and a wand or crook in left hand!), admittedly shows neither ears nor feet but, more importantly, it does show that Mary had an unmistakable *Le viens par ici* look which it is just possible Miss Hobart lacked. For Miss Hobart, according to court gossip, was a man.

Still, if stuck with large red ears and flat feet, there was absolutely no reason to be permanently attached to unsightly warts or wens. Although many considered warts, especially hairy ones, lucky,* they were not beautiful, but radishes shredded into a pewter dish, salted, covered, shaken madly, then rubbed on the wart three or four times a day would remove this blemish. Possibly salt, absorbing moisture from the radish, might act upon the metals in the pewter to produce a caustic solution which, with patience, would wear a wart away. At once more caustic and more deadly was a remover for an "unsightly Wen". Stone lime was put in water, when well-boiled it was mixed with "barrel" (barilla?) soap, spread on a cloth and applied to the growth. It "will eat any Wen away"[5] the recipe says cheerfully. The wonder is how the user endured the agony of an eating away process induced by slaked lime and lye.

*Can it be this and not lack of vanity which prompted Cromwell's famous request to Peter Lely to be painted warts and all? Cromwell had a great wart or wen on his chin—this signified riches, a good digestion and an ability to talk a lot. The two warts on his forehead were, fortunately, on the right side, and this also signified riches—had they been on the left side it would have meant poverty.

It is not surprising, then, that women took to patching furiously. Patches are said to have been invented by the mistress of a French king who wanted to hide an unsightly spot, and patches flourished here from around the beginning of the century. They, too, had their fashions and absurdities. Starting modestly as a simple dot of black taffeta or of red perfumed Spanish leather placed near the mouth, where the most stubborn spots appear, they soon changed shape and size and dotted the face with crescent moons, stars and diamonds. By mid-century the daring added a small silhouette of a coach and horses to forehead or cheek bone. Patching was a vanity which, like painting, was frowned upon by Parliament and by many women of Puritan persuasion who cultivated a simplicity of dress which eschewed all ornament. Yet not all women were Puritan and not all Puritan women wore regulation dress; they were not persuaded that a false red on cheek or lip was a symbol of Hell fire to come no matter how often they were told it was. Thus, in 1650, when Parliament ordered an Act against "the Vice of Painting* and wearing Black Patches and immodest Dresses of Women", it had singularly little effect.

Four years later John Evelyn notes, "women began to paint themselves, formerly a most ignominious thing and used only by prostitutes".[6] But here Evelyn is wrong. He was safely out of England in 1650 when Parliament ordered the Act and it is probable he observed painting for the first time in 1654 because fashion was then swinging from the light touch to the heavy hand in make-up, as it seems to do on an average of every twenty or thirty years unless wars, sumptuary laws or threats of Hell act as a deterrent.

In any event, patching and painting continued. Coaches and horses soon galloped out of favour, but at and after the Restor-

---

*A man wishing to discover if his beloved painted was advised to eat a great quantity of garlic or cummin seed and then breathe heavily in her face. If she were painted "the colour will vanish away, straight"— doubtless the beloved did too. This was an old trick and, one gathers, perhaps not much used in the seventeenth century.

ation patches—sometimes called "love spots" and, vulgarly, "mouches"—were so fashionable that Lady Castlemaine decreed they could be worn at all times, save when in mourning. They were still as useful as they were ornamental too, because the Duchess of Newcastle—who didn't give a "Harington" (brass farthing) for fashion, lived in the country for preference, wrote books and plays—once appeared in London wearing a justacorps, a black velvet cap, her curls about her ears and lavish patches about her mouth "because of the pimples".[7]

Late Stuart wigs and wig stands.

She was one of the sights of the town. Everyone talked of her "extravagancies", by which is meant that she was thought to be ridiculous, ludicrous and unfashionable; preferring books to gossip and her husband above other men.

In France, patches were worn only by the young. But in England, young, old, handsome, and ugly patched until they were "Bed-rid". "I have often counted fifteen patches or more upon the swarthy, wrinkled Phiz of an old Hag of three score and ten and upwards'', M. Misson says, not very gallantly for a Frenchman, but it was obviously true. And patches took on an additional significance in Queen Anne's day when women took to indicating which side they favoured politically by the side on which they patched. Astonishingly, Tory supporters patched on the left. Whigs on the right. The uncommitted—they were perhaps those who enjoyed being persuaded by men of both parties or liked being enigmatic—patched on both sides. This must have considerably reduced the utility of patching—a spot is no respector of political parties—or possibly women changed sides as frequently as maculae dictated. As they had no vote it can't have mattered much, and we do not know what influence a new preparation "A Certain Cure for Scabs, Pimples and the Old Invetcrate Itch"[8] which was published in 1714, may have have on the politics of the day. We do know, however, that it contained flowers of brimstone, butter and "red precipitate".

But patches provided only the final touch to a face already bleached by a wash, whitened with ceruse (white lead) which, despite the horrid side effects it frequently produced, remained the favourite paint of the century. The best ceruse these days came from Venice—that made in England was sophisticated with whiting and hadn't the covering qualities of pure white lead. Ceruse, mixed with a "sweet water" or white of egg, was applied with a rag or a brush exactly like paint. Red was often added—Indian lake* or cochineal—to a bit of the ceruse to produce a complexion "flowr'd with blush", although there was also a paper impregnated with a red dye called Spanish paper which, when wetted, could be rubbed on cheeks and lips. Later Spanish wool, also dye-impregnated, and a liquid known as "Bavarian Red" were used to superimpose the rose upon the lily—"rose and lily" was still the desired standard com-

---

*Lake is the English spelling of lākh, a crimson dye contained in the resin of East Indian trees of the acacia family and obtained through the sap-sucking activities of the Tacchardia lacca. A process of melting, straining and cooling turns the resin into thin brittle, shell-like plates, hence "shell-lac".

Of Cosmetics and Perfumes

plexion. A certain Mrs. Wetenhall (daughter of Sir Henry Bedingfield) who died in 1689, was a typical English beauty. Her colouring was "lilies and roses, snow and milk".[9] Arms, hands, bosom and feet were delicately modelled and her features were charming. But her face was totally devoid of expression and completely doll-like. This may be excused, perhaps, on the grounds that she lived "among cabbages and turkeys" at Peckham, which was boring; and with a bookish husband who had intended to enter the church but hadn't, which must have been even more boring. Or possibly, unlike Lady Wishfort, she preserved an expressionless face so there would never be any "cracks discernable in the white Vernish".[10] Indeed, many women did "lay(s) it on with a Trowel",[11] but not all were so lavish. Nor were they all apt to be caught by "Poetick Raptures", "High Heroick fustion" or "Fulhams of Poetick fiction" with which beauty was conventionally praised. Unfashionable women, in their dull way, might even agree with the tough cynical widow who says that most men will kick a woman in prose and yet adore and adorn her in verse with false, boring and silly clichés made to fit the poet's rhyme and not the woman's looks:

> "Her mouth compar'd t'an Oysters, with
> A row of Pearl in't stead of Teeth;
> Others make Posies of her Cheeks,
> Where red and whitest Colours mix;
> In which the Lilly, and the Rose,
> For Indian Lake, and Ceruse goes.
> The Sun and Moon by her bright Eyes
> Eclips'd and darken'd in the Skies,
> Are but Black-patches that she wears,
> Cut into Suns and Moons and Stars."[12]

This point of view, however, was exceptional, and the lily and rose went on being the fashionable complexion and cliché for years. But golden or red hair, once so popular, seems to have suffered a slight eclipse during the second half of the century.

The Pageant of Stuart England

Gentlemen may still have preferred blondes, but Charles, dark and swarthy himself, although his tastes were catholic, seems, on the whole, to have preferred brunettes. Judging by the countless recipes for dying hair black, many women must have decided that black hair was the thing wherein to catch the fancy of the king, even if Elizabeth Pepys did once madden her husband with flaxen hair. Both men and women meddled about with hair colour as they had always done, mostly out of vanity but sometimes for other reasons. James Butler, Earl (later Duke) of Ormonde disguised himself by dyeing his hair when he came to England during the last days of the Commonwealth to see what the possibilities were of a Royalist uprising. Unfortunately, the dye job went wrong. Ormonde's hair turned rainbow-coloured on top which must have been conspicuous, not to say unusual, in Puritan England. Possibly this very conspicuousness was a safeguard, a sort of double bluff. No spy could be such a ninny as to call attention to himself in this fashion.

To make the hair black "though any colour",[13] a groat* or sixpence was dissolved in aqua fortis and the liquid sponged on the hair, "but touch not the skin" admonishes the recipe. This seems advisable. Aqua fortis is nitric acid, and as groats and sixpences were of silver the liquid would be nitrate of silver. It was one thing to have raven tresses but quite another to look as if one were ebony-headed. Always provided hair and scalp remained after continued use of such stuff. Or, comb the hair with a comb dipped in warm oil of Tartar, dry by the fire, then rinse with Hyssop water, repeat daily and at the end of a week the hair was "a curious Black". One does not doubt this for an instant. But dyes grew less corrosive as time went on. The *Ladies Guide* for 1700 informs its readers that black hair can be achieved with "gum-dye" boiled with sage, myrtle, bay and

*The groat was worth 4d. It had been in circulation since the time of Edward III (1327-77). It was discontinued during Charles II's reign and not minted again until the days of William IV and Queen Victoria. The sixpence is much newer, it appeared first during the reign of Edward VI (1547-53).

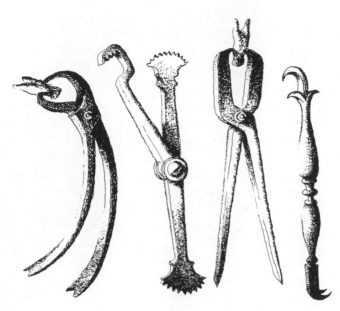

Dental instruments for levering and pulling teeth.

beet leaves plus walnut peelings. This was applied to wetted
hair—the face quickly washed in wine to remove any stain—
and allowed to dry by itself. Black hair, says the Guide, "is
particularly useful in setting off the whiteness of neck and skin."
So were small blackamoors kept as pages and attendants. Charles'
French mistress, Louise de Kéroualle, Duchess of Portsmouth,
thought so and had her picture painted with her page. She is
unadorned, but the page is richly dressed, wears a choker of fat
pearls and is offering his mistress equally large pearls from a
great shell.

No hair at all was less of a disadvantage after the Restoration
than during the first half of the century, for by then wigs and
false hair had come in again—rather excessively too—and for
the first time in modern history men took to wigs. Elizabethan
women had worn wigs but the Elizabethan male hadn't. He kept
his hair short, Roman fashion, until the latter part of the sixteenth century when he began to let it grow. Thus baldness

was neither desirable nor beautiful in the male (who also used cosmetics) and until wigs came in he tried, vainly no doubt, to keep baldness at bay with such things as Aqua Mellis,* which made the hair grow long and curly, or Ladanum (not to be confused with Laudanum) a gum which was thought to derive from dew falling upon a herb in Greece, or to be taken from the beard of a goat which had cropped the herb. Ladanum had other virtues too. It strengthened the skin, cured ear-ache and hardness of the womb. This hint, or rather the hair-growing part of it, was as up to date as Pliny who had mentioned Ladanum as a hair restorer and preserver of colour some sixteen centuries before.[14] A "Very good Pomatum"[15] to nourish and make the hair shining is such a long and complicated recipe that it is fortunate it would keep for three years—although why anyone would want to keep it, let alone make it, is a complete mystery. The basis for this early equivalent of brilliantine, or hair conditioner, was a pound of fat from a young dog (directions for killing included) and two pounds of lambs' caul. This obviously must be foreign. Not even our seventeenth-century ancestors would kill a dog for such a purpose—although they did not care much what happened to one used in bull or bear baiting.

Then there were those who had hair in the wrong places and this required work with "tiny tongs" or the use of a depilatory. A late century recipe recommends a mixture of "wax and rosin" (spelled as then pronounced and as still pronounced in the U.S.A. and Canada today) which is similar to our modern wax method, but users are advised "to wash ye place with temitry to keep ye hair from comeing again". Earlier in the century, fifty-two egg shells—beaten and distilled—were said to do the trick but one is a little doubtful although it is

*Although I am unable to discover what Aqua Mellis is, the name suggests it may have been honey water, a popular hair brightener and restorer in the previous century, or a decoction of balm (melissa officinalis). I incline to the latter because Aqua Mellis was to be used in the spring and the leaves of balm are more strongly scented in spring and early summer than at other times of year. All this is, however, pure guesswork on my part.

Of Cosmetics and Perfumes

certainly infinitely preferable to a recommended depilatory made of cat's dung dried, powdered and mixed with vinegar. Better, one feels, if the condition were desperate, to join a side-show as a bearded lady than remove superfluous hair by this method. Certainly Ursula Dyan must have thought so, for she exhibited herself, as such, in Holborn in 1688 together with a giantess who was six foot five inches tall.

As to hair styles generally, the Stuart century saw the rise of some very odd ones, and "rise" is the significant word. Men early began to glory in their hair and the Roundheads got their derisive name, not because they were particularly brachy-cephalic but because of the pudding-basin cut they affected at a time when long hair was in fashion. For after about 1625 men of the court party wore ringlets which cascaded down the back. One ringlet, known as a love-lock, was brought carelessly over one shoulder and tied with a ribbon bow. Charles I wore a long love-lock over his left shoulder and William Prynne took such a spite against it that he rushed into tactless and dangerous print in 1628 with The Unloveliness of Love-Locks". Women were in-volved in a hair style known as "tête de mouton", rather frizzled at the sides and with a high bun at the back of the head orna-mented with ribbon, pearls or flowers. By about 1650 both men and women were wearing a fringe which covered the forehead nearly to the eyebrows. Women wore it curled, men plain. These were court styles and were particularly fashionable in Cavalier circles.

After the Restoration, in 1663 to be exact, the King took to a black wig, possibly because at the age of thirty-three his hair was "mighty grey". This set the seal of approval upon wigs for men. Pepys, always a dressy fellow, had already ordered himself two periwigs, one costing £3 the other 40/- but he doesn't seem to have had courage enough to wear one until after he heard that the King was about to do so. He was much relieved when he appeared in church for the first time in his wig that "it did not prove so strange as I thought it would". Three guineas was a fair price for a wig but many cost as much as £40.

When first introduced, wigs were a mass of curls and ringlets, shoulder length at the sides and longer at the back. Black was the fashionable colour in emulation of the King—Charles once complained that all stage villains wore black wigs—but later brown shades were worn. There was a nasty scare in plague year when it was rumoured (probably correctly) that hair from plague victims was being used in the manufacture of wigs. By

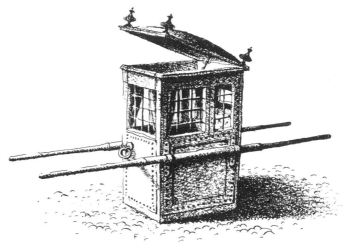

Sedan chair with opening lid.

the time of James II, wigs had a centre parting with great peaks of curls standing up on either side; these peaks grew higher and higher during the reign of William and Mary (and the tri-corne, for men, so typical of the Georgian era made its first tentative appearance then). By Anne's day wigs were yet higher with curls in a positive waterfall almost to the waist. Grey powdered wigs began to come in (they turned white, appropriately enough, in the time of George I); so did the tie and bob wig, but full-bottomed wigs were generally worn. Anne did not approve of the tie and bob. "I suppose his Lordship will come to court next time in his night cap" she said, when a Minister appeared in a new-fangled tie wig.

Of Cosmetics and Perfumes

Enormous wigs had great disadvantages, particularly in the English climate. High winds made a mess of them and they looked even worse when it rained.* Furthermore, there was some risk of fire. On his very first visit to the new house designed for Lord Burlington by Sir John Denham, Pepys accidentally set his wig alight. It made a very odd noise. Much smaller, neater wigs were worn for travelling and for sport. But a wig, large or small, had to be in perfect curl, so curling fluids were extensively advertised and men carried tortoiseshell combs about and could be seen in the park or theatre combing and curling their wigs.

During this time women's hair, naturally or unnaturally, went through a number of no less astonishing transformations. At the Restoration and for some years after, back hair was dressed high in a flat bun; side and side-back hair fell in ringlets. Side ringlets were short and wired to stand a little away from the face before falling parallel to the cheeks. In the mid-1670's wires disappeared, ringlets became longer, a centre parting was usual, and a feathering of rather moth-eaten pin curls fell with careful negligence about the forehead. Then, as men's wigs grew higher women's hair soared upward too. Higher and higher it mounted, tier piled upon tier and on top an equally high elaborate head-dress was placed so that

> "the face that erst near head was plac'd
> Imagine now about the waste."[16]

Obviously this "tour on tour" required a lot of hair and where nature faltered or failed artifice supplied a bogus tour which covered the forehead. Nature or artifice also had to supply a great number of curls, each had its own name and proper place in the edifice. "Cruches" were tiny pin curls on the

---

*Men despised the newly introduced umbrella. Heavy clumsy affairs, first used to hold over a bewigged parson as he conducted funeral rites at the graveside. Women did not despise them and some coffee houses even kept an umbrella which could be borrowed.

forehead; "Confidants" dangled about the ears; Passages or a "passagère" was a lock near the temple; "Berger", a lock "à la Shepherdesse", was turned up with a puff, and "crève-coeur" was the name for two small ringlets at the nape of the neck. It was perhaps the rape of one of these which Arabella Fermor (Belinda) suffered at the hands of Lord Petre, (the Baron).[17]

On the top of all this, literally, was the head-dress. It too in its hey-day,* which lasted from the time of William and Mary until about 1700, was a most complicated affair. Beginning simply enough as a white lace or silk cap with a fan of wired, fluted lace standing up in front, it soon changed shape and grew so elaborate that it needed a wire frame to support it. The frame, curiously, seems to have been called a commode, the head-dress itself was called a fontange—after Mlle Fontanges†, one of the French king's mistresses, who introduced it in France in 1679. At the height of its intricacy the fontange rose in tiers too, from hair swept high in front. One of the best portraits of Mary II (by Jan van der Vart) shows her wearing a tiered fontange and looking uncommonly attractive. The fontange also could be set to indicate political leanings and had as many bits of lace and ribbon added as the hair had curls. Long lappets fell down the back; the "cornet" drooped like hound's ears about the cheeks; various other separate pieces were known as "pinners", and to all this was added ribbon bows, sapphire or diamond bodkins, and, too often, lice. Hair was curled on irons (was the Calamister, or curling iron, brought here by the Romans?) or on curl papers fastened with lead. It will be remembered that Millamant swore she curled her hair on the love letters she received—not the prose ones, the ones containing poetry because they gave a better curl.[18]

---

*"There is not so Variable a thing in Nature as a Lady's Head-Dress: Within my own Memory I have known it rise and fall above Thirty Degrees", says Addison. (*Spectator* No. 98, June 22nd, 1711.)

†Mlle Fontanges was, it is said, poisoned by her rival Madame de Montespan.

Etui, 1700. Silver toilet box, 1680. Silver Tobacco box, 1699.

Combs were of box wood, scented wood, tortoise shell, ivory and sometimes of black lead—the latter kept the hair black. But if red or golden hair were preferred and nature had not obliged, German soap, ashes and quick lime made an excellent bleach. Some still probably preferred urine as a milder bleach for hair and cloth. It was collected by household servants and sold to cloth manufacturers as "old lant". What it was called when used on the hair I do not know.

A wig or false hair happily supplemented any lack, whether that lack was due to nature or quick lime, but when teeth fell out (due often to scurvy) or had to be removed, the loss was less happily sustained or disguised. Poets, ever gallant if inaccurate, went on comparing teeth to pearls in an endless sort of way—but more people possessed good pearls than good teeth. The English had such appalling teeth that foreigners frequently remarked on them. The Duke of Tuscany thought English women

351

were not inferior to Englishmen in stature or beauty. Their only defect was their teeth "which, generally speaking aren't very white". Goodness knows they tried hard enough to make them white with dentifrices guaranteed to remove discoloration. Mr. Ferene of the New Exchange had a rare Dentifrice, much approved at court, which contained Irios (orris) root, "Pomistone", cuttle bone, coral and fine alabaster, ground, sifted and made into a paste with "Gum Dragant" (tragacanth) and "Bread crums". Powdered brick replaced alabaster, "if you desire them red" (presumably "them" means gums not teeth) and the paste could be made into Dentifrices (the word means tooth-rub) of any shape "but rolls is the most commodious for your use".[19] A later and more simple method of cleansing "very foul spotted teeth"[20] was to tie a rag to a skewer, dip in Spirit of Salt, rub the teeth, being careful not to touch the gums, rinse the mouth with clear water—and the spots vanished. They very probably did and the teeth with them. Strong hydrochloric acid is highly corrosive. It was much better to prevent darkening with a "constant daily wash" of claret, Bole ammoniac, myrrh, "allum", Hungary water, honey of roses and Salt of Vitriol. This isn't so bad as it sounds; Salt of Vitriol is Glauber's* salt. Few followed the excellent and unusual example of John Bois (d. 1644) senior prebendary of Ely (he with Andrew Downes is responsible for much of the translation of the Apocrypha) who "after meat . . . was careful almost to curiosity in picking and rubbing his teeth, esteeming that a special preservation of health. By which means he carryed to his grave almost an Hebrew alphabet of teeth".[21] Nor did many take to the idea of rubbing the teeth with salt to prevent their becoming "worm-eaten" although some were, rather daringly, making a very tentative use of a small brush for cleaning. These three things would have avoided much trouble but they were by no means generally practised, and the usual methods of whitening teeth were such

*J. R. Glauber (1604-68) first described its preparation. It was called "sal mirabile". It is sodium sulphate and is the active principle of numerous mineral waters.

that, inevitably, remedies for toothache are as commonplace as recipes for tooth cleaners.

John Aubrey's cure for toothache was to make the gum bleed by scratching it with a new nail, then he drove the nail into an oak tree. This, he says "cured Sir William Neale's Son, a very Stout Gentleman, when he was almost Mad with Pain (and) had a mind to have Pistoll'd himself". As women rarely Pistoll themselves for any reason—possibly vanity leads them to choose less messy methods of *felo de se*—they may have found a paste of salt, alum and vinegar, put into an egg shell, charred to an ember and powdered, less drastic and less permanent than suicide. This preparation cured toothache and also sore gums, tongue and mouth. Even better, it fastened in loose teeth, although one had to be careful as a too frequent use would "flea the skin off". Of equal value was a remedy made of French flies, mithridate and vinegar applied behind the ear or to cheek bone. "'Twill blister" the user is warned "but rarely fails to cure". These were home remedies, but there were plenty of patent ones too, such as that advertised as "Sir Theodore Mayerne's (Physitian to King Charles) Opiate for the teeth; viz. makes them clean and white as Ivory, although never so black and rotten, fasteneth and preserveth them from Tooth-ach".[22] Here we have all the age-old elements of popular appeal in an advertisement. Science, a suggestion of a Royal user, and a definite promise. It did not matter that Sir Theodore had been dead for sixty-five years or that the king referred to was the first Charles not the second. What mattered was to sell the stuff. If it did no good, the sufferer could always have the tooth drawn.

If teeth, "tooth-ach" cures, and dentifrices were bad, dentisty was worse; as minor surgery it must have resembled mediaeval torture. To remove a tooth a terrible clawed lever called a "Pelican" was used, which ripped the tooth out of the socket and damaged adjacent teeth. Those gone beyond the gum line were "elevated" by a pointed metal shaft set in a handle. This also worked on the lever system—once the point had been driven in. As there was no such thing as a local anaesthetic, victims were bound or chained to chairs. Charles Fitzroy (Duke of Southampton) son of Charles and the rapacious Barbara, Countess of Castlemaine and Duchess of Cleveland, had "two unhandsome front teeth", so his mother had him bound to a chair with chains while the offending teeth were removed. This, according to Aubrey, affected the boy's intelligence. It

Silver toilet set, *c.* 1680.

may well have done. Hand drills were not unknown by the end of the century, but were probably more used in France than in England where they had already begun to fill teeth with hot lead. No wonder our ancestors would try almost anything— even suicide—rather than have a tooth drawn. An exception, however, was Lord William Howard. In January 1633 Dr. Foorde was called in to give his "openion" on his Lordships lip (the opinion cost £1) and prescribed an "oynetment" costing 1s. 6d. The condition did not improve and a week later

Of Cosmetics and Perfumes

Dr. Moore's advice was sought (it, too, cost £1). Although not stated, the advice is clear—for almost immediately we find that Mr. Clark "a tooth drawer" was paid 10/- and one hopes his Lordship had no more "toothatch". Later in the year an ominous and pathetic item appears. It is for a winding sheet for "Rich. Wilkinson with the soare face—5s.". Richard was possibly one of the gardeners at Naworth. Whether the sore face caused his death we do not know but it seems probable.

Apparently it never entered our heads that our teeth would have been better had we been willing to give up the prodigious number of sweet things of which we were so inordinately fond. Foreign visitors, right for once, had long thought this responsible for the bad teeth of the abominable English. Once the tooth was lost it could be replaced by one whittled out of bone or ivory, held in place by tying with gold wire to the flanking teeth, if any (walrus ivory was best because of its non-yellowing quality). Or a "rank of teeth" carved of bone or possibly wood, cumbersome, uncomfortable, and ill-fitting, would furnish a larger gap. It was a Frenchman (Jacques Guillemeau d. 1613) who first seems to have suggested a substitute for ivory with a recipe for making a false tooth out of mastic, white coral and prepared pearl. This would, indeed, provide pearly teeth for show if not for use. It is unlikely that the English, greedy as they might have been, took to it.

Sunken cheeks, due to loss of teeth or loss of youth, were counteracted by wearing "plumpers". They were much used, it is said, by elderly countesses and were "very thin, round and light balls".[23] Few can have been lean-cheeked by nature as overeating and going about in coaches and sedan chairs* instead of on horseback buried the century in flesh as it had never buried previous centuries, and it may be this which accounts for a recipe against bursting. This seems to have been chiefly a male affliction, but a "plaister" of baked fern roots, elecampane,

---

*Sedan chairs had to lower their seats and have a hinged top which lifted like the lid of a box to accommodate the high head-dresses and wigs of the day.

oils of bay and Exeter, applied to the relevant spot averted the danger.

Less painful, if more common, were corns. Not a visible defect these, but corns have never been an aid to beauty; they can contort and wrinkle or crack the paint of the face very quickly. Useful though they were in foretelling weather—"A coming show'r your shooting corns presage" as Swift points out—no fop could mince along in red-heeled, ornately buckled shoes; no woman could preserve a graceful port in high, curve-heeled shoes of brocade, satin, silk or leather when afflicted by corns. Fortunately "Mrs. Jones Reseit" for a "Plaister for Corns" made of Venice turpentine and virgin wax spread on a piece of Holland or Dowland, cut to size and left on the toe until it (the cloth) fell off softened the corn so that it could be cut.[24] By the end of the century many doctors advertised corn cutting as one of their accomplishments.

Hands were, of course, even more important than feet. Ideally they were required to "unite insensibly with the arms".[25] Even if unable to unite with sufficient insensibility they could be kept soft and white with "chicken-skin" gloves worn at night, or a paste of almonds, oxgall, and egg yolks mixed with oil of Tartar and, strangely, raisins. The Duchess of York (Anne Hyde) had a "most fine, white and fat hand" say Pepys who kissed it for the first time in 1666, but if Anthony à Wood can be believed (which too often he cannot) the Duchess "died (in 1681) with eating and drinking; died fast and fustie; salacious; lecherous."

Eyes were still made large and beautiful with belladonna, and eyebrows could be turned "a very curious black" with an ointment of burnt red filberts and goat's grease. Kohl was, possibly, used as an eye shadow and it may even be that a few experimented with lamp black and grease as an early form of mascara. It is surprising, at first sight, to read that in 1602 Queen Elizabeth, then nearing seventy, walked about at Oatlands "as freely as if she had only been eighteen years old" and allowed the visiting Duke of Stettin and his entourage to see her

Of Cosmetics and Perfumes

by "always taking off her mascara and bowing deeply to his princely Grace".[26] But mascara in those days meant a mask, and ladies in the Stuart era went on wearing masks outdoors against the ravages of sun, rain, wind and the killing glances of men—and also in the theatre when comedies were acted. Mascara, as we use the word, seems to have been originally Tuscan red! Here I can only guess, but it seems unlikely that it was used on eyelashes and more probable that if used at all,

Silver shell toilet box, *c.* 1620.

it was used on eyelids in the same way that Oriental women used henna occasionally. Red eyelids are no longer considered attractive, we prefer blue or green.

Tiny hand mirrors and toilet sets were carried about by both men and women but as, like Chaucer's Prioress, Madame Eglentyne—either out of a lamentable inability or a dogged refusal to learn—we still spoke "Frenssh . . . after the scole of Stratford atte Bow" we called these *étuis* "tweezes". Tweezes contained up to a dozen implements necessary for running repairs, including "tweezers"—hitherto known as "small tongs"—nail parers, cleaners and toothpicks. Sometimes the tools were hinged together like a Boy Scout's knife or a clutch of modern measuring spoons, sometimes they were separate, but always fitted into a case. Both tools and case were ornate or plain as money allowed. But, alas, the tooth-pick, plain or hinged —and in this era quite separated from its other end the ear-picker—lost much of its ornamental value. Gone were small golden lizards whose pointed tails relieved teeth of unwanted burdens and whose flattened heads de-waxed ears. No longer did Cupid's bejewelled arrow or a minute mermaid serve this dual purpose. Tooth-picks, always functional and often very beautiful, ceased to have an individuality when hinged to something else. It was the beginning of the end. In the next century when steel pens superseded quills, some use had to be found for the redundant quills and an anonymous genius thought up the quill tooth-pick.* Dull, impermanent quill picks were not a suitable or grand enough present for a sovereign, not worth handing down in families as were the beautiful, amusing and fantastic tooth-picks of the Renaissance and early seventeenth century. Tooth-picks were not, as they once had been, an important part of the knife and fork set, they had become merely an article of the toilet.

But articles of the toilet multiplied and became more ornate. Fashionable dressing-rooms were adorned and ornamented as never before. They were full

> "Of Toilet Plate, Gilt and Emboss'd
> And several other things of Cost,
> The Table Miroir, one Glue Pot,
>   One for Pomatum, and what not?
> Of Washes, Unguents and Cosmeticks,

*Perhaps fact followed fiction here. In Congreve's only novel, *Incognita*, published 1691, Aurelian, gazing upon his beloved, fancies he sees a young cupid "just pen-feather'd" employ "his naked quills to pick her teeth". It is possible that the quill toothpick began to make its appearance in polite society this early, although there is no evidence that metallic pens replaced quill pens until late in the eighteenth century.

Of Cosmetics and Perfumes

A Pair of Silver Candlesticks:
Snuffers and Snuff-dish, Boxes more
For Powders, Patches, Waters store . . .''[27]

This burlesque is undoubtedly based on fact and the fact carried to extreme can be seen in the magnificent, fantastic—and rather vulgar—silver bedroom furniture at Knole. There were few who could go in for this kind of ostentation, but grand toilet sets of silver (or silver gilt) such as that given by Sir Walter Calverley to his bride in 1706 were not uncommon. Sir Walter and his mother were "at cost" of £116 for this "fine set" of "dressing plate", but his wedding clothes including "a long wigg" cost "near £300". As his new coach, bought from George White-latch, cost £82.7.0, and the velvet for its lining came out at £30.7.0, coaches seem to have been cheaper than either clothes or dressing silver.[28]

Hand looking-glasses were as usual an essential, but table mirrors framed in silver, lacquer, or wood, according to one's income were rather newer and greatly in demand. Long mirrors, now used in all parts of a house, were also seen in the dressing-room. The wife of a Warden of Merton was thoroughly detested by Anthony à Wood chiefly it seems because she put the college to "un-necessary charges and very frivolous expences, among which was a very large Looking-Glass for her to see her ugly face, and body to the middle, and perhaps lower". But Anthony, an antiquarian to whom we owe much, was a little odd—particularly about sex and women. He also lived in an attic, was horrid to people, pinched a good deal of John Aubrey's original work and had a very low opinion of most members of the University. Tom Clayton, the husband of the lady with the long Looking-Glass was "a common Fornicator . . . the very Lol-poop of the University" while a new Master of Balliol "spent most of his time in bibbing and smoking, and nothing of a gent. to carry him off". Gents, perhaps, or at any rate fops, went in rather more for snuff than tobacco, and snuff boxes often contained a small mirror on the inside of the lid.

Pierced silver scissors case, 1670.

But if mirrors multiplied so did all sorts of boxes, baskets, bottles and pots which contained a woman's face, hair, ornaments, jewellery and so on. Powders were kept in sweet coffers of all shapes and sizes and made of silver, gold or scented wood. Fat flagons of crystal or silver, engraved or embossed, held scented waters, the most popular of which was Hungary Water. In the great country houses where the essence of spring and summer was distilled, Hungary water and other *eaux parfumeés* were made by hand. In town they could be bought ready made. "Hungary Water, right and fair, large half Pint (Flint) Bottles, Sold for 15d. per bottle" could be bought from Mr. Strahan the Bookseller. And to this advertisement[29] thoughtful and canny Mr. Strahan adds "Note, it is the same by which Isabella, Queen of Hungary, so long preserved her Life and Health". As everyone knew that constant use of this water (the recipe was given Isabella by a hermit in the late fourteenth century) had preserved the Queen to such an extent that at seventy-two she received an offer of marriage from the King of Poland, Mr. Strahan had no need to say more and Hungary water seems to have become the most popular of the lighter perfumes of the time. Together with orange water it replaces the rose water which was the favourite in the previous century.

Amber water too was still very popular. The Conde de

Of Cosmetics and Perfumes

Castel Melhor presented Lady Ann Fanshawe with a fine Brazil wood case containing crystal bottles full of "amber-water"; case and bottles were garnished with silver. Much earlier in the century, Marie de Medici sent Anna of Denmark a cabinet "very curiously wrought, and inlaid all over with musk and amber gris, which maketh a sweet savour" [30] Every box within the cabinet contained different jewels and "flowers for head tiring".

Still, despite time and money spent on beauty and adornment, on dress and jewels—particularly on diamonds which had become most popular*, our seventeenth-century ancestors, as we know, were not much given to washing either themselves or their clothes. Some women might and did bathe or wash in asses' milk as a beautifier, but unless it were washed off afterwards it too would become most ungrateful to the nose. The great unwashed included everyone. Literally, life stank. The real wonder is, that anyone ever noticed anything so trivial as what we with such euphemistic vulgarity call "B.O." and "halitosis". But they did, and personal reasons apart, there were medical grounds for trying to overcome or cancel out bad smells—evil odours bred diseases.

Nevertheless, the Stuart century loved perfumes and incense for their own sakes too; everything possible was perfumed—
—shoes, handkerchiefs, leather screens, boxes, books, gloves. Nor was darkest England forgotten. Travelling vendors found ample monetary compensation for the time spent in the country, peddling their wares at fairs, at markets and, even, in towns,

*The seventeenth century revealed the diamond as a beautiful stone. Up until then there was little a gem cutter could do other then grind it to a point or a rough table. Rose cutting is said to have been invented by Cardinal Mazarin, but this is doubtful. It probably originated in India. Here the base is left flat and the top cut with twenty-four or more facets. Even more popular was the brilliant cut of the late century with both crown and pavilion faceted. Diamonds were thought to be shewn off best by silver. Platinum although known was not used. It was thought to be unripe silver and of little value. But artificial pearls were invented, in France, in this century.

from house to house. That "brisk amorous, adventurous, unfortunate Coxcomb", Sir Samuel Harty, when disguised as an itinerant woman pedlar, tempts Clarinda and Miranda with "choice good Gloves, Amber, Orangery, Genoa, Romane, Frangipand, Neroly, Tuberose, Jessimine, and Marshal; all manner of Tires for the Head, Locks, Tours, Frowzes, and so forth; all manner of Washes, Almond-water, and Mercury-water for the Complexion; the best Peter and Spanish Paper that ever came over; the best Pomatums of Europe, but one rare one made of a Lamb's Caul and May-Dew. . . . Also all manner of Confections of Mercury and Hogs-Bones, to preserve present, and to restore lost Beauty".[31] In fact he carried the whole bag—or tray—of tricks. But he begins his tempting with the quite irresistible perfumed gloves.

Men wore gauntlet gloves; women's were lace or silk for everyday but on formal occasions they were of elbow-length white kid.* Perfumed gloves had certainly not lost their popularity since their introduction, in Elizabeth's day. Dryden's "Fair Corinna" (otherwise Elizabeth Thomas who wrote bad verse) tells a charming story of a pair of gloves given to her mother by a Dr. Glysson. They were of rich Spanish leather, fringed and embroidered with gold and of them the doctor said, "I do respect them for the last time I had the honour of approaching my mistress, Queen Elizabeth, she took them from her own Royal hands saying 'Here Glysson, wear them for my sake' ". By the time this incident took place (1684) Queen Elizabeth had been dead eighty-one years, Dr. Glysson was 100, and Elizabeth Thomas herself was only seven. Unfortunately, the Fair Corinna is not very trustworthy. She concocted a quite fictitious account of Dryden's death, and in later years seems

*The seventeenth century saw the development of the three-quarter sleeve, hence elbow-length gloves were invented to re-cover what had been bared by the new fashion. In the previous century, sleeves were always long and women wore gauntlet gloves. Women bought gloves by the dozen and gloves were also the usual "valentine" given by men to women in the seventeenth century.

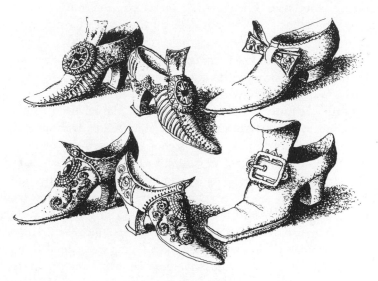

Women's and men's shoes, c. 1650-90.

to have subsisted on blackmail, of a not very lucrative kind as she died in poverty. Yet her story of Elizabeth's gloves may be true. If so, perhaps a faint trace of "the Earl of Oxford's Perfume", which the great Queen preferred above all others as a glove perfume, still lingered about them.

But if perfumed gloves were not new the perfumes used in them were. The old favourites, Musk, ambergris and civet continued to be popular but Orangery, Genoa, Romane, Frangipani, Neroli, Tuberose and "Marshall" were relatively new. Neroli, said to be the favourite perfume of the second wife of Flavio Orsini, Duke of Bracciano and Prince of Nerola, is mentioned in the sixteenth century but became a rage in the seventeenth. In Italy and France "Guanti di Neroli" and "Guanti di Frangipani" were much favoured, the latter were also said to get their name from a nobleman; the Marquis Frangipani, Marshal of the Armies of Louis XIII. He discovered a means of impregnating gloves with the perfume discovered by a botanist ancestor, Mercutio Frangipani.* Mercutio, or Mutio, accompanied Columbus and first noticed, off the coast of Antigua, the perfume of *Plumeria rubra* which he tried to imitate when he returned to Italy in 1493 or 1494. So the English were probably almost as tardy in taking to Frangipani as in taking to Hungary water. As for what was called in the Anglo-Saxon way "Marshall", it must have been Poudre à la Marèchale d'Aumont —for concocting perfumes was an art practised by rich amateurs —and was probably a powder or sachet to be used dry or turned to liquid in spirit of wine, or added to a greasy base as desired. It is probable that a greasy base was needed for glove perfume. All this sounds as if the most sought after perfumes came from abroad. They did. So did many other things. Sir Fopling Flutter, so eminent for being "bien-gante", wore gloves "fringed, large and graceful" and perfumed with Orangerie. He also wore nothing but "originals from the most famous hand in Paris". His suit was by Barroy (drap du Berri?), its garniture, Le Gras; his shoes, Piccat, and he wore a "Chedreux" (a "perruque" named for its inventor).[32]

Women were not to be outdone by the Sir Foplings of the day. Hungary water, although made at home, was also imported in casks from Amsterdam, so was "Jessaminy-butter" (oil) for gloves. Orange-flower water could be home-brewed but it was also imported from Calais and Dieppe. Various cosmetics came from Spain, and Spanish women from "the Queen to the cobbler's wife, old and young"[33] painted their faces white and red—widows excepted. Spanish widows had a dreary time. They never went out of heavy mourning or showed their hair after being widowed and they rarely married again. How very different from English widows who were much sought after, particularly if their defunct husbands had left them money or property! Although French women were said not to paint as

*The family was Roman. The name is believed to derive from the office, held by an early member of the family of supplying "broken" or "holy" bread for use in religious ceremonies. Mutio's recipe for Frangipani contains spices, orris root and musk.

Of Cosmetics and Perfumes

excessively as English or Spanish Women, we certainly imported large quantities of face creams from France—even English women must have known from 1675 on, that Ninon de Lenclos was boasting that she'd kept her beauty until her sixtieth year by the aid of the wonderful cosmetics she used. But Ninon must have been an exception, if we are to believe that "pragmatical" (busy) man John Evelyn. According to him French women were "extremely decayed" by the age of twenty, due he thought to the "siccity of the aire", drinking water, ill-diet or other "accident". Happily, English women decayed a trifle less quickly. If past her prime at twenty, she did not actually decay until four and twenty and was not "old and insufferable" until thirty.[34] After that, unmarried or unkept, she might as well be dead— and, in fact, very often was. But while alive she was going to lure the male—preferably in numbers:

> "Since painted or not painted all shall fade,
> And she who scorns a man must die a maid."[35]

Perfumes then, as always, were bait.

Dry, syrupy, aqueous or greasy; perfume was used in all forms and at all times. Perfumed powders or "pulvill" could be puffed by small bellows into any odorous corner much as we, today, use an aerosol air freshener. "Have you pulvill'd the Coachman and Postillion, that they may not Stink of the Stable"[36] was a constantly recurring question and was not asked in connection with coachmen, postillions or stables only. A favourite sweet powder of the beauties and bed-swervers of the court of Charles II was made of ambergris, musk and sandalwood. Chypre was popular as a dry—later as a liquid—perfume through-out the century. Although its name remained the same its formula must have changed, for it can have born little resem-blance to that original Chypre reputedly introduced into England by Richard "Yea and Nay" (better known to us as Coeur-de-Lion), who had, rather arrogantly, some 500 years before, assumed the title of King of Cyprus. Seventeenth- and early eighteenth-century Chypre seems to have been made of benzoin, storax, coriander, calaminth, and calamus root. Another kind, known as Red Chypre, must have had an entirely different scent as it was made from damask roses, red sandalwood, aloes, "giroffle" (cloves), musk, ambergris and civet. The best civet came from England—even the French admitted that. Both perfumes could be put into bags and used to sweeten linen or one's self. Or, with the addition of oil, could be made into a paste and, since pomanders were out, carried about in tiny bejewelled boxes of gold, silver or ivory with perforated lids.

Another sweet powder of orris, calamus, "benjamin" (benzoin), storax, civet, cloves, musk, aloes, rosewood and ambergris was mixed with orange-flower oil and added to rose leaves. This sounds like pot pourri, but the recipe specifically states that "the bag must be of Taffaty or else the powder will run through".[37] Yet another "excellent perfume" contained Damask roses, rose water, benjamin, civet and musk beaten together and made into little cakes which were placed, like a sandwich filling, between rose leaves and allowed to dry. Tincture of ambergris—a single drop would perfume anything and was also useful in cordials—required one oz. of ambergris, three drams of musk and a half-pint of spirit of wine. This was put in a glass stopped with "a cork and bladder" and set in horse dung for ten days to heat and mature.

These last three recipes have a rather old-fashioned, country, hereditary sound about them. Not that there weren't still plenty of rose leaves, spices and horse dung in the London of 300 years ago, but times had changed. Perfumes could be bought ready prepared in shops, and shops had become more tempting than ever. Merchants ransacked the whole world for new and wonderful things to add to the comfort, luxury and enjoyment of life. How had people managed before, with no arcaded new Exchange or without the Piazza? Here one could shop or "match-silk" (window shop); meet and gossip with one's friends; snub or encourage an ogle with one's fan; see and be seen by everyone. And for perfumes, there was, now, at the turn

Of Cosmetics and Perfumes

of the century, Mr. Charles Lillie's famous shop at the corner of Beaufort Buildings in the Strand. Mr. Lillie, who appears to be the first English perfumer, as such, in our annals, was also a newsagent and well patronized by both men and women. He seems also to have had an ironic sense of humour. One of his advertisements offers "snuffs and perfumes which refresh the brain in those who have too much for their quiet, and gladdens it in those who have too little to know the want of it". This, of course, may not be ironic, it may merely mean that snuff and perfume were the dexedrine and phenobarbital of the day.

It is not easy to say exactly when the word snuff became a synonym for powdered tobacco, but if snuff-taking did not become general with men and women until the first year of Anne's reign, powdered tobacco was known before then and was certainly sold in shops, even outside London, in the last decade of the seventeenth century. Before this men grated their own* on ivory graters but it is said that the vast quantity of snuff taken from Spanish ships at the battle of Vigo Bay (August 1702) which flooded onto the London market led to the general use of snuff. This is undoubtedly true, but it is also true that it was now beginning to be felt in certain circles that the smoking of pipes, particularly at balls and assemblies, was hardly *de rigueur* for a gentleman of fashion, whereas snuff was. If excuse were needed, snuff, like tobacco, was said to have medicinal qualities and it was therefore used as a preventive and a medicine —and was a great deal more pleasant than most remedies.

Various manufacturers had their own methods of perfuming snuff. The tobacco was probably first sweetened with an infusion of melilot and coloured with an infusion of cinnamon or India

---

*Perfumed tobacco was known a good deal earlier. In 1636 ten ounces of perfumed "Tobacka" cost John Hayne 15/6 which is far more expensive than any other tobacco mentioned in his book. It is significant, I think, that this is the only entry for perfumed tobacco and that 1636 was a bad plague year. As both tobacco and perfume were thought to ward off plague the two together must have been considered even more potent protection.

wood. It was then perfumed with jasmine, rose, orange-flower, tuberose, musk amber or civet. Often dried and powdered herbs were added, which made it more medicinal. Spices were added too—including pepper! As tobacco was very cheap, these were not adulterants, they were extra ingredients which also added to the price of snuff. So the taking of snuff—justified first on health grounds—became a fashion which, among the rich, called for the most exquisite workmanship on the part of

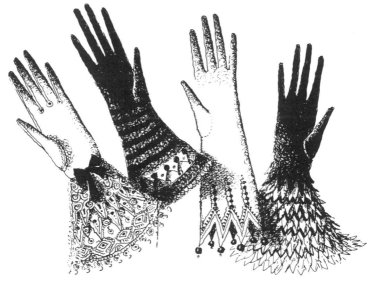

Women's gloves, c. 1630-90.

gold and silversmiths, jewellers, ivory workers and miniature painters to produce those works of art we call snuff boxes. The less rich made do with brass, tortoiseshell, ivory, wood . . . or a screw of paper. Early tobacco or snuff boxes were larger and less sophisticated and often bore a motto or legend. One of ivory, horn and boxwood dated 1664 says ''The Best is not too Good for You'' on its lid. Such boxes were often carved with arms and family motto.

In time, manoeuvring with a snuff box became for men as

Of Cosmetics and Perfumes

complicated as the "Airs, Motions . . . and Exercises of the Fan"[38] was for women; and Mr. Lillie, ironically obliging as ever, offered to teach young men and merchants "The Ceremony of the Snuff Box" to wit "Rules for Offering Snuff to a Stranger, a Friend, or a Mistress according to the Degrees of Familiarity or distance". He also undertook to give novices an explanation of the Scornful, Politick, and Surly Pinch.

Those who did not fancy Mr. Lillie's snuff—perhaps his advertisements offended those overburdened or undersupplied with brains, or perhaps it was not quite medicinal enough—had dozens of others to choose from. There was "Dr. Tyson's Apopletick Snuff" and "Angelick Snuff" to name but two. The latter not only removed "all manner of Disorders of the Head and Brain", it also eased pain immediately and did away with any feeling of "Swimming or Giddiness" due to "Vapours".[39] Vapours has an eminent Victorian sound, but it was an affliction of the seventeenth and eighteenth centuries, too, and was due then to bad air! Angelick Snuff could be had for "1/- a paper with Directions" and was sold only at Mr. Payne's Toyshop* at the Angel and Crown in St. Paul's Churchyard. Here one could buy an "unparallel'd Specifick Tincture . . . an assured Cure for leanness". Even at 3/6 a bottle Mr. Payne cannot have had enough thin customers to make the Specifick Tincture a profitable side line. He probably did well with the Angelic Snuff and one wonders if this were the brand favoured by women in church because so many women, regrettably, had gone too far with snuff-taking. Some took it all during a meal and made a horrid rattling noise in their noses. Others, perhaps more excusably, as sermons were apt to be so long—took it in church (so did men but that was different) and men did not approve. It might be pinched with perfect grace by a hand made soft and white by almond paste; it might be sniffed delicately by a nose

*Toys were not exclusively playthings for children. They were ornaments, trinkets and small commodities. Possibly the nearest equivalent of the seventeenth-century toy shop is the American Drug Store.

which had never needed a cure for shining and redness, and the attendant sneeze might be so delicate that no undue flushing of the Provence rose was discernable. But it *did* discolour the upper lip.

Early in the century Thomas Carew praised the pearliness of Celia's teeth and tears. In mid-century, handsome Richard Lovelace thought the sun had "butter'd with jessamine" Lucasta's hair and if, conversely, Sir John Suckling, in a rather coarse manner, had declared a preference for a deformed mistress, no one, as far as I know, went into Poetick Raptures or High Heroick Fustion about the nymph with the snuff-brown lip.

Nevertheless, nymphs and shepherds continued to populate and over-populate the pastoral poetry of Anne's reign as they had done throughout the century. And woman—painted to the dyed hair-line and over-fat—was still a nymph, living in a poet-created world where the props, the stage scenery, the sentiment was every bit as artificial and a good deal more worn and tattered. Death had not yet entered this Arcady, nor killed the non-existent golden age. We may be thankful it hadn't. Otherwise we should never have heard Ben Jonson, in a strangely lyric mood, addressing himself *To Celia* at the beginning of the Stuart era; nor a hump-backed "under-aged amorato"[40] singing *Where'er you walk* at its close.

CHAPTER TEN

Of Gardens and Gardeners

LIEUTENANT HAMMOND was neither important nor famous, but early in September 1635 he set out on a journey into "Westerne Counties". Being a man of his era, he took a lively interest in all sorts of things—people, places, antiquities, the countryside, churches, monuments, houses and gardens. Among the places he visited and described in his journal was the famous garden and grotto recently made at Enstone, Oxfordshire, by Thomas Bushell, an erstwhile page-secretary to Francis Bacon, Viscount St. Albans, dead these nine years.

A year later more important guests visited Enstone. They were King Charles and Queen Henrietta Maria who, on August 23rd, rode over from Oxford where they had been lavishly entertained at the "reformed" University by the new Chancellor, Archbishop Laud. Although the royal visit was reputedly unexpected, Mr. Bushell seems to have been uncommonly well prepared. Especially written verses of great length and limpness were sung to no less especially composed music by Simon Ive. But words could not—and, indeed, did not— express . . .

> ". . . the joy that hath been
> Since the King and the Queen
> Deigne to say
> They would pay
> A visit to this cell;"

This cell was the grotto where most of the entertainment took

Garden house and topiary work.

place—and the verse certainly suggests that the visit was no surprise. But Charles had seen the grotto before it was completed and had been so fascinated that he had promised to bring the Queen over one day. Perhaps he remembered, suddenly, that other grotto—the one designed by young, now elderly, Mr. Inigo Jones. He, Charles, had danced in the anti-masque of *Tethys' Festival* as Zephyr, clad in green satin with silver gossamer wings and crowned with flowers. Fair, strong, handsome Henry Frederick was newly Prince of Wales and no one had ever dreamed that shy, stammering, rickety-legged, ten year old Zephyr would become Charles I, by the Grace of God—and the death of the Young Phoenix—King . . . Defender of the Faith . . . etc.

But on this sultry day in late August 1636 the crown had become as light as a garland again—and for the last time—as he and the Queen ate the wonderful banquet prepared and served in the upper room of the grotto where a rock like a bear's head spouted water beneath a "Seiling . . . curiously and artificially painted" to show "the woman of Samaria drawing water for our

Of Gardens and Gardeners

Sauior",[1] the Angel giving directions to a parched Hagar and her son, and Susanna with the three peeping-Tom Elders. And, since there is always a love of the lugubrious and macabre in this century, the small rooms on either side of the banqueting room, all draped in black to symbolize the "melancholly retyr'd life like a Hermits",[2] must have pleased the guests too. One room was a study, the other a bed-chamber where, astonishingly, the black-draped bed was "hung by 4 Cordes covered with blak-bayes instead of bed-postes".*[3] Much, much more fascinating than this was the great Rock itself—or rather what the "ingenious Owner", as the Lieutenant calls him, had done to turn it into such a singular garden ornament—one of the first of its kind in England.

The rock had been discovered by accident when Mr. Bushell directed workmen to clear a boscage and dig a cave in a bank near a stream on his property; and in attempting the cave the rock was exposed. In its natural state it appears to have been about ten or twelve feet high and was full of cavities and hollows which dripped water, and "Pendants like Icecles as at Wokey Hole, Somerset".[4] As Bushell was a man of many and varied interests† he immediately enclosed the rock in a "faire 4 square Building of Freestone"[5] where it occupied all of one side of the lower room, with banqueting room, study and bed-chamber above. Even more cleverly, he concealed in the rock and about the vaulted room innumerable water pipes operated by cocks so that a waterworks display of great variety could be presented to amazed and delighted guests. One twist of the wrist and a

*Twenty-eight years later Evelyn visited the "famous wells, natural and artificial grotts . . . at Enstone". He says "it is an extraordinary solitude . . . (with) . . . a grot where he (Bushell) lay in a Hammock like an Indian". (Diary, Oct. 20th, 1664.)

†Thomas Bushell (1594-1674), one of Bacon's "Ganimedes" (Aubrey) was a smooth-tongued, highly intelligent rogue and mining engineer. He later became a great mining speculator and promoter and lost lots of money for himself and others. Aubrey gives an excellent picture of him and there is a most interesting modern biography by L. W. Gough.

373

great jet of water spouted up in front of the rock and juggled with a silver ball which rose and fell with the movement of the stream. Waterfalls flowed or dried up at a touch, and great jets spouted from each side to shatter themselves into a million sparkling pieces against opposite walls. By a trick of sunlight, seen through an artificial curtain of rain, a rainbow and strange flashes of lightning were observed. Nightingales bubbled, drums rolled, and other "rare and audible sounds and noyses"[6] were produced by water or air. And, when a spectator stood near the rock lost in admiration of its wonders and beauties, the way back could be cut off by a "plash'd Fence"[7] of water so that, sometimes, "faire ladies" could not get out without the water "flashing and dashing their smooth, soft, and tender thighs and knees".*[8]

It is unlikely that Queen Henrietta Maria was subjected to this sort of horse-play, which everyone in those days considered wildly hilarious, but she doubtless appreciated the joke as much as anyone else. Joke fountains had been quite a feature of Elizabethan (and Continental) gardens. This was much better than a simple joke-fountain which just hit one in the eye. It was more complicated, varied and amusing.

Although one visitor to the grotto thought it "a mad gimcracke sure, yet hereditary to these Hermeticall and Proiecticall Undertakers",[9] the Queen thought otherwise and ordered that

---

*I have taken the liberty of putting the descriptions of Hammond, Aubrey and Dr. Robert Plot (*The Natural History of Oxfordshire*) together to give a picture of the grotto. It is probably accurate enough as on Bushell's death the waterworks were taken over by the Earl of Lichfield who repaired Bushell's pipes and cisterns and, I believe, enlarged the "basin" outside the grotto into a larger pond. What the Earl seems to have added was largely outside, not in. I myself have investigated the site at Enstone in rubber boots and can find no visible trace of rock or buildings. The site is in the valley of the Glyme just east of A34 and near the Harrow Inn. There is now a farm house on the steep bank by the river, it is a small one but is built in part of golden stone, dressed. Most other buildings at Enstone are in the grey, not the golden, Cotswold stone.

grotto and gardens should henceforth be called "after her own princely name, Henrietta".[10] She further expressed her pleasure by presenting Mr. Bushell with "an entire Mummie from Egypt, a great raritie".[11] Unfortunately, it turned out to be a rather ephemeral gift. Mummies do not continue to remain mummies when transported to a damp grotto.

The significant thing about Thomas Bushell's grotto and water-works—the word had no municipal flavour then—is that it is one of the earliest on record in England.* Grottoes, new to the century, seem to have originated in Italy, probably in the mid-sixteenth century as a part of Renaissance detail—classical literature is full of grottoes and so is Renaissance poetry—and as an adjunct to the garden.

Probably the two most famous were the elaborate grottoes of the Villa d'Este and the Villa Aldobrandini which may have been responsible for the grotto craze which swept seventeenth-century Europe. Yet there were no hard and fast rules about grottoes. A grotto could be of any shape, size or form above or below ground. It could be a shallow niche in the bank of a stream containing a single statue or a bench; it could be splendidly raised in piled up rocks or cut from the living stone; it could be a pavilion attached to a house, or a small separate house in a secluded part of the garden, but all grottoes had one thing in common—water. Water was the *raison d'être* of every grotto, simple or fabulous. And so the Castalian spring of Delphi became the water-conceits of Tivoli, Frascati—and Enstone.

What is rather curious and odd is, that although early century gardens remained largely Elizabethan in character there was a sudden interest in garden tunnels, grottoes and caves. Dr. Harvey had caves dug in his Surrey garden to which he could retire and meditate, and, as we have seen, Thomas Bushell was bent on digging a cave to be used for the same purpose when he

*There was a grand one in the process of being built at Wilton House. Hammond saw this in 1635 and Celia Fiennes c. 1685. It seems to have disappeared by Defoe's day, whereas Bushell's Grotto continued until the mid-nineteenth century.

stumbled across the Enstone rock. One can dismiss this as merely a quirk of fashion—and undoubtedly fashion played its part. Or perhaps psychologists would explain it as a desire to return to the untroubled safety of the womb. But, I suggest, there is another factor here. I think people were afraid of the sun and remained afraid until our own century. Certainly everyone seems to have taken elaborate precautions against it.

Now it cannot be that the summer sun of the Stuart century was less tentative or infrequent or hotter than our twentieth-century sun, even if it did manage to ripen nectarines and peaches in quantity. Yet obviously, the song "Fear no more the heat o' the sun" was not written for an audience of Hagarenes. It was written for English ears and was sung by two early British princes who live in a cave in a forest in Wales which, even in midsummer, is decidedly on the cool side. So the fear of the sun, I believe, was very real. It was this which led our ancestors to build facing east, when possible (Lord Salisbury's own "lodgings" at Hatfield faced east), in order to escape a corrupting south wind, and to have both winter and summer parlours—the latter on the cool side of the hall. Further, they were constantly warning each other about the dangerous effects heat and sun had upon the head. A hot brain could scorch the blood or turn one mad. Heat caused the spontaneous generation of all sorts of horrid insects . . . poor James Harrington in his madness believed this happened to him. So in their gardens people created and built all sorts of shade traps as we now build "sun traps". There were arbours, simple and tunnelled; "shadow" houses, as summer houses began to be called around mid-century; tall hedges with niches and seats; avenues of trees; calculated wildernesses, coppices and boscages laid out with paths so that at any moment, and almost from any point in a garden, one could pop out of injurious sun into healthful shade. If we remember too that they also knew that plague, malaria and putrid fevers were more frequent in the summer and believed that evil odours bred diseases—even mildly hot weather could make the usual vile smells of the era even more vile—their fear of the

Garden frame and grindstone.

sun and their love of grottoes* caves, tunnels and shady places is understandable. How pleasant it was to be able to preserve health so fashionably, beautifully and amusingly.

Preserving health, by no means the sole reason for having a garden, was, nevertheless, a good and ancient one. Our British Pharmacopoeia no less than the science of Botany have a common ancestor in the Herbals and gardening books which began to be so popular from the late sixteenth century on. Such books were at pains to describe plants, soil, situation, manure, tools; they gave designs for gardens and garden houses; they told of the newest thing in bordering, such as boards, tiles, shank bones of sheep and "round blew or whitish pebbles stones"[12] but they were at equal pains to give information on the virtues of flowers and plants. Lavender, for example—and English Lavender is still the best in the world—was an extremely useful ornament in

*It is curious that grottoes were popular during the first half of the century, they then languished, to appear again in Anne's day. They reached a peak of beauty and ingenuity in the mid-eighteenth century.

any garden. It filled the interstices of the knot, had the great advantage of staying green in winter—and we had few plants which did at the beginning of the century—could be used to dry the linen on or to perfume it when dry. It was also fine for strewing and, even better, it was good for catalepsy, "a light megrim", the falling sickness and for those who "swoune much".[13] Alas, it was of no use in apoplexy, although "unlearned Physitians and divers rash and over-bold Apothecaries and other foolish women"[14] (which does not, I think, mean apothecaries were female) prescribed it with dire and often quite fatal results. It was Apoplexy which snatched away William Herbert, Earl of Pembroke, before 8 a.m. one morning in 1630—"a distemper that has proved fatal to many who have been too excessive in their pleasure". William may have been excessive, but he was the patron of many famous men, among them Inigo Jones. It was his father, Aubrey says, who built the wonderful grotto at Wilton—persuaded to it by King Charles I.

Apothecaries, bold or timid, were medical men and more often than not had their own gardens. They dealt in and used medicinal herbs. But so did grocers. In fact the Apothecaries Society and the Grocers Company were affiliated. This led to trouble and one suspects that it may have been the untrained Grocers rather than the trained Apothecaries who were so rash and overbold as to include Lavender in a cure for Apoplexy. In any event there were many men "not well instructed in the Art or Mystery of Apothecaries" who made and compounded "many unwholesome, deceitful, corrupt and dangerous medicines . . . to the great peril and daily hazard" of the subjects of James I. There were enough perils and hazards without this. So James firmly supported the Apothecaries in their desire to break away from the Grocers, and granted them a charter (1617) which disunited and disassociated "the Apothecaries of our City of London from the Freemen of the Mystery of Grocers". As the charter referred to the Grocers by implication as "Empericks and unskillfull and ignorant men" and used the uncomplimentary phrases quoted above, the Grocers were, not unnaturally, extremely annoyed and in 1624 they, rather meanly, induced the Lord Mayor of London to petition James to revoke the Apothecaries' Charter. The poor Apothecaries were in a panic, but James stood staunchly by them. He informed the Lord Mayor in even more precise terms exactly why he had granted the charter. "Grocers" said the King—and one is inclined to agree—"are not competent judges of the practice of medicine". The Lord Mayor was so put out by this that for seven solid years afterwards no Lord Mayor of London ever invited the poor Apothecaries to hear the Christmas sermon at St. Paul's.

Indeed the Apothecaries had a thin time of it all round until late in the century. Their first home after the split was Cobham House, Blackfriars, where they taught physic—qualification for membership was made much more strict than before— and it wasn't until 1673 that they obtained a sixty-one year lease of, roughly, $3\frac{1}{2}$ acres of land at a rental of £5 per annum from Charles Cheyne (later Lord Cheyne). Here they began a new physic garden where they grew and observed plants, trees and shrubs—native and foreign—and where Stewards of the Society arranged botanical excursions as practical work for student Apothecaries. One of these students was young Hans Sloane.*

The new gardens stood in Paradise Row (now Royal Hospital Road) and their beginnings were very difficult. The gardens were a long way from the watchful eye of Master and wardens at Blackfriars. The gardener, who was given a house and £30 a year, demanded (and got) higher wages. Plants were stolen. Workmen cheated. Everything became almost as involved, difficult and expensive as it is today. The Apothecaries nearly gave up, but private members came to the rescue with funds. A high wall was built to keep out thieves no less than the thieving wind. Plants growing in the physic garden of one Mrs. Gape of Westminster (the Apothecaries had bought the lease)

---

*In 1722 Sir Hans Sloane who had bought the lease of the Manor of Chelsea in 1712 conveyed the Physic Garden to the Apothecaries for-ever on an annual rent of £5.

were transferred to Chelsea. A greenhouse was erected in 1680
—it cost £138. The south wall was festooned with nectarines
of all sorts, peaches, plums and apricots and, around 1683,
four cedars of Lebanon, the first* to bear cones in England,
were planted. Two became the famous Chelsea cedars and lived
until 1878 and 1903, but those who planted them were so
doubtful of their survival† that they did not even record the
exact date of planting. These cone-producing cedars were, it is
believed, the direct parents of the Lebanon cedars which became
common throughout the country in the eighteenth century
and which today, raising their great, green, tabled heights are
still the glory of many an English garden. So the Chelsea Physic
Garden, one of the two earliest in England (the first is the
Oxford Botanic Garden), became famous. It attracted amateurs
and professionals alike. Innumerable rarities were to be seen,
such as the tree bearing the Jesuit's bark and the cucumber
tree‡ whose fruit was said to make useful corks. James II, in his
silly way, revoked the Society's charter—for political reasons
but it was later re-granted. Henry Hyde, second Earl of Clarendon
and as Protestant as his great father, simply couldn't stomach his
royal brother-in-law James II, nor William and Mary for that
matter. So he often took refuge in the Chelsea Physic Garden
where, among the variety of plants, the green hedges, the

*But note, Sir Thomas Hanmer writing before 1659 says that some
cedars of Lebanon had been raised from seed in England but that
plantations were as yet very small. We don't know what happened to
these or if they survived, but this would seem to be the first mention of
Cedars of Lebanon produced from seed and growing in England. The
Rev. Edward Pococke imported plants of the tree in 1642, but they
probably did not survive.

†So tender and difficult was the cedar, that the great French
botanist, Dr. Jussieu, brought one from Syria carefully potted up in
his second best hat. He nursed it carefully and shared with it the meagre
daily allowance of water on the long voyage home.

‡Von Uffenbach mentions this in 1710, but there must be some confusion here as he says the "bark" makes useful corks. The true
cucumber tree *Magnolia acumenata* was not, as far as I can ascertain,
introduced until some years later.

"herbs of every leaf, that sudden flowered, opening their various colours and made gay"[15] the banks where they were set "Irish-stitch fashion," he found balm for his troubled soul. It is in the seventeenth century that the name Chelsea first became associated in people's minds with flowers and plants of great beauty and variety.* It still is. All because of a quarrel between the Grocers and the Apothecaries.

But to return to James I and the early years of a century which, although rich in private gardens, is perhaps more important because gardens plus the "new" scientific attitude spelled the equally new study of Botany. James was a great patron of gardens, gardeners, and gardening. In fact the one wholly endearing characteristic possessed by all the Stuarts was their interest in and their love of gardens. James did much to the gardens of Theobalds. He clipped hedges, put in neat linden avenues, fountains, a mount of Venus set within a labyrinth, and he en-circled the park with miles of high wall. He was interested in receiving new and strange plants and seeds for his gardens and, in 1622, Sir Henry Wotton sent him melon seeds from Venice "the choisest . . . of all kinds which his Majesty doth expect". James evidently did not know that melons were not to be trusted as food (they were difficult enough to grow and all gardeners exchanged ideas on how best to do so . . . steeping the seed in milk was thought a help). Over-indulgence in melons had brought Sophia, Queen of Poland, into a "numb'd Palsie" and, back in 1471, had given Pope Paul II his congé with a "mortal apoplexy". James also decided to import innumerable mulberry trees, promote their culture and start a silk industry in England . . . which was a worthy thought. So, in November 1609, he sent off a circular letter to all the Lords Lieutenant—and a pam-phlet on mulberry culture—ordering them to make public announcement that, in the following May, 1,000 mulberry trees would be delivered to each county and all who were able were to buy them at 3d. to 4d. a plant or 6/- per hundred. James

*One does not forget Sir Thomas More's famous garden at Chelsea in the previous century but it was a private garden.

led the way by having four acres at or near Westminster put under mulberries. It cost £935 to level the ground, build a wall and plant the trees. It was not a success. Later on it was to become the famous Mulberry Gardens, a pleasure ground, closed in 1673 when Charles II granted the land to Henry Bennet, Earl of Arlington. Today, Buckingham Palace stands on the site.

James also, in 1605, formed a Guild of Gardeners in the city of London for alas, many so-called gardeners (we call them nurserymen) were fearful swindlers who sold dead trees and bad seeds "to the great deceit and loss" of the buyer. It was hoped that a Guild would put a stop to this fraud. It didn't. So a second Charter was granted in 1616 and this one had real teeth in it. It provided that no one not licensed by the Company could "use or exercise the art or Mystery of Gardening" within a specified area. No person who had not served his apprenticeship and received the freedom of the Company was permitted to sell any garden stuff, save during certain specified hours, and in such places and markets open to other "foreigners" who had not the freedom of the city. Further, the company could seize any "plants, herbs or roots" exposed for sale by an unlicensed person and distribute them among the poor of the district where the offence had taken place; and, lastly, members could inspect anything in any market in the city and within a six-mile radius and were empowered "to burn or otherwise consume" all those plants, etc. found to be "unwholesome, dry, rotten, deceitful or unprofitable". Unprofitable that is to the buyer not to the vendor.

James' own "herbarist" who, incidentally, had no high opinion of melons, was John Parkinson. Parkinson's life, like that of Inigo Jones, stretches from the reign of Elizabeth to the rigours of the Commonwealth and Protectorate. There is a terrible poignancy about the lives of those who were old enough to have heard the great Tilbury speech in their youth and in old age the last words of Charles I upon the scaffold. But Parkinson was a gardener, and gardening, like art and history, is a continuous process. Parkinson is as much a part of the sixteenth as of the seventeenth century. His best known book, *Paradisi in Sole** dedicated to Henrietta Maria, was not published until 1629 (the title is surely a pun on his name?) and, like the old Herbalists, he is careful to stress the virtues of the plants he describes, although he is also careful to do away with some of the more fanciful absurdities of that great plagiarist Gerard. Parkinson is a fine observer as well as a practical gardener. He describes

Portable orange tree and wheeled water butt and pump.

the best roots, plants and shrubs for kitchen gardens, he deals with orchards and grafting, but he was also keenly aware that plants, although "useful for physic", were to be "admired for beauty" too. Yet his *Theatrum Botanicum* (1640) dedicated to Charles I is, as he rightly says, "a Herball of Large Extent". It runs to 149 chapters, weighs $11\frac{1}{2}$ lb. and has a "Table of Virtues" listing above 1,700 different remedies "to cure and prevent diseases". The chapters on "new strange and rare plants" from all parts of the world are full of unbelievably fascinating—and often fascinatingly unbelievable—information.

The year of the *Paradisi* was also marked by the "herbarizing"

**Paradisi in Sole Paradisus Terrestris*: 1629, 1635, 1656.

(botanical) expeditions made into deepest Kent by Thomas Johnson of Snow Hill (we met him in Chapter Six) and several intrepid companions. The results were published under the title *Iter . . . in Agrum Cantianum*.* Yet another of Johnson's expeditions was into Hampstead Heath where he listed the flowers found there. Johnson was a great man for such excursions, and the very first lists of local wild flowers ever published in England belong to this century. How strange to learn that wild Bugloss grew on the dry banks of "Piccadilla" and that Belladonna was found in Islington. But how sad that this great botanist-royalist died of wounds received at the siege of Basing House in 1644.

Herbarizing or botanizing expeditions, as such, were for all practical purposes new to this century. The great sixteenth-century adventurers who sailed around the world for the first time discovered and explored strange new lands, opened up new trade routes and, whenever possible, brought back booty from Spanish treasure ships, also brought home innumerable plants hitherto unheard of in England. This "side-line", as it were, was brilliantly successful as we learn from Parson Harrison who writes, sometime around 1577 how wonderful it is "to see how many strange herbs, plants, and annual fruits are daily brought unto us from the Indies, Americas, Taprobane (Ceylon), Canary Isles and all parts of the world". Noblemen and gentlemen had "great store of these flowers" which had begun to do so well that once "aquainted with our soils" they almost seemed indigenous.

By the seventeenth century England was no longer chasing Spain all over the place. But it was sending embassies to all parts of the world, and it became usual for anyone going almost anywhere to be commissioned to search out new plants. In addition, practical gardeners and herbarizers now took to joining a ship bound for foreign parts for the primary purpose of collecting plants, although they might find themselves engaged in other and less welcome activities such as fighting pirates on

Iter Plantarum investigationis Ergo susceptum . . . in Ager Cantianum.

the Barbary coast as John Tradescant the elder did. Nevertheless, he brought back the "Argier Apricock" with him which
soon became England's favourite apricock.

The Tradescants, father and son, are great gardening names
of the century from its beginning until the death of the younger
John in 1662, but at the beginning of the century John, the
elder, was gardener to Robert Cecil who was busy building his
new house at Hatfield where as much trouble was taken with
the garden as with the house—which would have pleased Robert's
cousin, Francis Bacon, although there was little love lost between
them. Robert spent vast sums on his garden and also received
magnificent gifts from those who desired his favour. The Queen
of France sent 500 fruit trees; the French Minister's wife,
Mme. de la Boderye (or Broderie) sent 30,000 vines; the elder
Tradescant himself sent a variety of plants, bulbs and trees
from Holland and France—but he sent bills too. One for
"Routes, flowers, seedes, trees and plantes" dated 1611 shows
"roots of flowers of Rosasses and shrubs, strang and rare—£3",
a description which is almost as perplexing as the spelling.
Among many other items invoiced at this time are "fortye
frittelarias" at 3d. each; and 800 tulips at 10/- per hundred.*
There was an "excedying great cherye called the boores cherye"
for 12/- and among other trees and shrubs there were oranges,
"olyander" trees, a "Myrtel and two fyg trees". Mulberry
trees at 3/- each cost much more than those supplied to King
James but they were probably large and well grown.

Hatfield's gardens were particularly splendid. The main one,
lying below a railed terrace, had as its chief feature a wildly
expensive waterworks (French engineers were employed for
this) where a prodigy of a marble basin held an enormous
artificial rock, built around an iron core and surmounted by a
statue painted to resemble copper. This basin fed a highly

*During the wild tulip speculation in Holland (1634-37) which
ended in a financial disaster of South Sea Bubble proportions, tulips
were bought and sold (on paper as it were) for thousands of florins
apiece.

artificial stream—a veritable Meander in little—which snaked its way to a valley where a dam made a lake, complete with an island planted with briar roses and hawthorn, and reached by a painted wooden bridge (stone bridges were not common then). Fish, snakes, and leaves—in lead—lurked in correct places on the stream's bank or on its bed which glowed and glittered with coloured stones and pebbles, and strange, exotic sea shells. These Tradescant had sent by the boxful from Paris.

But Robert, Earl of Salisbury, did not live long enough to enjoy his new house and garden, he died in 1612, deeply in debt and deeply detested:

> "Here lies Robin Crookback, unjustly reckoned,
> A Richard the Third, he was Judas the second"[16]

summed up popular opinion of the day. His famous gardener survived for another quarter of a century* and his name lives for us, rather inadequately in my opinion, in the *Tradescantia virginiana* and far less inadequately in a fine double daffodil *narcissus roseus Tradescanti*. "This prince of Daffodils, belongeth primarily to John Tradescant" (the elder) Parkinson says, "as the first founder thereof that we know." Son John succeeded his father as gardener to the king, travelled much in Virginia, and the *Aster Tradescanti*† better known to us as the Michaelmas Daisy was introduced by him. He also brought over the acacia, the American walnut, the American plane, the red maple, the deciduous cypress and probably the tulip tree. This with its delicate, fragrant flowers and bright green, saddle-shaped leaves must have delighted the century as it still delights us.

But the Tradescants, father and son, collected things other than plants on their travels, and around 1629 they set up their

---

*After the Earl's death Tradescant became gardener to Lord Wotton (not to be confused with Sir Henry Wotton), later to the Duke of Buckingham and in 1629 to Charles I. In 1618 he joined Sir Dudley Digges' mission to Archangel and made the first list of Russian flora.

†This now seems to be the name given to the white variety.

Of Gardens and Gardeners

museum of Curiosities—commonly known as Tradescant's Ark—at Lambeth where they had a large physic garden. Ark and garden were visited by many notables of the day—Charles and Henrietta Maria, the Duke of Buckingham and Archbishop Laud among them. During the Commonwealth and Protectorate John the younger avoided the flood, retired to his Ark and catalogued the *Musaeum Tradescantianum* (published 1656). Although the Museum went to Elias Ashmole and from him to the University of Oxford, it seems only just to point out that the first of our public museums, the Ashmolean, owes its origin to the interest and enterprise of two seventeenth-century gardener-botanist-collectors.

There were many in England like the younger Tradescant who, during the Civil War, Commonwealth and Cromwell, retired from the scene to cultivate their gardens. John Fetherston, unable to decide which side to take, avoided the issue, remained at Packwood House and laid out those strange topiary gardens which symbolize the sermon on the Mount—a less unusual subject for topiary work then than now.* Lord Scudamore, a royalist, after the King's execution sought consolation at Holme Lacy in planting and grafting apple trees and introduced the Red Streak Pippin, a famous cider apple—at the beginning of the eighteenth century we find Dr. Claver Morris buying "Red Streak Pippin Sider" for £1.13.0 the half hog's head. Sir Thomas Hanmer, the Cavalier, went on breeding tulips, kept his now famous gardening journal, and sent off various parcels of plants and seeds with great impartiality to royalist and roundhead alike. One of his friends was John Evelyn who, in 1652, scurried back (permanently this time) from the Continent and was busy rebuilding the old Tudor House, Sayes Court, and turning a 100-acre field into a charming garden. The Republican Parliamentary General, John Lambert, was also a tulip fancier (as Charles I had been) and, in 1655, Sir Thomas sent him "a great mother-

---

*Packwood House and its topiary gardens are now National Trust Property. It also has a charming and typical mid-century gateway on either side of which, in the brick wall, are alcoves for bees.

root of Agate Hanmer" his pride and joy among tulips. General Lambert, in the year Evelyn returned, bought Wimbledon House—once belonging to Robert Cecil's elder half-brother, Thomas, first Earl of Exeter, but by this time only "a late parcel of the possession of Henrietta Maria, the relict and late Queen of Charles Stuart".[17] He paid £7,000 for it. In 1657 the Republican General, not surprisingly, fell out with Cromwell over the business of whether the Lord Protector should be given the title of King and retired to grow tulips and Guernsey lilies in relative peace.* He sent a Guernsey lily to Alexander Marshall from Wimbledon and Marshall's painting of it is the first record of this flower in England.†

It must not be thought that during the Commonwealth and Protectorate gardening was one of the forbidden pleasures. It wasn't. Although few great gardens were laid out and others, such as those of Nonsuch and Wimbledon, were sold along with the houses (Theobalds was destroyed) gardening was encouraged. There was a greater emphasis laid on the more practical aspects such as market gardening, the improvement of orchards, and the growing of economic plants—although this is a rather risky statement, because the whole period covers only eleven years of an era full of books about how to improve gardening and husbandry. Nevertheless, a glance at a few of what might be called "gardening-for-profit" books so popular in mid-century, suggests that this is so. Adam Speed, a Puritan, wrote *Adam out of Eden*, ‡ and in many ways this post-lapsarian Adam is still a complete innocent—at least in gardening knowledge. White

---

*Peace did not last long. Lambert supported Richard Cromwell; opposed Monck; was arrested, imprisoned, escaped; attempted to raise troops to oppose Monck; failed, arrested, imprisoned; tried for high treason, condemned to death, sentence not implemented, exiled to Guernsey; died 1683.

†Tradescant's Ark contained among its treasures "A booke of . . . choicest Flowers and Plants exquisitely limned . . . by Mr. Alex. Marshall" (Catalogue, Section VIII).

‡First published, it is said, in 1626, but I have not seen this edition. Published again in 1649.

Garden rollers, earth-sifter and line.

lilies may be turned red by drilling a hole in the root (bulb) and filling with any red powder. Roses will turn yellow when planted among broom. Even more innocent—and the innocent are often so deadly dangerous—is his idea that rabbits are great improvers and can raise the value of land tenfold—from £200 to £2,000 a year. Plant thistles to support rabbits, he urges, as well as for the benefit of calves, lambs and pigs. Domestic animals must have been far less choosy about food than their modern descendants. We spend a fortune on trying to get rid of thistles—and rabbits. But perhaps Adam meant sow thistles, which certainly pigs will eat, though they won't touch other kinds. None of this sounds in the least practical, but Speed did recommend the planting of potatoes, thoroughly good advice which was, as we know, almost wholly ignored.

Walter Blith, or Blythe, a Yorkshire yeoman in Cromwell's army and self described as "another lover of ingenuity", tells his countrymen to follow the West Country's example and plant "the Vine, the Plumb, the Cherry, Pear and Apple".* He also urges the planting of more useful vegetables—cabbage, carrot, onion, parsnip, artichoke and "Turnep". This too was good advice, most people with gardens—and most people had gardens—did not grow enough fruit and vegetables. The rich, with large orchards and gardens and better able to experiment, were better supplied, but enormous quantitites of fruit and salad crops were imported from the Continent, particularly from Holland. The first Dutch War (1652-54) interfered with this source of supply.

Ralph Austen, also a Puritan—and at various times proctor, deputy registrary and registrary to visitors of Magdalen College, Oxford—also wrote improving books on gardening.† Most of his arguments are based on scriptural authority and his book is lavishly illustrated with biblical texts. Every process of culture is compared to some aspect of Christian life. This is rather tedious. Adam, generally acknowledged by all to be the first gardener and alluded to so frequently as such, was, after all, not a Christian. This never seemed to strike anyone. Austen, however, unlike his contemporary Speed, does try to do away with certain vulgar errors and it probably astonished and disappointed many to learn that writing a word or verse on a peach stone did not result—once the stone had become a tree—in a crop of peaches inscribed with the same message. Nor did immersing apple grafts in pike's blood make apples redder, nor did soaking fruit stones in one's favourite tipple or cordial produce fruit flavoured with whatever liquid the parent stone had been soaked in.

As keen on fruit trees as Austen or Alcinous is William Lawson—a most endearing writer on how to make a garden pay. Lawson, about whom we know virtually nothing, published the fruit of his forty-eight years of experience "in the North Part of England" in 1618—which means he was born early in the

*The English Improver or a New Survey of Husbandry (1649).
†The Spiritual Use of an Orchard or Garden of Fruit Trees.

Of Gardens and Gardeners

reign of Queen Elizabeth. We don't know when he died but his book remained popular for a good sixty years* after publication —not surprisingly as he creates an ideal orchard so dream-like, so childlike and so enchanting that one can hardly believe it existed even in this other Eden.

An orchard to Lawson is "a delight". It is Paradise, "for what was Paradise other than that?"—and a purely English Paradise too. No exotics, no vineyard. What could be better than "our own English Syder or Perry"? Further, an orchard for profit is as good as a cornfield and, unlike a cornfield, gives one "unspeakable pleasure". To turn a pleasure into a profit has always been part of the Englishness of the English. So Lawson is practical about planting, soil feeding and pruning but, says he, the first requirement for a "Pleasant and Profitable Orchard is a Fruiterer". The Fruiterer must not be a "lazy lubber" but a man who is "Religious, Honest and Skillful" (the order of virtues is revealing). Yet Lawson was not writing for the rich or near rich because he says "if you be not able, nor willing, to have a gardener, keep your profits to yourself, but then you must take all the pains". Still, it is a little difficult to see how even the most zealous and painstaking lover of fruit could produce, single-handed, Lawson's orchard-garden-Paradise; well hedged, on low ground (high ground isn't "fat" and if it is, is soon "eroded", besides it is windy) with a stream running through it, if possible. Apples, pears, cherries "Filberds" (red and white), plums and bullaces were best for the north as "we meddle not with Apricocks and Peaches". The orchard-garden should contain a mount† or two, "curiously wrought" inside and out— which makes the mount sound rather like a grotto—or made solid of earth and planted over with cherry trees. Here, in or

---

*A New Garden and Orchard (1618-19). After several editions of its own it was included in Markham's A Way to Get Wealth and this too went into a number of editions. I have drawn chiefly upon the 1676 edition. The last edition appeared in 1683.

†Mounts, a great feature of Elizabethan gardens, persisted in the first half of the century, but fell into desuetude after that.

on the mount, one could sit near the advised stream and "angle a peckled Trout, sleighty Eel or some other daintie fish". Failing a natural stream, one simply dug a moat (hardly single-handed) stocked it, and fished with boat and net. A labyrinth or maze of fruiting trees or shrubs "well framed to a man's height" was a useful and ornamental adjunct to any garden. Friends, happily lost within, picked fruit—presumably for the owner—and were quite unable to escape until shewn the way. A pretty knot garden, a bowling alley and butts were other features; also a "conduit" (fountain). Benches, and banks of "chamomile" were provided to sit on; raised gravelled or sanded paths (but gravel was better) to walk on. These walks were edged with fruiting bushes. What pure bliss to have "borders on every side hanging and dropping with Fe'berries,* Raspberras, Barberries, Currans and the roots of your trees powdered with Strawberries, Red, White and Green".[18]

In his small, solid way, Lawson is saying:

> "What won'drous life is this I lead!
> Ripe apples drop about my head;
> The luscious clusters of the vine
> Upon my mouth do crush their wine;
> The nectarine and curious peach,
> Into my hands themselves do reach;
> Stumbling on melons, as I pass,
> Insnar'd with flowers, I fall on grass."[19]

But this lush garden of Marvell's is based, most probably, on that belonging to Lord Fairfax whose "drowsy, dull, Presbyterian humour", as Lord Clarendon describes him, certainly did not prevent his having one of the most beautiful gardens in England —and in the north too. Lawson's garden on the other hand, is either wholly or partly within reach of everyman. And if Marvell's nightingale

*Dialect for Gooseberry, perhaps from Theve berry (Theve. ME = prickly shrub).

Of Gardens and Gardeners

"doth here make choice
To sing the tryals of her voice;"[20]

Lawson's nightingale, a less poetic but more practical bird, has "a strong delightsome voice out of a weak body and will cleanse trees of Catarpillars and noysome worms and flies", ably assisted by the "gentle" Robin redbreast, the "silly" wren with her "sweet" whistle, the Blackbird and Throstle.

It is through Lawson that we learn what flowers, vegetables and herbs were grown by—or recommended to—the ordinary everyday people of England, and he lists many of them in *The Countrie Housewife's Garden*, the very first gardening book ever written exclusively for women. It must always be remembered that in those days by far the greatest number of people were just plain, anonymous, country folk; traditional in their likes and dislikes; suspicious and slow to accept new things and new ways of doing things; thus Lawson's lists when set against the wealth of "outlandish" and "exotick" plants introduced during the century are certainly old-fashioned. Yet we cannot possibly

Cart, wheelbarrow, double-spouted watering can
and garden "sighter".

doubt that he is speaking of the favourites of the time and describing the usual type of small garden of the period. He suggests two gardens, one for flowers and a "Kitchin" or "Summer" garden, because flowers, although they can be mingled with certain herbs, would suffer "some disgrace" if intermingled with onions or parsnips or other coarse vegetables. Old-fashioned knot gardens—a Tudor innovation—are still very popular even if fashionable gardens now favoured the much looser parterres. Lawson says there are so many designs for knots that he leaves it to the Countrie Housewife to please herself. Just in case she can't, he suggests a few—the Cink-foyle, Flower-de-Luce, Tre-foyl, Cross-Bow, Diamond—many might equally well have been carried out in a plaster work ceiling.

The woodbine is a "seemly ornament" about doorways and windows, he says, with rosemary planted close to the house. The flower garden, proper, should contain roses—red, damask, velvet, double-double provence or musk and, among other things (depending on area), purple cowslips, primroses, violets, french mallow, lilies, flower-de-luce, wallflowers, Mary-golds, daisies, "Holihocks", bachelor's buttons, "Daffadowndillies", small "paunces", or heart's ease, and strange flowers such as "the Crowne Imperial . . . Tulippos, Narcissus, Hyacinthes, Heletropians . . . whose colours being glorious and different" make such a "brave checked mixture that it is both wond'rous pleasant and delectable to behold". And—almost best of all— "Clove gilly flowers" the "King of flowers . . . except the Rose". Of varieties, he recommends "Queens July-flower (July was then pronounced, logically, with the first syllable accented as in Julius), he himself has nine or ten "of several (separate) colours" and "divers of them as big as Roses". This too is part of the Englishness of the English. The longest and most faithful love affair in England's gardening history is her passion for the rose and the pink.

As for herbs, he urges fennel, angelica, tansy, lovage, elecampane (the dried root kills itches), succory "Burrage", bugloss, parsley, savoury "Licoras" and chives. Times had changed. In the previous century "Licoras" is not found as a usual herb, while chives were thought by some to disorder the brain— which may account for Nero's quite extraordinary behaviour. He kept his voice dulcet—if dulcet it were—by eating chives or so Pliny says. Useful vegetables are leeks, onions, parsnips, "carrets", endive, "Pompions" (probably marrows not pump- kins)—a warning about frost here—"skerets" artichoke, cab- bage—but watch out for "catarpillars"—turnips, lettuce for salad and radish. The latter makes a fine sauce for a "cloyed" stomach. Peas and beans had long been known and were grown in variety, but the Scarlet Runner introduced in the very late sixteenth or early seventeenth century remained, it seems, a purely ornamental vine until the reign of the last Stuart when it was discovered that it was edible. It is still regarded as purely ornamental in many parts of Canada and the U.S.A. today.* The beet was now more eaten for its root, hitherto we'd chiefly used its leaves. This is probably why we call it beetroot, al- though in the seventeenth century, as in N. America today, it was called beet.

Even farther north than Lawson's Yorkshire garden was that at Naworth Castle, near Carlisle. Here, between 1629 and 1633, Belted Will Howard's gardeners, at an average wage of 10d. per day, were planting endless "cabidge" and sowing parsley, "beete" and "garlick". With "10 spades and 2 shoofles", at 1/6 each, they set out young pear trees which cost 2/4 each; apples and plums at 2/6 apiece and "meddled" with a few apricots at 4/- the tree. Ignoring the joys of—or perhaps as a supplement to—"our own English Syder and Perry" they cautiously planted six "vine trees" at 2/- each, while two old women weeded the garden. At least they were doing so in 1630 for exactly a penny a day apiece.† The vegetables planted

*I have not known it eaten in either country, but it is a large continent and may be eaten in parts where I have never been.

†Head gardener, Lawrence Worth, received £4 per year in 1612 and was receiving exactly the same fourteen years later. He doubtless lived on the estate in a rent-free cottage as most of the gardeners and assistants did. And probably the old women did too. One hopes so.

sound rather limited and unimaginative and one wonders, rather, about all that garlic! Was it grown as a vegetable, a pot herb, a medicine or because it was believed to have the ability to cancel the attractive power of magnets?—a vulgar error soon to be exposed by Sir Thomas Browne.

Sir Thomas, himself, had a house and garden near the market place in Norwich, a city long famous for flowers, market gardens and annual "Florists Feasts". John Evelyn described house and garden as a "Paradise and cabinet of rarities" when he visited there the day before Sir Thomas's sixty-sixth birthday in 1671. And by 1671 a very great change indeed had taken place in great gardens as in most other things. The English version of the Italian Renaissance garden—with Tudor and Gothic touches was now out. The formal French style, based on the work of the great Le Nôtre was firmly established. It called for enormous, sweeping, uninterrupted vistas to and through distant and carefully organized "wood works", where geometrically-angled paths led to such surprise features (within the wood) as small secret gardens, a hunting lodge, fountain courts, and grottoes. In fact the park became, in a sense, a part of the garden. Only of course one did not do much walking in it, one rode, either on a horse or in a carriage. Immediately in front of the house, vast symmetrical parterres, in pairs, were placed. These had to serve a dual purpose, for they were viewed not only outdoors at ground level, but also from first-floor (piano nobile) windows. There were many, many types of parterre from which to choose, but *parterres de broderie*, correctly, must be nearest the house or palace. These contained no flowers at all and

> ". . . the rathe primrose that forsaken dies
> The tufted crow-toe, and pale jessamine,
> The white pink, and the pansy freaked with jet,
> The glowing violet,
> The musk rose, and the well attired woodbine."[21]

Of Gardens and Gardeners

had no place in or near the *parterres de broderie* where "embroidery" was usually carried out in clipped box (Queen Anne couldn't abide the smell of box and had all the box hedges which William III had planted at Hampton Court torn out). Most designs were curly and scroll-like, with the bare surfaces or interstices filled with coloured sands, brick dust, crushed shells, marble chips (crushed) and just plain iron rust.* Everything was as formal, as elaborate and uniform as the rigid code of etiquette which prevailed at the court of Louis *le Grand*. Ornamental lakes became perfect circles or squares or straight canals. Huge fountains forced tons of water into the air (the only use to which the water pump was put in this era, as far as I know). The dreary *patte d'oie*, with its middle "toe" a canal, and flanking toes, one on each side, composed of angled, tree-lined avenues all radiating from a semicircle of trees, was high fashion. The restored Charles could hardly wait to impose this monstrous, great goose-foot on St. James's Park (admittedly the old Park was pretty boggy and often flooded). Pepys was delighted with what was going on there as early as September 1660 and by July 1662 sat under a tree in a corner one Sunday "and there sang some songs".

Evelyn observed "the strange and wonderful dexterity of the sliders" on the new canal in December of that year. They performed "with skates, after the manner of the Hollanders" and before their Majesties too. But he has little to say about the new park in his Diary. He may have admired it, but being something of a pickthank he certainly would have overpraised it in his diary had he found anything to praise. Evelyn had seen and noted wonderful gardens in Italy and France during his conti-

*Other types of parterre were the water and the compartment parterre. They usually adjoined the embroidered parterre. There was also the *parterre fleuriste*, or cut work parterre, which actually contained flowers. In France the latter were not set too near the house and came under the kitchen garden department. The worst parterre of all, the French thought, was an English invention and called *Parterre à l'Anglais*—plain, mean little things, said the French, being mostly grass plots without much involved pattern.

nental wanderings, and was still busy creating his own at Sayes Court, Deptford (no garden is ever finished) which combined, he thought, the best points of Italian, French and even Tudor Gardens into one charming whole. He shaped his plan "to the nature of the place"—others didn't, they removed hills and even villages for the sake of a vista. Old Parkinson would have been astonished, and probably disapproving. He believed, poor innocent, that "the severall situations of mens dwellings, are for the most part unavoidable and irremovable".[22] But then he had also believed that "the Apricock is without question a kind of Plumme rather than a Peach". John Evelyn was better informed, particularly about trees, which he loved in variety and upon which he was an expert.* His hedges too were famous, particularly his holly hedges which Peter Mikhailov—a volunteer sailor as he styled himself—ruined when he became a tenant of Sayes Court. Mikhailov liked to have himself trundled through the hedge in a wheelbarrow. Tenant and friends did much damage to house and garden. They were "a house full of people and right nasty", Evelyn's bailiff writes; not without reason. Indoors, paint work, tiles and 200 window panes had to be renewed; sheets and curtains were torn; tables and chairs broken to bits. Outside, great pot holes were made in the two bowling greens lying to the south of the house. Wall fruit trees and border boards were damaged. Mikhailov—better known to us as Peter the Great, Tsar of Muscovy—was not an ideal tenant.† But he did create the Russian Navy, learned much about shipbuilding at Deptford and was a remarkable man in many ways.

Evelyn, it hardly needs saying, was a great amateur of gardens and wrote and translated many books on the subject. His own garden—small by royal or noble standards, large by ordinary

*Evelyn's book on Trees, *Sylva*, remained the standard work on the subject until the last quarter of the eighteenth century

†This was in 1696. Evelyn had let Sayes Court to Admiral Benbow who, at the request of William III, sub-let it to the Tsar. Damages paid to Evelyn and Benbow by the Treasury (and not very quickly either) amounted to £300.

Ornamental garden house, c. 1680.

ones—must have been charming, judging from its plan, for he does not seem to have been entirely converted to the fashionable French school of design which ended in a perfectly deadly, baleful and boring symmetry. Yet, like Lawson but on a different scale and in a larger era, he too had his vision of Paradise. Of an *Elysium Britannicum*: A Royal Garden. An ideal. It was to be his magnum opus, this book on grand gardens, but it never got finished (though separate parts were published). This "Elysium" must be full of "stupendous" and wonderful plants and must contain a very great variety of other things too—groves, labyrinths, "dedals"* cabinets (bowers or summer houses?), cradles, close work, pavilions, porticoes, lanterns and "relievos of topiary and hortulan architecture". That he based some of his ideas on the magnificent and beautiful gardens he'd seen in

*A trifle confusing, a daedal was a labyrinth anyway, deriving its name from the first builder Daedalus. But perhaps a daedal was a subterranean labyrinth as opposed to a terranean one like a maze.

Italy in 1645 is apparent, because he includes in his Paradise "artificial echoes", automata, hydraulic music, to say nothing of canals, baths, cascades, rocks, grottoes, crypts, mounts (these were terribly *vieux jeu* by now), "conservatories of ice and snow", theatres, amphitheatres and—precipices! It sounds preposterously extravagant and probably not all *extravaganze* were to be used at once. But perhaps they were! People were very fond of stupendous plants and all sorts of artifices by then, while some of the "extravagancies" of the previous period had become almost commonplace in post-Cromwellian England.

Orangeries,* once so rare, were now usual in great gardens and, after Parliament had turned William of Orange into William III, they positively flourished in silent flattery of the new monarch. Orangeries were elaborately built and heated in winter. The trees stood in tubs and were moved out in summer to an "orangerie parterre" or were regimented onto terraces. "Bring your orange trees out boldly in May", Evelyn advises to our horror. But the difference of eleven days in the calendar, particularly in May, would account for there being small danger of ruin by May frosts. It also explains, when we read gardening books of the time, why everything seems to "come on" so much earlier than nowadays.

Even so, there was much less danger of frost affecting any tender plant or small tree because greenhouses were so much more usual after the Restoration. Before, there had been the infrequent "stove-house"; that is, a house where plants were over-wintered and were kept warm by open fireplaces or pans of charcoal or, even more advanced, by pipes running from a stove. Stove plants, as we still call them, must have been a lot warmer in winter than their owners. A stove house did not

---

*The first orangery in England is said to have been made by Sir Frances Carew at Beddington in the time of Elizabeth I. It was still famous, much enlarged, and is reported to have produced 10,000 oranges in 1690. The trees were destroyed in the hard winter of 1739-40.

Of Gardens and Gardeners

necessarily have much glass in it. Windows, yes, with shutters because it was thought that air kept plants green. But at some point during the Stuart century heat and glass were combined to make the heated glass-house or greenhouse, a combination which must have excited as much wonder and amazement then as its mammoth successor, the Crystal Palace did, two centuries later.

Garden houses multiplied too. If there was but one, it was often put near the road where it made a handy room to wait for, or to look out at, passing coaches (the word gazebo does not appear to have been used until *circa* 1750). There were probably eight summer houses of assorted kinds at Wimbledon when Henrietta Maria owned it, including several shadow houses, the orange house, and two banqueting houses. One of the latter, a very grand one, stood at the east end of the turfed "terras" with benches, a table of polished "artificial stone", and handsome statues disposed about inside. The doors were carved and coloured, but the whole house appears to have been painted green, inside and out, which sounds rather a mistake. Banqueting houses waned in popularity as time went on, but pavilions— either as solid wings to a house or separate and small like butterflies—settled here and there. It is doubtful if any were portable like the pavilion of the great "Chan Cublay" first revealed to the English in 1625.* This was "gilded and vernished" and around each pillar a dragon wound itself, its head "bearing up the loft" and its wings displayed on both sides of the pillars; the whole pavilion was "sustained with two hundred silken cords" so it could be "sundered and taken down like a Tent".[23]

Even more essential and usual than pavilions were fountains. There were splendid ones in new gardens everywhere, such as those at Wilton. But the Wilton fountains had been there ever since Charles I's day and were now, many thought, outclassed

*Sir Christopher Wren did indeed design a portable house to be put up as and where one liked. But this was for William III to use when he went across to mow down the unfortunate Irish.

by the amazing waterworks at Chatsworth where the enthusiastic
first Duke laid out new gardens to suit his newly altered house.
Here, formal parterres of great size and symmetry embroidered
the ground; the old orchard was uprooted to make way for
greenhouse and "Birdhouse"; a mountain was "removed and
perfectly carried away"[24] to make a grand vista; but the greatest
wonder of all was the Cascade. Celia Fiennes saw it around
1697. It was torn up, deepened and enlarged in 1701 and Thomas
Archer's beautiful Cascade House was set at its head.* The
gardens were full of fountains, fed from a great reservoir of
thirty acres, Defoe tells us, and seems to have thought it one
of the wonders of the Peak that such a house and garden should
have been built in a "houling winderness".[25] But Venus, Boreas,
Neptune, Triton, Sea Horses and Dolphins at Chatsworth and
similar "waterworks" in other gardens were to the day what
fireworks were at night. Celia Fiennes who, some say, is the
original "fine lady upon a white horse" for Fiennes is pronounced
"fines", was particularly delighted with Chatsworth's "Willow
Tree", "the leaves barke and all looks very naturall" she writes,
"the roote is full of rubbish or great stones to appearance and
all on a sudden by turning a sluce it raines from each leafe and
from the branches like a shower; it being made of brass and pipes
to each leafe but in appearance is exactly like any Willow".†
It was, indeed, a weeping willow and just possibly the idea came
from Spain from the gardens of Aranjuez (chiefly laid out by
Mary Tudor's nasty husband). This garden contained many of
the highest trees ever seen by Lady Anne Fanshawe, some,
bored through, had pipes inserted so that when water was
forced through them the trees became living fountains. Great

---

*The Cascade has been rebuilt since then, but the Cascade House
with the addition of four lions—is the original. Archer's garden house
in Wrest Park (Beds.) still stands. It was built 1709-12. Archer
subsequently seems to have given up architecture for the lucrative
office of groom porter which he held under Queen Anne and George I.

†The present Willow fountain is not the original made by Ibeck in
1692, but the Sea horse and Triton fountains are original.

Of Gardens and Gardeners

English gardens were not complete without elaborate and novel fountains plus lakes and/or canals or—if house and garden were middling—ponds stocked with fish which "show to the sun their waved coats dropped with gold".[26]

At his new house, Esholt Hall, Sir Walter Calverley in 1704 stocked his pond with "4 score tench and 20 carps" given him by Mr. Arthington—a compliment which the receiver returned in the shape of two dozen partridge either for Mr. Arthington's

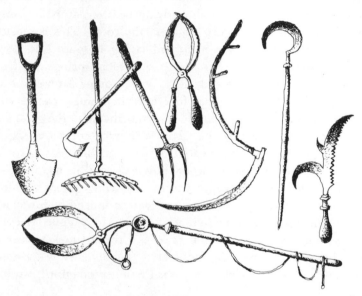

Garden tools in common use.

park or larder. Considering that twice as a child, Sir Walter had narrowly escaped an aqueous death—first, in 1671 when at the age of two he "fell into a tube of Water and had like to have been drowned"; and second, in the very next year when he "fell into a panfull of milk and was taken oute for dead"[27]— it was really brave of him to have such a personally dangerous ornament as a large pond in his new garden.

A lawn was much safer; and lawns as we know them today

began in the seventeenth century. Mediaeval lawns imitated flower-sprinkled meadows. Tudor lawns were small "green plots" of camomile or grass. But the Stuart century improved on these and possibly the first description of how to make a large lawn, is given by Gervase Markham.[28] The lawn area must be cleared of stones and weeds (boiling water poured over the roots of the latter was an excellent eradicator) the earth must be beaten and "trod down mightily", then turfs laid—curiously enough, grass side down. These were then "danced upon with the feet" and pressed down lightly with a paving beetle. After this, small hair-like grass began to peep up from the roots. This is sensible advice. Turf was full of weeds and laying it grass side down would smother weeds but not grass which springs up from exposed roots. John Rea (not Ray, who comes later) is even more specific. The area must first be railed and covered with hungry sand unless the ground is barren, otherwise the grass will grow too rank. The turf, cut from a hungry common, should be laid, green side up, beaten with a mallet and watered copiously. Camomile lawns were, however, still in use and continued so until the nineteenth century. Bowling greens required —and got—perfectly level surfaces greatly admired by foreigners because cutting lawns and bowling greens had to be done by scythe and swept clean with a broom (two and three times a week at great houses). Hence the popularity of low, slow growing camomile. The lawn mower wasn't invented until around 1830.

Garden tools and implements are very recognizably the ancestors of our own. Rollers of wood or stone; spades, shovels, picks, mattocks, forks; riddles of wood and of wire; hoes and trowels of various kinds; clippers for low shrubs and tall trees; wheelbarrows and carts; pruning knives, grafting knives and small delicate knives especially for layering gillyflowers; water carts; fruit picking platforms and "pockets"; baskets and besoms and various sorts of garden frames, were all part of the necessary equipment. Some garden frames look exactly like bedsteads with posts, tester and ornaments at the four corners

Of Gardens and Gardeners

complete with curtains to be drawn at night against the frost. They lack only mattress and "coverlids". Bell glasses were used, lead watering cans frequent, and bird scarers—bells strung on a line—must have been less devastating in sound if less effective than that awful line of squibs on the burning rope which we use today. Paradise, like every mundane paradise, had its snags. Birds were only one of them.

There were snags which could not be coped with. Terrible winters for one thing, and there were several of these during the century. But there were also compensating mild ones such as that of 1679/80 when as far north as Crosby, William Blundell* picked white violets from his garden on January 30th, found his daffodils in bud, and the tansy "about a finger long".[29] In February the "apricock buds" were red, and on New Year's Day—that is March 25th, 1680—the pears were fully flowered and "in their greatest lustre". Apart from the weather, about which one could do nothing—and fortunately can still do nothing —there were the usual garden pests which had to be dealt with. "Moles, Catts, Earewiggs, snailes and Mice", were the chief ones bothering Sir Thomas Hanmer. Moles always were and always had been a great nuisance and "Remedies against Moles"[30] were many, varied and, one fears, largely ineffective. Those who could afford to, employed mole catchers—usually on a strictly cash basis. No moles no money. The average rate was around 12d. a dozen for "olde moles"; 6d. a dozen for young ones. To employ a catcher to "gette a single mole in a howse, garden and the like"[31] was more costly at 2d. or 3d. per lone mole. Henry Best who farmed in the East Riding seems to have had a real bargain when, in 1628, he paid John Pearson 13½d.

*There is a link here with Thomas Bushell. Blundell, a Roman Catholic, retired to the Isle of Man in 1646 or 1648 and busied himself with writing about its antiquities. Bushell occupied a cave or cell on the Calf of Man in 1626 where, after Bacon's death, he thought of becoming a hermit . . . and Blundell describes the cave and hut which Bushell occupied. People there were still talking about Bushell's "Pendant Bed".

for a dozen old moles but only 6d. for two dozen young ones Do-it-yourself remedies included pouring water down the run either to drown the animals or drive them into a narrow passage where they could be caught (Sir Thomas Hanmer says this is useless even when the water is boiling or poisoned), and Adam Speed says that pieces of red herring burned on top of molehills, or bits of garlic and leek stuck in them will cause the moles to hurry above ground where they can be caught. But he frankly admits he hasn't tried this himself and advises the reader to make "his own tryal, belief or doubt". Failing these, good hefty thorny rose branches pushed through the runs were reputed to do the trick. It is extremely unlikely that such was the case.

But the mole's one brief hour of fame came in this century when, in 1702, an anonymous "little gentleman in black velvet" caused William III to be thrown from his horse, an accident which indirectly caused his death shortly afterwards. Although because of this the mole became, theoretically, the favourite animal of extreme Tories—one might say even their heraldic beast—no general amnesty was declared. Whig and Tory, so divided on all else, were united in persecuting moles.

Caterpillars too were "noysome". Lawson, assisted by nightingale, robin and silly wren, preferred to pick the excess off by hand and crush them underfoot. He did not approve of smoking the trees to get rid of them, "un-naturall heates are nothing good for naturall trees" he says, and although he does not mention "the parsimonious emmet" as a particular pest he recommends soot, ashes and other refuse to prevent "pismires" and other insects from invading fruit, which sounds dubious. Evelyn recommends coarse honey and glass beaten with copperas[32] which is more hopeful, while Sir Thomas Hanmer recommends that snails be taken at night with a candle—which sounds positively exhausting. Sheep's hooves on poles, he also says, will effectively trap earwigs, which indeed they will. Today we use old tin cans instead of sheep's hooves—one is slightly macabre, the other perfectly hideous, but both work.

Of Gardens and Gardeners

Among other things gardeners had to cope with were canker, animals (including deer), "poysonful smoke",[33] weeds, filth, worms, boisterous blasts, cold, some birds and "evil neighbours". Lawson recommends a strong fence, a greyhound, a stone-bow (catapult) a "gunne" against most animals and, with unbelievable cruelty, "an apple with a hook" against deer. "Justice and Liberality" are recommended—a trifle optimistically one feels—to "put away evil neighbours".*

But to return to happier aspects of the garden. New to the century was the "pheasant garden". Pheasant were not at all new, but someone around this time had the idea that they should be hand reared and the pheasant garden, usually adjacent to the park and enclosed by walls or a hedge, was the result. Live birds in the garden or in the house increased prodigiously and the canary† became almost common. Everyone, even Cromwell, seemed passionately addicted to having birds about, and a variety of aquatic ones ornamented new ponds, lakes and canals— even if Evelyn found the Pelican in St. James's Park a "melancholy water fowl".[34] Peacocks of uncorruptible flesh no longer

---

*It is doubtful if justice or liberality would have overcome the evil designs of the Earl of Lincoln. He removed the protecting pale from his neighbour Ludowic Bryskett's garden at Chelsea, in 1604, and sent in workmen to remove all the Bryskett cabbages, and cattle to spoil the Bryskett barley. In 1606 the neighbourly Earl taking a scunner against Sir Robert Stapleton who lived nearby, hired a jakes farmer to dump his dung into the Thames near enough to Sir Robert's house to make the air offensive and to pollute his water supply.

†The canary, or sugar bird, so called because it loved sugar and sugar cane, was known in the sixteenth century but was rare and expensive in Europe both because it came from the Canary Islands and because sugar was then very expensive. The Spanish had a monopoly on canaries and, it is said, refused to allow male birds to be exported. But in mid-seventeenth century a ship with a load of canaries bound for Leghorn was shipwrecked off the Italian coast, and the birds escaped, flew to Elba where in the favourable climate, they multiplied quickly, were snared and exported to the European mainland. Thus the Spanish monopoly of canaries (though not of Canary) was broken.

kept watch in the inner courtyard of a house to cry the approach of strangers as they had done for centuries, they now danced delicate pavanes down broad, tree-lined avenues, or displayed Argus-eyed tail coverts on the great green terraces of new houses. Aviaries, more commonly called Birdcages (hence Birdcage Walk at the Buckingham Palace end of St. James's Park) became usual. Indoors they were large, beautifully built and cupola-ed. Outdoors they were grand garden features. There was a fine birdcage in the gardens at Wimbledon with three open turrets "very well wrought . . . for the setting and perching of birds". It contained a handsome court and a fountain. Court, fountain, and turrets were all covered with "strong iron wire" and this birdcage was, the surveyors say, such "a great ornament to the house and garden" that they valued it at £25.4.0. Very unlike Sir Thomas Fowler's aviary near Hackney which was "a poor business".[35] The Duchess of Mazarin, who remained in England after the death of her royal lover (Charles II), had a large aviary at her house, No. 4 Paradise Row. In 1696 Saint Evremond writes to console her for the disappearance of Boulé, her bullfinch. Saint-Evremond, himself, held the sinecure appointment of Keepership of the Ducks in the Decoy of St. James's Park with a salary, which amounted to a pension, of £300 per year. Much earlier, in 1667, Lady Castelmaine rushed out into her aviary in a smock to see the great Earl of Clarendon (whom she hated) sadly cross the courtyard after being dismissed from office by Charles. There is still a charming birdcage to be seen today at Melbourne Hall, Derbyshire, in the gardens originally laid out by Sir Thomas Coke with the aid of that famous pair, London and Wise, "to suit with Versailles".[36] This is really an "iron arbour" made in the shape of a French Birdcage by Robert Bakewell a pupil of Jean Tijou.* Thomas Coke married the

---

*Tijou's wrought iron work is unsurpassed and can still be seen in the great gates at Hampton Court. The beautiful gates at Burley-on-the-Hill are probably his work too, although they no longer show to advantage since Repton was allowed a free hand with house and garden in 1796.

Gateway to Oxford physic garden.

Earl of Chesterfield's daughter and the Earl had a notable garden which in 1698 contained that rarity, a cedar of Lebanon as well as a great tall tulip tree near the wilderness, also "a great avery of birds which stands like a sumer house open". There were also "many close averys of birds".[37] Presumably this open aviary was also an iron arbour and not meant for birds, whereas "close" (wired) ones were.

As for automata and mechanical devices, such garden conceits became more and more popular as the Stuart century drew to its close. It is true that Bishop Wilkins, when Warden of Wadham, had been able to make a rainbow appear by means of an artificial mist and by an involved calculation of where to stand to see it properly, but this was in its way a scientific toy. More in line with the taste of the time was a water clock in Sir Anthony Cope's garden at Hanwell which showed the hours "by the rise of a new gilded sun",[38] one for each hour. These numbered (and unscientific) suns rose successively within an arch which marked the half-hour at its zenith.* Even better, and probably no more accurate, was the Earl of Chesterfield's water-worked garden clock which struck the hours and chimed the quarters. It also played "*Lilliburlero*"† on the chimes at the Earl's pleasure. It was nothing to have metal birds sing, statues weep, or brazen heads seem to speak. And topiary work, although not mechanical in the usual sense of the word, became almost a mania with anyone who possessed a shrub, a tree and a pair of shears. One, Mr. Cox, a rich dealer in flax who lived near London, had all sorts of topiary work in his garden;[39] animals, men considerably larger than life, ships in full sail, and even a sundial with stylus of clipped box. Clever Mr. Cox also managed to combine an automaton and topiary in one figure which spoke (by means of a hollow tube).

Among the mildly eccentric gardeners of the day there was the old parson at Banstead who devoted himself to his garden for fifty years (gardening and natural history in England owe much to parsons and Bishops). He was, in 1703, "old and doates" and his garden presented a rather strange appearance as various plots contained stones which he called gods and goddesses. One large white stone surrounded by nine small ones, apparently placed on a table in a tree, represented Apollo and the nine Muses on Parnassus. Painted heads representing the mogul, the Cham of Tartary, the "Zarr of Muscovy" and others stood about. The topiary work was slightly on the bizarre side too. Benches and seats were cut out of quickset hedges, one ivy-covered tree was "cut even" (level) and called "Tenneriff". It had a stair leading to the top where, it appears from Miss Fiennes' description, there was "an eight square bench"—which sounds suitable for the Quangle Wangle and his gay friends of the

---

*Vitruvius describes similar waterclocks (Bk. IX, Ch. 8) made by Ctesibus of Alexandria *circa* 250 B.C.

†"Lilliburlero" or "Lillibulero" is England's Marseillaise! The song of the "Glorious Revolution". It is supposedly the work of the Marquis of Wharton. Purcell, some say, wrote the music. Joseph Addison was, at one time, Wharton's secretary.

Of Gardens and Gardeners

Crumpety Tree—but hardly for an elderly parson. Yet another tree was cut in the shape of a huge rose so that seated under it people could talk "sub-Rosa".*

By this late date, however, it was really old-fashioned not to say vulgar to clip trees in human or animal form as poor Mr. Cox and the parson of Banstead did. The Joneses all over the country had been surpassing each other with the new "mathematical" mode of clipping with such frenzy that satiety inevitably resulted. Trees became obelisks, spheres, pyramids of green, and it was particularly smart to have a row of slender trees which looked like a line of poles each topped by a large, perfectly round green ball. Or to alternate these heads on pikes with equally perfect pyramids. Such things could be bought large and ready clipped from the great nurseries of London and Wise at Brompton, if one were rich enough. They could be raised oneself if one weren't.

The death knell of topiary, of dead formalization, of unnatural symmetry imposed upon trees was sounded in 1712 when Addison tells his readers that he prefers to "look upon a Tree in all its Luxuriancy and Diffusion of Boughs and Branches" and not cut into "a Mathematical Figure". "Our British Gardeners" he writes, "instead of humouring Nature, love to deviate from it as much as possible. Our Trees rise in Cones, Globes and Pyramids. We see the mark of the Scissors upon every Plant and Bush".[40] This is doubtless an exaggeration, by 1712 there were so many new trees, bushes, shrubs and plants that a few must surely have escaped disfigurement. John Aubrey says that 7,000 "exotick Plants" were brought into England between the Restoration and 1691 and "especially since about 1683". Even if we regard this figure with suspicion (and there's no need to do so) we know that from beginning to end the Stuart century was filled with new kinds of plants and trees. Evergreens

*The parson may have been old, but I wonder if he was really in his dotage? It sounds more as if he had a rather oblique sense of humour. Miss Fiennes, although I am her devoted admirer, does not appear to have been humoristically inclined.

The Pageant of Stuart England

of many sorts now carried a part of summer into winter. It is said that Sir Isaac Wake (d. 1632) first planted "Pine and Firres in England" which may or may not be true, but it is certain that the horse chestnut with its pale pyramids of flowers was not seen here before 1625. How difficult to imagine England now without evergreens, horse chestnuts or the Lebanon cedar . . . yet these were just a few of the trees new to the century while in contemporary records such a wealth of new plants appears that gardeners both amateur and "Mercenarie"—as Evelyn calls professional ones—must have been hard put to find room for them all.

Botanist-gardeners must have been equally hard pressed trying to classify them.* As early as 1648 the Physic Garden at Oxford† contained about 1,600 species and in 1650 the young science of botany took a leap forward when William How tried to distinguish, in his *Phytologia Britannica*, indigenous from outlandish plants. John Ray (1627-1705) (not to be confused with John Rea) and Robert Morison (1620-83) were the first to classify plants by the observation of similarities of fruit and flower. Hitherto, a crude system based on the external appearance of plants or their place of growth had been used as a method of classification, with wildly inaccurate results. Ray, a zoologist as well, is the originator of a natural system of classification. He separated non-flowering plants (i.e. fungi, seaweeds, mosses, ferns) from flowering and divided the latter into Dicotyledons and Monocotyledons. His *Methodus Plantarum* is one of the great

*That book written by Solomen which told of "all plants from the cedar of Libanus to the moss that groweth out of the wall" was in the process of becoming a fact. It was foreshadowed by Francis Bacon in *The New Atlantis*, first published 1629.

†Founded 1621 by a grant of land given by Henry, Earl of Danby. Its fine gate is by Nicholas Stone after a design by Inigo Jones. Its first gardener was Jacob Brobart the Elder, an ugly man with a hideous wife. His hands were black and coarse as any field labourers, his dress was mean and so was his hat. It seems hardly necessary to state that these derogatory personal remarks are by that endearing fellow, von Uffenbach.

Of Gardens and Gardeners

land-marks in botany. Robert Morison, physician, scientist, botanist to Charles II, and first professor of Botany at Oxford also produced a systematic arrangement. It was based to a certain extent (as was Ray's) on the system evolved by Andrea Caesalpini* of the famous Botanic Gardens, Pisa, who had, as early as 1583, taken the 1,500 botanic plants then known and, remembering no doubt the sixteenth verse of the seventh Chapter of Matthew, classified accordingly. Nehemiah Grew with his microscope investigated plant anatomy† (so did Malpighi) but no one followed in his footsteps for another century. Even Samuel Morland the inventor (and a former tutor of Sam Pepys) interested himself in botany and in 1703 arrived at the startling conclusion that the "farina" (pollen) was the fertilizing agent; "congeries of seminal plants, one of which must be conveyed into every ovum before it can become prolific"—a statement so nearly right as to make no difference.

In addition to all this activity, amateurs and professional botanists were collecting, drying and pressing plants in their specimen books, or making beautiful drawings of them, observing and recording in a way that would have delighted Francis Bacon. The amusing but crude wood-cuts illustrating the old Herbals gave way to accurate drawings and engravings. These are very much better than the century's efforts to depict birds and beasts . . . for the very simple reason that plants, trees, and shrubs stand still. James Petiver (1663-1718), Demonstrator of Botany at the Chelsea Physic Garden, a famous Apothecary with a large practice in Aldersgate and also Apothecary to St. Bartholomew's and the Charterhouse, accumulated, as we know, a wonderful natural history collection. In addition, he published two folio volumes with very beautiful engravings.

*Caesalpini (1519-1603) was second director of the Pisa Gardens, which were the earliest in Europe devoted to the study of Botany. They were founded in 1543 by Cosimo I, Duke of Tuscany.

†It is possible that credit for Grew's theory of sexuality should be given to Sir Thomas Millington, Sedlian Professor of natural philosophy at Oxford.

The Pageant of Stuart England

His neat volumes of dried plants are still preserved in the Natural History Museum. Plant collecting, drying and so on was not a job for professionals alone, amateurs took to it too. The absolutely indefatigable Mr. Evelyn, when abroad, had collected and arranged hundreds of pressed simples from the Padua Botanic Garden in a large folio volume. When Sam Pepys saw the book he observed, quite correctly, it was "better than a Herball".[41] Queen Mary II was most interested in gardens and in collecting rare plants. She sent people off to Virginia, to the Canaries and other spots to collect rare and exotic flowers— one, a Century plant, didn't bloom until two centuries later, and in 1689 she paid "To James Read, Gardiner for going to Virginia to make a collection of Foreign Plantes £234.11.9". Whether she ever dried or pressed flowers into an album I cannot say. Nevertheless the fashion for books of pressed flowers—a fashion which reached its apogee in Victorian times —began here.

But to return from dried plants to living post-Restoration and late Stuart gardens. As we have seen, great gardens now followed the French fashion as they had once followed the Italian. But great gardens were still vastly outnumbered by small ones and when we remember that during the last quarter or so of the Stuart century (that is 1680-1714), there was a great increase in houses built for small gentlemen, it is clear there must have been a comparable increase in new gardens which were neither of the grand nor simple cottage variety. The enormous vistas down which one looked, expecting almost to see an apotheosis of Louis XIV painted on the clouds above; the splendid and fabulous waterworks; the elephantine *patte d'oie*, can hardly have been thought suitable garden planning for the charming, beautifully proportioned, small houses which were so very English—even had their owners been able to afford them. Unfortunately, we have virtually no documentary evidence of what such gardens were like (plans do not exist as they do of great gardens) but fortunately we have John Rea who advised on lawns and published a number of gardening books (*Complete*

Garden ornaments, *c.* 1630-80.

Florilage, 1665, enlarged to *Flora Ceres and Pomona* 1678) which, like Lawson's books earlier on, went on being popular long after his death which occurred in 1681. Rea lived at Kinlet near Bewdley, was an expert on bulbs, a friend of Thomas Hanmer, and a firm believer in the small garden. Large gardens were too often ill-furnished and ill-kept and he thinks for a "private gentleman 40 square yards fruit and 20 flowers is enough" (even a nobleman needed no more than eighty for fruit and thirty for flowers).

Ideally, the garden should lie on the south of the house, encompassed by a nine-foot wall; another wall five feet high of bricks or of pales painted brick colour should separate orchard from flower garden with a good opening in the wall for easy access from one to the other. So, safe enclosed within the wall, flowers and fruit can flourish without fear of nibbling deer or evil neighbours. Here, in this small area, the owner could create his own small Elysium. The component parts of this Eden are however, explained in some detail by Rea. The orchard is to be farthest from the house, the flowers nearest and set in square beds or parterres more simply designed than Lawson's knots. Square beds are railed with painted wood or with box; recommended centre-pieces are "great tufts of pionies" set round with varieties of cyclamen, daffodils, hyacinths and other low-growing flowers. At the corners are tall bulbs; crown imperials, or martagons. Straight beds are best for tulips, he says and thereby conjures up the regimented rows still so favoured in the Royal Parks.

Walls are to support climbing plants and fruit trees—such as pears grafted on quince and, strangely to us, the double-flowered pomegranate. In between these are standard roses, so grafted that a succession of colours is achieved. Below, in wide borders he would have the gardener plant auriculas (Mistress Bugges in Battersea raised a fine purple one and Jacob Brobart the Elder, "Keeper of the Public Gardens" in Oxford, was an auricula expert); red primroses, rose campion, dame's violet (hesperis), the best wallflowers, double nonsuch, stock gilliflowers and a host of other things. A lattice-work for roses made a very pretty background for snowdrops in spring or for potted plants in summer. We already know Rea's views on lawn making and he had equally strong ones on the very necessary gravel paths. Sandy gravel was the worst, "cat-brain" gravel was the best. But, like Bishop Burnet, when puzzled, "I cannot pretend to determine" what is meant by "cat-brain" gravel. Rea, while admitting noble fountains, statues, grottoes and the like to be very fine and magnificent ornaments, feels that such "dead works in gardens ill-done, are little better than blocks in the way to interrupt sight". Again we are a little puzzled to determine what is ill-done—dead works or garden? Or does he mean dead works badly placed? Probably the latter, for he leaves us in no doubt at all that a summer house—a prime requisite of any garden—must be placed to one side of the garden. He is quite specific as to the kind of summer house too, "a handsom, octangular somer-house", it must be "roofed every way and

Of Gardens and Gardeners

finely painted with Landskips* and other conceits". This house has a dual purpose. Besides being furnished with tables and chairs for great delight and entertainment, it is also useful as a place in which to put bulbs and other plants when lifted. Here one could label, wrap and stow them away in boxes until needed again.

Rea gives us a great deal of information on small gardens of the time, together with much sensible advice. No doubt some of his readers produced fine gardens, and no doubt some didn't. No doubt small gentlemen experimented with different designs and added their own touches—which is really how English gardens become English. New flowers and plants would be introduced from time to time—for once the botanists and the rich had imported "wonderful and splendid flowers" they became established and soon found their way into smaller gardens. Perhaps by now the nasturtium (*tropaeolum majus*) which Parkinson† once mixed with "Corn or Gillo flowers" to make "a delicate Tussie-mussie" and which he had described, so long ago, as being "of so great beauty and sweetness withall that my Garden of Delight cannot be unfurnished of it", had become common. As common as the once rare red lily which Rea's son-in-law, also a gardener, describes as "vulgar"; or as common as the formerly treasured martagons which he, unlike his father-in-law, does not recommend. They are "rustick . . . a rambling flower fit only for flower pots or chimneys" (that is to be set in the empty fireplace in summer) or to be planted, presumably, out of sight under hedges. It is doubtful if any but the fashionable despised the martagon for these reasons. Certainly they were greatly loved by country folk and were to be seen in medium, small and minute gardens everywhere.

*The earliest surviving English Landskip is in the Ashmolean. It was painted (on copper) by an amateur, Sir Nathaniel Bacon.

†An echo of Parkinson is found in 1908 when the Worshipful Company of Gardeners presented the Lord Mayor of London with a nosegay of thirty-eight of the flowers mentioned in the *Paradisi*. The flowers were grown by Sander and Son, St. Albans. (sc. P.R.O. Reade 30/18.)

The Pageant of Stuart England

For even if, long, long ago the great Lord Burghley had delighted to "ride private in his garden upon a little muile"[42] and a hundred years or so later William III borrowed a little horse to ride about the gardens of Burghley House; even if at Castle Howard the gardens were to reach "the highest pitch that Nature and Polite gardening can ever arrive to",[43] unnatural and rude gardening still persisted. It persisted about tiny cottages and in rural districts all over England—and only a trifle less naturally and rudely in the sixty square yards recommended as being a suitable size for a private gentleman who needed no mule nor horse to enable him to enjoy his own private paradise.

In those days our ancestors, blindly, foolishly, obstinately—and despite any or all evidence to the contrary—believed that if one Paradise had been lost another had been gained. It did not lie in some far, fabled country inhabited by foreigners. It was not somewhere in the airy acres of the sky or in a Heaven "sowed with stars . . . thick as a field"[44] and occupied by angels. It was here. It was now. It was England. They lived in it!

"We liue, breath and haue our beeing in a second Paradice" says Lieutenant Hammond who saw the grotto at Enstone when he, it, and the Stuart century were still young, "a delightful Garden and a plentifully furnish'd Magazine and Store-house of all terrestriall felicitie and sublunary happiness" he continues, touching us with his own wonder, awe and joy, "soe enrich'd and ouer mantled with Plenty and Pleasure, soe happie, glorious and triumphant . . . as makes all Strangers ouer the whole face of the Vniuerse to gaze and wonder . . .

> Oh formosa triumphans fortunata resplendens,
> Insula Regio magna Brittania gloria Mundi."

CHAPTER ELEVEN

The Queen is Dead—Long Live the King

IT is curious, perhaps, that the Stuart century should have opened and closed with the death of a Queen Regnant. Curious that both Queen Elizabeth and Queen Anne should have been succeeded by foreigners. But Anne was not Elizabeth although, for some obscure reason, she sometimes fancied she was like her and once, even, toyed with the idea of taking her great predecessor's personal motto *semper eadem* as her own.

Distanced in time, from a cold Thursday in March 1603 to a hot Sunday in August 1714, by a century of monarchs and eleven years of Commonwealth and Protectorate, the two queens gaze at each other without recognition as they do in wax effigy in Westminster Abbey. Between them lies the Stuart era, one of the most brilliant in English history—yet the tragedy of the House of Stuart is, perhaps, one of the saddest things in that history, too. No sovereigns had more or better opportunities to emerge as great kings; none failed so completely and abysmally. And when Charles II and James II sought the protection and the money of absolutism personified in Louis XIV of France—and France was England's greatest trade rival—the result was 1689 and the true end of the old world of Elizabeth. One cannot imagine her as a pensioner of Spain.

So from the Glorious Revolution on we are in a world which becomes year by year recognizably our modern one. A world of constitutional monarchs, of political parties, of higher taxes upon landowners and the poor—and of lower ones on industrialists. It is a new world of banks, of eating bread and butter, of coffee-houses and the stock exchange, of Cabinet Ministers, better street lighting and drinking Bohea tea. It is a world of developing political institutions and disappearing yeomanry; of emerging industrialization and declining family industry and of patriarchal family life.

We are in the age of Pope whose glittering, polished couplets and bright malice are to Shakespeare what a crystal drop of water is to a raging torrent. The beauty and barbarity of the Renaissance, which persisted until the end of James I's reign, is long over. England is at once more polished and less poetic. More civilized, more comfortable and more self-conscious. It is, in Anne's reign, much more prosperous too. The harvests are good and fewer are hungry. There is more freedom; freedom from arbitrary arrest and freedom from religious persecution. There is also freedom from arbitrary taxation— at least for men of property—for a man rich enough can always buy his way into Parliament. When Elizabeth died, none of these things was true.

When Elizabeth died, a sapphire ring was dropped from a window—or passed through an outer door of Richmond Palace —to Sir Robert Carey. And Carey, with this pre-arranged signal in his pocket, galloped off to Scotland to tell James VI, King of Scots, that he was King James, the first of that name, of England. When Anne died at Kensington Palace, Dr. Arbuthnot signalled her death by waving a white pocket handkerchief at a pre-arranged window—and George Lewis of Hanover was proclaimed King George, the first of that name, of England. So between a sapphire ring and a white pocket handkerchief the Stuart century is contained. A pocket handkerchief is, after all, of more real use than a sapphire ring.

Thus Queen Anne was "Mrs. Morley" to her one-time favourite, Sarah, Duchess of Marlborough. But Queen Elizabeth had been Gloriana to the whole of England.

SELECTED BIBLIOGRAPHY

Adams, W. Bridges: *The Irresistible Theatre,* Vol. I.

Amherst, Alicia: *A History of Gardening in England.*

Archer, John: *Everyman his own Doctor.*

Ashley, Maurice: *The Greatness of Oliver Cromwell.*

Ashley, Maurice: *England in the 17th Century.*

Ashmole, Elias: *Diary and Will,* ed. R. T. Gunther. *Old Ashmolean reprints II.*

Aubrey, John: *Brief Lives* (ed. O. L. Dick).

Bacon, Francis: *Essays or Counsells, Civill and Moral.*

Bacon, Francis: *New Atlantis.*

Baker, Richard: *A Chronicle of the Kings of England* (1635 2nd ed.).

Baxter, Richard: *Autobiography.*

Beckmann, John: *A History of Inventions* (trans.: Wm. Johnston, revised: 1816, W. Frances and J. W. Griffith).

Behn, Aphra: *Oroonoko.*

Blencowe, Anne: *The Receipt Book* (ed. Geo. Saintsbury).

Boyle, Robert: *The Sceptical Chymist.*

Browne, Thomas: *Religio Medici.*

Browne, Thomas: *Pseudodoxia Epidemica.*

Browne, Thomas: *Hydriotaphia.*

Brushfield, T. N.: *The Financial Diary of a Citizen of Exeter* (pamphlet, Transactions; Devonshire Assn. for the Advancement of Science and Literature, etc. 1901).

Burnet, Gilbert: *A History of My Own Times* (ed. Osmund Airy, 1887).

Burton, Robert: *The Anatomy of Melancholy.*

Selected Bibliography

Camden Society: *A Description of a Journie into Westerne Counties* (Lieut. Hammond).

Camden Society: *Lismore Papers.*

Camden Society: *Diary of Marmeduke Rawdon of York.*

Camden Society: *Robert Loder's Farm Accounts.*

Camden Society: *The State of England in 1600* (Thomas Wilson).

Camden Society: *Ralph Josselin's Diary.*

Carlyle, Thomas: *The Letters and Speeches of Oliver Cromwell* (ed. S. C. Lomas).

Campbell, Mildred: *The English Yeoman.*

Chamberlain, John: *Letters* (ed. N. E. McClure.

Chatsworth Settlement: MSS. Account book of R. W.

Chatsworth Settlement: MSS. Account books (probably) of Sir John Bankes.

Clark, Andrew: *The Life and Times of Anthony Wood*, (Oxford Hist. Soc.).

Clark, G. N.: *The Seventeenth Century.*

Clarendon (Earl of): Extracts from his *History of the Rebellion.*

Cotton, Charles (?): *The Compleat Gamester, etc.*

Crosby Records: *A Cavalier's Note Book* (ed. T. Ellison Gibson).

Defoe, Daniel: *A Tour Through England and Wales.*

de Gramont: *Memoirs* (ed. & trans. Quennell).

de Gramont: *Memoirs* (trans. & notes Horace Walpole).

de Gramont: *Memoirs* (ed. Allan Fea).

Dirks, Henry: *Inventors and Inventions.*

Dirks, Henry: *The Life, Times and Scientific Labours of the second Marquis of Worcester.*

Donaldson, John (comp. & ed.): *Agricultural Biography.*

Drummond, J. C. and Wilbraham, Anne: *The Englishman's Food* (revised, D. Hollingworth, 1958).

Evelyn, John: *Diary* (ed. E. S. de Beer: and also Everyman).

Evelyn, John: *Acetaria, A Discourse of Sallets.*

Evelyn, John: *Miscellaneous Writings,* collected by Wm. Upcott, 1825.

Selected Bibliography

Evelyn, John: *Fumifugium* (facsimile copy ed. 1772) Old Ashmolean Reprints VIII.

Ellis, Henry: *Original Letters*, 2nd series, vols. 3 & 4; 3rd series, vol. 4.

Fanshawe, Anne: *Diary of*. John Lane, the Bodley Head, 1907.

Fiennes, Celia: MSS. "Journeys" (Broughton Castle).

Fiennes, Celia: *The Journeys of Celia Fiennes*, (ed. Christopher Morris).

Fuller, Thomas: *A History of the Worthies of England*.

Fussell, G. E.: *The English Rural Labourer*.

Gardiner, S. R. (ed.): *Constitutional Documents of the Puritan Revolution 1625-1666*.

Gerard, John: *The Great Herball*.

Godwin, Francis: *The Man in the Moone*.

Gough, J. W.: *The Superlative Prodigall*.

Guizot, F. P. G.: *Histoire de Richard Cromwell et du Rétablissement des Stuarts*.

Guizot, F. P. G.: *Histoire de la République d'Angleterre et de Cromwell*.

Guthrie, Douglas: *A History of Medicine*.

Green, David: *Gardener to Queen Anne*.

Green, J. R.: *A Short History of the English People*.

Hadfield, Miles: *Gardening in Britain*.

Hanmer, Thomas: *The Garden Book* (written 1659, ed. I. Elstob, 1935).

Harington, John: *Nugae Antiquae*.

Harrington, James: *Oceana*.

Harrison, G. B.: *A Jacobean Journal for the Years 1603-1606*

Harrison, G. B.: *A Second Jacobean Journal (1607-1610)*.

Hayward, John (ed.): *The Letters of Saint Evremond*.

Hicks, George: *The Gentleman Instructed*.

Hiscock, W. G.: *John Evelyn and his Family Circle*.

Hobhouse, Edmund (ed.) *The Diary of a West Country Physician*.

Selected Bibliography

Jordan, W. K.: *Philanthrophy in England 1480-1660.*

Kenyon, J. P.: *The Stuarts.*

Law, E.: *The History of Hampton Court Palace.*
Ludlow, Edmund: *Memoirs (1625-1672)* (ed. C. H. Firth, 1884).
Lucas, Margaret (Margaret Cavendish, Duchess of Newcastle): *The Sociable Letters.*
Lucas, Margaret: *The Life of the Most Illustrious Prince William, Duke of Newcastle.*
Lucas, Margaret: *A True Relation of My Birth and Life.*
Lucas, Theophilus: *Memoirs of the Lives, Intrigues and Comical Adventures of the Most Famous Gamesters and Celebrated Sharpers in the Reigns of Charles II, James II, William III and Queen Anne.*
Luttrell, Narcissus: *A Brief Historical Relation of State Affairs 1678-1714.*

Maitland, F. W.: *The Constitutional History of England.*
Manley, M. de la Rivière: *Secret Memoirs and Manners of Several Persons of Quality of Both Sexes, from the New Atlantis.*
Magalotti, Lorenzo: *Travels of Cosimo the Third, Grand Duke of Tuscany.*
Markham, Gervase: *A Way to Get Wealth* (ed. 1647).
Misson, Henri: *Memoirs and Observations in his Travels over England* (trans. Ozell).
Muffet, Thomas: *Health's Improvements* (as revised by Dr. Christopher Bennett, 1655).

Nef, John U.: *Cultural Foundations of Industrial Civilization.*
Nef, John U.: *The Rise of the British Coal Industry.*
Neill, Stephen: *Anglicanism.*
Newton, E. (ed.): *The Lyme Letters.*
Nichols, John: *The Progresses, Processions and Magnificent Festivities of King James the First.*
Notestein, Wallace: *Four Worthies.*
Notestein, Wallace: *English Folk.*

Selected Bibliography

Oglander, John: *A Royalist's Notebook.*
Ogg, David: *England in the Reign of Charles II.*

Parkinson, John: *Paradisi in Sole, Paradisus Terrestris.*
Parkinson, John: *Theatrum Botanicum.*
Peck, Francis: *Desiderata Curiosa.*
Pepys, Samuel: *Diary* (ed. H. B. Wheatley: and also Everyman).
Platt, Hugh: *Delights for Ladies* (1594).
Platt, Hugh: *The Jewel House of Art and Nature* (printed for Elizabeth Allsop, 1653).
Plot, Robert: *The Natural History of Oxfordshire.*

Reresby, John: *Memoirs* (ed. Andrew Browning).
Rohde, E. S.: *The Story of the Garden.*
Robinson, Victor: *The Story of Medicine.*
Rowse, A. L.: *The Early Churchills.*
Rowse, A. L.: *The Elizabethans and America.*
Rye, W. B. (comp. & ed.): *England as seen by Foreigners in the days of Elizabeth and James I.*

Sackville-West, V.: *Aphra Behn.*
Sackville-West, V.: *Knole and the Sackvilles.*
Scott Thomson, G.: *Life of a Noble Household.*
Selden, John: *Table Talk* (ed. S. H. Reynolds).
Singer, Charles: *A Short History of Scientific Ideas.*
Stow, John: *The Survey of London.*
Strickland, Agnes: *Lives of the Queens of England.* Vols: v, vi, vii, viii.
Surtees Society: *Memorandum Book of Sir Walter Calverley, Bart.*
Surtees Society: *Selections from the Household Books of Lord Wm. Howard.*

Tanner, J. R.: *English Constitutional Conflicts of the Seventeenth Century. (1603-1689).*
Tawney, R. H.: *Religion and the Rise of Capitalism.*

Selected Bibliography

Tradescant, John (the younger): *Musaeum Tradescantianum,* Old Ashmolean Reprints I.

Trevelyan, G. M.: *England Under the Stuarts.*

Trevelyan, G. M.: *England in the Time of Queen Anne.*

Trevelyan, G. M.: *English Social History.*

Trevor Roper, H.: *The Gentry, 1540-1600.*

Verney Family: *Memoirs* (col. & ed. Parthenope, Lady Verney).

Verney Family: *Memoirs,* Vol. IV (ed. Margaret M. Verney).

Vitruvius (Marcus Vitruvius Pollio): *The Ten Books of Architecture* (trans. M. H. Morgan).

Von Uffenbach, Z. C.: *Diary* (trans. & ed. J. E. B. Meyer).

Von Uffenbach, Z. C.: *Diary and Travels* ("London 1710", trans. & ed. W. Quarrell and M. Mare).

Watkin, E. I.: *Roman Catholicism in England from the Reformation to 1950.*

Wilkins, John: *The Mathematical and Philosophical Works* (ed. Whittington 1802), Vol. I.

Willson, D. H.: *James VI and I*

Wren, Christopher: *Parentalia, or Memoirs of the Family of Wrens, but chiefly of Sir C. Wren* (pub. 1750 by Stephen Wren).

Miscellaneous

Pharmacopoeia Radcliffiana: or Dr. *Radcliff's prescriptions faithfully gather'd from his Original Receipts, etc.,* printed for Charles Rivington, 1716.

A Collection of Above Three Hundred Receipts in Cookers, Physick and Surgerys for the Use of All Good Wives, Tender Mothers and Careful Nurses, by Several Hands; printed for Richard Wilkins, London, 1714.

The Queen's Closet Opened (incomparable Secrets in Physick, Chyrugery, Preserving, Candying, etc.); corrected and revised with many new and large Additions, etc.; printed London, 1683.

SOURCES

CHAPTER I

[1] John Manningham: *Diary.*
[2] John Nichols: *The Progresses, Processions and Magnificent Festivities of King James I.*
[3] Andrew Marvell: *Music's Empire.*
[4] John Nichols: op. cit.
[5] John Nichols: op. cit.
[6] John Nichols: op. cit.
[7] John Nichols: op. cit.
[8] John Nichols: op. cit.
[9] G. M. Trevelyan: *England Under the Stuarts.*
[10] Thomas Wilson: *The State of England.*
[11] Thomas Wilson: op. cit.
[12] Thomas Fuller: *A History of the Worthies of England* (from which all quotations in this paragraph are taken).
[13] Hoole Jackson: *Discomforts of Early Travellers* (*Country Life*—September 28th, 1961).
[14] Lieut. Hammond: *A Journie into Westerne Counties.*
[15] Samuel Pepys: see *Diary*, entry June 11th, 1668, for all quotations in this paragraph.
[16] C.S.P. Dom. Feb. 4th, 1640.
[17] Thomas Wilson: Ellis: *Letters*, 2nd series Letter CCXLVI.
[18] Quoted by John Nichols: op. cit.
[19] *The Bible:* King James version, preface.
[20] Thomas Carlyle: *Letters and Speeches of Oliver Cromwell*: (ed. Mrs. S. C. Lomas: ex introduction, C. H. Firth).

428

Sources

21 J. R. Tanner: *English Constitutional Conflicts of the Seventeenth Century, 1603-1688.*

22 Robert Burton: *The Anatomy of Melancholy* (Part 1. Section 2, Subsection XV Digression of the Misery of Scholars).

23 Edward Hyde, Earl of Clarendon: *History of the Rebellion.*

24 John Milton: *Comus—A Masque.*

25 John Milton: op. cit.

26 Francis Peck: *Desiderata Curiosa.*

27 Melfort: Ellis. op. cit. Letter CCCLXXXV.

28 Prince George of Hanover: Ellis. op. cit. Letter CCXCVIII.

29 A. C. Edwards: *English History from Essex Sources.*

30 Essex Record Office.

31 Essex Record Office.

32 John Taylor: *A Discovery by Sea from London to Salisbury.* 1623.

33 Sir Thomas Browne: *Hydriotaphia or Urne Buriall.*

CHAPTER II

1 John Nichols: *The Progresses etc. of King James I.*

2 Lieut. Hammond: *A Short Survey of 26 Counties* (1634).

3 Celia Fiennes: *Journals.*

4 Celia Fiennes: op. cit.

5 John Evelyn: *Diary*: entry Aug. 30th, 1654.

6 John Evelyn: op. cit. Oct. 22nd, 1644.

7 John Aubrey: *Brief Lives.*

8 Christopher Wren (son): *Parentalia.*

9 John Evelyn: op. cit. Aug. 17th, 1666.

10 Gilbert Burnet: *A History of My Own Times.*

11 John Evelyn: op. cit. Sept. 7th, 1666.

CHAPTER III

1 Samuel Pepys: *Diary*, entry Jan. 1st, 1662.

2 John Evelyn: *Diary*, entry Aug. 14th, 1662.

Sources

[3] J. W. (probably James Wheldon): MSS. accounts, Chatsworth Settlement.

[4] Ralph Josselin: *Diary*, entry March 1st, 1662.

[5] Parliament Bill, 1649.

[6] John Evelyn: *Diary*, entry May 30th, 1662.

[7] Agnes Strickland: *Lives of the Queens of England*, Vol. V (Letter of Thomas Maynard to Sir Edward Nichols).

[8] Hampton Court inventory, 1659.

[9] F. W. Steer: Farm & Cottage Inventories of Mid-Essex (1635-1749).

[10] Agnes Strickland: *Lives of the Queens of England*, Vol. V.

[11] Francis Peck: *Desiderata Curiosa*.

[12] Lady Verney: *Memoirs of the Verney Family*.

[13] John Evelyn: *The State of France* (1652).

[14] George Etherege: *The Man of Mode*, Act 5, Scene 2.

[15] John Aubrey: *Natural History of Wiltshire* (MS. Bodleian Lib.).

[16] Celia Fiennes: *Journeys*.

[17] John Aubrey: *Brief Lives*.

CHAPTER IV

[1] H. Misson: *Memoirs and Observations* etc.

[2] John Evelyn: *Fumifugium*.

[3] William Shakespeare: *Cymbeline*, Act 1, Scene 4.

[4] A. de la Pryme: *Diary*

[5] John Evelyn: *Diary*, entry June 26th, 1676.

[6] MSS. Accounts, Chatsworth Settlement.

[7] Henry Savile: Ellis: *Letters*, 2nd series. Letter CCCXI.

[8] William Congreve: *The Way of the World*, Act 1, Scene 9.

[9] Alexander Pope: *The Rape of the Lock*.

[10] John Smith: *Horological Dialogues*.

[11] Alexander Pope: *Essay on Criticism*.

[12] William Wycherley: *The Country Wife*, Act 4, Scene 3.

Sources

[13] Daniel Defoe: *A Tour Through England and Wales.*

[14] Thomas Shadwell: *The Humorist,* Act 3.

[15] Thomas Shadwell: *The Sullen Lovers,* Act 5.

[16] Mrs. M. de la R. Manley: *Secret Memoirs & Manners from The New Atlantis,* Vol. 1 (7th Ed. 1741).

[17] E. Law: *The History of Hampton Court Palace.*

[18] Celia Fiennes: *Journeys.*

[19] William Shakespeare: *Measure for Measure,* Act 3, Scene 2.

[20] William Shakespeare: *Timon of Athens,* Act 4, Scene 3.

CHAPTER V

[1] John Chamberlain: Letter to Sir Dudley Carleton, Jan. 10th, 1617-18.

[2] John Milton: *Comus—a Masque.*

[3] Ben Jonson: *Neptune's Triumph.*

[4] John Milton: *Paradise Regained,* Book IV.

[5] Gervase Markham: *The Good Housewife.*

[6] John Chamberlain: Letter to Sir Dudley Carleton, March 27th, 1616.

[7] Robert Loder: Farm Accounts.

[8] Philip Massinger: *The City Madam* (1632).

[9] Henri Misson: *Memoirs and Observations in his Travels* (trans. and ed. by Ozell).

[10] Leeds MS.; PRO 30/32: 55 & 56.

[11] E. Ward: *The London Spy.*

[12] Samuel Pepys: *Diary,* entry Nov. 2nd, 1667.

[13] *The Tatler* (No. 97).

[14] Robert Burton: *The Anatomy of Melancholy* (Part 2, Section 5).

[15] Andrew Clark: *Life of Anthony à Wood.*

[16] Elizabeth Burton: *The Pageant of Elizabethan England*

[17] Margaret (Lucas) Cavendish: *Natures Dissert.*

Sources

[18] Frederick Slare: *A Vindication of Sugars against the Charges of Dr. Willis and other Physicians and Common Prejudice* (1715).

[19] By Several Hands: *A Collection of Above Three Hundred Receipts, etc.*

[20] Anne Blencowe: *The Receipt Book.*

[21] Joseph Addison: *The Spectator* (No. 195).

[22] Joseph Addison: ibid.

[23] John Clarke or Clerk: *Paroemiologia.*

CHAPTER VI

[1] Francis Bacon: *The Advancement of Learning.*

[2] Samuel Pepys: *Diary,* entry Oct. 19th, 1663.

[3] Daniel Defoe: *A Journal of the Plague Years.*

[4] Hugh Platt and others: *The Queen's Closet Opened* (corrected and revised London 1683).

[5] William Shakespeare: *Macbeth,* Act 4, Scene 1.

[6] By Several Hands: *A Collection of Above Three Hundred Receipts etc.* (1714).

[7] Thomas Fuller: *Good Thoughts in Bad Times Together with Good Thoughts in Worse Times.*

[8] Margaret M. Verney: *Memoirs of the Verney Family.*

[9] Francis Bacon: *New Atlantis.*

[10] John Chamberlain: Letters to Alice Carleton, Feb. 16th, 1614-15.

[11] Thomas Fuller: *A History of the Worthies of England.*

[12] Thomas Fuller: ibid.

[13] Thomas Fuller: ibid.

[14] John Aubrey: *Brief Lives.*

[15] John Aubrey: op. cit.

[16] John Aubrey: op. cit.

[17] Robert Burton: *The Anatomy of Melancholy.*

[18] Thomas Fuller: *A History of the Worthies of England.*

[19] Thomas Fuller: op. cit.

Sources

[20] Advertisement: *Spectator* (Nos. 331, 231).

[21] Advertisement: *Spectator* (No. 404).

[22] Advertisement: *Spectator* (No. 602).

[23] Francis Bacon: *Novum Organum.*

CHAPTER VII

[1] Samuel Pepys: *Diary,* entry Feb. 1st, 1664.

[2] Christopher Wren: *Parentalia.*

[3] Christopher Wren: op. cit.

[4] Thomas Powell: *Human Industry,* 1661.

[5] Samuel Pepys: *Diary,* entry March 23rd, 1663.

[6] Compiled by W. B. Rye: *England as seen by Foreigners in the days of Elizabeth and James I.*

[7] Ben Jonson: *Epicoene or The Silent Woman.*

[8] Ben Jonson: *The Staple of News.*

[9] John Bate: *Mysteries of Art and Nature.*

[10] Christopher Wren: op. cit.

[11] Ed. S. W. Singer (1820): *Anecdotes of Joseph Spencer* (1699-1768).

[12] Christopher Wren: op. cit.

[13] John U. Nef: *The Rise of the British Coal Industry.*

[14] Thomas Power: *Experimental Philosophy.*

[15] Samuel Pepys: *Diary,* entry Nov. 1st, 1660.

[16] John Aubrey: *Brief Lives.*

[17] John Evelyn: *Diary,* entry Aug. 28th, 1655.

[18] John Aubrey: op. cit.

[19] John Evelyn: *Diary,* entry Oct. 25th, 1696.

[20] John Evelyn: *Diary,* entry Aug. 6th, 1651.

[21] Francis Bacon: *Essays "Of Innovations".*

[22] John Chamberlain: Letter to Sir Dudley Carleton, May 18th, 1616.

[23] Francis Godwin or Godwyn: *The Man in the Moone* or a *Discourse of a Voyage Thither,* (2nd ed. 1657).

Sources

CHAPTER VIII

1 John Aubrey: *Brief Lives.*

2 (perhaps) Charles Cotton: *The Compleat Gamestere.*

3 Gilbert Burnet: *A History of My Own Times.*

4 Theophilus Lucas: *Memoirs of The Lives, Intrigues and Comical Adventures,* etc.

5 John Aubrey: *Brief Lives.*

6 Charles Cotton: op. cit.

7 Henry Dircks: *The Life, Times and Scientific Labours of the Second Marquis of Worcester.*

8 George Swinnock: *The Life and Death of Thomas Wilson* (1672).

9 John Chamberlayne: *The Present State of England.*

10 Essex Record Office: Complaint of the Inhabitants of Thaxted (July 1610).

11 Margaret Cavendish: *The Sociable Letters.*

12 G. M. Trevelyan: *England Under the Stuarts.*

13 Andrew Marvell: *Poems on Affairs of State,* etc.

14 Samuel Pepys: *Diary,* entry Jan. 4th, 1664.

15 John Earle: *Microcosmographie.*

16 Charles Cotton: op. cit.

17 Charles Cotton: op. cit.

18 Henri Missiou: *Memoirs and Observations,* etc.

19 *Annalia Dubrencia* and other sources on site.

20 John Pory: Letter to Sir Thomas Puckering, Feb. 23rd, 1631.—Ellis: *Letters,* 2nd series, Letter CCLXXI.

21 Jonathan Swift: Letter to Stella, July 31st, 1711.

22 John Northbrooke: *A Treatise against Idleness, Idle Pastimes and Players.*

23 George Gresley: Letter to Sir Thomas Puckering–Ellis: *Letters,* 2nd series, Letter CCLXXV.

24 George Villiers, Second Duke of Buckingham: *The Rehearsal,* Act 3, Scene 5.

25 John Selden: *Table Talk* (ed. S. H. Reynolds, 1892).

Sources

[26] John Selden: ibid.

[27] Richard Steele: *Spectator* (No. 324).

[28] George Hicks: *The Gentleman Instructed.*

[29] Preface: *Coryat's Crudities.*

[30] L. C. von Uffenbach: *Travels* (trans. and ed. Quarrell and Mare. Also *Diary,* trans. and ed. by J. E. B. Meyer).

[31] John Dryden: *All for Love,* Act 5, Scene 1.

CHAPTER IX

[1] Richard Lovelace: *Aramantha,* from which all quotations in the paragraph are taken.

[2] William Congreve: *The Old Bachelor,* Act 4, Scene 8.

[3] Samuel Pepys: *Diary,* entry March 8th, 1664

[4] de Gramont: *Memoirs.*

[5] Hugh Platt & others: *The Queen's Closet Opened* (1683 ed.).

[6] John Evelyn: *Diary,* entry May 11th, 1654.

[7] Samuel Pepys: *Diary,* entry April 26th, 1667.

[8] By Several Hands: *A Collection of Above Three Hundred Receipts,* etc.

[9] de Gramont: *Memoirs.*

[10] William Congreve: *The Way of the World,* Act 3, Scene 5.

[11] William Congreve: *The Double Dealer,* Act 3, Scene 10.

[12] Samuel Butler: *Hudibras,* Second Part, Canto I.

[13] Hugh Platt & others: *The Queen's Closet Opened.*

[14] Gaius Plinius Secundus: *Natural History,* Book XXVI.

[15] Hugh Platt & others: *The Queen's Closet Opened.*

[16] Mary (or John) Evelyn: *Mundus Muliebris.*

[17] Alexander Pope: *The Rape of the Lock.*

[18] William Congreve: *The Way of the World,* Act 2, Scene 4.

[19] Hugh Platt & others: *The Queen's Closet Opened.*

[20] By Several Hands: *A Collection of Above Three Hundred Receipts,* etc.

Sources

21 Francis Peck: *Desiderata Curiosa.*

22 Advertisements: *Spectator* (Nos. 48, 104, 116, etc.).

23 John Evelyn: *The Fop's Dictionary.*

24 Anne Blencowe: *Receipt Book.*

25 *The Ladies Guide,* 1700.

26 *The Diary of the Duke of Stettin* (Royal Historical Society Transactions, Vol. VI. Ed. and comp. Frederic Gershow).

27 Mary Evelyn: op. cit.

28 Walter Calverley: *Memorandum Book.*

29 Advertisement: *Spectator* (Nos. 209, 219, etc.).

30 Agnes Strickland: *Lives of the Queens of England,* Vol. V.

31 Thomas Shadwell: *The Virtuoso,* Act 3.

32 George Etherege: *The Man of Mode,* Act 3, Scene 2.

33 Lady Anne Fanshawe: *Diary.*

34 George Etherege: op. cit., Act 4, Scene 1.

35 Alexander Pope: *The Rape of the Lock.*

36 William Congreve: *The Way of the World,* Act 4, Scene 1.

37 Hugh Platt & others: *The Queen's Closet Opened.*

38 Advertisement: (*Spectator* No. 138).

39 Advertisement: (*Spectator* No. 348).

40 E. Burnaby Greene: *An Essay on Pastoral Poetry.*

CHAPTER X

1 Lieut. Hammond: *Description of a Journie made into Westerne Counties.*

2 Lieut. Hammond: op. cit.

3 John Aubrey: *Brief Lives.*

4 John Aubrey: ibid.

5 Lieut. Hammond: op. cit.

6 Lieut. Hammond: op. cit.

7 Lieut. Hammond: op. cit.

8 Lieut. Hammond: ibid.

Sources

[9] Lieut. Hammond: ibid.

[10] John Aubrey: op. cit.

[11] John Aubrey: op. cit.

[12] John Parkinson: *Paradisi in Sole, Paradisus Terrestris.*

[13] John Gerard: *Great Herball.*

[14] John Gerard: *Great Herball.*

[15] John Milton: *Paradise Lost,* Book VII.

[16] Tanner: MSS. CCXCIX: Bodleian Library.

[17] Parliamentary Survey, 1649.

[18] William Lawson: *A New Orchard and Garden.*

[19] Andrew Marvell: *The Garden.*

[20] Andrew Marvell: *Upon Appleton House.*

[21] John Milton: *Lycidas.*

[22] John Parkinson: op. cit.

[23] Samuel Purchas: *Hakluytus Posthumus or Purchas his Pilgrimes.*

[24] Daniel Defoe: *A Tour Through England and Wales* (Letter VIII).

[25] Daniel Defoe: ibid.

[26] John Milton: *Paradise Lost,* Book VII.

[27] Surtees Society: *Memorandum Book of Sir Walter Calverley Bart.*

[28] Gervase Markham: *The English Husbandman.*

[29] Crosby Records: *A Cavalier's Note Book.*

[30] Alicia Amherst: *A History of Gardening in England.*

[31] Surtees Society: *Rural Economy in Yorkshire.*

[32] John Evelyn: *Gardeners' Almanack.*

[33] William Lawson: op. cit.

[34] John Evelyn: *Diary,* entry Feb. 19th, 1665.

[35] John Evelyn: *Diary,* entry May 10th, 1654.

[36] David Green: *Gardener to Queen Anne.*

[37] Celia Fiennes: *Journeys.*

[38] Robert Plot: *The Natural History of Oxfordshire.*

[39] L. C. von Uffenbach: *Diary* (London 1710 trans. and ed. Quarrell and Mare).

[40] Joseph Addison: *Spectator* (No. 414).

Sources

[41] W. G. Hiscock: *John Evelyn and His Family Circle.*

[42] Francis Peck: *Desiderata Curiosa.*

[43] Alicia Amherst: op. cit.

[44] John Milton: *Paradise Lost,* Book VII.

INDEX

Index

Index

Index

Index

Index

Index

Index

446

Index

Index